P9-CMF-229

Thomas H. Huxley

THE HARVARD CLASSICS
EDITED BY CHARLES W ELIOT LL D

ESSAYS

ENGLISH AND AMERICAN

WITH INTRODUCTIONS AND NOTES

VOLUME 28

P F COLLIER & SON
NEW YORK

Designed, Printed, and Bound at
The Collier Press, New York

CONTENTS

INTRODUCTORY NOTE

William Makepeace Thackeray, *one of the greatest of English novelists, was born at Calcutta, India, on July 18, 1811, where his father held an administrative position. He was sent to England at six for his education, which he received at the Charterhouse and Cambridge, after which he began, but did not prosecute, the study of law. Having lost his means, in part by gambling, he made up his mind to earn his living as an artist, and went to Paris to study. He had some natural gift for drawing, which he had already employed in caricature, but, though he made interesting and amusing illustrations for his books, he never acquired any marked technical skill.*

He now turned to literature, and, on the strength of an appointment as Paris correspondent of a short-lived radical newspaper, he married. On the failure of the newspaper he took to miscellaneous journalism and the reviewing of books and pictures, his most important work appearing in "Fraser's Magazine" and "Punch." In 1840 his wife's mind became clouded, and, though she never recovered, she lived on till 1894.

Success came to Thackeray very slowly. "Catherine," "The Great Hoggarty Diamond," "Barry Lyndon," and several volumes of travel had failed to gain much attention before the "Snob Papers," issued in "Punch" in 1846, brought him fame. In the January of the next year "Vanity Fair" began to appear in monthly numbers, and by the time it was finished Thackeray had taken his place in the front rank of his profession. "Pendennis" followed in 1850, and sustained the prestige he had won.

The next year he began lecturing, and delivered in London the lectures on the "English Humourists," which he repeated the following winter in America with much success. "Esmond" had appeared on the eve of his setting sail, and revealed his style at its highest point of perfection, and a tenderer if less powerful touch than "Vanity Fair" had displayed. In 1855 "The Newcomes" appeared, and was followed by a second trip to America, when he lectured on the "Four Georges." After an unsuccessful attempt to enter Parliament, the novelist resumed his writing with "The Virginians" (1857-59), in which he availed himself of his American experiences.

In the January of 1860 the "Cornhill Magazine" was founded, with Thackeray as first editor, and launched on a distinguished career. Most of his later work was published in its pages, but "Lovel the Widower" and the "Adventures of Philip" have not taken a place beside his greater work. In the essays constituting the "Roundabout Papers," however, he appeared at his easiest and most charming. After a little more than two years he resigned the editorship; and on December 23, 1863, he died.

Thackeray's greatest distinction is, of course, as a novelist, and an estimate of his work in this field is not in place here. But as an essayist he is also great. The lectures on the "English Humourists," of which the following paper on "Swift" was the first, were the fruit of an intimate knowledge of the time of Queen Anne, and a warm sympathy with its spirit. And here, as in all his mature work, Thackeray is the master of a style that for ease, suppleness, and range of effect has seldom been equaled in English.

JONATHAN SWIFT[1]

BY WILLIAM MAKEPEACE THACKERAY

IN treating of the English humourists of the past age, it is of the men and of their lives, rather than of their books, that I ask permission to speak to you; and in doing so, you are aware that I cannot hope to entertain you with a merely humourous or facetious story. Harlequin without his mask is known to present a very sober countenance, and was himself, the story goes, the melancholy patient whom the Doctor advised to go and see Harlequin—a man full of cares and perplexities like the rest of us, whose Self must always be serious to him, under whatever mask or disguise or uniform he presents it to the public. And as all of you here must needs be grave when you think of your own past and present, you will not look to find, in the histories of those whose lives and feelings I am going to try and describe to you, a story that is otherwise than serious, and often very sad. If Humour only meant laughter, you would scarcely feel more interest about humourous writers than about the private life of poor Harlequin just mentioned, who possesses in common with these the power of making you laugh. But the men regarding whose lives and stories your kind presence here shows that you have curiosity and sympathy, appeal to a great number of our other faculties, besides our mere sense of ridicule. The humourous writer professes to awaken and direct your love, your pity, your kindness—your scorn for untruth, pretension, imposture—your tenderness for the weak, the poor, the oppressed, the unhappy. To the best of his means and ability he comments on all the ordinary actions and passions of life almost. He

[1] From the English Humourists of the Eighteenth Century.

takes upon himself to be the week-day preacher, so to speak. Accordingly, as he finds, and speaks, and feels the truth best we regard him, esteem him—sometimes love him. And, as his business is to mark other people's lives and peculiarities, we moralize upon *his* life when he is gone—and yesterday's preacher becomes the text for to-day's sermon.

Of English parents, and of a good English family of clergymen, Swift was born in Dublin in 1667, seven months after the death of his father, who had come to practise there as a lawyer. The boy went to school at Kilkenny, and afterwards to Trinity College, Dublin, where he got a degree with difficulty, and was wild, and witty, and poor. In 1688, by the recommendation of his mother, Swift was received into the family of Sir William Temple, who had known Mrs. Swift in Ireland. He left his patron in 1694, and the next year took orders in Dublin. But he threw up the small Irish preferment which he got and returned to Temple, in whose family he remained until Sir William's death in 1699. His hopes of advancement in England failing, Swift returned to Ireland, and took the living of Laracor. Hither he invited Hester Johnson, Temple's natural daughter, with whom he had contracted a tender friendship, while they were both dependants of Temple's. And with an occasional visit to England, Swift now passed nine years at home.

In 1709 he came to England, and, with a brief visit to Ireland, during which he took possession of his deanery of St. Patrick, he now passed five years in England, taking the most distinguished part in the political transactions which terminated with the death of Queen Anne. After her death, his party disgraced, and his hopes of ambition over, Swift returned to Dublin, where he remained twelve years. In this time he wrote the famous "Drapier's Letters" and "Gulliver's Travels." He married Hester Johnson, Stella, and buried Esther Vanhomrigh, Vanessa, who had followed him to Ireland from London, where she had contracted a violent passion for him. In 1726 and 1727 Swift was in England, which he quitted for the last time on hearing of his wife's illness. Stella died in January, 1728, and Swift not until 1745, having passed the last five of the seventy-eight years of his life with an impaired intellect and keepers to watch him.

You know, of course, that Swift has had many biographers; his life has been told by the kindest and most good-natured of men, Scott, who admires but can't bring himself to love him; and by stout old Johnson, who, forced to admit him into the company of poets, receives the famous Irishman, and takes off his hat to him with a bow of surly recognition, scans him from head to foot, and passes over to the other side of the street. Dr. Wilde of Dublin, who has written a most interesting volume on the closing years of Swift's life, calls Johnson "the most malignant of his biographers:" it is not easy for an English critic to please Irishmen—perhaps to try and please them. And yet Johnson truly admires Swift: Johnson does not quarrel with Swift's change of politics, or doubt his sincerity of religion: about the famous Stella and Vanessa controversy the Doctor does not bear very hardly on Swift. But he could not give the Dean that honest hand of his; the stout old man puts it into his breast, and moves off from him.

Would we have liked to live with him? That is a question which, in dealing with these people's works, and thinking of their lives and peculiarities, every reader of biographies must put to himself. Would you have liked to be a friend of the great Dean? I should like to have been Shakspeare's shoeblack—just to have lived in his house, just to have worshipped him—to have run on his errands, and seen that sweet serene face. I should like, as a young man, to have lived on Fielding's staircase in the Temple, and after helping him up to bed perhaps, and opening his door with his latch-key, to have shaken hands with him in the morning, and heard him talk and crack jokes over his breakfast and his mug of small beer. Who would not give something to pass a night at the club with Johnson, and Goldsmith, and James Boswell, Esq., of Auchinleck? The charm of Addison's companionship and conversation has passed to us by fond tradition—but Swift? If you had been his inferior in parts (and that, with a great respect for all persons present, I fear is only very likely), his equal in mere social station, he would have bullied, scorned, and insulted you; if, undeterred by his great reputation, you had met him like a man, he would have quailed before you, and not had the pluck to reply, and gone home, and years after written a foul epigram about you—watched for you in a sewer, and come out to assail you with a coward's blow and a dirty bludgeon. If you had been a lord with a blue riband, who flattered his vanity, or could help his ambition, he would have been the most delightful company in the world. He would have been so manly, so sarcastic, so bright, odd, and original, that you might think he had no object in view but the indulgence of his humour and that he was the most reckless, simple creature in the world. How he would have torn your enemies to pieces for you! and made fun of the Opposition! His servility was so boisterous that it looked like independence; he would have done your errands, but with the air of patronizing you, and after fighting your battles, masked, in the street or the press, would have kept on his hat before your wife and daughters in the drawing-room, content to take that sort of pay for his tremendous services as a bravo.

He says as much himself in one of his letters to Bolingbroke:—"All my endeavours to distinguish myself were only for want of a great title and fortune, that I might be used like a lord by those who have an opinion of my parts; whether right or wrong is no great matter. And so the reputation of wit and great learning does the office of a blue riband or a coach and six."

Could there be a greater candour? It is an outlaw, who says, "These are my brains; with these I'll win titles and compete with fortune. These are my bullets; these I'll turn into gold;" and he hears the sound of coaches and six, takes the road like Macheath, and makes society stand and deliver. They are all on their knees before him. Down go my lord bishop's apron, and his Grace's blue riband, and my lady's brocade petticoat in the mud. He eases the one of a living, the other of a patent place, the third of a little snug post about the Court, and gives them over to followers of his own. The great prize has not come yet. The coach with the mitre and crosier in it, which he intends to have for *his* share, has been delayed on the way from St. James's; and he waits and waits until nightfall, when his runners come and tell him that the coach has taken a different road, and escaped him. So he fires his pistols into the air with a curse, and rides away into his own country.

Swift's seems to me to be as good a name to point a moral or adorn a tale of ambition, as any hero's that ever lived and failed. But we must remember that the morality was lax—that other gentlemen besides himself took the road in his day—that public society was in a strange disordered condition, and the State was ravaged by other condottieri. The Boyne was being fought and won, and lost—the bells rung in William's victory, in the very same tone with which they would have pealed for James's. Men were loose upon politics, and had to shift for themselves. They, as well as old beliefs and institutions, had lost their moorings and gone adrift in the storm. As in the South Sea Bubble, almost everybody gambled; as in the Railway mania—not many centuries ago—almost every one took his unlucky share: a man of that time, of the vast talents and ambition of Swift, could scarce do otherwise than grasp at his prize, and make his spring at his opportunity. His bitterness, his scorn, his rage, his subsequent misanthropy, are ascribed by some panegyrists to a deliberate conviction of mankind's unworthiness, and a desire to amend them by castigating. His youth was bitter, as that of a great genius bound down by ignoble ties, and powerless in a mean dependence; his age was bitter, like that of a great genius that had fought the battle and nearly won it, and lost it, and thought of it afterwards writhing in a lonely exile. A man may attribute to the gods, if he likes, what is caused by his own fury, or disappointment, or self-will. What public man—what statesman projecting a *coup*—what king determined on an invasion of his neighbour—what satirist meditating an onslaught on society or an individual, can't give a pretext for his move? There was a French general the other day who proposed to march into this country and put it to sack and pillage, in revenge for humanity outraged by our conduct at Copenhagen: there is always some excuse for men of the aggressive turn. They are of their nature warlike, predatory, eager for fight, plunder, dominion.

As fierce a beak and talon as ever struck—as strong a wing as ever beat, belonged to Swift. I am glad, for one, that fate wrested the prey out of his claws, and cut his wings and chained him. One can gaze, and not without awe and pity, at the lonely eagle chained behind the bars.

That Swift was born at No. 7, Hoey's Court, Dublin, on the 30th November, 1667, is a certain fact, of which nobody will deny the sister island the honour and glory; but, it seems to me, he was no more an Irishman than a man born of English parents at Calcutta is a Hindoo. Goldsmith was an Irishman, and always an Irishman: Steele was an Irishman, and always an Irishman: Swift's heart was English and in England, his habits English, his logic eminently English; his statement is elaborately simple; he shuns tropes and metaphors, and uses his ideas and words with a wise thrift and economy, as he used his money: with which he could be generous and splendid upon great occasions, but which he husbanded when there was no need to spend it. He never indulges in needless extravagance of rhetoric, lavish epithets, profuse imagery. He lays his opinion before you with a grave simplicity and a perfect neatness. Dreading ridicule too, as a man of his humour—above all an Englishman of his humour—certainly would, he is afraid to use the poetical power which he really possessed; one often fancies in reading him that he dares not be eloquent when he might; that he does not speak above his voice, as it were, and the tone of society.

His initiation into politics, his knowledge of business, his knowledge of polite life, his acquaintance with literature even, which he could not have pursued very sedulously during that reckless career at Dublin, Swift got under the roof of Sir William Temple. He was fond of telling in after life what quantities of books he devoured there, and how King William taught him to cut asparagus in the Dutch fashion. It was at Shene and at Moor Park, with a salary of twenty pounds and a dinner at the upper servants' table, that this great and lonely Swift passed a ten years' apprenticeship—wore a cassock that was only not a livery—bent down a knee as proud as Lucifer's to supplicate my lady's good graces, or run on his honour's errands. It was here, as he was writing at Temple's table, or following his patron's walk, that he saw and heard the men who had governed the great world—measured himself with them, looking up from his silent corner, gauged their brains, weighed their wits, turned them, and tried them, and marked them. Ah! what platitudes he must have heard! what feeble jokes! what pompous commonplaces! what small men they must have seemed under those enormous periwigs, to the swarthy, uncouth, silent Irish secretary. I wonder whether it ever struck Temple, that that Irishman was his master? I suppose that dismal conviction did not present itself under the ambrosial wig, or Temple could never have lived with Swift. Swift sickened, rebelled, left the service—ate humble pie and came back again; and so for ten years went on, gathering learning, swallowing scorn, and submitting with a stealthy rage to his fortune.

Temple's style is the perfection of practised and easy good-breeding. If he does not penetrate very deeply into a subject, he professes a very gentlemanly acquaintance with it; if he makes rather a parade of Latin, it was the custom of his day, as it was the custom for a gentleman to envelope his head in a periwig and his hands in lace ruffles. If he wears buckles and square-toed shoes, he steps in them with a consummate grace, and you never hear their creak, or find them treading upon any lady's train or any rival's heels in the Court crowd. When that grows too hot or too agitated for him, he politely leaves it. He retires to his retreat of Shene or Moor Park; and lets the King's party and the Prince of Orange's party battle it out among themselves. He reveres the Sovereign (and no man perhaps ever testified to his loyalty by so elegant a bow); he admires the Prince of Orange; but there is one person whose ease and comfort he loves more than all the princes in Christendom, and that valuable member of society is himself, Gulielmus Temple, Baronettus. One sees him in his retreat; between his study-chair and his tulip-beds, clipping his apricots and pruning his essays,—the statesman, the ambassador no more; but the philosopher, the Epicurean, the fine gentleman and courtier at St. James's as at Shene; where in place of kings and fair ladies, he pays his court to the Ciceronian majesty; or walks a minuet with the Epic Muse; or dallies by the south wall with the ruddy nymph of gardens.

Temple seems to have received and exacted a prodigious deal of veneration from his household, and to have been coaxed, and warmed, and cuddled by the people round about him, as delicately as any of the plants which he loved. When he fell ill in 1693, the household was aghast at his indisposition: mild Dorothea, his wife, the best companion of the best of men—

> "Mild Dorothea, peaceful, wise, and great,
> Trembling beheld the doubtful hand of fate."

As for Dorinda, his sister,—

> "Those who would grief describe, might come and trace
> Its watery footsteps in Dorinda's face.
> To see her weep, joy every face forsook,
> And grief flung sables on each menial look.
> The humble tribe mourned for the quickening soul,
> That furnished spirit and motion through the whole."

Isn't that line in which grief is described as putting the menials into a mourning livery, a fine image? One of the menials wrote it, who did not like that Temple livery nor those twenty-pound wages. Cannot one fancy the uncouth young servitor, with downcast eyes, books and papers in hand, following at his honour's heels in the garden walk; or taking his honour's orders as he stands by the great chair, where Sir William has the gout, and his feet all blistered with moxa? When Sir William has the gout or scolds it must be hard work at the second table; the Irish secretary owned as much afterwards: and when he came to dinner, how he must have lashed and growled and torn the household with his gibes and scorn! What would the steward say about the pride of them Irish schollards—and this one had got no great credit even at his Irish college, if the truth were known—and what a contempt his Excellency's own gentleman must have had for Parson Teague from Dublin. (The valets and chaplains were always at war. It is hard to say which Swift thought the more contemptible.) And what must have been the sadness, the sadness and terror, of the housekeeper's little daughter with the curling black ringlets and the sweet smiling face, when the secretary who teaches her to read and write, and whom she loves and reverences above all things—above mother, above mild Dorothea, above that tremendous Sir William in his square-toes and periwig,—when *Mr. Swift* comes down from his master with rage in his heart, and has not a kind word even for little Hester Johnson?

Perhaps, for the Irish secretary, his Excellency's condescension was even more cruel than his frowns. Sir William *would* perpetually quote Latin and the ancient classics *àpropos* of his gardens and his Dutch statues and *plates-bandes,* and talk about Epicurus and Diogenes Lærtius, Julius Cæsar, Semiramis, and the gardens of the Hesperides, Mæcenas, Strabo describing Jericho, and the Assyrian kings. *Àpropos* of beans, he would mention Pythagoras's precept to abstain from beans, and that this precept probably meant that wise men should abstain from public affairs. *He* is a placid Epicurean; *he* is a Pythagorean philosopher; *he* is a wise man—that is the deduction. Does not Swift think so? One can imagine the downcast eyes lifted up for a moment, and the flash of scorn which they emit. Swift's eyes were as azure as the heavens; Pope says nobly (as everything Pope said and thought of his friend was good and noble), "His eyes are as azure as the heavens, and have a charming archness in them." And one person in that household, that pompous, stately, kindly Moor Park, saw heaven nowhere else.

But the Temple amenities and solemnities did not agree with Swift. He was half-killed with a surfeit of Shene pippins; and in a garden-seat which he devised for himself at Moor Park, and where he devoured greedily the stock of books within his reach, he caught a vertigo and deafness which punished and tormented him through life. He could not bear the place or the servitude. Even in that poem of courtly condolence, from which we have quoted a few lines of mock melancholy, he breaks out of the funereal procession with a mad shriek, as it were, and rushes away crying his own grief, cursing his own fate, foreboding madness, and forsaken by fortune, and even hope.

I don't know anything more melancholy than the letter to Temple, in which, after having broke from his bondage, the poor wretch crouches piteously towards his cage again, and deprecates his master's anger. He asks for testimonials for orders. "The particulars required of me are what relate to morals and learning; and the reasons of quitting your honour's family—that is, whether the last was occasioned by any ill action. They are left entirely to your honour's mercy, though in the first I think I cannot reproach myself for anything further than for *infirmities*. This is all I dare at present beg from your honour, under circumstances of life not worth your regard: what is left me to wish (next to the health and prosperity of your honour and family) is that Heaven would one day allow me the opportunity of leaving my acknowledgments at your feet. I beg my most humble duty and service be presented to my ladies, your honour's lady and sister."—Can prostration fall deeper? could a slave bow lower?

Twenty years afterwards Bishop Kennet, describing the same man, says, "Dr. Swift came into the coffee-house and had a bow from everybody but me. When I came to the antechamber [at Court] to wait before prayers, Dr. Swift was the principal man of talk and business. He was soliciting the Earl of Arran to speak to his brother, the Duke of Ormond, to get a place for a clergyman. He was promising Mr. Thorold to undertake, with my Lord Treasurer, that he should obtain a salary of 200*l*. per annum as member of the English Church at Rotterdam. He stopped F. Gwynne, Esq., going into the Queen with the red bag, and told him aloud, he had something to say to him from my Lord Treasurer. He took out his gold watch, and telling the time of day, complained that it was very late. A gentleman said he was too fast. 'How can I help it,' says the Doctor, 'if the courtiers give me a watch that won't go right?' Then he instructed a young nobleman, that the best poet in England was Mr. Pope (a Papist), who had begun a translation of Homer into English, for which he would have them all subscribe: 'For,' says he, 'he shall not begin to print till I have a thousand guineas for him.' Lord Treasurer, after leaving the Queen, came through the room, beckoning Dr. Swift to follow him,—both went off just before prayers." There's a little malice in the Bishop's "just before prayers."

This picture of the great Dean seems a true one, and is

harsh, though not altogether unpleasant. He was doing good, and to deserving men too, in the midst of these intrigues and triumphs. His journals and a thousand anecdotes of him relate his kind acts and rough manners. His hand was constantly stretched out to relieve an honest man—he was cautious about his money, but ready.—If you were in a strait would you like such a benefactor? I think I would rather have had a potato and a friendly word from Goldsmith than have been beholden to the Dean for a guinea and a dinner. He insulted a man as he served him, made women cry, guests look foolish, bullied unlucky friends, and flung his benefactions into poor men's faces. No; the Dean was no Irishman—no Irishman ever gave but with a kind word and a kind heart.

It is told, as if it were to Swift's credit, that the Dean of St. Patrick's performed his family devotions every morning regularly, but with such secrecy that the guests in his house were never in the least aware of the ceremony. There was no need surely why a church dignitary should assemble his family privily in a crypt, and as if he was afraid of heathen persecution. But I think the world was right, and the bishops who advised Queen Anne, when they counselled her not to appoint the author of the "Tale of a Tub" to a bishopric, gave perfectly good advice. The man who wrote the arguments and illustrations in that wild book, could not but be aware what must be the sequel of the propositions which he laid down. The boon companion of Pope and Bolingbroke, who chose these as the friends of his life, and the recipients of his confidence and affection, must have heard many an argument, and joined in many a conversation over Pope's port, or St. John's burgundy, which would not bear to be repeated at other men's boards.

I know of few things more conclusive as to the sincerity of Swift's religion than his advice to poor John Gay to turn clergyman, and look out for a seat on the Bench. Gay, the author of the "Beggar's Opera"—Gay, the wildest of the wits about town—it was this man that Jonathan Swift advised to take orders—to invest in a cassock and bands—just as he advised him to husband his shillings and put his thousand pounds out at interest. The Queen, and the bishops, and the world, were right in mistrusting the religion of that man.

I am not here, of course, to speak of any man's religious views, except in so far as they influence his literary character, his life, his humour. The most notorious sinners of all those fellow-mortals whom it is our business to discuss—Harry Fielding and Dick Steele, were especially loud, and I believe really fervent, in their expressions of belief; they belaboured freethinkers, and stoned imaginary atheists on all sorts of occasions, going out of their way to bawl their own creed, and persecute their neighbour's, and if they sinned and stumbled, as they constantly did with debt, with drink, with all sorts of bad behaviour, they got upon their knees and cried "Peccavi" with a most sonorous orthodoxy. Yes; poor Harry Fielding and poor Dick Steele were trusty and undoubting Church of England men; they abhorred Popery, Atheism, and wooden shoes, and idolatries in general; and hiccupped Church and State with fervour.

But Swift? *His* mind had had a different schooling, and possessed a very different logical power. *He* was not bred up in a tipsy guard-room, and did not learn to reason in a Covent Garden tavern. He could conduct an argument from beginning to end. He could see forward with a fatal clearness. In his old age, looking at the "Tale of a Tub," when he said, "Good God, what a genius I had when I wrote that book!" I think he was admiring not the genius, but the consequences to which the genius had brought him—a vast genius, a magnificent genius, a genius wonderfully bright, and dazzling, and strong,—to seize, to know, to see, to flash upon falsehood and scorch it into perdition, to penetrate into the hidden motives, and expose the black thoughts of men,—an awful, an evil spirit.

Ah man! you, educated in Epicurean Temple's library, you whose friends were Pope and St. John—what made you to swear to fatal vows, and bind yourself to a life-long hypocrisy before the Heaven which you adored with such real wonder, humility, and reverence? For Swift was a reverent, was a pious spirit—for Swift could love and could pray. Through the storms and tempests of his furious mind, the stars of religion and love break out in the blue, shining serenely, though hidden by the driving clouds and the maddened hurricane of his life.

It is my belief that he suffered frightfully from the consciousness of his own scepticism, and that he had bent his pride so far down as to put his apostasy out to hire. The paper left behind him, called "Thoughts on Religion," is merely a set of excuses for not professing disbelief. He says of his sermons that he preached pamphlets: they have scarce a Christian characteristic; they might be preached from the steps of a synagogue, or the floor of a mosque, or the box of a coffee-house almost. There is little or no cant—he is too great and too proud for that; and, in so far as the badness of his sermons goes, he is honest. But having put that cassock on, it poisoned him: he was strangled in his bands. He goes through life, tearing, like a man possessed with a devil. Like Abudah in the Arabian story, he is always looking out for the Fury, and knows that the night will come and the inevitable hag with it. What a night, my God, it was! what a lonely rage and long agony—what a vulture that tore the heart of that giant! It is awful to think of the great sufferings of this great man. Through life he always seems alone, somehow. Goethe was so. I can't fancy Shakspeare otherwise. The giants must live apart. The kings can have no company. But this man suffered so; and deserved so to suffer. One hardly reads anywhere of such a pain.

The "sæva indignatio" of which he spoke as lacerating his heart, and which he dares to inscribe on his tombstone—as if the wretch who lay under that stone waiting God's judgment had a right to be angry,—breaks out from him in a thousand pages of his writing, and tears and rends him. Against men in office, he having been overthrown; against men in England, he having lost his chance of preferment there, the furious exile never fails to rage and curse. Is it fair to call the famous "Drapier's Letters" patriotism? They are masterpieces of dreadful humour and invective: they are reasoned logically enough too, but the proposition is as monstrous and fabulous as the Lilliputian island. It is not that the grievance is so great, but there is his enemy—the assault is wonderful for its activity and terrible rage. It is Samson, with a bone in his hand, rushing on his enemies and felling them: one admires not the cause so much as the strength, the anger, the fury of the champion. As is the case with madmen, certain subjects provoke him, and awaken his fits of wrath. Marriage is one of these; in a hundred passages in his writings he rages against it; rages against children; an object of constant satire, even more contemptible in his eyes than a lord's chaplain, is a poor curate with a large family. The idea of this luckless paternity never fails to bring down from him gibes and foul language. Could Dick Steele, or Goldsmith, or Fielding, in his most reckless moment of satire, have written anything like the Dean's famous "modest proposal" for eating children? Not one of these but melts at the thoughts of childhood, fondles and caresses it. Mr. Dean has no such softness, and enters the nursery with the tread and gaiety of an ogre. "I have been assured," says he in the "Modest Proposal," "by a very knowing American of my acquaintance in London, that a young healthy child, well nursed, is, at a year old, a most delicious, nourishing, and wholesome food, whether stewed, roasted, baked, or boiled; and I make no doubt it will equally serve in a *ragoût*." And taking up this pretty joke, as his way is, he argues it with perfect gravity and logic. He turns and twists this subject in a score of different ways: he hashes it; and he serves it up cold; and he garnishes it; and relishes it always. He describes the little animal as "dropped from its dam," advising that the mother should let it suck plentifully in the last month, so as to render it plump and fat for a good table!

"A child," says his Reverence, "will make two dishes at an entertainment for friends; and when the family dines alone, the fore or hind quarter will make a reasonable dish," and so on; and, the subject being so delightful that he can't leave it, he proceeds to recommend, in place of venison for squires' tables, "the bodies of young lads and maidens not exceeding fourteen or under twelve." Amiable humourist! laughing castigator of morals! There was a process well known and practised in the Dean's gay days: when a lout entered the coffee-house, the wags proceeded to what they called "roasting" him. This is roasting a subject with a vengeance. The Dean had a native genius for it. As the "Almanach des Gourmands" says, *On naît rôtisseur.*

And it was not merely by the sarcastic method that Swift exposed the unreasonableness of loving and having children. In Gulliver, the folly of love and marriage is urged by graver arguments and advice. In the famous Lilliputian kingdom, Swift speaks with approval of the practice of instantly removing children from their parents and educating them by the State; and amongst his favourite horses, a pair of foals are stated to be the very utmost a well-regulated equine couple would permit themselves. In fact, our great satirist was of opinion that conjugal love was unadvisable, and illustrated the theory by his own practice and example—God help him—which made him about the most wretched being in God's world.

The grave and logical conduct of an absurd proposition, as exemplified in the cannibal proposal just mentioned, is our author's constant method through all his works of humour. Given a country of people six inches or sixty feet high, and by the mere process of the logic, a thousand wonderful absurdities are evolved, at so many stages of the calculation. Turning to the first minister who waited behind him with a white staff near as tall as the mainmast of the "Royal Sovereign," the King of Brobdingnag observes how contemptible a thing human grandeur is, as represented by such a contemptible little creature as Gulliver. "The Emperor of Lilliput's features are strong and masculine" (what a surprising humour there is in this description!)—"The Emperor's features," Gulliver says, "are strong and masculine, with an Austrian lip, an arched nose, his complexion olive, his countenance erect, his body and limbs well proportioned, and his deportment majestic. He is taller *by the breadth of my nail* than any of his court, which alone is enough to strike an awe into beholders."

What a surprising humour there is in these descriptions! How noble the satire is here! how just and honest! How perfect the image! Mr. Macaulay has quoted the charming lines of the poet, where the king of the pigmies is measured by the same standard. We have all read in Milton of the spear that was like "the mast of some tall admiral," but these images are surely likely to come to the comic poet originally. The subject is before him. He is turning it in a thousand ways. He is full of it. The figure suggests itself naturally to him, and comes out of his subject, as in that wonderful passage when Gulliver's box having been dropped by the eagle into the sea, and Gulliver having been received into the ship's cabin, he calls upon the crew to bring the box into the cabin, and put it on the table, the cabin being only a quarter the size of the box. It is the *veracity* of the blunder which is so admirable. Had a man come from such a country as Brobdingnag he would have blundered so.

But the best stroke of humour, if there be a best in that abounding book, is that where Gulliver, in the unpronounceable country, describes his parting from his master the horse. "I took," he says, "a second leave of my master, but as I was going to prostrate myself to kiss his hoof, he did me the honour to raise it gently to my mouth. I am not ignorant how much I have been censured for mentioning this last particular. Detractors are pleased to think it improbable that so illustrious a person should descend to give so great a mark of distinction to a creature so inferior as I. Neither have I forgotten how apt some travellers are to boast of extraordinary favours they have received. But if these censurers were better acquainted with the noble and courteous disposition of the Houyhnhnms they would soon change their opinion."

The surprise here, the audacity of circumstantial evidence, the astounding gravity of the speaker, who is not ignorant how much he has been censured, the nature of the favour conferred, and the respectful exultation at the receipt of it, are surely complete; it is truth topsy-turvy, entirely logical and absurd.

As for the humour and conduct of this famous fable, I suppose there is no person who reads but must admire; as for the moral, I think it horrible, shameful, unmanly, blasphemous; and giant and great as this Dean is, I say we should hoot him. Some of this audience mayn't have read the last part of Gulliver, and to such I would recall the advice of the venerable Mr. Punch to persons about to marry, and say "Don't." When Gulliver first lands among the Yahoos, the naked howling wretches clamber up trees and assault him, and he describes himself as "almost stifled with the filth which fell about him." The reader of the fourth part of "Gulliver's Travels" is like the hero himself in this instance. It is Yahoo language: a monster gibbering shrieks, and gnashing imprecations against mankind—tearing down all shreds of modesty, past all sense of manliness and shame; filthy in word, filthy in thought, furious, raging, obscene.

And dreadful it is to think that Swift knew the tendency of his creed—the fatal rocks towards which his logic desperately drifted. That last part of "Gulliver" is only a consequence of what has gone before; and the worthlessness of all mankind, the pettiness, cruelty, pride, imbecility, the general vanity, the foolish pretension, the mock greatness, the pompous dulness, the mean aims, the base successes—all these were present to him; it was with the din of these curses of the world, blasphemies against heaven, shrieking in his ears, that he began to write his dreadful allegory—of which the meaning is that man is utterly wicked, desperate and imbecile, and his passions are so monstrous, and his boasted powers so mean, that he is and deserves to be the slave of brutes, and ignorance is better than his vaunted reason. What had this man done? what secret remorse was rankling at his heart? what fever was boiling in him, that he should see all the world blood-shot? We view the world with our own eyes, each of us; and we make from within us the world we see. A weary heart gets no gladness out of sunshine; a selfish man is sceptical about friendship, as a man with no ear doesn't care for music. A frightful self-consciousness it must have been, which looked on mankind so darkly through those keen eyes of Swift.

A remarkable story is told by Scott, of Delany, who interrupted Archbishop King and Swift in a conversation which left the prelate in tears, and from which Swift rushed away with marks of strong terror and agitation in his countenance, upon which the Archbishop said to Delany, "You have just met the most unhappy man on earth; but on the subject of his wretchedness you must never ask a question."

The most unhappy man on earth;—Miserrimus—what a character of him! And at this time all the great wits of England had been at his feet. All Ireland had shouted after him, and worshipped him as a liberator, a saviour, the greatest Irish patriot and citizen. Dean Drapier Bickerstaff Gulliver—the most famous statesmen, and the greatest poets of his day, had applauded him, and done him homage; and at this time, writing over to Bolingbroke from Ireland, he says, "It is time for me to have done with the world, and so I would if I could get into a better before I was called into the best, *and not die here in a rage, like a poisoned rat in a hole.*"

We have spoken about the men, and Swift's behaviour to them; and now it behoves us not to forget that there are certain other persons in the creation who had rather intimate relations with the great Dean. Two women whom he loved and injured are known by every reader of books so familiarly that if we had seen them, or if they had been relatives of our own, we scarcely could have known them better. Who hasn't in his mind an image of Stella? Who does not love her? Fair and tender creature: pure and affectionate heart! Boots it to you, now that you have been at rest for a hundred and twenty years, not divided in death from the cold heart which caused yours, whilst it beat, such faithful pangs of love and grief—boots it to you now, that the whole world loves and deplores you? Scarce any man, I believe, ever thought of that grave, that did not cast a flower of pity on it, and write over it a sweet epitaph. Gentle lady, so lovely, so loving, so unhappy! you have had countless champions; millions of manly hearts mourning for you. From generation to generation we take up the fond tradition of your beauty; we watch and follow your tragedy, your bright morning love and purity, your constancy, your grief, your sweet martyrdom. We know your legend by heart. You are one of the saints of English story.

And if Stella's love and innocence are charming to contemplate, I will say that in spite of ill-usage, in spite of drawbacks, in spite of mysterious separation and union, of hope delayed and sickened heart—in the teeth of Vanessa, and that little episodical aberration which plunged Swift into such woful pitfalls and quagmires of amorous perplexity—in spite of the verdicts of most women, I believe, who, as far as my experience and conversation go, generally take Vanessa's part in the controversy—in spite of the tears which Swift caused Stella to shed, and the rocks and barriers which fate and temper interposed, and which prevented the pure course of that true love from running smoothly—the brightest part of Swift's story, the pure star in that dark and tempestuous life of Swift's, is his love for Hester Johnson. It has been my business, professionally of course, to go through a deal of sentimental reading in my time, and to acquaint myself with love-making, as it has been described in various languages, and at various ages of the world; and I know of nothing more manly, more tender, more exquisitely touching, than some of these brief notes, written in what Swift calls "his little language" in his journal to Stella.

He writes to her night and morning often. He never sends away a letter to her but he begins a new one on the same day. He can't bear to let go her kind little hand, as it were. He knows that she is thinking of him, and longing for him far away in Dublin yonder. He takes her letters from under his pillow and talks to them, familiarly, paternally, with fond epithets and pretty caresses—as he would to the sweet and artless creature who loved him. "Stay," he writes one morning—it is the 14th of December, 1710—"Stay, I will answer some of your letter this morning in bed. Let me see. Come and appear, little letter! Here I am, says he, and what say you to Stella this morning fresh and fasting? And can Stella read this writing without hurting her dear eyes?" he goes on, after more kind prattle and fond whispering. The dear eyes shine clearly upon him then—the good angel of his life is with him and blessing him. Ah, it was a hard fate that wrung from them so many tears, and stabbed pitilessly that pure and tender bosom. A hard fate: but would she have changed it? I have heard a woman say that she would have taken Swift's cruelty to have had his tenderness. He had a sort of worship for her whilst he wounded her. He speaks of her after she is gone; of her wit, of her kindness, of her grace, of her beauty, with a simple love and reverence that are indescribably touching; in contemplation of her goodness his hard heart melts into pathos; his cold rhyme kindles and glows into poetry, and he falls down on his knees, so to speak, before the angel whose life he had embittered, confesses his own wretchedness and unworthiness, and adores her with cries of remorse and love:—

> "When on my sickly couch I lay,
> Impatient both of night and day,
> And groaning in unmanly strains,
> Called every power to ease my pains,
> Then Stella ran to my relief,
> With cheerful face and inward grief,
> And though by heaven's severe decree
> She suffers hourly more than me,
> No cruel master could require
> From slaves employed for daily hire,
> What Stella, by her friendship warmed,
> With vigour and delight performed.
> Now, with a soft and silent tread,
> Unheard she moves about my bed:
> My sinking spirits now supplies
> With cordials in her hands and eyes.
> Best pattern of true friends! beware;
> You pay too dearly for your care
> If, while your tenderness secures
> My life, it must endanger yours:
> For such a fool was never found
> Who pulled a palace to the ground,
> Only to have the ruins made
> Materials for a house decayed."

One little triumph Stella had in her life—one dear little piece of injustice was performed in her favour, for which I confess, for my part, I can't help thanking fate and the Dean. *That other person* was sacrificed to her—that—that young woman, who lived five doors from Dr. Swift's lodgings in Bury Street, and who flattered him, and made love to him in such an outrageous manner—Vanessa was thrown over.

Swift did not keep Stella's letters to him in reply to those he wrote to her. He kept Bolingbroke's, and Pope's, and

Harley's, and Peterborough's: but Stella, "very carefully," the Lives say, kept Swift's. Of course: that is the way of the world: and so we cannot tell what her style was, or of what sort were the little letters which the Doctor placed there at night, and bade to appear from under his pillow of a morning. But in Letter IV. of that famous collection he describes his lodging in Bury Street, where he has the first-floor, a dining-room and bed-chamber, at eight shillings a week; and in Letter VI. he says "he has visited a lady just come to town," whose name somehow is not mentioned; and in Letter VIII. he enters a query of Stella's—"What do you mean 'that boards near me, that I dine with now and then?' What the deuce! You know whom I have dined with every day since I left you, better than I do." Of course she does. Of course Swift has not the slightest idea of what she means. But in a few letters more it turns out that the Doctor has been to dine "gravely" with a Mrs. Vanhomrigh: then that he has been to "his neighbour:" then that he has been unwell, and means to dine for the whole week with his neighbour! Stella was quite right in her previsions. She saw from the very first hint, what was going to happen; and scented Vanessa in the air. The rival is at the Dean's feet. The pupil and teacher are reading together, and drinking tea together, and going to prayers together, and learning Latin together, and conjugating *amo, amas, amavi* together. The little language is over for poor Stella. By the rule of grammar and the course of conjugation, doesn't *amavi* come after *amo* and *amas?*

The loves of Cadenus and Vanessa you may peruse in Cadenus's own poem on the subject, and in poor Vanessa's vehement expostulatory verses and letters to him; she adores him, implores him, admires him, thinks him something god-like, and only prays to be admitted to lie at his feet. As they are bringing him home from church, those divine feet of Dr. Swift's are found pretty often in Vanessa's parlour. He likes to be admired and adored. He finds Miss Vanhomrigh to be a woman of great taste and spirit, and beauty and wit, and a fortune too. He sees her every day; he does not tell Stella about the business: until the impetuous Vanessa becomes too fond of him, until the Doctor is quite frightened by the young woman's ardour, and confounded by her warmth. He wanted to marry neither of them—that I believe was the truth; but if he had not married Stella, Vanessa would have had him in spite of himself. When he went back to Ireland, his Ariadne, not content to remain in her isle, pursued the fugitive Dean. In vain he protested, he vowed, he soothed, and bullied; the news of the Dean's marriage with Stella at last came to her, and it killed her—she died of that passion.

And when she died, and Stella heard that Swift had written beautifully regarding her, "That doesn't surprise me," said Mrs. Stella, "for we all know the Dean could write beautifully about a broomstick." A woman—a true woman! Would you have had one of them forgive the other?

In a note in his biography, Scott says that his friend Dr. Tuke of Dublin, has a lock of Stella's hair, enclosed in a paper by Swift, on which are written, in the Dean's hand, the words: "*Only a woman's hair.*" An instance, says Scott, of the Dean's desire to veil his feelings under the mask of cynical indifference.

See the various notions of critics! Do those words indicate indifference or an attempt to hide feeling? Did you ever hear or read four words more pathetic? Only a woman's hair: only love, only fidelity, only purity, innocence, beauty; only the tenderest heart in the world stricken and wounded, and passed away now out of reach of pangs of hope deferred, love insulted, and pitiless desertion:—only that lock of hair left; and memory and remorse, for the guilty, lonely wretch, shuddering over the grave of his victim.

And yet to have had so much love, he must have given some. Treasures of wit and wisdom, and tenderness, too, must that man have had locked up in the caverns of his gloomy heart, and shown fitfully to one or two whom he took in there. But it was not good to visit that place. People did not remain there long, and suffered for having been there. He shrank away from all affections sooner or later. Stella and Vanessa both died near him, and away from him. He had not heart enough to see them die. He broke from his fastest friend, Sheridan; he slunk away from his fondest admirer, Pope. His laugh jars on one's ear after seven score years. He was always alone—alone and gnashing in the darkness, except when Stella's sweet smile came and shone upon him. When that went, silence and utter night closed over him. An immense genius: an awful downfall and ruin. So great a man he seems to me, that thinking of him is like thinking of an empire falling. We have other great names to mention—none I think, however, so great or so gloomy.

THE IDEA OF A UNIVERSITY

BY
JOHN HENRY NEWMAN

INTRODUCTORY NOTE

JOHN HENRY NEWMAN *was born in London, February 21, 1801. Going up to Oxford at sixteen, he gained a scholarship at Trinity College, and after graduation became fellow and tutor of Oriel, then the most alive, intellectually, of the Oxford colleges. He took orders, and in 1828 was appointed vicar of St. Mary's, the university church. In 1832 he had to resign his tutorship on account of a difference of opinion with the head of the college as to his duties and responsibilities, Newman regarding his function as one of a "substantially religious nature."*

Returning to Oxford the next year from a journey on the Continent, he began, in cooperation with R. H. Froude and others, the publication of the "Tracts for the Times," a series of pamphlets which gave a name to the "Tractarian" or "Oxford" movement for the defence of the "doctrine of apostolical succession and the integrity of the Prayer-Book." After several years of agitation, during which Newman came to exercise an extraordinary influence in Oxford, the movement and its leader fell under the official ban of the university and of the Anglican bishops, and Newman withdrew from Oxford, feeling that the Anglican Church had herself destroyed the defences which he had sought to build for her. In October, 1845, he was received into the Roman Church.

The next year he went to Rome, and on his return introduced into England the institute of the Oratory. In 1854 he went to Dublin for four years as rector of the new Catholic university, and while there wrote his volume on the "Idea of a University," in which he expounds with wonderful clearness of thought and beauty of language his view of the aim of education. In 1879 he was created cardinal in recognition of his services to the cause of religion in England, and in 1890 he died. Of the history of Newman's religious opinions and influence no hint can be given here. The essays which follow do, indeed, imply important and fundamental elements of his system of belief; but they can be taken in detachment as the exposition of a view of the nature and value of culture by a man who was himself the fine flower of English university training and a master of English prose.

THE IDEA OF A UNIVERSITY

I. WHAT IS A UNIVERSITY?

IF I were asked to describe as briefly and popularly as I could, what a University was, I should draw my answer from its ancient designation of a *Studium Generale,* or "School of Universal Learning." This description implies the assemblage of strangers from all parts in one spot;—*from all parts;* else, how will you find professors and students for every department of knowledge? and *in one spot;* else, how can there be any school at all? Accordingly, in its simple and rudimental form, it is a school of knowledge of every kind, consisting of teachers and learners from every quarter. Many things are requisite to complete and satisfy the idea embodied in this description; but such as this a University seems to be in its essence, a place for the communication and circulation of thought, by means of personal intercourse, through a wide extent of country.

There is nothing far-fetched or unreasonable in the idea thus presented to us; and if this be a University, then a University does but contemplate a necessity of our nature, and is but one specimen in a particular medium, out of many which might be adduced in others, of a provision for that necessity. Mutual education, in a large sense of the word, is one of the great and incessant occupations of human society, carried on partly with set purpose, and partly not. One generation forms another; and the existing generation is ever acting and reacting upon itself in the persons of its individual members. Now, in this process, books, I need scarcely say, that is, the *litera scripta,* are one special instrument. It is true; and emphatically so in this age. Considering the prodigious powers of the press, and how they are developed at this time in the never-intermitting issue of periodicals, tracts, pamphlets, works in series, and light literature, we must allow there never was a time which promised fairer for dispensing with every other means of information and instruction. What can we want more, you will say, for the intellectual education of the whole man, and for every man, than so exuberant and diversified and persistent a promulgation of all kinds of knowledge? Why, you will ask, need we go up to knowledge, when knowledge comes down to us? The Sibyl wrote her prophecies upon the leaves of the forest, and wasted them; but here such careless profusion might be prudently indulged, for it can be afforded without loss, in consequence of the almost fabulous fecundity of the instrument which these latter ages have invented. We have sermons in stones, and books in the running brooks; works larger and more comprehensive than those which have gained for ancients an immortality, issue forth every morning, and are projected onwards to the ends of the earth at the rate of hundreds of miles a day. Our seats are strewed, our pavements are powdered, with swarms of little tracts; and the very bricks of our city walls preach wisdom, by informing us by their placards where we can at once cheaply purchase it.

I allow all this, and much more; such certainly is our popular education, and its effects are remarkable. Nevertheless, after all, even in this age, whenever men are really serious about getting what, in the language of trade, is called "a good article," when they aim at something precise, something refined, something really luminous, something really large, something choice, they go to another market; they avail themselves, in some shape or other, of the rival method, the ancient method, of oral instruction, of present communication between man and man, of teachers instead of learning, of the personal influence of a master, and the humble initiation of a disciple, and, in consequence, of great centres of pilgrimage and throng, which such a method of education necessarily involves. This, I think, will be found to hold good in all those departments or aspects of society, which possess an interest sufficient to bind men together, or to constitute what is called "a world."

It holds in the political world, and in the high world, and in the religious world; and it holds also in the literary and scientific world.

If the actions of men may be taken as any test of their convictions, then we have reason for saying this, viz.:—that the province and the inestimable benefit of the *literæ scripta* is that of being a record of truth, and an authority of appeal, and an instrument of teaching in the hands of a teacher; but that, if we wish to become exact and fully furnished in any branch of knowledge which is diversified and complicated, we must consult the living man and listen to his living voice. I am not bound to investigate the cause of this, and anything I may say will, I am conscious, be short of its full analysis;—perhaps we may suggest, that no books can get through the number of minute questions which it is possible to ask on any extended subject, or can hit upon the very difficulties which are severally felt by each reader in succession. Or again, that no book can convey the special spirit and delicate peculiarities of its subject with that rapidity and certainty which attend on the sympathy of mind with mind, through the eyes, the look, the accent, and the manner, in casual expressions thrown off at the moment, and the unstudied turns of familiar conversation. But I am already dwelling too long on what is but an incidental portion of my main subject. Whatever be the cause, the fact is undeniable. The general principles of any study you may learn by books at home; but the detail, the colour, the tone, the air, the life which makes it live in us, you must catch all these from those in whom it lives already. You must imitate the student in French or German, who is not content with his grammar, but goes to Paris or Dresden: you must take example from the young artist, who aspires to visit the great Masters in Florence and in Rome. Till we have discovered some intellectual daguerreotype, which takes off the course of thought, and the form, lineaments, and features of truth, as completely and minutely, as the optical instrument reproduces the sensible object; we must come to the teachers of wisdom to learn wisdom, we must repair to the fountain, and drink there. Portions of it may go from thence to the ends of the earth by means of books;

but the fulness is in one place alone. It is in such assemblages and congregations of intellect that books themselves, the masterpieces of human genius, are written, or at least originated.

The principle on which I have been insisting is so obvious, and instances in point are so ready, that I should think it tiresome to proceed with the subject, except that one or two illustrations may serve to explain my own language about it, which may not have done justice to the doctrine which it has been intended to enforce.

For instance, the polished manners and high-bred bearing which are so difficult of attainment, and so strictly personal when attained,—which are so much admired in society, from society are acquired. All that goes to constitute a gentleman,—the carriage, gait, address, gestures, voice; the ease, the self-possession, the courtesy, the power of conversing, the talent of not offending; the lofty principle, the delicacy of thought, the happiness of expression, the taste and propriety, the generosity and forbearance, the candour and consideration, the openness of hand;—these qualities, some of them come by nature, some of them may be found in any rank, some of them are a direct precept of Christianity; but the full assemblage of them, bound up in the unity of an individual character, do we expect they can be learned from books? are they not necessarily acquired, where they are to be found, in high society? The very nature of the case leads us to say so; you cannot fence without an antagonist, nor challenge all comers in disputation before you have supported a thesis; and in like manner, it stands to reason, you cannot learn to converse till you have the world to converse with; you cannot unlearn your natural bashfulness, or awkwardness, or stiffness, or other besetting deformity, till you serve your time in some school of manners. Well, and is it not so in matter of fact? The metropolis, the court, the great houses of the land, are the centres to which at stated times the country comes up, as to shrines of refinement and good taste; and then in due time the country goes back again home, enriched with a portion of the social accomplishments, which those very visits serve to call out and heighten in the gracious dispensers of them. We are unable to conceive how the "gentlemanlike" can otherwise be maintained; and maintained in this way it is.

And now a second instance: and here too I am going to speak without personal experience of the subject I am introducing. I admit I have not been in Parliament, any more than I have figured in the *beau monde;* yet I cannot but think that statesmanship, as well as high breeding, is learned, not by books, but in certain centres of education. If it be not presumption to say so, Parliament puts a clever man *au courant* with politics and affairs of state in a way surprising to himself. A member of the Legislature, if tolerably observant, begins to see things with new eyes, even though his views undergo no change. Words have a meaning now, and ideas a reality, such as they had not before. He hears a vast deal in public speeches and private conversation, which is never put into print. The bearings of measures and events, the action of parties, and the persons of friends and enemies, are brought out to the man who is in the midst of them with a distinctness, which the most diligent perusal of newspapers will fail to impart to them. It is access to the fountain-heads of political wisdom and experience, it is daily intercourse, of one kind or another, with the multitude who go up to them, it is familiarity with business, it is access to the contributions of fact and opinion thrown together by many witnesses from many quarters, which does this for him. However, I need not account for a fact, to which it is sufficient to appeal; that the Houses of Parliament and the atmosphere around them are a sort of University of politics.

As regards the world of science, we find a remarkable instance of the principle which I am illustrating, in the periodical meetings for its advance, which have arisen in the course of the last twenty years, such as the British Association. Such gatherings would to many persons appear at first sight simply preposterous. Above all subjects of study, Science is conveyed, is propagated, by books, or by private teaching; experiments and investigations are conducted in silence; discoveries are made in solitude. What have philosophers to do with festive celebrities, and panegyrical solemnities with mathematical and physical truth? Yet on a closer attention to the subject, it is found that not even scientific thought can dispense with the suggestions, the instruction, the stimulus, the sympathy, the intercourse with mankind on a large scale, which such meetings secure. A fine time of year is chosen, when days are long, skies are bright, the earth smiles, and all nature rejoices; a city or town is taken by turns, of ancient name or modern opulence, where buildings are spacious and hospitality hearty. The novelty of place and circumstance, the excitement of strange, or the refreshment of well-known faces, the majesty of rank or of genius, the amiable charities of men pleased both with themselves and with each other; the elevated spirits, the circulation of thought, the curiosity; the morning sections, the outdoor exercise, the well-furnished, well-earned board, the not ungraceful hilarity, the evening circle; the brilliant lecture, the discussions or collisions or guesses of great men one with another, the narratives of scientific processes, of hopes, disappointments, conflicts, and successes, the splendid eulogistic orations; these and the like constituents of the annual celebration, are considered to do something real and substantial for the advance of knowledge which can be done in no other way. Of course they can but be occasional; they answer to the annual Act, or Commencement, or Commemoration of a University, not to its ordinary condition; but they are of a University nature; and I can well believe in their utility. They issue in the promotion of a certain living and, as it were, bodily communication of knowledge from one to another, of a general interchange of ideas, and a comparison and adjustment of science with science, of an enlargement of mind, intellectual and social, of an ardent love of the particular study, which may be chosen by each individual, and a noble devotion to its interests.

Such meetings, I repeat, are but periodical, and only partially represent the idea of a University. The bustle and whirl which are their usual concomitants, are in ill keeping with the order and gravity of earnest intellectual education. We desiderate means of instruction which involve no interruption of our ordinary habits; nor need we seek it long, for the natural course of things brings it about, while we debate over it. In every great country, the metropolis itself becomes a sort of necessary University, whether we will or no. As the chief city is the seat of the court, of high society, of politics, and of law, so as a matter of course is it the seat of letters also; and at this time, for a long term of years, London and Paris are in fact and in operation Universities, though in Paris its famous University is no more, and in London a University scarcely exists except as a board of administration. The newspapers, magazines, reviews, journals, and periodicals of all kinds, the publishing trade, the libraries, museums, and academies there found, the learned and scientific societies, necessarily invest it with the functions of a University; and that atmosphere of intellect, which in a former age hung over Oxford or Bologna or Salamanca, has, with the change of times, moved away to the centre of civil government. Thither come up youths from all parts of the country, the students of law, medicine, and the fine arts, and the *employés and attachés* of literature. There they live, as chance determines; and they are satisfied with their temporary home, for they find in it all that was promised to them there. They have not come in vain, as far as their own object in coming is concerned. They have not learned any particular religion, but they have learned their own particular profession well. They have, moreover, become acquainted with the habits, manners, and opinions of their place of sojourn, and done their part in maintaining the tradition of them. We cannot then be without virtual Universities; a metropolis is such: the simple question is, whether the education sought and given should be based on principle, formed upon rule, directed to the highest ends, or left to the random succession of masters and schools, one after another, with a melancholy waste of thought and an extreme hazard of truth.

Religious teaching itself affords us an illustration of our subject to a certain point. It does not indeed seat itself merely in centres of the world; this is impossible from the nature of the case. It is intended for the many, not the few; its subject matter is truth necessary for us, not truth recondite and rare; but it concurs in the principle of a University so far as this, that its great instrument, or rather organ, has ever been that which nature prescribes in all education, the personal presence of a teacher, or, in theological language, Oral Tradition. It is the living voice, the breathing form, the expressive countenance, which preaches, which catechises. Truth, a subtle, invisible, manifold spirit, is poured into the mind of the scholar by his eyes and ears, through his affections, imagination, and reason; it is poured into his mind and is sealed up there in perpetuity, by propounding and repeating it, by questioning and requestioning, by correcting and explaining, by progressing and then recurring to first principles, by all those ways which are implied in the word "catechising." In the first ages, it was a work of long time; months, sometimes years, were devoted to the arduous task of disabusing the mind of the incipient Christian of its pagan errors, and of moulding it upon the Christian faith. The Scriptures indeed were at hand for the study of those who could avail themselves of them; but St. Irenæus does not hesitate to speak of whole races, who had been converted to Christianity, without being able to read them. To be unable to read or write was in those times no evidence of want of learning: the hermits of the deserts were, in this sense of the word, illiterate; yet the great St. Anthony, though he knew not letters, was a match in disputation for the learned philosophers who came to try him. Didymus again, the great Alexandrian theologian, was blind. The ancient discipline, called the *Disciplina Arcani,* involved the same principle. The more sacred doctrines of Revelation were not committed to books but passed on by successive tradition. The teaching on the Blessed Trinity and the Eucharist appears to have been so handed down for some hundred years; and when at length reduced to writing, it has filled many folios, yet has not been exhausted.

But I have said more than enough in illustration; I end as I began;—a University is a place of concourse, whither students come from every quarter for every kind of knowledge. You cannot have the best of every kind everywhere; you must go to some great city or emporium for it. There you have all the choicest productions of nature and art all together, which you find each in its own separate place elsewhere. All the riches of the land, and of the earth, are carried up thither; there are the best markets, and there the best workmen. It is the centre of trade, the supreme court of fashion, the umpire of rival talents, and the standard of things rare and precious. It is the place for seeing galleries of first-rate pictures, and for hearing wonderful voices and performers of transcendent skill. It is the place for great preachers, great orators, great nobles, great statesmen. In the nature of things, greatness and unity go together; excellence implies a centre. And such, for the third or fourth time, is a University; I hope I do not weary out the reader by repeating it. It is the place to which a thousand schools make contributions; in which the intellect may safely range and speculate, sure to find its equal in some antagonist activity, and its judge in the tribunal of truth. It is a place where inquiry is pushed forward, and discoveries verified and perfected, and rashness rendered innocuous, and error exposed, by the collision of mind with mind, and knowledge with knowledge. It is the place where the professor becomes eloquent, and is a missionary and a preacher, displaying his science in its most complete and most winning form, pouring it forth with the zeal of enthusiasm, and lighting up his own love of it in the breasts of his hearers. It is the place where the catechist makes good his ground as he goes, treading in the truth day by day into the ready memory, and wedging and tightening it into the expanding reason. It is a place which wins the admiration of the young by its celebrity, kindles the affections of the middle-aged by its beauty, and rivets the fidelity of the old by its associations. It is a seat of wisdom, a light of the world, a minister of the faith, an Alma Mater of the rising generation. It is this and a great deal more, and demands a somewhat better head and hand than mine to describe it well.

Such is a University in its idea and in its purpose; such in good measure has it before now been in fact. Shall it ever be again? We are going forward in the strength of the Cross, under the patronage of the Blessed Virgin, in the name of St. Patrick, to attempt it.

II. SITE OF A UNIVERSITY

IF we would know what a University is, considered in its elementary idea, we must betake ourselves to the first and most celebrated home of European literature and source of European civilization, to the bright and beautiful Athens,—Athens, whose schools drew to her bosom, and then sent back again to the business of life, the youth of the Western World for a long thousand years. Seated on the verge of the continent, the city seemed hardly suited for the duties of a central metropolis of knowledge; yet, what it lost in convenience of approach, it gained in its neighbourhood to the traditions of the mysterious East, and in the loveliness of the region in which it lay. Hither, then, as to a sort of ideal land, where all archetypes of the great and the fair were found in substantial being, and all departments of truth explored, and all diversities of intellectual power exhibited, where taste and philosophy were majestically enthroned as in a royal court, where there was no sovereignty but that of mind, and no nobility but that of genius, where professors were rulers, and princes did homage, hither flocked continually from the very corners of the *orbis terrarum,* the many-tongued generation, just rising, or just risen into manhood, in order to gain wisdom.

Pisistratus had in an early age discovered and nursed the infant genius of his people, and Cimon, after the Persian war, had given it a home. That war had established the naval supremacy of Athens; she had become an imperial state; and the Ionians, bound to her by the double chain of kindred and of subjection, were importing into her both their merchandize and their civilization. The arts and philosophy of the Asiastic coast were easily carried across the sea, and there was Cimon, as I have said, with his ample fortune, ready to receive them with due honours. Not content with patronizing their professors, he built the first of those noble porticos, of which we hear so much in Athens, and he formed the groves, which in process of time became the celebrated Academy. Planting is one of the most graceful, as in Athens it was one of the most beneficent, of employments. Cimon took in hand the wild wood, pruned and dressed it, and laid it out with handsome walks and welcome fountains. Nor, while hospitable to the authors of the city's civilization, was he ungrateful to the instruments of her prosperity. His trees extended their cool, umbrageous branches over the merchants, who assembled in the Agora, for many generations.

Those merchants certainly had deserved that act of bounty; for all the while their ships had been carrying forth the intellectual fame of Athens to the western world. Then commenced what may be called her University existence. Pericles, who succeeded Cimon both in the government and in the patronage of art, is said by Plutarch to have entertained the idea of making Athens the capital of federated Greece: in this he failed, but his encouragement of such men as Phidias and Anaxagoras led the way to her acquiring a far more lasting sovereignty over a far wider empire. Little understanding the sources of her own greatness, Athens would go to war: peace is the interest of a seat of commerce and the arts; but to war she went; yet to her, whether peace or war, it mattered not. The political power of Athens waned and disappeared; kingdoms rose and fell; centuries rolled away,—they did but bring fresh triumphs to the city of the poet and the sage. There at length the swarthy Moor and Spaniard were seen to meet the blue-eyed Gaul; and the Cappadocian, late subject of Mithridates, gazed without alarm at the haughty conquering Roman. Revolution after revolution passed over the face of Europe, as well as of Greece, but still she was there,—Athens, the city of mind,—as radiant, as splendid, as delicate, as young, as ever she had been.

Many a more fruitful coast or isle is washed by the blue Ægean, many a spot is there more beautiful or sublime to see, many a territory more ample; but there was one charm in Attica, which in the same perfection was nowhere else.

The deep pastures of Arcadia, the plain of Argos, the Thessalian vale, these had not the gift; Bœotia, which lay to its immediate north, was notorious for its very want of it. The heavy atmosphere of that Bœotia might be good for vegetation, but it was associated in popular belief with the dulness of the Bœotian intellect: on the contrary, the special purity, elasticity, clearness, and salubrity of the air of Attica, fit concomitant and emblem of its genius, did that for it which earth did not;—it brought out every bright hue and tender shade of the landscape over which it was spread, and would have illuminated the face even of a more bare and rugged country.

A confined triangle, perhaps fifty miles its greatest length, and thirty its greatest breadth; two elevated rocky barriers, meeting at an angle; three prominent mountains, commanding the plain,—Parnes, Pentelicus, and Hymettus; an unsatisfactory soil; some streams, not always full;—such is about the report which the agent of a London company would have made of Attica. He would report that the climate was mild; the hills were limestone; there was plenty of good marble; more pasture land than at first survey might have been expected, sufficient certainly for sheep and goats; fisheries productive; silver mines once, but long since worked out; figs fair; oil first-rate; olives in profusion. But what he would not think of noting down, was, that that olive tree was so choice in nature and so noble in shape, that it excited a religious veneration; and that it took so kindly to the light soil, as to expand into woods upon the open plain, and to climb up and fringe the hills. He would not think of writing word to his employers, how that clear air, of which I have spoken, brought out, yet blended and subdued the colours on the marble, till they had a softness and harmony, for all their richness, which in a picture looks exaggerated, yet is after all within the truth. He would not tell, how that same delicate and brilliant atmosphere freshened up the pale olive, till the olive forgot its monotony, and its cheek glowed like the arbutus or beech of the Umbrian hills. He would say nothing of the thyme and thousand fragrant herbs which carpeted Hymettus; he would hear nothing of the hum of its bees; nor take much account of the rare flavour of its honey, since Gozo and Minorca were sufficient for the English demand. He would look over the Ægean from the height he had ascended; he would follow with his eye the chain of islands, which, starting from the Sunian headland, seemed to offer the fabled divinities of Attica, when they would visit their Ionian cousins, a sort of viaduct thereto across the sea; but that fancy would not occur to him, nor any admiration of the dark violet billows with their white edges down below; nor of those graceful, fanlike jets of silver upon the rocks, which slowly rise aloft like water spirits from the deep, then shiver, and break, and spread, and shroud themselves, and disappear, in a soft mist of foam; nor of the gentle, incessant heaving and panting of the whole liquid plain; nor of the long waves, keeping steady time, like a line of soldiery, as they resound upon the hollow shore,—he would not deign to notice that restless living element at all, except to bless his stars that he was not upon it. Nor the distinct detail, nor the refined colouring, nor the graceful outline and roseate golden hue of the jutting crags, nor the bold shadows cast from Otus or Laurium by the declining sun;—our agent of a mercantile firm would not value these matters even at a low figure. Rather we must turn for the sympathy we seek to yon pilgrim student come from a semi-barbarous land to that small corner of the earth, as to a shrine, where he might take his fill of gazing on those emblems and coruscations of invisible unoriginate perfection. It was the stranger from a remote province, from Britain or from Mauritania, who in a scene so different from that of his chilly, woody swamps, or of his fiery choking sands, learned at once what a real University must be, by coming to understand the sort of country, which was its suitable home.

Nor was this all that a University required, and found in Athens. No one, even there, could live on poetry. If the students at that famous place had nothing better than bright hues and soothing sounds, they would not have been able or disposed to turn their residence there to much account. Of course they must have the means of living, nay, in a certain sense, of enjoyment, if Athens was to be an Alma Mater at the time, or to remain afterwards a pleasant thought in their memory. And so they had: be it recollected Athens was a port, and a mart of trade, perhaps the first in Greece; and this was very much to the point, when a number of strangers were ever flocking to it, whose combat was to be with intellectual, not physical difficulties, and who claimed to have their bodily wants supplied, that they might be at leisure to set about furnishing their minds. Now, barren as was the soil of Attica, and bare the face of the country, yet it had only too many resources for an elegant, nay luxurious abode there. So abundant were the imports of the place, that it was a common saying, that the productions, which were found singly elsewhere, were brought all together in Athens. Corn and wine, the staple of subsistence in such a climate, came from the isles of the Ægean; fine wool and carpeting from Asia Minor; slaves, as now, from the Euxine, and timber too; and iron and brass from the coasts of the Mediterranean. The Athenian did not condescend to manufactures himself, but encouraged them in others; and a population of foreigners caught at the lucrative occupation both for home consumption and for exportation. Their cloth, and other textures for dress and furniture, and their hardware—for instance, armour—were in great request. Labour was cheap; stone and marble in plenty; and the taste and skill, which at first were devoted to public buildings, as temples and porticos, were in course of time applied to the mansions of public men. If nature did much for Athens, it is undeniable that art did much more.

Here some one will interrupt me with the remark: "By the bye, where are we, and whither are we going?—what has all this to do with a University? at least what has it to do with education? It is instructive doubtless; but still how much has it to do with your subject?" Now I beg to assure the reader that I am most conscientiously employed upon my subject; and I should have thought every one would have seen this: however, since the objection is made, I may be allowed to pause awhile, and show distinctly the drift of what I have been saying, before I go farther. *What* has this to do with my subject! why, the question of the *site* is the very first that comes into consideration, when a *Stadium Generale* is contemplated; for that site should be a liberal and noble one; who will deny it? All authorities agree in this, and very little reflection will be sufficient to make it clear. I recollect a conversation I once had on this very subject with a very eminent man. I was a youth of eighteen, and was leaving my University for the Long Vacation, when I found myself in company in a public conveyance with a middle-aged person, whose face was strange to me. However, it was the great academical luminary of the day, whom afterwards I knew very well. Luckily for me, I did not suspect it; and luckily too, it was a fancy of his, as his friends knew, to make himself on easy terms especially with stage-coach companions. So, what with my flippancy and his condescension, I managed to hear many things which were novel to me at the time; and one point which he was strong upon, and was evidently fond of urging, was the material pomp and circumstance which should environ a great seat of learning. He considered it was worth the consideration of the government, whether Oxford should not stand in a domain of its own. An ample range, say four miles in diameter, should be turned into wood and meadow, and the University should be approached on all sides by a magnificent park, with fine trees in groups and groves and avenues, and with glimpses and views of the fair city, as the traveller drew near it. There is nothing surely absurd in the idea, though it would cost a round sum to realise it. What has a better claim to the purest and fairest possessions of nature, than the seat of wisdom? So thought my coach companion; and he did but express the tradition of ages and the instinct of mankind.

For instance, take the great University of Paris. That famous school engrossed as its territory the whole south bank of the Seine, and occupied one half, and that the pleasanter half, of the city. King Louis had the island pretty well as his own,—it was scarcely more than a fortification; and the north of the river was given over to the nobles and citizens to do what they could with its marshes; but the eligible south, rising from the stream, which swept around its base, to the fair summit of St. Genevieve, with its broad meadows, its vineyards and its gardens, and with the sacred elevation of Montmartre confronting it, all this was the inheritance of the University. There was that pleasant Pratum, stretching along the river's bank, in which the students for centuries took their recreation, which Alcuin seems to mention in his farewell verses to Paris, and which has given a name to the great Abbey of St. Germain-des-Prés. For long years it was devoted to the purposes of innocent and healthy enjoyment; but evil times came on the University; disorder arose within its precincts, and the fair meadow became the scene of party brawls; heresy stalked through Europe, and Germany and England no longer sending their contingent of students, a heavy debt was the consequence to the academical body. To let their land was the only resource left to them: buildings rose upon it, and spread along the green sod, and the country at length became town. Great was the grief and indignation of the doctors and masters, when this catastrophe occurred. "A wretched sight," said the Proctor of the German nation, "a wretched sight, to witness the sale of that ancient manor, whither the Muses were wont to wander for retirement and pleasure. Whither shall the youthful student now betake himself, what relief will he find for his eyes, wearied with intense reading, now that the pleasant stream is taken from him?" Two centuries and more have passed since this complaint was uttered; and time has shown that the outward calamity, which it recorded, was but the emblem of the great moral revolution, which was to follow; till the institution itself has followed its green meadows, into the region of things which once were and now are not.

And in like manner, when they were first contemplating a University in Belgium, some centuries ago, "Many," says Lipsius, "suggested Mechlin, as an abode salubrious and clean, but Louvain was preferred, as for other reasons, so because no city seemed from the disposition of place and people, more suitable for learned leisure. Who will not approve the decision? Can a site be healthier or more pleasant? The atmosphere pure and cheerful; the spaces open and delightful; meadows, fields, vines, groves, nay, I may say, a *rus in urbe*. Ascend and walk round the walls; what do you look down upon? Does not the wonderful and delightful variety smooth the brow and soothe the mind? You have corn, and apples, and grapes; sheep and oxen; and birds chirping or singing. Now carry your feet or your eyes beyond the walls; there are streamlets, the river meandering along; country-houses, convents, the superb fortress; copses or woods fill up the scene, and spots for simple enjoyment." And then he breaks out into poetry:

> Salvete Athenæ nostræ, Athenæ Belgicæ,
> Te Gallus, te Germanus, et te Sarmata
> Invisit, et Britannus, et te duplicis
> Hispaniæ alumnus, etc.

Extravagant, then, and wayward as might be the thought of my learned coach companion, when, in the nineteenth century, he imagined, Norman-wise, to turn a score of villages into a park or pleasaunce, still, the waywardness of his fancy is excused by the justness of his principle; for certainly, such as he would have made it, a University ought to be. Old Antony-à-Wood, discoursing on the demands of a University, had expressed the same sentiment long before him; as Horace in ancient times, with reference to Athens itself, when he spoke of seeking truth "in the *groves* of Academe." And to Athens, as will be seen, Wood himself appeals, when he would discourse of Oxford. Among "those things which are required to make a University," he puts down,—

"First, a good and pleasant site, where there is a wholesome and temperate constitution of the air; composed with waters, springs or wells, woods and pleasant fields; which being obtained, those commodities are enough to invite students to stay and abide there. As the Athenians in ancient times were happy for their conveniences, so also were the Britons, when by a remnant of the Grecians that came amongst them, they or their successors selected such a place in Britain to plant a school or schools therein, which for its pleasant situation was afterwards called Bellositum or Bellosite, now Oxford, privileged with all those conveniences before mentioned."

By others the local advantages of that University have been more philosophically analyzed;—for instance, with a reference to its position in the middle of southern England;

its situation on several islands in a broad plain, through which many streams flowed; the surrounding marshes, which, in times when it was needed, protected the city from invaders; its own strength as a military position; its easy communication with London, nay with the sea, by means of the Thames; while the London fortifications hindered pirates from ascending the stream, which all the time was so ready and convenient for a descent.

Alas! for centuries past that city has lost its prime honour and boast, as a servant and soldier of the Truth. Once named the second school of the Church, second only to Paris, the foster-mother of St. Edmund, St. Richard, St. Thomas Cantilupe, the theatre of great intellects, of Scotus the subtle Doctor, of Hales the irrefragable, of Occam the special, of Bacon the admirable, of Middleton the solid, and of Bradwardine the profound, Oxford has now lapsed to that level of mere human loveliness, which in its highest perfection we admire in Athens. Nor would it have a place, now or hereafter, in these pages, nor would it occur to me to speak its name, except that, even in its sorrowful deprivation, it still retains so much of that outward lustre, which, like the brightness on the prophet's face, ought to be a ray from an illumination within, as to afford me an illustration of the point on which I am engaged, viz., what should be the material dwelling-place and appearance, the local circumstances, and the secular concomitants of a great University. Pictures are drawn in tales of romance, of spirits seemingly too beautiful in their fall to be really fallen, and the holy Pope at Rome, Gregory, in fact, and not in fiction, looked upon the blue eyes and golden hair of the fierce Saxon youth in the slave market, and pronounced them Angels, not Angles; and the spell which this once loyal daughter of the Church still exercises upon the foreign visitor, even now when her true glory is departed, suggests to us how far more majestic and more touching, how brimful of indescribable influence would be the presence of a University, which was planted within, not without Jerusalem,—an influence, potent as her truth is strong, wide as her sway is world-wide, and growing, not lessening, by the extent of space over which its attraction would be exerted.

Let the reader then listen to the words of the last learned German, who has treated of Oxford, and judge for himself if they do not bear me out, in what I have said of the fascination which the very face and smile of a University possess over those who come within its range.

"There is scarce a spot in the world," says Huber, "that bears an historical stamp so deep and varied as Oxford; where so many noble memorials of moral and material power coöperating to an honourable end, meet the eye all at once. He who can be proof against the strong emotions which the whole aspect and genius of the place tend to inspire, must be dull, thoughtless, uneducated, or of very perverted views. Others will bear us witness, that, even side by side with the Eternal Rome, the Alma Mater of Oxford may be fitly named, as producing a deep, a lasting, and peculiar impression.

"In one of the most fertile districts of the Queen of the Seas, whom nature has so richly blessed, whom for centuries past no footstep of foreign armies has desecrated, lies a broad green vale, where the Cherwell and the Isis mingle their full, clear waters. Here and there primeval elms and oaks overshadow them; while in their various windings they encircle gardens, meadows, and fields, villages, cottages, farm-houses, and country-seats, in motley mixture. In the midst rises a mass of mighty buildings, the general character of which varies between convent, palace, and castle. Some few Gothic church-towers and Romaic domes, it is true, break through the horizontal lines; yet the general impression at a distance and at first sight, is essentially different from that of any of the towns of the middle ages. The outlines are far from being so sharp, so angular, so irregular, so fantastical; a certain softness, a peculiar repose, reigns in those broader, terrace-like rising masses. Only in the creations of Claude Lorraine or Poussin could we expect to find a spot to compare with the prevailing character of this picture, especially when lit up by a favourable light. The principal masses consist of Colleges, the University buildings, and the city churches; and by the side of these the city itself is lost on distant view. But on entering the streets, we find around us all the signs of an active and prosperous trade. Rich and elegant shops in profusion afford a sight to be found nowhere but in England; but with all this glitter and show, they sink into a modest, and, as it were, a menial attitude, by the side of the grandly severe memorials of the higher intellectual life, memorials which have been growing out of that life from almost the beginning of Christianity itself. Those rich and elegant shops are, as it were, the domestic offices of these palaces of learning, which ever rivet the eye of the observer, while all besides seems perforce to be subservient to them. Each of the larger and more ancient Colleges looks like a separate whole—an entire town, whose walls and monuments proclaim the vigorous growth of many centuries; and the town itself has happily escaped the lot of modern beautifying, and in this respect harmonizes with the Colleges."

There are those who, having felt the influence of this ancient School, and being smit with its splendour and its sweetness, ask wistfully, if never again it is to be Catholic, or whether at least some footing for Catholicity may not be found there. All honour and merit to the charitable and zealous hearts who so inquire! Nor can we dare to tell what in time to come may be the inscrutable purposes of that grace, which is ever more comprehensive than human hope and aspiration. But for me, from the day I left its walls, I never, for good or bad, have had anticipation of its future; and never for a moment have I had a wish to see again a place, which I have never ceased to love, and where I lived for nearly thirty years. Nay, looking at the general state of things at this day, I desiderate for a School of the Church, if an additional School is to be granted to us, a more central position than Oxford has to show. Since the age of Alfred and of the first Henry, the world has grown, from the west and south of Europe, into four or five continents; and I look for a city less inland than that old sanctuary, and a country closer upon the highway of the seas. I look towards a land both old and young; old in its Christianity, young in the promise of its future; a nation, which received grace before the Saxon came to Britain, and which has never quenched it; a Church, which comprehends in its history the rise and fall of Canterbury and York, which Augustine and Paulinus found, and Pole and Fisher left behind them. I contemplate a people which has had a long night, and will have an inevitable day. I am turning my eyes towards a hundred years to come, and I dimly see the island I am gazing on, become the road of passage and union between two hemispheres, and the centre of the world. I see its inhabitants rival Belgium in populousness, France in vigour, and Spain in enthusiasm; and I see England taught by advancing years to exercise in its behalf that good sense which is her characteristic towards every one else. The capital of that prosperous and hopeful land is situate in a beautiful bay and near a romantic region; and in it I see a flourishing University, which for a while had to struggle with fortune, but which, when its first founders and servants were dead and gone, had successes far exceeding their anxieties. Thither, as to a sacred soil, the home of their fathers, and the fountain-head of their Christianity, students are flocking from East, West, and South, from America and Australia and India, from Egypt and Asia Minor, with the ease and rapidity of a locomotion not yet discovered, and last, though not least, from England,—all speaking one tongue, all owning one faith, all eager for one large true wisdom; and thence, when their stay is over, going back again to carry over all the earth "peace to men of good will."

III. UNIVERSITY LIFE AT ATHENS

HOWEVER apposite may have been the digression into which I was led when I had got about half through the foregoing Chapter, it has had the inconvenience of what may be called running me off the rails; and now that I wish to proceed from the point at which it took place, I shall find some trouble, if I may continue the metaphor, in getting up the steam again, or if I may change it, in getting into the swing of my subject.

It has been my desire, were I able, to bring before the reader what Athens may have been, viewed as what we have since called a University; and to do this, not with any purpose of writing a panegyric on a heathen city, or of denying its many deformities, or of concealing what was morally base in what was intellectually great, but just the contrary, of representing things as they really were; so far, that is, as to enable him to see what a University is, in the very constitution of society and in its own idea, what is its nature and object, and what it needs of aid and support external to itself to complete that nature and to secure that object.

So now let us fancy our Scythian, or Armenian, or African, or Italian, or Gallic student, after tossing on the Saronic waves, which would be his more ordinary course to Athens, at last casting anchor at Piræus. He is of any condition or rank of life you please, and may be made to order, from a prince to a peasant. Perhaps he is some Cleanthes, who has been a boxer in the public games. How did it ever cross his brain to betake himself to Athens in search of wisdom? or, if he came thither by accident, how did the love of it ever touch his heart? But so it was, to Athens he came with three drachms in his girdle, and he got his livelihood by drawing water, carrying loads, and the like servile occupations. He attached himself, of all philosophers, to Zeno the Stoic,—to Zeno, the most high-minded, the most haughty of speculators; and out of his daily earnings the poor scholar brought his master the daily sum of an obolus, in payment for attending his lectures. Such progress did he make, that on Zeno's death he actually was his successor in his school; and, if my memory does not play me false, he is the author of a hymn to the Supreme Being, which is one of the noblest effusions of the kind in classical poetry. Yet, even when he was the head of a school, he continued in his illiberal toil as if he had been a monk; and, it is said, that once, when the wind took his pallium, and blew it aside, he was discovered to have no other garment at all;—something like the German student who came up to Heidelberg with nothing upon him but a great coat and a pair of pistols.

Or it is another disciple of the Porch,—Stoic by nature, earlier than by profession,—who is entering the city; but in what different fashion he comes! It is no other than Marcus, Emperor of Rome and philosopher. Professors long since were summoned from Athens for his service, when he was a youth, and now he comes, after his victories in the battle field, to make his acknowledgments at the end of life, to the city of wisdom, and to submit himself to an initiation into the Eleusinian mysteries.

Or it is a young man of great promise as an orator, were it not for his weakness of chest, which renders it necessary that he should acquire the art of speaking without over-exertion, and should adopt a delivery sufficient for the display of his rhetorical talents on the one hand, yet merciful to his physical resources on the other. He is called Cicero; he will stop but a short time, and will pass over to Asia Minor and its cities, before he returns to continue a career which will render his name immortal; and he will like his short sojourn at Athens so well, that he will take good care to send his son thither at an earlier age than he visited it himself.

But see where comes from Alexandria (for we need not

be very solicitous about anachronisms), a young man from twenty to twenty-two, who has narrowly escaped drowning on his voyage, and is to remain at Athens as many as eight or ten years, yet in the course of that time will not learn a line of Latin, thinking it enough to become accomplished in Greek composition, and in that he will succeed. He is a grave person, and difficult to make out; some say he is a Christian, something or other in the Christian line his father is for certain. His name is Gregory, he is by country a Cappadocian, and will in time become preëminently a theologian, and one of the principal Doctors of the Greek Church.

Or it is one Horace, a youth of low stature and black hair, whose father has given him an education at Rome above his rank in life, and now is sending him to finish it at Athens; he is said to have a turn for poetry: a hero he is not, and it were well if he knew it; but he is caught by the enthusiasm of the hour, and goes off campaigning with Brutus and Cassius, and will leave his shield behind him on the field of Philippi.

Or it is a mere boy of fifteen: his name Eunapius; though the voyage was not long, sea sickness, or confinement, or bad living on board the vessel, threw him into a fever, and, when the passengers landed in the evening at Piræus, he could not stand. His countrymen who accompanied him, took him up among them and carried him to the house of the great teacher of the day, Proæresius, who was a friend of the captain's, and whose fame it was which drew the enthusiastic youth to Athens. His companions understand the sort of place they are in, and, with the license of academic students, they break into the philosopher's house, though he appears to have retired for the night, and proceed to make themselves free of it, with an absence of ceremony, which is only not impudence, because Proæresius takes it so easily. Strange introduction for our stranger to a seat of learning, but not out of keeping with Athens; for what could you expect of a place where there was a mob of youths and not even the pretence of control; where the poorer lived any how, and got on as they could, and the teachers themselves had no protection from the humours and caprices of the students who filled their lecture-halls? However, as to this Eunapius, Proæresius took a fancy to the boy, and told him curious stories about Athenian life. He himself had come up to the University with one Hephæstion, and they were even worse off than Cleanthes the Stoic; for they had only one cloak between them, and nothing whatever besides, except some old bedding; so when Proæresius went abroad, Hephæstion lay in bed, and practised himself in oratory; and then Hephæstion put on the cloak, and Proæresius crept under the coverlet. At another time there was so fierce a feud between what would be called "town and gown" in an English University, that the Professors did not dare lecture in public, for fear of ill treatment.

But a freshman like Eunapius soon got experience for himself of the ways and manners prevalent in Athens. Such a one as he had hardly entered the city, when he was caught hold of by a party of the academic youth, who proceeded to practise on his awkwardness and his ignorance. At first sight one wonders at their childishness; but the like conduct obtained in the medieval Universities; and not many months have passed away since the journals have told us of sober Englishmen, given to matter-of-fact calculations, and to the anxieties of money-making, pelting each other with snowballs on their own sacred territory, and defying the magistracy, when they would interfere with their privilege of becoming boys. So I suppose we must attribute it to something or other in human nature. Meanwhile, there stands the new-comer, surrounded by a circle of his new associates, who forthwith proceed to frighten, and to banter, and to make a fool of him, to the extent of their wit. Some address him with mock politeness, others with fierceness; and so they conduct him in solemn procession across the Agora to the Baths; and as they approach, they dance about him like madmen. But this was to be the end of his trial, for the Bath was a sort of initiation; he thereupon received the pallium, or University gown, and was suffered by his tormentors to depart in peace. One alone is recorded as having been exempted from this persecution; it was a youth graver and loftier than even St. Gregory himself: but it was not from his force of character, but at the instance of

Gregory, that he escaped. Gregory was his bosom-friend, and was ready in Athens to shelter him when he came. It was another Saint and Doctor; the great Basil, then, (it would appear,) as Gregory, but a catechumen of the Church.

But to return to our freshman. His troubles are not at an end, though he has got his gown upon him. Where is he to lodge? whom is he to attend? He finds himself seized, before he well knows where he is, by another party of men, or three or four parties at once, like foreign porters at a landing, who seize on the baggage of the perplexed stranger, and thrust half a dozen cards into his unwilling hands. Our youth is plied by the hangers-on of professor this, or sophist that, each of whom wishes the fame or the profit of having a houseful. We will say that he escapes from their hands, —but then he will have to choose for himself where he will put up; and, to tell the truth, with all the praise I have already given, and the praise I shall have to give, to the city of mind, nevertheless, between ourselves, the brick and wood which formed it, the actual tenements, where flesh and blood had to lodge (always excepting the mansions of great men of the place), do not seem to have been much better than those of Greek or Turkish towns, which are at this moment a topic of interest and ridicule in the public prints. A lively picture has lately been set before us of Gallipoli. Take, says the writer, a multitude of the dilapidated outhouses found in farm-yards in England, of the rickety old wooden tenements, the cracked, shutterless structures of planks and tiles, the sheds and stalls, which our bye lanes, or fish-markets, or river-sides can supply; tumble them down on the declivity of a bare bald hill; let the spaces between house and house, thus accidentally determined, be understood to form streets, winding of course for no reason, and with no meaning, up and down the town; the roadway always narrow, the breadth never uniform, the separate houses bulging or retiring below, as circumstances may have determined, and leaning forward till they meet overhead;—and you have a good idea of Gallipoli. I question whether this picture would not nearly correspond to the special seat of the Muses in ancient times. Learned writers assure us distinctly that the houses of Athens were for the most part small and mean; that the streets were crooked and narrow; that the upper stories projected over the roadway; and that staircases, balustrades, and doors that opened outwards, obstructed it;—a remarkable coincidence of description. I do not doubt at all, though history is silent, that that roadway was jolting to carriages, and all but impassable; and that it was traversed by drains, as freely as any Turkish town now. Athens seems in these respects to have been below the average cities of its time. "A stranger," says an ancient, "might doubt, on the sudden view, if really he saw Athens."

I grant all this, and much more, if you will; but, recollect, Athens was the home of the intellectual, and beautiful; not of low mechanical contrivances, and material organization. Why stop within your lodgings counting the rents in your wall or the holes in your tiling, when nature and art call you away? You must put up with such a chamber, and a table, and a stool, and a sleeping board, any where else in the three continents; one place does not differ from another indoors; your magalia in Africa, or your grottos in Syria are not perfection. I suppose you did not come to Athens to swarm up a ladder, or to grope about a closet: you came to see and to hear, what hear and see you could not elsewhere. What food for the intellect is it possible to procure indoors, that you stay there looking about you? do you think to read there? where are your books? do you expect to purchase books at Athens—you are much out in your calculations. True it is, we at this day, who live in the nineteenth century, have the books of Greece as a perpetual memorial; and copies there have been, since the time that they were written; but you need not go to Athens to procure them, nor would you find them in Athens. Strange to say, strange to the nineteenth century, that in the age of Plato and Thucydides, there was not, it is said, a bookshop in the whole place: nor was the book trade in existence till the very time of Augustus. Libraries, I suspect, were the bright invention of Attalus or the Ptolemies; I doubt whether Athens had a library till the reign of Hadrian. It was what the student gazed on, what he heard, what he caught by the magic of sympathy, not what he read, which was the education furnished by Athens.

He leaves his narrow lodging early in the morning; and not till night, if even then, will he return. It is but a crib or kennel,—in which he sleeps when the weather is inclement or the ground damp; in no respect a home. And he goes out of doors, not to read the day's newspaper, or to buy the gay shilling volume, but to imbibe the invisible atmosphere of genius, and to learn by heart the oral traditions of taste. Out he goes; and, leaving the tumble-down town behind him, he mounts the Acropolis to the right, or he turns to the Areopagus on the left. He goes to the Parthenon to study the sculptures of Phidias; to the temple of the Dioscuri to see the paintings of Polygnotus. We indeed take our Sophocles or Æschylus out of our coat-pocket; but, if our sojourner at Athens would understand how a tragic poet can write, he must betake himself to the theatre on the south, and see and hear the drama literally in action. Or let him go westward to the Agora, and there he will hear Lysias or Andocides pleading, or Demosthenes haranguing. He goes farther west still, along the shade of those noble planes, which Cimon has planted there; and he looks around him at the statues and porticos and vestibules, each by itself a work of genius and skill, enough to be the making of another city. He passes through the city gate, and then he is at the famous Ceramicus; here are the tombs of the mighty dead; and here, we will suppose, is Pericles himself, the most elevated, the most thrilling of orators, converting a funeral oration over the slain into a philosophical panegyric of the living.

Onwards he proceeds still; and now he has come to that still more celebrated Academe, which has bestowed its own name on Universities down to this day; and there he sees a sight which will be graven on his memory till he dies. Many are the beauties of the place, the groves, and the statues, and the temple, and the stream of the Cephissus flowing by; many are the lessons which will be taught him day after day by teacher or by companion; but his eye is just now arrested by one object; it is the very presence of Plato. He does not hear a word that he says; he does not care to hear; he asks neither for discourse nor disputation; what he sees is a whole, complete in itself, not to be increased by addition, and greater than anything else. It will be a point in the history of his life; a stay for his memory to rest on, a burning thought in his heart, a bond of union with men of like mind, ever afterwards. Such is the spell which the living man exerts on his fellows, for good or for evil. How nature impels us to lean upon others, making virtue, or genius, or name, the qualification for our doing so! A Spaniard is said to have travelled to Italy, simply to see Livy; he had his fill of gazing, and then went back again home. Had our young stranger got nothing by his voyage but the sight of the breathing and moving Plato, had he entered no lecture-room to hear, no gymnasium to converse, he had got some measure of education, and something to tell of to his grandchildren.

But Plato is not the only sage, nor the sight of him the only lesson to be learned in this wonderful suburb. It is the region and the realm of philosophy. Colleges were the inventions of many centuries later; and they imply a sort of cloistered life, or at least a life of rule, scarcely natural to an Athenian. It was the boast of the philosophic statesman of Athens, that his countrymen achieved by the mere force of nature and the love of the noble and the great, what other people aimed at by laborious discipline; and all who came among them were submitted to the same method of education. We have traced our student on his wanderings from the Acropolis to the Sacred Way; and now he is in the region of the schools. No awful arch, no window of many-coloured lights marks the seats of learning there or elsewhere; philosophy lives out of doors. No close atmosphere oppresses the brain or inflames the eyelid; no long session stiffens the limbs. Epicurus is reclining in his garden; Zeno looks like a divinity in his porch; the restless Aristotle, on the other side of the city, as if in antagonism to Plato, is walking his pupils off their legs in his Lyceum by the Ilyssus. Our student has determined on entering himself as a disciple of Theophrastus, a teacher of marvellous popularity, who has brought together two thousand pupils from all parts of the world. He himself is of Lesbos; for masters, as well as students, come hither from all regions of the earth,—as befits a University. How could Athens have collected hearers in such numbers, unless she had selected teachers of such power? it was the range of territory, which the notion of a University implies, which furnished both the quantity of the one, and the quality of the other. Anaxagoras was from Ionia, Carneades from Africa, Zeno from Cyprus, Protagoras from Thrace, and Gorgias from Sicily. Andromachus was a Syrian, Proæresius an Armenian, Hilarius a Bithynian, Philiscus a Thessalian, Hadrian a Syrian. Rome is celebrated for her liberality in civil matters; Athens was as liberal in intellectual. There was no narrow jealousy, directed against a Professor, because he was not an Athenian; genius and talent were the qualifications; and to bring them to Athens, was to do homage to it as a University. There was a brotherhood and a citizenship of mind.

Mind came first, and was the foundation of the academical polity; but it soon brought along with it, and gathered round itself, the gifts of fortune and the prizes of life. As time went on, wisdom was not always sentenced to the bare cloak of Cleanthes; but beginning in rags, it ended in fine linen. The Professors became honourable and rich; and the students ranged themselves under their names, and were proud of calling themselves their countrymen. The University was divided into four great nations, as the medieval antiquarian would style them; and in the middle of the fourth century, Proæresius was the leader or proctor of the Attic, Hephæstion of the Oriental, Epiphanius of the Arabic, and Diophantus of the Pontic. Thus the Professors were both patrons of clients, and hosts and *proxeni* of strangers and visitors, as well as masters of the schools: and the Cappadocian, Syrian, or Sicilian youth who came to one or other of them, would be encouraged to study by his protection, and to aspire by his example.

Even Plato, when the schools of Athens were not a hundred years old, was in circumstances to enjoy the *otium cum dignitate*. He had a villa out at Heraclea; and he left his patrimony to his school, in whose hands it remained, not only safe, but fructifying, a marvellous phenomenon in tumultuous Greece, for the long space of eight hundred years. Epicurus too had the property of the Gardens where he lectured; and these too became the property of his sect. But in Roman times the chairs of grammar, rhetoric, politics, and the four philosophies, were handsomely endowed by the State; some of the Professors were themselves statesmen or high functionaries, and brought to their favourite study senatorial rank or Asiatic opulence.

Patrons such as these can compensate to the freshman, in whom we have interested ourselves, for the poorness of his lodging and the turbulence of his companions. In every thing there is a better side and a worse; in every place a disreputable set and a respectable, and the one is hardly known at all to the other. Men come away from the same University at this day, with contradictory impressions and contradictory statements, according to the society they have found there; if you believe the one, nothing goes on there as it should be: if you believe the other, nothing goes on as it should *not*. Virtue, however, and decency are at least in the minority everywhere, and under some sort of a cloud or disadvantage; and this being the case, it is so much gain whenever an Herodes Atticus is found, to throw the influence of wealth and station on the side even of a decorous philosophy. A consular man, and the heir of an ample fortune, this Herod was content to devote his life to a professorship, and his fortune to the patronage of literature. He gave the sophist Polemo about eight thousand pounds, as the sum is calculated, for three declamations. He built at Athens a stadium six hundred feet long, entirely of white marble, and capable of admitting the whole population. His theatre, erected to the memory of his wife, was made of cedar wood curiously carved. He had two villas, one at Marathon, the place of his birth, about ten miles from Athens, the other at Cephissia, at the distance of six; and thither he drew to him the *élite*, and at times the whole body of the students. Long arcades, groves of trees, clear pools for the bath, delighted and recruited the summer visitor. Never was so brilliant a lecture-room as his evening banqueting-hall; highly connected students from Rome mixed with the sharp-witted provincial of Greece or Asia

Minor; and the flippant sciolist, and the nondescript visitor, half philosopher, half tramp, met with a reception, courteous always, but suitable to his deserts. Herod was noted for his repartees; and we have instances on record of his setting down, according to the emergency, both the one and the other.

A higher line, though a rarer one, was that allotted to the youthful Basil. He was one of those men who seem by a sort of fascination to draw others around them even without wishing it. One might have deemed that his gravity and his reserve would have kept them at a distance; but, almost in spite of himself, he was the centre of a knot of youths, who, pagans as most of them were, used Athens honestly for the purpose for which they professed to seek it; and, disappointed and displeased with the place himself, he seems nevertheless to have been the means of their profiting by its advantages. One of these was Sophronius, who afterwards held a high office in the State: Eusebius was another, at that time the bosom-friend of Sophronius, and afterwards a Bishop. Celsus too is named, who afterwards was raised to the government of Cilicia by the Emperor Julian. Julian himself, in the sequel of unhappy memory, was then at Athens, and known at least to St. Gregory. Another Julian is also mentioned, who was afterwards commissioner of the land tax. Here we have a glimpse of the better kind of society among the students of Athens; and it is to the credit of the parties composing it, that such young men as Gregory and Basil, men as intimately connected with Christianity, as they were well known in the world, should hold so high a place in their esteem and love. When the two saints were departing, their companions came around them with the hope of changing their purpose. Basil persevered; but Gregory relented, and turned back to Athens for a season.

THE STUDY OF POETRY

BY
MATTHEW ARNOLD

INTRODUCTORY NOTE

Matthew Arnold *was the son of the well-known English schoolmaster, Thomas Arnold of Rugby. He was born at Laleham in 1822, and went to school at Winchester and Rugby. Going up to Balliol College, Oxford, in 1841, he won a scholarship, took the Newdigate prize for English verse, and was elected fellow of Oriel in 1845. After some years as a private secretary, he became an Inspector of Schools and performed the routine duties of this office for thirty-five years. For ten years he was Professor of Poetry at Oxford, and in 1883-84 he lectured in America. He died in 1888.*

Arnold is notable among modern men of letters as being almost equally distinguished in poetry and prose. His poetical work belongs to the earlier part of his career, and was practically finished by 1867. At the time of its first publication it appealed to only a narrow public; but it rose steadily in esteem through Arnold's life, though he ceased to add to it, and now many critics hold that it will outlive his prose. The best of it is refined in feeling, lofty in thought, and exquisite in expression; its prevailing note, a subdued melancholy.

In prose Arnold wrote on many themes—educational, social, political, and, especially, literary and religious. His attacks on dogmatic Christianity promise to be the most short-lived of his works; and perhaps deservedly so, as here Arnold was dealing with technical matters in which he was not an expert. In literary criticism he has been and still is a vital influence, urging especially the value of an outlook over the literatures of other countries and the cultivating of an intimacy with the great classics of the past. In the following essay on the "Study of Poetry," one of the most famous of his utterances, there may be found exemplified his characteristically vivacious and memorable style, his delicate appreciations brilliantly and precisely expressed, his concrete and persuasive argument. Perhaps no single critical document of our time has contributed so many phrases to the current literary vocabulary, or has stimulated so many readers to the use of lofty and definite standards of judgment.

THE STUDY OF POETRY[1]

'THE future of poetry is immense, because in poetry, where it is worthy of its high destinies, our race, as time goes on, will find an ever surer and surer stay. There is not a creed which is not shaken, not an accredited dogma which is not shown to be questionable, not a received tradition which does not threaten to dissolve. Our religion has materialised itself in the fact, in the supposed fact; it has attached its emotion to the fact, and now the fact is failing it. But for poetry the idea is everything; the rest is a world of illusion, of divine illusion. Poetry attaches its emotion to the idea; the idea *is* the fact. The strongest part of our religion to-day is its unconscious poetry.'

Let me be permitted to quote these words of my own, as uttering the thought which should, in my opinion, go with us and govern us in all our study of poetry. In the present work it is the course of one great contributory stream to the world-river of poetry that we are invited to follow. We are here invited to trace the stream of English poetry. But whether we set ourselves, as here, to follow only one of the several streams that make the mighty river of poetry, or whether we seek to know them all, our governing thought should be the same. We should conceive of poetry worthily, and more highly than it has been the custom to conceive of it. We should conceive of it as capable of higher uses, and called to higher destinies, than those which in general men have assigned to it hitherto. More and more mankind will discover that we have to turn to poetry to interpret life for us, to console us, to sustain us. Without poetry, our science will appear incomplete; and most of what now

[1] Published in 1880 as the General Introduction to 'The English Poets,' edited by T. H. Ward.

passes with us for religion and philosophy will be replaced by poetry. Science, I say, will appear incomplete without it. For finely and truly does Wordsworth call poetry 'the impassioned expression which is in the countenance of all science'; and what is a countenance without its expression? Again, Wordsworth finely and truly calls poetry 'the breath and finer spirit of all knowledge'; our religion, parading evidences such as those on which the popular mind relies now; our philosophy, pluming itself on its reasonings about causation and finite and infinite being; what are they but the shadows and dreams and false shows of knowledge? The day will come when we shall wonder at ourselves for having trusted to them, for having taken them seriously; and the more we perceive their hollowness, the more we shall prize 'the breath and finer spirit of knowledge' offered to us by poetry.

But if we conceive thus highly of the destinies of poetry, we must also set our standard for poetry high, since poetry, to be capable of fulfilling such high destinies, must be poetry of a high order of excellence. We must accustom ourselves to a high standard and to a strict judgment. Sainte-Beuve relates that Napoleon one day said, when somebody was spoken of in his presence as a charlatan: 'Charlatan as much as you please; but where is there *not* charlatanism?' —'Yes,' answers Sainte-Beuve, 'in politics, in the art of governing mankind, that is perhaps true. But in the order of thought, in art, the glory, the eternal honour is that charlatanism shall find no entrance; herein lies the inviolableness of that noble portion of man's being.' It is admirably said, and let us hold fast to it. In poetry, which is thought and art in one, it is the glory, the eternal honour, that charlatanism shall find no entrance; that this noble sphere be kept inviolate and inviolable. Charlatanism is for confusing or obliterating the distinctions between excellent and inferior, sound and unsound or only half-sound, true and untrue or only half-true. It is charlatanism, conscious or unconscious, whenever we confuse or obliterate these. And in poetry, more than anywhere else, it is unpermissible to confuse or obliterate them. For in poetry the distinction between excellent and inferior, sound and unsound or only half-sound, true and untrue or only half-true, is of paramount importance. It is of paramount importance because of the high destinies of poetry. In poetry, as in criticism of life under the conditions fixed for such a criticism by the laws of poetic truth and poetic beauty, the spirit of our race will find, we have said, as time goes on and as other helps fail, its consolation and stay. But the consolation and stay will be of power in proportion to the power of the criticism of life. And the criticism of life will be of power in proportion as the poetry conveying it is excellent rather than inferior, sound rather than unsound or alf-sound, true rather than untrue or half-true.

The best poetry is what we want; the best poetry will be found to have a power of forming, sustaining, and delighting us, as nothing else can. A clearer, deeper sense of the best in poetry, and of the strength and joy to be drawn from it, is the most precious benefit which we can gather from a poetical collection such as the present. And yet in the very nature and conduct of such a collection there is inevitably something which tends to obscure in us the consciousness of what our benefit should be, and to distract us from the pursuit of it. We should therefore steadily set it before our minds at the outset, and should compel ourselves to revert constantly to the thought of it as we proceed.

Yes; constantly in reading poetry, a sense for the best, the really excellent, and of the strength and joy to be drawn from it, should be present in our minds and should govern our estimate of what we read. But this real estimate, the only true one, is liable to be superseded, if we are not watchful, by two other kinds of estimate, the historic estimate and the personal estimate, both of which are fallacious. A poet or a poem may count to us historically, they may count to us on grounds personal to ourselves, and they may count to us really. They may count to us historically. The course of development of a nation's language, thought, and poetry, is profoundly interesting; and by regarding a poet's work as a stage in this course of development we may easily bring ourselves to make it of more importance as poetry than in itself it really is, we may come to use a language of quite exaggerated praise in criticising it; in short, to over-rate it. So arises in our poetic judgments the fallacy caused by the estimate which we may call historic. Then, again, a poet or poem may count to us on grounds personal to ourselves. Our personal affinities, likings and circumstances, have great power to sway our estimate of this or that poet's work, and to make us attach more importance to it as poetry than in itself it really possesses, because to us it is, or has been, of high importance. Here also we over-rate the object of our interest, and apply to it a language of praise which is quite exaggerated. And thus we get the source of a second fallacy in our poetic judgments—the fallacy caused by an estimate which we may call personal.

Both fallacies are natural. It is evident how naturally the study of the history and development of poetry may incline a man to pause over reputations and works once conspicuous but now obscure, and to quarrel with a careless public for skipping, in obedience to mere tradition and habit, from one famous name or work in its national poetry to another, ignorant of what it misses, and of the reason for keeping what it keeps, and of the whole process of growth in its poetry. The French have become diligent students of their own early poetry, which they long neglected; the study makes many of them dissatisfied with their so-called classical poetry, the court-tragedy of the seventeenth century, a poetry which Pellisson long ago reproached with its want of the true poetic stamp, with its *politesse stérile et rampante,* but which nevertheless has reigned in France as absolutely as if it had been the perfection of classical poetry indeed. The dissatisfaction is natural; yet a lively and accomplished critic, M. Charles d'Héricault, the editor of Clément Marot, goes too far when he says that 'the cloud of glory playing round a classic is a mist as dangerous to the future of a literature as it is intolerable for the purposes of history.' 'It hinders,' he goes on, 'it hinders us from seeing more than one single point, the culminating and exceptional point; the summary, fictitious and arbitrary, of a thought and of a work. It substitutes a halo for a physiognomy, it puts a statue where there was once a man, and hiding from us all trace of the labour, the attempts, the weaknesses, the failures, it claims not study but veneration; it does not show us how the thing is done, it imposes upon us a model. Above all, for the historian this creation of classic personages is inadmissible; for it withdraws the poet from his time, from his proper life, it breaks historical relationships, it blinds criticism by conventional admiration, and renders the investigation of literary origins unacceptable. It gives us a human personage no longer but a God seated immovable amidst His perfect work, like Jupiter on Olympus; and hardly will it be possible for the young student to whom such work is exhibited at such a distance from him, to believe that it did not issue ready made from that divine head.'

All this is brilliantly and tellingly said, but we must plead for a distinction. Everything depends on the reality of a poet's classic character. If he is a dubious classic, let us sift him; if he is a false classic, let us explode him. But if he is a real classic, if his work belongs to the class of the very best (for this is the true and right meaning of the word *classic, classical*), then the great thing for us is to feel and enjoy his work as deeply as ever we can, and to appreciate the wide difference between it and all work which has not the same high character. This is what is salutary, this is what is formative; this is the great benefit to be got from the study of poetry. Everything which interferes with it, which hinders it, is injurious. True, we must read our classic with open eyes, and not with eyes blinded with superstition; we must perceive when his work comes short, when it drops out of the class of the very best, and we must rate it, in such cases, at its proper value. But the use of this negative criticism is not in itself, it is entirely in its enabling us to have a clearer sense and a deeper enjoyment of what is truly excellent. To trace the labour, the attempts, the weaknesses, the failures of a genuine classic, to acquaint oneself with his time and his life and his historical relationships, is mere literary dilettantism unless it has that clear sense and deeper enjoyment for its end. It may be said that the more we know about a classic the better we shall enjoy him; and, if we lived as long as Methuselah and had all of us heads of perfect clearness and wills of perfect steadfastness, this might be true in fact as it is plausible in theory. But the case here is much the same as the case with the Greek and Latin studies of our schoolboys. The elaborate philological groundwork which we require them to lay is in theory an admirable preparation for appreciating the Greek and Latin authors worthily. The more thoroughly we lay the groundwork, the better we shall be able, it may be said, to enjoy the authors. True, if time were not so short, and schoolboys' wits not so soon tired and their power of attention exhausted; only, as it is, the elaborate philological preparation goes on, but the authors are little known and less enjoyed. So with the investigator of 'historic origins' in poetry. He ought to enjoy the true classic all the better for his investigations; he often is distracted from the enjoyment of the best, and with the less good he overbusies himself, and is prone to over-rate it in proportion to the trouble which it has cost him.

The idea of tracing historic origins and historical relationships cannot be absent from a compilation like the present. And naturally the poets to be exhibited in it will be assigned to those persons for exhibition who are known to prize them highly, rather than to those who have no special inclination towards them. Moreover, the very occupation with an author, and the business of exhibiting him, disposes us to affirm and amplify his importance. In the present work, therefore, we are sure of frequent temptation to adopt the historic estimate, or the personal estimate, and to forget the real estimate; which latter, nevertheless, we must employ if we are to make poetry yield us its full benefit. So high is that benefit, the benefit of clearly feeling and of deeply enjoying the really excellent, the truly classic in poetry, that we do well, I say, to set it fixedly before our minds as our object in studying poets and poetry, and to make the desire of attaining it the one principle to which, as the *Imitation* says, whatever we may read or come to know, we always return. *Cum multa legeris et cognoveris, ad unum semper oportet redire principium.*

The historic estimate is likely in especial to affect our

judgment and our language when we are dealing with ancient poets; the personal estimate when we are dealing with poets our contemporaries, or at any rate modern. The exaggerations due to the historic estimate are not in themselves, perhaps, of very much gravity. Their report hardly enters the general ear; probably they do not always impose even on the literary men who adopt them. But they lead to a dangerous abuse of language. So we hear Cædmon, amongst our own poets, compared to Milton. I have already noticed the enthusiasm of one accomplished French critic for 'historic origins.' Another eminent French critic, M. Vitet, comments upon that famous document of the early poetry of his nation, the *Chanson de Roland.* It is indeed a most interesting document. The *joculator* or *jongleur* Taillefer, who was with William the Conqueror's army at Hastings, marched before the Norman troops, so said the tradition, singing 'of Charlemagne and of Roland and of Oliver, and of the vassals who died at Roncevaux'; and it is suggested that in the *Chanson de Roland* by one Turoldus or Théroulde, a poem preserved in a manuscript of the twelfth century in the Bodleian Library at Oxford, we have certainly the matter, perhaps even some of the words, of the chant which Taillefer sang. The poem has vigour and freshness; it is not without pathos. But M. Vitet is not satisfied with seeing in it a document of some poetic value, and of very high historic and linguistic value; he sees in it a grand and beautiful work, a monument of epic genius. In its general design he finds the grandiose conception, in its details he finds the constant union of simplicity with greatness, which are the marks, he truly says, of the genuine epic, and distinguish it from the artificial epic of literary ages. One thinks of Homer; this is the sort of praise which is given to Homer, and justly given. Higher praise there cannot well be, and it is the praise due to epic poetry of the highest order only, and to no other. Let us try, then, the *Chanson de Roland* at its best. Roland, mortally wounded, lay himself down under a pine-tree, with his face turned towards Spain and the enemy—

> 'De plusurs choses à remembrer li prist,
> De tantes teres cume li bers cunquist,

De dulce France, des humes de sun lign,
De Carlemagne sun seignor ki l'nurrit.'[2]

That is primitive work, I repeat, with an undeniable poetic quality of its own. It deserves such praise, and such praise is sufficient for it. But now turn to Homer—

"Ὡς φάτο· τοὺς δ ἤδη κατέχεν φυσίζοος αἶα
ἐν Λακεδαίμονι αὖθι, φίλῃ ἐν πατρίδι γαίῃ.[3]

We are here in another world, another order of poetry altogether; here is rightly due such supreme praise as that which M. Vitet gives to the *Chanson de Roland.* If our words are to have any meaning, if our judgments are to have any solidity, we must not heap that supreme praise upon poetry of an order immeasurably inferior.

Indeed there can be no more useful help for discovering what poetry belongs to the class of the truly excellent, and can therefore do us most good, than to have always in one's mind lines and expressions of the great masters, and to apply them as a touchstone to other poetry. Of course we are not to require this other poetry to resemble them; it may be very dissimilar. But if we have any tact we shall find them, when we have lodged them well in our minds, an infallible touchstone for detecting the presence or absence of high poetic quality, and also the degree of this quality, in all other poetry which we may place beside them. Short passages, even single lines, will serve our turn quite sufficiently. Take the two lines which I have just quoted from Homer, the poet's comment on Helen's mention of her brothers;—or take his

Ἆ δειλώ, τί σφῶϊ δόμεν Πηλῆϊ ἄνακτι
θνητῷ; ὑμεῖς δ' ἐστὸν ἀγήρω τ' ἀθανάτω τε.
ἦ ἵνα δυστήνοισι μετ' ἀνδράσιν ἄλγε' ἔχητον;[4]

the address of Zeus to the horses of Peleus;—or take finally his

[2] 'Then began he to call many things to remembrance,—all the lands which his valour conquered, and pleasant France, and the men of his lineage, and Charlemagne his liege lord who nourished him.'—'Chanson de Roland,' iii. 939-942.

[3] 'So said she; they long since in Earth's soft arms were reposing,
There, in their own dear land, their fatherland, Lacedæmon.'
—'Iliad,' iii. 243, 244 (translated by Dr. Hawtrey).

[4] 'Ah, unhappy pair, why gave we you to King Peleus, to a mortal? but

Καὶ σέ, γέρον, τὸ πρὶν μὲν ἀκούομεν ὄλβιον εἶναι[5]

the words of Achilles to Priam, a suppliant before him. Take that incomparable line and a half of Dante, Ugolino's tremendous words—

> 'Io no piangeva; sì dentro impietrai.
> Piangevan elli . . .'[6]

take the lovely words of Beatrice to Virgil—

> 'Io son fatta da Dio, sua mercè, tale,
> Che la vostra miseria non mi tange,
> Nè fiamma d'esto incendio non m'assale . . .'[7]

take the simple, but perfect, single line—

> 'In la sua volontade è nostra pace.'[8]

Take of Shakespeare a line or two of Henry the Fourth's expostulation with sleep—

> 'Wilt thou upon the high and giddy mast
> Seal up the ship-boy's eyes, and rock his brains
> In cradle of the rude imperious surge . . .'

and take, as well, Hamlet's dying request to Horatio—

> 'If thou didst ever hold me in thy heart,
> Absent thee from felicity awhile,
> And in this harsh world draw thy breath in pain
> To tell my story . . .'

Take of Milton that Miltonic passage:

> 'Darken'd so, yet shone
> Above them all the archangel; but his face
> Deep scars of thunder had intrench'd, and care
> Sat on his faded cheek . . .'

add two such lines as—

> 'And courage never to submit or yield
> And what is else not to be overcome . . .'

and finish with the exquisite close to the loss of Proserpine, the loss

ye are without old age, and immortal. Was it that with men born to misery ye might have sorrow?'—'Iliad,' xvii. 443-445.

[5] 'Nay, and thou too, old man, in former days wast, as we hear, happy.'—'Iliad,' xxiv. 543.

[6] 'I wailed not, so of stone grew I within;—*they* wailed.'—'Inferno,' xxxiii. 39, 40.

[7] 'Of such sort hath God, thanked be His mercy, made me, that your misery toucheth me not, neither doth the flame of this fire strike me.'—'Inferno,' ii. 91-93.

[8] 'In His will is our peace.'—'Paradiso,' iii. 85.

'... which cost Ceres all that pain
To seek her through the world.'

These few lines, if we have tact and can use them, are enough even of themselves to keep clear and sound our judgments about poetry, to save us from fallacious estimates of it, to conduct us to a real estimate.

The specimens I have quoted differ widely from one another, but they have in common this: the possession of the very highest poetical quality. If we are thoroughly penetrated by their power, we shall find that we have acquired a sense enabling us, whatever poetry may be laid before us, to feel the degree in which a high poetical quality is present or wanting there. Critics give themselves great labour to draw out what in the abstract constitutes the characters of a high quality of poetry. It is much better simply to have recourse to concrete examples;—to take specimens of poetry of the high, the very highest quality, and to say: The characters of a high quality of poetry are what is expressed *there*. They are far better recognized by being felt in the verse of the master, than by being perused in the prose of the critic. Nevertheless if we are urgently pressed to give some critical account of them, we may safely, perhaps, venture on laying down, not indeed how and why the characters arise, but where and in what they arise. They are in the matter and substance of the poetry, and they are in its manner and style. Both of these, the substance and matter on the one hand, the style and manner on the other, have a mark, an accent, of high beauty, worth, and power. But if we are asked to define this mark and accent in the abstract, our answer must be: No, for we should thereby be darkening the question, not clearing it. The mark and accent are as given by the substance and matter of that poetry, by the style and manner of that poetry, and of all other poetry which is akin to it in quality.

Only one thing we may add as to the substance and matter of poetry, guiding ourselves by Aristotle's profound observation that the superiority of poetry over history consists in its possessing a higher truth and a higher seriousness (*φιλοσοφώτερον καὶ σπουδαιότερον*). Let us add, therefore, to what we have said, this: that the substance and matter of the best poetry acquire their special character from possessing, in an eminent degree, truth and seriousness. We may add yet further, what is in itself evident, that to the style and manner of the best poetry their special character, their accent, is given by their diction, and, even yet more, by their movement. And though we distinguish between the two characters, the two accents, of superiority, yet they are nevertheless vitally connected one with the other. The superior character of truth and seriousness, in the matter and substance of the best poetry, is inseparable from the superiority of diction and movement marking its style and manner. The two superiorities are closely related, and are in steadfast proportion one to the other. So far as high poetic truth and seriousness are wanting to a poet's matter and substance, so far also, we may be sure, will a high poetic stamp of diction and movement be wanting to his style and manner. In proportion as this high stamp of diction and movement, again, is absent from a poet's style and manner, we shall find, also, that high poetic truth and seriousness are absent from his substance and matter.

So stated, these are but dry generalities; their whole force lies in their application. And I could wish every student of poetry to make the application of them for himself. Made by himself, the application would impress itself upon his mind far more deeply than made by me. Neither will my limits allow me to make any full application of the generalities above propounded; but in the hope of bringing out, at any rate, some significance in them, and of establishing an important principle more firmly by their means, I will, in the space which remains to me, follow rapidly from the commencement the course of our English poetry with them in my view.

Once more I return to the early poetry of France, with which our own poetry, in its origins, is indissolubly connected. In the twelfth and thirteenth centuries, that seed-time of all modern language and literature, the poetry of France had a clear predominance in Europe. Of the two divisions of that poetry, its productions in the *langue d'oil* and its productions in the *langue d'oc,* the poetry of the *langue d'oc,* of southern France, of the troubadours, is of importance because of its effect on Italian literature;—the first literature of modern Europe to strike the true and grand note, and to bring forth, as in Dante and Petrarch it brought forth, classics. But the predominance of French poetry in Europe, during the twelfth and thirteenth centuries, is due to its poetry of the *langue d'oil,* the poetry of northern France and of the tongue which is now the French language. In the twelfth century the bloom of this romance-poetry was earlier and stronger in England, at the court of our Anglo-Norman kings, than in France itself. But it was a bloom of French poetry; and as our native poetry formed itself, it formed itself out of this. The romance-poems which took possession of the heart and imagination of Europe in the twelfth and thirteenth centuries are French; 'they are,' as Southey justly says, 'the pride of French literature, nor have we anything which can be placed in competition with them.' Themes were supplied from all quarters; but the romance-setting which was common to them all, and which gained the ear of Europe, was French. This constituted for the French poetry, literature, and language, at the height of the Middle Age, an unchallenged predominance. The Italian Brunetto Latini, the master of Dante, wrote his *Treasure* in French because, he says, 'la parleure en est plus délitable et plus commune à toutes gens.' In the same century, the thirteenth, the French romance-writer, Christian of Troyes, formulates the claims, in chivalry and letters, of France, his native country, as follows:—

'Or vous ert par ce livre apris,
Que Gresse ot de chevalerie
Le premier los et de clergie;
Puis vint chevalerie à Rome,
Et de la clergie la some,
Qui ore est en France venue.
Diex doinst qu'ele i soit retenue,
Et que li lius li abelisse
Tant que de France n'isse
L'onor qui s'i est arestée!'

'Now by this book you will learn that first Greece had the renown for chivalry and letters: then chivalry and the primacy in letters passed to Rome, and now it is come to France.

God grant it may be kept there; and that the place may please it so well, that the honour which has come to make stay in France may never depart thence!'

Yet it is now all gone, this French romance-poetry of which the weight of substance and the power of style are not unfairly represented by this extract from Christian of Troyes. Only by means of the historic estimate can we persuade ourselves not to think that any of it is of poetical importance.

But in the fourteenth century there comes an Englishman nourished on this poetry, taught his trade by this poetry, getting words, rhyme, metre from this poetry; for even of that stanza which the Italians used, and which Chaucer derived immediately from the Italians, the basis and suggestion was probably given in France. Chaucer (I have already named him) fascinated his contemporaries, but so too did Christian of Troyes and Wolfram of Eschenbach. Chaucer's power of fascination, however, is enduring; his poetical importance does not need the assistance of the historic estimate; it is real. He is a genuine source of joy and strength, which is flowing still for us and will flow always. He will be read, as time goes on, far more generally than he is read now. His language is a cause of difficulty for us; but so also, and I think in quite as great a degree, is the language of Burns. In Chaucer's case, as in that of Burns, it is a difficulty to be unhesitatingly accepted and overcome.

If we ask ourselves wherein consists the immense superiority of Chaucer's poetry over the romance-poetry—why it is that in passing from this to Chaucer we suddenly feel ourselves to be in another world, we shall find that his superiority is both in the substance of his poetry and in the style of his poetry. His superiority in substance is given by his large, free, simple, clear yet kindly view of human life,—so unlike the total want, in the romance-poets, of all intelligent command of it. Chaucer has not their helplessness; he has gained the power to survey the world from a central, a truly human point of view. We have only to call to mind the Prologue to *The Canterbury Tales*. The right comment upon it is Dryden's: 'It is sufficient to say, according to the proverb, that *here is God's plenty.*' And again: 'He is a perpetual fountain of good sense.' It is by a large, free, sound representation of things, that poetry, this high criticism of life, has truth of substance; and Chaucer's poetry has truth of substance.

Of his style and manner, if we think first of the romance-poetry and then of Chaucer's divine liquidness of diction, his divine fluidity of movement, it is difficult to speak temperately. They are irresistible, and justify all the rapture with which his successors speak of his 'gold dew-drops of speech.' Johnson misses the point entirely when he finds fault with Dryden for ascribing to Chaucer the first refinement of our numbers, and says that Gower also can show smooth numbers and easy rhymes. The refinement of our numbers means something far more than this. A nation may have versifiers with smooth numbers and easy rhymes, and yet may have no real poetry at all. Chaucer is the father of our splendid English poetry; he is our 'well of English undefiled,' because by the lovely charm of his diction, the lovely charm of his movement, he makes an epoch and founds a tradition. In Spenser, Shakespeare, Milton, Keats, we can follow the tradition of the liquid diction, the fluid movement of Chaucer; at one time it is his liquid diction of which in these poets we feel the virtue, and at another time it is his fluid movement. And the virtue is irresistible.

Bounded as is my space, I must yet find room for an example of Chaucer's virtue, as I have given examples to show the virtue of the great classics. I feel disposed to say that a single line is enough to show the charm of Chaucer's verse; that merely one line like this—

'O martyr souded[9] in virginitee!'

has a virtue of manner and movement such as we shall not find in all the verse of romance-poetry;—but this is saying nothing. The virtue is such as we shall not find, perhaps, in all English poetry, outside the poets whom I have named as the special inheritors of Chaucer's tradition. A single line, however, is too little if we have not the strain of

[9] The French *soudé;* soldered, fixed fast.

Chaucer's verse well in our memory; let us take a stanza. It is from *The Prioress's Tale,* the story of the Christian child murdered in a Jewry—

> 'My throte is cut unto my nekke-bone
> Saidè this child, and as by way of kinde
> I should have deyd, yea, longè time agone;
> But Jesu Christ, as ye in bookès finde,
> Will that his glory last and be in minde,
> And for the worship of his mother dere
> Yet may I sing *O Alma* loud and clere.'

Wordsworth has modernised this Tale, and to feel how delicate and evanescent is the charm of verse, we have only to read Wordsworth's first three lines of this stanza after Chaucer's—

> 'My throat is cut unto the bone, I trow,
> Said this young child, and by the law of kind
> I should have died, yea, many hours ago.'

The charm is departed. It is often said that the power of liquidness and fluidity in Chaucer's verse was dependent upon a free, a licentious dealing with language, such as is now impossible; upon a liberty, such as Burns too enjoyed, of making words like *neck, bird,* into a dissyllable by adding to them, and words like *cause, rhyme,* into a dissyllable by sounding the *e* mute. It is true that Chaucer's fluidity is conjoined with this liberty, and is admirably served by it; but we ought not to say that it was dependent upon it. It was dependent upon his talent. Other poets with a like liberty do not attain to the fluidity of Chaucer; Burns himself does not attain to it. Poets, again, who have a talent akin to Chaucer's, such as Shakespeare or Keats, have known how to attain his fluidity without the like liberty.

And yet Chaucer is not one of the great classics. His poetry transcends and effaces, easily and without effort, all the romance-poetry of Catholic Christendom; it transcends and effaces all the English poetry contemporary with it, it transcends and effaces all the English poetry subsequent to it down to the age of Elizabeth. Of such avail is poetic truth of substance, in its natural and necessary union with poetic truth of style. And yet, I say, Chaucer is not one of the great classics. He has not their accent. What is wanting to him is suggested by the mere mention of the name of the first great classic of Christendom, the immortal poet who died eighty years before Chaucer,—Dante. The accent of such verse as

'In la sua volontade è nostra pace . . .'

is altogether beyond Chaucer's reach; we praise him, but we feel that this accent is out of the question for him. It may be said that it was necessarily out of the reach of any poet in the England of that stage of growth. Possibly; but we are to adopt a real, not a historic, estimate of poetry. However we may account for its absence, something is wanting, then, to the poetry of Chaucer, which poetry must have before it can be placed in the glorious class of the best. And there is no doubt what that something is. It is the *σπουδαιότης* the high and excellent seriousness, which Aristotle assigns as one of the grand virtues of poetry. The substance of Chaucer's poetry, his view of things and his criticism of life, has largeness, freedom, shrewdness, benignity; but it has not this high seriousness. Homer's criticism of life has it, Dante's has it, Shakespeare's has it. It is this chiefly which gives to our spirits what they can rest upon; and with the increasing demands of our modern ages upon poetry, this virtue of giving us what we can rest upon will be more and more highly esteemed. A voice from the slums of Paris, fifty or sixty years after Chaucer, the voice of poor Villon out of his life of riot and crime, has at its happy moments (as, for instance, in the last stanza of *La Belle Heaulmière*[10]) more of this important poetic virtue of

[10] The name *Heaulmière* is said to be derived from a head-dress (helm) worn as a mark by courtesans. In Villon's ballad, a poor old creature of this class laments her days of youth and beauty. The last stanza of the ballad runs thus—

'Ainsi le bon temps regretons
Entre nous, pauvres vieilles sottes,
Assises bas, à croppetons,
Tout en ung tas comme pelottes;
A petit feu de chenevottes
Tost allumées, tost estainctes.
Et jadis fusmes si mignottes!
Ainsi en prend à maintz et maintes.'

'Thus amongst ourselves we regret the good time, poor silly old things, low-seated on our heels, all in a heap like so many balls; by a little fire of hemp-stalks, soon lighted, soon spent. And once we were such darlings! So fares it with many and many a one.'

seriousness than all the productions of Chaucer. But its apparition in Villon, and in men like Villon, is fitful; the greatness of the great poets, the power of their criticism of life, is that their virtue is sustained.

To our praise, therefore, of Chaucer as a poet there must be this limitation; he lacks the high seriousness of the great classics, and therewith an important part of their virtue. Still, the main fact for us to bear in mind about Chaucer is his sterling value according to that real estimate which we firmly adopt for all poets. He has poetic truth of substance, though he has not high poetic seriousness, and corresponding to his truth of substance he has an exquisite virtue of style and manner. With him is born our real poetry.

For my present purpose I need not dwell on our Elizabethan poetry, or on the continuation and close of this poetry in Milton. We all of us profess to be agreed in the estimate of this poetry; we all of us recognise it as great poetry, our greatest, and Shakespeare and Milton as our poetical classics. The real estimate, here, has universal currency. With the next age of our poetry divergency and difficulty begin. An historic estimate of that poetry has established itself; and the question is, whether it will be found to coincide with the real estimate.

The age of Dryden, together with our whole eighteenth century which followed it, sincerely believed itself to have produced poetical classics of its own, and even to have made advance, in poetry, beyond all its predecessors. Dryden regards as not seriously disputable the opinion 'that the sweetness of English verse was never understood or practised by our fathers.' Cowley could see nothing at all in Chaucer's poetry. Dryden heartily admired it, and, as we have seen, praised its matter admirably; but of its exquisite manner and movement all he can find to say is that 'there is the rude sweetness of a Scotch tune in it, which is natural and pleasing, though not perfect.' Addison, wishing to praise Chaucer's numbers, compares them with Dryden's own. And all through the eighteenth century, and down even into our own times, the stereotyped phrase of approbation for good verse found in our early poetry has been, that it even approached the verse of Dryden, Addison, Pope, and Johnson.

Are Dryden and Pope poetical classics? Is the historic estimate, which represents them as such, and which has been so long established that it cannot easily give way, the real estimate? Wordsworth and Coleridge, as is well known, denied it; but the authority of Wordsworth and Coleridge does not weigh much with the young generation, and there are many signs to show that the eighteenth century and its judgments are coming into favour again. Are the favourite poets of the eighteenth-century classics?

It is impossible within my present limits to discuss the question fully. And what man of letters would not shrink from seeming to dispose dictatorially of the claims of two men who are, at any rate, such masters in letters as Dryden and Pope; two men of such admirable talent, both of them, and one of them, Dryden, a man, on all sides, of such energetic and genial power? And yet, if we are to gain the full benefit from poetry, we must have the real estimate of it. I cast about for some mode of arriving, in the present case, at such an estimate without offence. And perhaps the best way is to begin, as it is easy to begin, with cordial praise.

When we find Chapman, the Elizabethan translator of Homer, expressing himself in his preface thus: 'Though truth in her very nakedness sits in so deep a pit, that from Gades to Aurora and Ganges few eyes can sound her, I hope yet those few here will so discover and confirm that, the date being out of her darkness in this morning of our poet, he shall now gird his temples with the sun,'—we pronounce that such a prose is intolerable. When we find Milton writing: 'And long it was not after, when I was confirmed in this opinion, that he, who would not be frustrate of his hope to write well hereafter in laudable things, ought himself to be a true poem,'—we pronounce that such a prose has its own grandeur, but that it is obsolete and inconvenient. But when we find Dryden telling us: 'What Virgil wrote in the vigour of his age, in plenty and at ease, I have undertaken to translate in my declining years; struggling with wants, oppressed with sickness, curbed in my genius, liable to be misconstrued in all I write,'—then we exclaim that here at last we have the true English prose, a prose such as we would all gladly use if we only knew how. Yet Dryden was Milton's contemporary.

But after the Restoration the time had come when our nation felt the imperious need of a fit prose. So, too, the time had likewise come when our nation felt the imperious need of freeing itself from the absorbing preoccupation which religion in the Puritan age had exercised. It was impossible that this freedom should be brought about without some negative excess, without some neglect and impairment of the religious life of the soul; and the spiritual history of the eighteenth century shows us that the freedom was not achieved without them. Still, the freedom was achieved; the preoccupation, an undoubtedly baneful and retarding one if it had continued, was got rid of. And as with religion amongst us at that period, so it was also with letters. A fit prose was a necessity; but it was impossible that a fit prose should establish itself amongst us without some touch of frost to the imaginative life of the soul. The needful qualities for a fit prose are regularity, uniformity, precision, balance. The men of letters, whose destiny it may be to bring their nation to the attainment of a fit prose, must of necessity, whether they work in prose or in verse, give a predominating, an almost exclusive attention to the qualities of regularity, uniformity, precision, balance. But an almost exclusive attention to these qualities involves some repression and silencing of poetry.

We are to regard Dryden as the puissant and glorious founder, Pope as the splendid high priest, of our age of prose and reason, of our excellent and indispensable eighteenth century. For the purposes of their mission and destiny their poetry, like their prose, is admirable. Do you ask me whether Dryden's verse, take it almost where you will, is not good?

> 'A milk-white Hind, immortal and unchanged,
> Fed on the lawns and in the forest ranged.'

I answer: Admirable for the purposes of the inaugurator of an age of prose and reason. Do you ask me whether Pope's verse, take it almost where you will, is not good?

> 'To Hounslow Heath I point, and Banstead Down
> Thence comes your mutton, and these chicks my own.'

I answer: Admirable for the purposes of the high priest of an age of prose and reason. But do you ask me whether such verse proceeds from men with an adequate poetic criticism of life, from men whose criticism of life has a high seriousness, or even, without that high seriousness, has poetic largeness, freedom, insight, benignity? Do you ask me whether the application of ideas to life in the verse of these men, often a powerful application, no doubt, is a powerful *poetic* application? Do you ask me whether the poetry of these men has either the matter or the inseparable manner of such an adequate poetic criticism; whether it has the accent of

> 'Absent thee from felicity awhile . . .'

or of

> 'And what is else not to be overcome . . .'

or of

> 'O martyr souded in virginitee!'

I answer: It has not and cannot have them; it is the poetry of the builders of an age of prose and reason. Though they may write in verse, though they may in a certain sense be masters of the art of versification, Dryden and Pope are not classics of our poetry, they are classics of our prose.

Gray is our poetical classic of that literature and age; the position of Gray is singular, and demands a word of notice here. He has not the volume or the power of poets who, coming in times more favourable, have attained to an independent criticism of life. But he lived with the great poets, he lived, above all, with the Greeks, through perpetually studying and enjoying them; and he caught their poetic point of view for regarding life, caught their poetic manner. The point of view and the manner are not self-sprung in him, he caught them of others; and he had not the free and abundant use of them. But, whereas Addison and Pope never had the use of them, Gray had the use of them at times. He is the scantiest and frailest of classics in our poetry, but he is a classic.

And now, after Gray, we are met, as we draw towards the end of the eighteenth century, we are met by the great name of Burns. We enter now on times where the personal estimate of poets begins to be rife, and where the real estimate of them is not reached without difficulty. But in spite of the disturbing pressures of personal partiality, of national partiality, let us try to reach a real estimate of the poetry of Burns.

By his English poetry Burns in general belongs to the eighteenth century, and has little importance for us.

> 'Mark ruffian Violence, distain'd with crimes,
> Rousing elate in these degenerate times;
> View unsuspecting Innocence a prey,
> As guileful Fraud points out the erring way;
> While subtle Litigation's pliant tongue
> The life-blood equal sucks of Right and Wrong!'

Evidently this is not the real Burns, or his name and fame would have disappeared long ago. Nor is Clarinda's love-poet, Sylvander, the real Burns either. But he tells us himself: 'These English songs gravel me to death. I have not the command of the language that I have of my native tongue. In fact, I think that my ideas are more barren in English than in Scotch. I have been at *Duncan Gray* to dress it in English, but all I can do is desperately stupid.' We English turn naturally, in Burns, to the poems in our own language, because we can read them easily; but in those poems we have not the real Burns.

The real Burns is of course in his Scotch poems. Let us boldly say that of much of this poetry, a poetry dealing perpetually with Scotch drink, Scotch religion, and Scotch manners, a Scotchman's estimate is apt to be personal. A Scotchman is used to this world of Scotch drink, Scotch religion, and Scotch manners; he has a tenderness for it; he meets its poet half way. In this tender mood he reads pieces like the *Holy Fair* or *Halloween*. But this world of Scotch drink, Scotch religion, and Scotch manners is against a poet, not for him, when it is not a partial countryman who reads him; for in itself it is not a beautiful world, and no one can deny that it is of advantage to a poet to deal with a beautiful world. Burns's world of Scotch drink, Scotch religion, and Scotch manners, is often a harsh, a sordid, a repulsive world: even the world of his *Cotter's Saturday Night* is not a beautiful world. No doubt a poet's criticism of life may have such truth and power that it triumphs over its world and delights us. Burns may triumph over his world, often he does triumph over his world, but let us observe how and where. Burns is the first case we have had where the bias of the personal estimate tends to mislead; let us look at him closely, he can bear it.

Many of his admirers will tell us that we have Burns, convivial, genuine, delightful, here—

> 'Leeze me on drink! it gies us mair
>   Than either school or college;
> It kindles wit, it waukens lair,
>   It pangs us fou o' knowledge.
> Be't whisky gill or penny wheep
>   Or ony stronger potion,
> It never fails, on drinking deep,
>   To kittle up our notion
>   By night or day.

There is a great deal of that sort of thing in Burns, and it is unsatisfactory, not because it is bacchanalian poetry, but because it has not that accent of sincerity which bacchanalian poetry, to do it justice, very often has. There is something in it of bravado, something which makes us feel that we have not the man speaking to us with his real voice; something, therefore, poetically unsound.

With still more confidence will his admirers tell us that we have the genuine Burns, the great poet, when his strain asserts the independence, equality, dignity, of men, as in the famous song *For a' that, and a' that*—

> 'A prince can mak' a belted knight,
>   A marquis, duke, and a' that;
> But an honest man's aboon his might,
>   Guid faith he mauna fa' that!
>   For a' that, and a' that,
>   Their dignities, and a' that,
>   The pith o' sense, and pride o' worth,
>   Are higher rank than a' that.'

Here they find his grand, genuine touches; and still more, when this puissant genius, who so often set morality at defiance, falls moralising—

> The sacred lowe o' weel-placed love
>   Luxuriantly indulge it;

But never tempt th' illicit rove,
Tho' naething should divulge it.
I waive the quantum o' the sin,
The hazard o' concealing,
But och! it hardens a' within,
And petrifies the feeling.'

Or in a higher strain—

'Who made the heart, 'tis He alone
Decidedly can try us;
He knows each chord, its various tone;
Each spring, its various bias.
Then at the balance let's be mute,
We never can adjust it;
What's *done* we partly may compute,
But know not what's resisted.'

Or in a better strain yet, a strain, his admirers will say, unsurpassable—

'To make a happy fire-side clime
To weans and wife,
That's the true pathos and sublime
Of human life.'

There is criticism of life for you, the admirers of Burns will say to us; there is the application of ideas to life! There is, undoubtedly. The doctrine of the last-quoted lines coincides almost exactly with what was the aim and end, Xenophon tells us, of all the teaching of Socrates. And the application is a powerful one; made by a man of vigorous understanding, and (need I say?) a master of language.

But for supreme poetical success more is required than the powerful application of ideas to life; it must be an application under the conditions fixed by the laws of poetic truth and poetic beauty. Those laws fix as an essential condition, in the poet's treatment of such matters as are here in question, high seriousness;—the high seriousness which comes from absolute sincerity. The accent of high seriousness, born of absolute sincerity, is what gives to such verse as

'In la sua volontade è nostra pace . . .'

to such criticism of life as Dante's, its power. Is this accent felt in the passages which I have been quoting from Burns? Surely not; surely, if our sense is quick, we must perceive that we have not in those passages a voice from the very inmost soul of the genuine Burns; he is not speaking to us from these depths, he is more or less preaching. And the compensation for admiring such passages less, from missing the perfect poetic accent in them, will be that we shall admire more the poetry where that accent is found.

No; Burns, like Chaucer, comes short of the high seriousness of the great classics, and the virtue of matter and manner which goes with that high seriousness is wanting to his work. At moments he touches it in a profound and passionate melancholy, as in those four immortal lines taken by Byron as a motto for *The Bride of Abydos,* but which have in them a depth of poetic quality such as resides in no verse of Byron's own—

> 'Had we never loved sae kindly,
> Had we never loved sae blindly,
> Never met, or never parted,
> We had ne'er been broken-hearted.'

But a whole poem of that quality Burns cannot make; the rest, in the *Farewell to Nancy,* is verbiage.

We arrive best at the real estimate of Burns, I think, by conceiving his work as having truth of matter and truth of manner, but not the accent or the poetic virtue of the highest masters. His genuine criticism of life, when the sheer poet in him speaks, is ironic; it is not—

> 'Thou Power Supreme, whose mighty scheme
> These woes of mine fulfil,
> Here firm I rest, they must be best
> Because they are Thy will!'

It is far rather: *Whistle owre the lave o't!* Yet we may say of him as of Chaucer, that of life and the world, as they come before him, his view is large, free, shrewd, benignant,—truly poetic therefore; and his manner of rendering what he sees is to match. But we must note, at the same time, his great difference from Chaucer. The freedom of Chaucer is heightened, in Burns, by a fiery, reckless energy; the benignity of Chaucer deepens, in Burns, into an overwhelming sense of the pathos of things;—of the pathos of human nature, the pathos, also, of non-human nature. Instead of the fluidity of Chaucer's manner, the manner of Burns has spring, boundless swiftness. Burns is by far the greater force, though he has perhaps less charm. The world of Chaucer is fairer, richer, more significant than that of Burns; but when the largeness and freedom of Burns get full sweep, as in *Tam o' Shanter,* or still more in that puissant and splendid production, *The Jolly Beggars,* his world may be what it will, his poetic genius triumphs over it. In the world of *The Jolly Beggars* there is more than hideousness and squalor, there is bestiality; yet the piece is a superb poetic success. It has a breadth, truth, and power which make the famous scene in Auerbach's Cellar, of Goethe's *Faust,* seem artificial and tame beside it, and which are only matched by Shakespeare and Aristophanes.

Here, where his largeness and freedom serve him so admirably, and also in those poems and songs where to shrewdness he adds infinite archness and wit, and to benignity infinite pathos, where his manner is flawless, and a perfect poetic whole is the result,—in things like the address to the mouse whose home he had ruined, in things like *Duncan Gray, Tam Glen, Whistle and I'll come to you my Lad, Auld Lang Syne* (this list might be made much longer),—here we have the genuine Burns, of whom the real estimate must be high indeed. Not a classic, nor with the excellent σπουδαιότης of the great classics, nor with a verse rising to a criticism of life and a virtue like theirs; but a poet with thorough truth of substance and an answering truth of style, giving us a poetry sound to the core. We all of us have a leaning towards the pathetic, and may be inclined perhaps to prize Burns most for his touches of piercing, sometimes almost intolerable, pathos; for verse like—

> 'We twa hae paidl't i' the burn
> From mornin' sun till dine;
> But seas between us braid hae roar'd
> Sin auld lang syne . . .'

where he is as lovely as he is sound. But perhaps it is by the perfection of soundness of his lighter and archer masterpieces that he is poetically most wholesome for us. For the votary misled by a personal estimate of Shelley, as so many of us have been, are, and will be,—of that beautiful spirit building his many-coloured haze of words and images

> 'Pinnacled dim in the intense inane'—

no contact can be wholesomer than the contact with Burns at his archest and soundest. Side by side with the

> 'On the brink of the night and the morning
> My coursers are wont to respire,
> But the Earth has just whispered a warning
> That their flight must be swifter than fire . . .'

of *Prometheus Unbound,* how salutary, how very salutary, to place this from *Tam Glen*—

> 'My minnie does constantly deave me
> And bids me beware o' young men;
> They flatter, she says, to deceive me;
> But wha can think sae o' Tam Glen?'

But we enter on burning ground as we approach the poetry of times so near to us—poetry like that of Byron, Shelley, and Wordsworth—of which the estimates are so often not only personal, but personal with passion. For my purpose, it is enough to have taken the single case of Burns, the first poet we come to of whose work the estimate formed is evidently apt to be personal, and to have suggested how we may proceed, using the poetry of the great classics as a sort of touchstone, to correct this estimate, as we had previously corrected by the same means the historic estimate where we met with it. A collection like the present, with its succession of celebrated names and celebrated poems, offers a good opportunity to us for resolutely endeavouring to make our estimates of poetry real. I have sought to point out a method which will help us in making them so, and to exhibit it in use so far as to put any one who likes in a way of applying it for himself.

At any rate the end to which the method and the estimate are designed to lead, and from leading to which, if they do lead to it, they get their whole value,—the benefit of being able clearly to feel and deeply to enjoy the best, the truly classic, in poetry,—is an end, let me say it once more at parting, of supreme importance. We are often told that an era is opening in which we are to see multitudes of a common sort of readers, and masses of a common sort of literature; that such readers do not want and could not relish anything better than such literature, and that to provide it is becoming a vast and profitable industry. Even if good literature entirely lost currency with the world, it would still be abundantly worth while to continue to enjoy it by oneself. But it never will lose currency with the world, in spite of monetary appearances; it never will lose supremacy. Currency and supremacy are insured to it, not indeed by the world's deliberate and conscious choice, but by something far deeper,—by the instinct of self-preservation in humanity.

SESAME AND LILIES

BY

JOHN RUSKIN

INTRODUCTORY NOTE

JOHN RUSKIN *(1819-1900), the greatest master of ornate prose in the English language, was born in London and educated at Oxford. He studied painting, and became a graceful and accurate draftsman, but he early transferred his main energies from the production to the criticism and teaching of art. In 1843 appeared the first volume of "Modern Painters," and succeeding volumes continued to be published till it was completed by the fifth in 1860. The startling originality of this work, both in style and in the nature of its esthetic theories, brought the author at once into prominence, though for some time he was more attacked than followed. Meanwhile he extended his scope to include other fields. In "The Seven Lamps of Architecture" (1849) and "The Stones of Venice" (1851-53) he applied his theories to architecture; in "Pre-Raphaelitism" (1851) he came to the defense of the new school of art then beginning to agitate England; in "Unto this Last" (1861) and many other writings he attacked the current political economy.*

In spite of the great variety of the themes of Ruskin's numerous volumes, there are to be found, underlying the eloquent argument, exposition, and exhortation of all, a few persistent principles. The application of these principles in one place is often inconsistent with that in another, and Ruskin frankly reversed his opinion with great frequency in successive editions of the same work; yet he continued to use a dogmatic tone which is at once his strength and his weakness.

The two lectures which constitute "Sesame and Lilies" deal ostensibly with the reading of books; but in characteristic fashion the author brings into the discussion his favorite ideas on ethics, esthetics, economics, and many other subjects. It thus gives a fairly comprehensive idea of the nature of the widespread influence which he exerted on English life and thought during the whole of the second half of the nineteenth century. Its style also, in its earnestness, its richness, and its lofty eloquence, exemplifies the pitch to which he brought the tradition of the highly decorated prose cultivated by De Quincey in the previous generation, a pitch of gorgeousness in color and cadence which has been surpassed by none.

SESAME AND LILIES

LECTURE I.—SESAME

OF KINGS' TREASURIES[1]

"You shall each have a cake of sesame,—and ten pound."

LUCIAN: *The Fisherman.*

MY FIRST duty this evening is to ask your pardon for the ambiguity of title under which the subject of this lecture has been announced: for indeed I am not going to talk of kings, known as regnant, nor of treasuries, understood to contain wealth; but of quite another order of royalty, and another material of riches, than those usually acknowledged. I had even intended to ask your attention for a little while on trust, and (as sometimes one contrives, in taking a friend to see a favorite piece of scenery) to hide what I wanted most to show, with such imperfect cunning as I might, until we unexpectedly reached the best point of view by winding paths. But—and as also I have heard it said, by men practiced in public address, that hearers are never so much fatigued as by the endeavour to follow a speaker who gives them no clue to his purposes,—I will take the slight mask off at once, and tell you plainly that I want to speak to you about the treasures hidden in books; and about the way we find them, and the way we lose them. A grave subject, you will say; and a wide one! Yes; so wide that I shall make no effort to touch the compass of it. I will try only to bring before you a few simple thoughts about reading, which press themselves upon me every day more deeply, as I watch the course of the public mind with respect to our daily enlarging means of education; and the answer-

[1] This lecture was given December 6, 1864, at Rusholme Town Hall, Manchester, in aid of a library fund for the Rusholme Institute.

ingly wider spreading on the levels, of the irrigation of literature.

2. It happens that I have practically some connection with schools for different classes of youth; and I receive many letters from parents respecting the education of their children. In the mass of these letters I am always struck by the precedence which the idea of a "position in life" takes above all other thoughts in the parents'—more especially in the mothers'—minds. "The education befitting such and such a *station in life*"—this is the phrase, this the object, always. They never seek, as far as I can make out, an education good in itself; even the conception of abstract rightness in training rarely seems reached by the writers. But, an education "which shall keep a good coat on my son's back;—which shall enable him to ring with confidence the visitors' bell at doubled-belled doors; which shall result ultimately in establishment of a doubled-belled door to his own house;—in a word, which shall lead to 'advancement in life';—*this* we pray for on bent knees—and this is *all* we pray for." It never seems to occur to the parents that there may be an education which, in itself, *is* advancement in Life;—that any other than that may perhaps be advancement in Death; and tha' this essential education might be more easily got, or given, than they fancy, if they set about it in the right way; while it is for no price, and by no favor, to be got, if they set about it in the wrong.

3. Indeed, among the ideas most prevalent and effective in the mind of this busiest of countries, I suppose the first—at least that which is confessed with the greatest frankness, and put forward as the fittest stimulus to youthful exertion—is this of "Advancement in Life." May I ask you to consider with me what this idea practically includes, and what it should include?

Practically, then, at present, "advancement in life" means, becoming conspicuous in life;—obtaining a position which shall be acknowledged by others to be respectable or honorable. We do not understand by this advancement in general, the mere making of money, but the being known to have made it; not the accomplishment of any great aim, but the being seen to have accomplished it. In a word, we mean the gratification of our thirst for applause. That thirst, if the last infirmity of noble minds, is also the first infirmity of weak ones; and, on the whole, the strongest impulsive influence of average humanity: the greatest efforts of the race have always been traceable to the love of praise, as its greatest catastrophes to the love of pleasure.

4. I am not about to attack or defend this impulse. I want you only to feel how it lies at the root of effort; especially of all modern effort. It is the gratification of vanity which is, with us, the stimulus of toil, and balm of repose; so closely does it touch the very springs of life that the wounding of our vanity is always spoken of (and truly) as in its measure *mortal;* we call it "mortification," using the same expression which we should apply to a gangrenous and incurable bodily hurt. And although few of us may be physicians enough to recognize the various effect of this passion upon health and energy, I believe most honest men know, and would at once acknowledge, its leading power with them as a motive. The seaman does not commonly desire to be made captain only because he knows he can manage the ship better than any other sailor on board. He wants to be made captain that he may be *called* captain. The clergyman does not usually want to be made a bishop only because he believes no other hand can, as firmly as his, direct the diocese through its difficulties. He wants to be made bishop primarily that he may be called "My Lord." And a prince does not usually desire to enlarge, or a subject to gain, a kingdom, because he believes that no one else can as well serve the State, upon its throne; but, briefly, because he wishes to be addressed as "Your Majesty," by as many lips as may be brought to such utterance.

5. This, then, being the main idea of "advancement in life," the force of it applies, for all of us, according to our station, particularly to that secondary result of such advancement which we call "getting into good society." We want to get into good society, not that we may have it, but that we may be seen in it; and our notion of its goodness depends primarily on its conspicuousness.

Will you pardon me if I pause for a moment to put what I fear you may think an impertinent question? I never can go on with an address unless I feel, or know, that my audience are either with me or against me: I do not much care which, in beginning; but I must know where they are; and I would fain find out, at this instant, whether you think I am putting the motives of popular action too low. I am resolved, to-night, to state them low enough to be admitted as probable; for whenever, in my writings on Political Economy, I assume that a little honesty, or generosity—or what used to be called "virtue"—may be calculated upon as a human motive of action, people always answer me, saying, "You must not calculate on that: that is not in human nature: you must not assume anything to be common to men but acquisitiveness and jealousy; no other feeling ever has influence on them, except accidentally, and in matters out of the way of business." I begin, accordingly, to-night low in the scale of motives; but I must know if you think me right in doing so. Therefore, let me ask those who admit the love of praise to be usually the strongest motive in men's minds in seeking advancement, and the honest desire of doing any kind of duty to be an entirely secondary one, to hold up their hands. (*About a dozen of hands held up—the audience, partly not being sure the lecturer is serious, and, partly, shy of expressing opinion.*) I am quite serious—I really do want to know what you think; however, I can judge by putting the reverse question. Will those who think that duty is generally the first, and love of praise the second, motive, hold up their hands? (*One hand reported to have been held up, behind the lecturer.*) Very good; I see you are with me, and that you think I have not begun too near the ground. Now, without teasing you by putting farther question, I venture to assume that you will admit duty as at least a secondary or tertiary motive. You think that the desire of doing something useful, or obtaining some real good, is indeed an existent collateral idea, though a secondary one, in most men's desire of advancement. You will grant that moderately honest men desire place and office, at least in some measure, for the sake of beneficent power; and would wish to associate rather with sensible and well-informed persons than with fools and ignorant persons, whether they are seen in the company of the sensible ones or not. And finally, without being troubled by repetition of any common truisms about the preciousness of friends, and the influence of companions, you will admit, doubtless that according to the sincerity of our desire that our friends may be true, and our companions wise,—and in proportion to the earnestness and discretion with which we choose both, will be the general chances of our happiness and usefulness.

6. But, granting that we had both the will and the sense to choose our friends well, how few of us have the power! or, at least, how limited, for most, is the sphere of choice! Nearly all our associations are determined by chance, or necessity; and restricted within a narrow circle. We cannot know whom we would; and those whom we know, we cannot have at our side when we most need them. All the higher circles of human intelligence are, to those beneath, only momentarily and partially open. We may, by good fortune, obtain a glimpse of a great poet, and hear the sound of his voice; or put a question to a man of science, and be answered good-humoredly. We may intrude ten minutes' talk on a cabinet minister, answered probably with words worse than silence, being deceptive; or snatch, once or twice in our lives, the privilege of throwing a bouquet in the path of a Princess, or arresting the kind glance of a Queen. And yet these momentary chances we covet; and spend our years, and passions, and powers in pursuit of little more than these; while, meantime, there is a society continually open to us, of people who will talk to us as long as we like, whatever our rank or occupation;—talk to us in the best words they can choose, and of the things nearest their hearts. And this society, because it is so numerous and so gentle, and can be kept waiting round us all day long,—kings and statesmen lingering patiently, not to grant audience, but to gain it!—in those plainly furnished and narrow anterooms, our bookcase shelves,—we make no account of that company,—perhaps never listen to a word they would say, all day long!

7. You may tell me, perhaps, or think within yourselves, that the apathy with which we regard this company of the noble, who are praying us to listen to them; and the passion

with which we pursue the company, probably of the ignoble who despise us, or who have nothing to teach us, are grounded in this,—that we can see the faces of the living men, and it is themselves, and not their sayings, with which we desire to become familiar. But it is not so. Suppose you never were to see their faces;—suppose you could be put behind a screen in the statesman's cabinet, or the prince's chamber, would you not be glad to listen to their words, though you were forbidden to advance beyond the screen? And when the screen is only a little less, folded in two instead of four, and you can be hidden behind the cover of the two boards that bind a book, and listen all day long, not to the casual talk, but to the studied, determined, chosen addresses of the wisest of men;—this station of audience, and honorable privy council, you despise!

8. But perhaps you will say that it is because the living people talk of things that are passing, and are of immediate interest to you, that you desire to hear them. Nay; that cannot be so, for the living people will themselves tell you about passing matters, much better in their writings than in their careless talk. But I admit that this motive does influence you, so far as you prefer those rapid and ephemeral writings to slow and enduring writings,—books, properly so called. For all books are divisible into two classes, the books of the hour, and the books of all time. Mark this distinction—it is not one of quality only. It is not merely the bad book that does not last, and the good one that does. It is a distinction of species. There are good books for the hour, and good ones for all time; bad books for the hour, and bad ones for all time. I must define the two kinds before I go farther.

9. The good book of the hour, then,—I do not speak of the bad ones,—is simply the useful or pleasant talk of some person whom you cannot otherwise converse with, printed for you. Very useful often, telling you what you need to know; very pleasant often, as a sensible friend's present talk would be. These bright accounts of travels; good-humored and witty discussions of question; lively or pathetic story-telling in the form of novel; firm fact-telling, by the real agents concerned in the events of passing history;—all these

books of the hour, multiplying among us as education becomes more general, are a peculiar possession of the present age; we ought to be entirely thankful for them, and entirely ashamed of ourselves if we make no good use of them. But we make the worst possible use if we allow them to usurp the place of true books: for strictly speaking, they are not books at all, but merely letters or newspapers in good print. Our friend's letter may be delightful, or necessary, to-day: whether worth keeping or not, is to be considered. The newspaper may be entirely proper at breakfast time, but assuredly it is not reading for all day. So, though bound up in a volume, the long letter which gives you so pleasant an account of the inns, and roads, and weather last year at such a place, or which tells you that amusing story, or gives you the real circumstances of such and such events, however valuable for occasional reference, may not be, in the real sense of the word, a "book" at all, nor in the real sense, to be "read." A book is essentially not a talked thing, but a written thing; and written, not with the view of mere communication, but of permanence. The book of talk is printed only because its author cannot speak to thousands of people at once; if he could, he would—the volume is mere *multiplication* of his voice. You cannot talk to your friend in India; if you could, you would; you write instead: that is mere *conveyance* of voice. But a book is written, not to multiply the voice merely, not to carry it merely, but to perpetuate it. The author has something to say which he perceives to be true and useful, or helpfully beautiful. So far as he knows, no one has yet said it; so far as he knows, no one else can say it. He is bound to say it, clearly and melodiously if he may; clearly, at all events. In the sum of his life he finds this to be the thing, or group of things, manifest to him;—this, the piece of true knowledge, or sight, which his share of sunshine and earth has permitted him to seize. He would fain set it down forever; engrave it on rock, if he could; saying, "This is the best of me; for the rest, I ate, and drank, and slept, loved, and hated, like another; my life was as the vapor and is not; but this I saw and knew: this if anything of mine, is worth your memory." That is his "writing"; it is, in his small human way, and with whatever degree of true inspiration is in him, his inscription, or scripture. That is a "Book."

10. Perhaps you think no books were ever so written.

But, again, I ask you, do you at all believe in honesty, or at all in kindness? or do you think there is never any honesty or benevolence in wise people? None of us, I hope, are so unhappy as to think that. Well, whatever bit of a wise man's work is honestly and benevolently done, that bit is his book, or his piece of art.[2] It is mixed always with evil fragments—ill-done, redundant, affected work. But if you read rightly, you will easily discover the true bits, and those *are* the book.

11. Now books of this kind have been written in all ages by their greatest men:—by great readers, great statesmen, and great thinkers. These are all at your choice; and Life is short. You have heard as much before;—yet have you measured and mapped out this short life and its possibilities? Do you know, if you read this, that you cannot read that—that what you lose to-day you cannot gain to-morrow? Will you go and gossip with your housemaid, or your stable-boy, when you may talk with queens and kings; or flatter yourselves that it is with any worthy consciousness of your own claims to respect that you jostle with the hungry and common crowd for *entrée* here, and audience there, when all the while this eternal court is open to you, with its society, wide as the world, multitudinous as its days, the chosen, and the mighty, of every place and time? Into that you may enter always; in that you may take fellowship and rank according to your wish; from that, once entered into it, you can never be outcast but by your own fault; by your aristocracy of companionship there, your own inherent aristocracy will be assuredly tested, and the motives with which you strive to take high place in the society of the living, measured, as to all the truth and sincerity that are in them, by the place you desire to take in this company of the Dead.

12. "The place you desire," and the place you *fit yourself for,* I must also say; because, observe, this court of the past differs from all living aristocracy in this:—it is open

[2] Note this sentence carefully, and compare the "Queen of the Air," § 106.

to labor and to merit, but to nothing else. No wealth will bribe, no name overawe, no artifice deceive, the guardian of those Elysian gates. In the deep sense, no vile or vulgar person ever enters there. At the portières of that silent Faubourg St. Germain, there is but brief question, Do you deserve to enter? Pass. Do you ask to be the companion of nobles? Make yourself noble, and you shall be. Do you long for the conversation of the wise? Learn to understand it, and you shall hear it. But on other terms?—no. If you will not rise to us, we cannot stoop to you. The living lord may assume courtesy, the living philosopher explain his thought to you with considerate pain; but here we neither feign nor interpret; you must rise to the level of our thoughts if you would be gladdened by them, and share our feelings, if you would recognize our presence."

13. This, then, is what you have to do, and I admit that it is much. You must, in a word, love these people, if you are to be among them. No ambition is of any use. They scorn your ambition. You must love them, and show your love in these two following ways:

I.—First, by a true desire to be taught by them, and to enter into their thoughts. To enter into theirs, observe; not to find your own expressed by them. If the person who wrote the book is not wiser than you, you need not read it; if he be, he will think differently from you in many respects.

Very ready we are to say of a book, "How good this is—that's exactly what I think!" But the right feeling is, "How strange that is! I never thought of that before, and yet I see it is true; or if I do not now, I hope I shall, some day." But whether thus submissively or not, at least be sure that you go to the author to get at *his* meaning, not to find yours. Judge it afterwards, if you think yourself qualified to do so; but ascertain it first. And be sure also, if the author is worth anything, that you will not get at his meaning all at once;—nay, that at his whole meaning you will not for a long time arrive in any wise. Not that he does not say what he means, and in strong words too; but he cannot say it all; and what is more strange, *will* not, but in a hidden way and in parables, in order that he may be sure you want it. I cannot quite see the reason of this, nor analyze that cruel reticence in the breasts of wise men which makes them always hide their deeper thought. They do not give it to you by way of help, but of reward; and will make themselves sure that you deserve it before they allow you to reach it. But it is the same with the physical type of wisdom, gold. There seems, to you and me, no reason why the electric forces of the earth should not carry whatever there is of gold within it at once to the mountain tops, so that kings and people might know that all the gold they could get was there; and without any trouble of digging, or anxiety, or chance, or waste of time, cut it away, and coin as much as they needed. But Nature does not manage it so. She puts it in little fissures in the earth, nobody knows where: you may dig long and find none; you must dig painfully to find any.

14. And it is just the same with men's best wisdom. When you come to a good book, you must ask yourself, "Am I inclined to work as an Australian miner would? Are my pickaxes and shovels in good order, and am I in good trim myself, my sleeves well up to the elbow, and my breath good, and my temper?" And, keeping the figure a little longer, even at the cost of tiresomeness, for it is a thoroughly useful one, the metal you are in search of being the author's mind or meaning, his words are as the rock which you have to crush and smelt in order to get at it. And your pickaxes are your own care, wit, and learning; your smelting-furnace is your own thoughtful soul. Do not hope to get at any good author's meaning without those tools and that fire; often you will need sharpest, finest chiseling, and patientest fusing, before you can gather one grain of the metal.

15. And therefore, first of all, I tell you, earnestly and authoritatively (I *know* I am right in this), you must get into the habit of looking intensely at words, and assuring yourself of their meaning, syllable by syllable—nay letter by letter. For though it is only by reason of the opposition of letters in the function of signs, to sounds in the function of signs, that the study of books is called "literature," and that a man versed in it is called, by the consent of nations, a man of letters instead of a man of books, or of words, you

may yet connect with that accidental nomenclature this real fact;—that you might read all the books in the British Museum (if you could live long enough) and remain an utterly "illiterate," uneducated person; but that if you read ten pages of a good book, letter by letter,—that is to say, with real accuracy,—you are forevermore in some measure an educated person. The entire difference between education and non-education (as regards the merely intellectual part of it) consists in this accuracy. A well-educated gentleman may not know many languages,—may not be able to speak any but his own,—may have read very few books. But whatever language he knows, he knows precisely; whatever word he pronounces, he pronounces rightly; above all, he is learned in the *peerage* of words; knows the words of true descent and ancient blood at a glance, from words of modern canaille; remembers all their ancestry, their intermarriages, distant relationships, and the extent to which they were admitted, and offices they held, among the national noblesse of words at any time, and in any country. But an uneducated person may know, by memory, many languages, and talk them all, and yet truly know not a word of any,—not a word even of his own. An ordinarily clever and sensible seaman will be able to make his way ashore at most ports; yet he has only to speak a sentence of any language to be known for an illiterate person: so also the accent, or turn of expression of a single sentence, will at once mark a scholar. And this is so strongly felt, so conclusively admitted by educated persons, that a false accent or a mistaken syllable is enough, in the parliament of any civilized nation, to assign to a man a certain degree of inferior standing forever.

16. And this is right; but it is a pity that the accuracy insisted on is not greater, and required to a serious purpose. It is right that a false Latin quantity should excite a smile in the House of Commons; but it is wrong that a false English *meaning* should *not* excite a frown there. Let the accent of words be watched; and closely: let their meaning be watched more closely still, and fewer will do the work. A few words well chosen and distinguished, will do work that a thousand cannot, when every one is acting, equivo-

cally, in the function of another. Yes; and words, if they are not watched, will do deadly work sometimes. There are masked words droning and skulking about us in Europe just now,—(there never were so many, owing to the spread of a shallow, blotching, blundering, infectious "information," or rather deformation, everywhere, and to the teaching of catechisms and phrases at schools instead of human meanings)—there are masked words abroad, I say, which nobody understands, but which everybody uses, and most people will also fight for, live for, or even die for, fancying they mean this or that, or the other, of things dear to them: for such words wear chameleon cloaks—"groundlion" cloaks, of the color of the ground of any man's fancy: on that ground they lie in wait, and rend him with a spring from it. There never were creatures of prey so mischievous, never diplomatists so cunning, never poisoners so deadly, as these masked words; they are the unjust stewards of all men's ideas: whatever fancy or favorite instinct a man most cherishes, he gives to his favorite masked word to take care of for him; the word at last comes to have an infinite power over him,—you cannot get at him but by its ministry.

17. And in languages so mongrel in breed as the English, there is a fatal power of equivocation put into men's hands, almost whether they will or no, in being able to use Greek or Latin words for an idea when they want it to be awful; and Saxon or otherwise common words when they want it to be vulgar. What a singular and salutary effect, for instance, would be produced on the minds of people who are in the habit of taking the Form of the "Word" they live by, for the Power of which that Word tells them, if we always either retained, or refused, the Greek form "biblos," or "biblion," as the right expression for "book"—instead of employing it only in the one instance in which we wish to give dignity to the idea, and translating it into English everywhere else. How wholesome it would be for many simple persons, if, in such places (for instance) as Acts xix. 19, we retained the Greek expression, instead of translating it, and they had to read—"Many of them also which used curious arts, brought their bibles together, and burnt them before all men; and they counted the price of them, and

found it fifty thousand pieces of silver!" Or, if, on the other hand, we translated where we retain it, and always spoke of "The Holy Book," instead of "Holy Bible," it might come into more heads than it does at present, that the Word of God, by which the heavens were, of old, and by which they are now kept in store,[8] cannot be made a present of to anybody in morocco binding; nor sown on any wayside by help either of steam plough or steam press; but is nevertheless being offered to us daily, and by us with contumely refused; and sown in us daily, and by us, as instantly as may be, choked.

18. So, again, consider what effect has been produced on the English vulgar mind by the use of the sonorous Latin form "damno," in translating the Greek κατακρίνω, when people charitably wish to make it forcible; and the substitution of the temperate "condemn" for it, when they choose to keep it gentle; and what notable sermons have been preached by illiterate clergymen on—"He that believeth not shall be damned"; though they would shrink with horror from translating Heb. xi. 7, "The saving of his house, by which he damned the world"; or John viii. 10, 11, "Woman, hath no man damned thee? She saith, No man, Lord. Jesus answered her, Neither do I damn thee; go and sin no more." And divisions in the mind of Europe, which have cost seas of blood and in the defense of which the noblest souls of men have been cast away in frantic desolation, countless as forest leaves—though, in the heart of them, founded on deeper causes—have nevertheless been rendered practicably possible, namely, by the European adoption of the Greek word for a public meeting, "ecclesia," to give peculiar respectability to such meetings, when held for religious purposes; and other collateral equivocations, such as the vulgar English one of using the word "priest" as a contraction for "presbyter."

19. Now, in order to deal with words rightly, this is the habit you must form. Nearly every word in your language has been first a word of some other language—of Saxon, German, French, Latin, or Greek (not to speak of eastern and primitive dialects). And many words have been all

[8] 2 Peter, iii. 5-7.

these;—that is to say, have been Greek first, Latin next, French and German next, and English last: undergoing a certain change of sense and use on the lips of each nation; but retaining a deep vital meaning, which all good scholars feel in employing them, even at this day. If you do not know the Greek alphabet, learn it; young or old—girl or boy—whoever you may be, if you think of reading seriously (which, of course, implies that you have some leisure at command), learn your Greek alphabet; then get good dictionaries of all these languages, and whenever you are in doubt about a word, hunt it down patiently. Read Max Müller's lectures thoroughly, to begin with; and, after that, never let a word escape you that looks suspicious. It is severe work; but you will find it, even at first, interesting, and at last, endlessly amusing. And the general gain to your character, in power and precision, will be quite incalculable.

Mind, this does not imply knowing, or trying to know, Greek or Latin, or French. It takes a whole life to learn any language perfectly. But you can easily ascertain the meanings through which the English word has passed; and those which in a good writer's work it must still bear.

20. And now, merely for example's sake, I will, with your permission, read a few lines of a true book with you, carefully; and see what will come out of them. I will take a book perfectly known to you all. No English words are more familiar to us, yet few perhaps have been read with less sincerity. I will take these few following lines of Lycidas:

"Last came, and last did go,
The pilot of the Galilean lake;
Two massy keys he bore of metals twain,
(The golden opes, the iron shuts amain),
He shook his mitred locks, and stern bespake,
'How well could I have spar'd for thee, young swain,
Enow of such as for their bellies' sake
Creep, and intrude, and climb into the fold!
Of other care they little reckoning make,
Than how to scramble at the shearers' feast,
And shove away the worthy bidden guest;
Blind mouths! that scarce themselves know how to hold

A sheep-hook, or have learn'd aught else, the least
That to the faithful herdsman's art belongs!
What recks it them? What need they? They are sped;
And when they list, their lean and flashy songs
Grate on their scrannel pipes of wretched straw;
The hungry sheep look up, and are not fed,
But, swoln with wind, and the rank mist they draw,
Rot inwardly, and foul contagion spread;
Besides what the grim wolf with privy paw
Daily devours apace, and nothing said.' "

Let us think over this passage, and examine its words.

First, is it not singular to find Milton assigning to St. Peter, not only his full episcopal function, but the very types of it which Protestants usually refuse most passionately? His "mitred" locks! Milton was no Bishop-lover; how comes St. Peter to be "mitred"? "Two massy keys he bore." Is this, then, the power of the keys claimed by the Bishops of Rome, and is it acknowledged here by Milton only in a poetical license, for the sake of its picturesqueness, that he may get the gleam of the golden keys to help his effect? Do not think it. Great men do not play stage tricks with doctrines of life and death: only little men do that. Milton means what he says; and means it with his might too—is going to put the whole strength of his spirit presently into the saying of it. For though not a lover of false bishops, he *was* a lover of true ones; and the Lake-pilot is here, in his thoughts, the type and head of true episcopal power. For Milton reads that text, "I will give unto thee the keys of the kingdom of Heaven" quite honestly. Puritan though he be, he would not blot it out of the book because there have been bad bishops; nay, in order to understand *him,* we must understand that verse first; it will not do to eye it askance, or whisper it under our breath, as if it were a weapon of an adverse sect. It is a solemn, universal assertion, deeply to be kept in mind by all sects. But perhaps we shall be better able to reason on it if we go on a little farther, and come back to it. For clearly this marked insistence on the power of the true episcopate is to make us feel more weightily what is to be charged against the false claimants of episcopate; or generally, against false claimants of power and rank in the body of the clergy; they who, "for their bellies' sake, creep, and intrude, and climb into the fold."

21. Never think Milton uses those three words to fill up his verse, as a loose writer would. He needs all the three; specially those three, and no more than those—"creep," and "intrude," and "climb"; no other words would or could serve the turn, and no more could be added. For they exhaustively comprehend the three classes, correspondent to the three characters, of men who dishonestly seek ecclesiastical power. First, those who *"creep"* into the fold; who do not care for office, nor name, but for secret influence, and do all things occultly and cunningly, consenting to any servility of office or conduct, so only that they may intimately discern, and unawares direct, the minds of men. Then those who "intrude" (thrust, that is) themselves into the fold, who by natural insolence of heart, and stout eloquence of tongue, and fearlessly perseverant self-assertion, obtain hearing and authority with the common crowd. Lastly, those who "climb," who by labor and learning, both stout and sound, but selfishly exerted in the cause of their own ambition, gain high dignities and authorities, and become "lords over the heritage," though not "ensamples to the flock."

22. Now go on:—

> "Of other care they little reckoning make,
> Than how to scramble at the shearers' feast.
> *Blind mouths—*"

I pause again, for this is a strange expression; a broken metaphor, one might think, careless and unscholarly.

Not so: its very audacity and pithiness are intended to make us look close at the phrase and remember it. Those two monosyllables express the precisely accurate contraries of right character, in the two great offices of the Church—those of bishop and pastor.

A "Bishop" means a "person who sees."

A "Pastor" means a "person who feeds."

The most unbishoply character a man can have is therefore to be Blind.

The most unpastoral is, instead of feeding, to want to be fed,—to be a Mouth.

Take the two reverses together, and you have "blind mouths." We may advisably follow out this idea a little. Nearly all the evils in the Church have arisen from bishops desiring *power* more than *light*. They want authority, not outlook. Whereas their real office is not to rule; though it may be vigorously to exhort and rebuke; it is the king's office to rule; the bishop's office is to *oversee* the flock; to number it, sheep by sheep; to be ready always to give full account of it. Now it is clear he cannot give account of the souls, if he has not so much as numbered the bodies of his flock. The first thing, therefore, that a bishop has to do is at least to put himself in a position in which, at any moment, he can obtain the history, from childhood, of every living soul in his diocese, and of its present state. Down in that back street, Bill and Nancy, knocking each other's teeth out!—Does the bishop know all about it? Has he his eye upon them? Has he *had* his eye upon them? Can he circumstantially explain to us how Bill got into the habit of beating Nancy about the head? If he cannot, he is no bishop, though he had a mitre as high as Salisbury steeple; he is no bishop,—he has sought to be at the helm instead of the masthead; he has no sight of things. "Nay," you say, "it is not his duty to look after Bill in the back street." What! the fat sheep that have full fleeces—you think it is only those he should look after, while (go back to your Milton) "the hungry sheep look up, and are not fed, besides what the grim wolf with privy paw" (bishops knowing nothing about it) "daily devours apace, and nothing said"?

"But that's not our idea of a bishop."[4] Perhaps not; but it was St. Paul's; and it was Milton's. They may be right, or we may be; but we must not think we are reading either one or the other by putting our meaning into their words.

23. I go on.

"But, swollen with wind, and the rank mist they draw."

This is to meet the vulgar answer that "if the poor are not looked after in their bodies, they are in their souls; they have spiritual food."

[4] Compare the 13th Letter in "Time and Tide."

And Milton says, "They have no such thing as spiritual food; they are only swollen with wind." At first you may think that is a coarse type, and an obscure one. But again, it is a quite literally accurate one. Take up your Latin and Greek dictionaries, and find out the meaning of "Spirit." It is only a contraction of the Latin word "breath," and an indistinct translation of the Greek word for "wind." The same word is used in writing, "The wind bloweth where it listeth"; and in writing, "So is every one that is born of the Spirit"; born of the *breath,* that is; for it means the breath of God, in soul and body. We have the true sense of it in our words "inspiration" and "expire." Now, there are two kinds of breath with which the flock may be filled; God's breath, and man's. The breath of God is health, and life, and peace to them, as the air of heaven is to the flocks on the hills; but man's breath—the word which *he* calls spiritual,—is disease and contagion to them, as the fog of the fen. They rot inwardly with it; they are puffed up by it, as a dead body by the vapors of its own decomposition. This is literally true of all false religious teaching; the first and last, and fatalest sign of it is that "puffing up." Your converted children, who teach their parents; your converted convicts, who teach honest men; your converted dunces, who, having lived in cretinous stupefaction half their lives, suddenly awakening to the fact of there being a God, fancy themselves therefore His peculiar people and messengers; your sectarians of every species, small and great, Catholic or Protestant, of high church or low, in so far as they think themselves exclusively in the right and others wrong; and preëminently, in every sect, those who hold that men can be saved by thinking rightly instead of doing rightly, by word instead of act, and wish instead of work:—these are the true fog children—clouds, these, without water; bodies, these, of putrescent vapor and skin, without blood or flesh: blown bag-pipes for the fiends to pipe with—corrupt, and corrupting,—"Swollen with wind, and the rank mist they draw."

24. Lastly, let us return to the lines respecting the power of the keys, for now we can understand them. Note the difference between Milton and Dante in their interpretation

of this power: for once, the latter is weaker in thought; he supposes *both* the keys to be of the gate of heaven; one is of gold, the other of silver: they are given by St. Peter to the sentinel angel; and it is not easy to determine the meaning either of the substances of the three steps of the gate, or of the two keys. But Milton makes one, of gold, the key of heaven; the other, of iron, the key of the prison in which the wicked teachers are to be bound who "have taken away the key of knowledge, yet entered not in themselves."

We have seen that the duties of bishop and pastor are to see and feed; and, of all who do so it is said, "He that watereth, shall be watered also himself." But the reverse is truth also. He that watereth not, shall be *withered* himself, and he that seeth not, shall himself be shut out of sight,—shut into the perpetual prison-house. And that prison opens here, as well as hereafter: he who is to be bound in heaven must first be bound on earth. That command to the strong angels, of which the rock-apostle is the image, "Take him, and bind him hand and foot, and cast him out," issues, in its measure, against the teacher, for every help withheld, and for every truth refused, and for every falsehood enforced; so that he is more strictly fettered the more he fetters, and farther outcast, as he more and more misleads, till at last the bars of the iron cage close upon him, and as "the golden opes, the iron shuts amain."

25. We have got something out of the lines, I think, and much more is yet to be found in them; but we have done enough by way of example of the kind of word-by-word examination of your author which is rightly called "reading"; watching every accent and expression, and putting ourselves always in the author's place, annihilating our own personality, and seeking to enter into his, so as to be able assuredly to say, "Thus Milton thought," not "Thus *I* thought, in mis-reading Milton." And by this process you will gradually come to attach less weight to your own "Thus I thought" at other times. You will begin to perceive that what *you* thought was a matter of no serious importance;—that your thoughts on any subject are not perhaps the clearest and wisest that could be arrived at thereupon:—in fact,

that unless you are a very singular person, you cannot be said to have any "thoughts" at all; that you have no materials for them, in any serious matters;[5]—no right to "think," but only to try to learn more of the facts. Nay, most probably all your life (unless, as I said, you are a singular person) you will have no legitimate right to an "opinion" on any business, except that instantly under your hand. What must of necessity be done, you can always find out, beyond question, how to do. Have you a housc to keep in order, a commodity to sell, a field to plough, a ditch to cleanse. There need be no two opinions about these proceedings; it is at your peril if you have not much more than an "opinion" on the way to manage such matters. And also, outside of your own business, there are one or two subjects on which you are bound to have but one opinion. That roguery and lying are objectionable, and are instantly to be flogged out of the way whenever discovered;—that covetousness and love of quarreling are dangerous dispositions even in children, and deadly dispositions in men and nations;—that in the end, the God of heaven and earth loves active, modest, and kind people, and hates idle, proud, greedy, and cruel ones;—on these general facts you are bound to have but one and that a very strong, opinion. For the rest, respecting religions, governments, sciences, arts, you will find that, on the whole, you can know NOTHING,—judge nothing; that the best you can do, even though you may be a well-educated person, is to be silent, and strive to be wiser every day, and to understand a little more of the thoughts of others, which so soon as you try to do honestly, you will discover that the thoughts even of the wisest are very little more than pertinent questions. To put the difficulty into a clear shape, and exhibit to you the grounds for *in*decision, that is all they can generally do for you!—and well for them and for us, if indeed they are able "to mix the music with our thoughts, and sadden us with heavenly doubts." This writer, from whom I have been reading to you, is not among the first or wisest: he sees shrewdly as far as he sees, and therefore

[5] Modern "education" for the most part signifies giving people the faculty of thinking wrong on every conceivable subject of importance to them.

it is easy to find out his full meaning; but with the greater men, you cannot fathom their meaning; they do not even wholly measure it themselves,—it is so wide. Suppose I had asked you, for instance, to seek for Shakespeare's opinion, instead of Milton's, on this matter of Church authority?—or for Dante's? Have any of you, at this instant, the least idea what either thought about it? Have you ever balanced the scene with the bishops in Richard III. against the character of Cranmer? the description of St. Francis and St. Dominic against that of him who made Virgil wonder to gaze upon him,—"disteso, tanto vilmente, nell' eterno esilio"; or of him whom Dante stood beside, "come 'l frate che confessa lo perfido assassin?"[6] Shakespeare and Alighieri knew men better than most of us, I presume! They were both in the midst of the main struggle between the temporal and spiritual powers. They had an opinion, we may guess. But where is it? Bring it into court! Put Shakespeare's or Dante's creed into articles, and send *it* up for trial by the Ecclesiastical Courts!

26. You will not be able, I tell you again, for many and many a day, to come at the real purposes and teaching of these great men; but a very little honest study of them will enable you to perceive that what you took for your own "judgment" was mere chance prejudice, and drifted, helpless, entangled weed of castaway thought: nay, you will see that most men's minds are indeed little better than rough heath wilderness, neglected and stubborn, partly barren, partly overgrown with pestilent brakes, and venomous, wind-sown herbage of evil surmise; that the first thing you have to do for them, and yourself, is eagerly and scornfully to set fire to *this;* burn all the jungle into wholesome ash heaps, and then plough and sow. All the true literary work before you, for life, must begin with obedience to that order, "Break up your fallow ground, and *sow not among thorns.*"

27. II.[7]—Having then faithfully listened to the great teachers, that you may enter into their Thoughts, you have yet this higher advance to make;—you have to enter into their Hearts. As you go to them first for clear sight, so you must stay with them, that you may share at last their

[6] "Inferno," xxiii. 125, 126; xix. 49, 50. [7] Compare ¶ 13 above.

just and mighty Passion. Passion, or "sensation." I am not afraid of the word; still less of the thing. You have heard many outcries against sensation lately; but, I can tell you, it is not less sensation we want, but more. The ennobling difference between one man and another,—between one animal and another,—is precisely in this, that one feels more than another. If we were sponges, perhaps sensation might not be easily got for us; if we were earth-worms, liable at every instant to be cut in two by the spade, perhaps too much sensation might not be good for us. But, being human creatures, *it is* good for us; nay, we are only human in so far as we are sensitive, and our honor is precisely in proportion to our passion.

28. You know I said of that great and pure society of the dead, that it would allow "no vain or vulgar person to enter there." What do you think I meant by a "vulgar" person? What do you yourselves mean by "vulgarity"? You will find it a fruitful subject of thought; but, briefly, the essence of all vulgarity lies in want of sensation. Simple and innocent vulgarity is merely an untrained and undeveloped bluntness of body and mind; but in true inbred vulgarity, there is a deathful callousness, which, in extremity, becomes capable of every sort of bestial habit and crime, without fear, without pleasure, without horror, and without pity. It is in the blunt hand and the dead heart, in the diseased habit, in the hardened conscience, that men become vulgar; they are forever vulgar, precisely in proportion as they are incapable of sympathy,—of quick understanding,—of all that, in deep insistence on the common, but most accurate term, may be called the "tact" or "touch-faculty" of body and soul; that tact which the Mimosa has in trees, which the pure woman has above all creatures;—fineness and fullness of sensation beyond reason;—the guide and sanctifier of reason itself. Reason can but determine what is true:—it is the God-given passion of humanity which alone can recognize what God has made good.

29. We come then to the great concourse of the Dead, not merely to know from them what is True, but chiefly to feel with them what is just. Now, to feel with them, we must be like them; and none of us can become that without

pains. As the true knowledge is disciplined and tested knowledge,—not the first thought that comes,—so the true passion is disciplined and tested passion,—not the first passion that comes. The first that come are the vain, the false, the treacherous; if you yield to them they will lead you wildly and far in vain pursuit, in hollow enthusiasm, till you have no true purpose and no true passion left. Not that any feeling possible to humanity is in itself wrong, but only wrong when undisciplined. Its nobility is in its force and justice; it is wrong when it is weak, and felt for paltry cause. There is a mean wonder, as of a child who sees a juggler tossing golden balls, and this is base, if you will. But do you think that the wonder is ignoble, or the sensation less, with which every human soul is called to watch the golden balls of heaven tossed through the night by the Hand that made them? There is a mean curiosity, as of a child opening a forbidden door, or a servant prying into her master's business;—and a noble curiosity, questioning, in the front of danger, the source of the great river beyond the sand,—the place of the great continents beyond the sea;—a nobler curiosity still, which questions of the source of the River of Life, and of the space of the Continent of Heaven,—things which "the angels desire to look into." So the anxiety is ignoble, with which you linger over the course and catastrophe of an idle tale; but do you think the anxiety is less, or greater, with which you watch, or *ought* to watch, the dealings of fate and destiny with the life of an agonized nation? Alas! it is the narrowness, selfishness, minuteness, of your sensation that you have to deplore in England at this day;—sensation which spends itself in bouquets and speeches; in revelings and junketings; in sham fights and gay puppet shows, while you can look on and see noble nations murdered, man by man, without an effort or a tear.

30. I said "minuteness" and "selfishness" of sensation, but in a word, I ought to have said "injustice" or "unrighteousness" of sensation. For as in nothing is a gentleman better to be discerned from a vulgar person, so in nothing is a gentle nation (such nations have been) better to be discerned from a mob, than in this,—that their feelings

are constant and just, results of due contemplation, and of equal thought. You can talk a mob into anything; its feelings may be—usually are—on the whole, generous and right; but it has no foundation for them, no hold of them; you may tease or tickle it into any, at your pleasure; it thinks by infection, for the most part, catching an opinion like a cold, and there is nothing so little that it will not roar itself wild about, when the fit is on;—nothing so great but it will forget in an hour, when the fit is past. But a gentleman's or a gentle nation's, passions are just, measured and continuous. A great nation, for instance, does not spend its entire national wits for a couple of months in weighing evidence of a single ruffian's having done a single murder; and for a couple of years see its own children murder each other by their thousands or tens of thousands a day, considering only what the effect is likely to be on the price of cotton, and caring nowise to determine which side of battle is in the wrong. Neither does a great nation send its poor little boys to jail for stealing six walnuts; and allow its bankrupts to steal their hundreds or thousands with a bow, and its bankers, rich with poor men's savings, to close their doors "under circumstances over which they have no control," with a "by your leave"; and large landed estates to be bought by men who have made their money by going with armed steamers up and down the China Seas, selling opium at the cannon's mouth, and altering, for the benefit of the foreign nation, the common highwayman's demand of "your money *or* your life," into that of "your money *and* your life." Neither does a great nation allow the lives of its innocent poor to be parched out of them by fog fever, and rotted out of them by dunghill plague, for the sake of sixpence a life extra per week to its landlords;[8] and then debate, with driveling tears, and diabolical sympathies, whether it ought not piously to save, and nursingly cherish, the lives of its murderers. Also, a great nation having made up its mind that hanging is quite the wholesomest process for its homicides in general, can yet with mercy distinguish between the degrees of guilt in homicides; and does not yelp like a pack

[8] See note at end of lecture. I have put it in large type, because the course of matters since it was written has made it perhaps better worth attention.

of frost-pinched wolf-cubs on the blood-track of an unhappy crazed boy, or gray-haired clodpate Othello, "perplexed i' the extreme," at the very moment that it is sending a Minister of the Crown to make polite speeches to a man who is bayoneting young girls in their father's sight, and killing noble youths in cool blood, faster than a country butcher kills lambs in spring. And, lastly, a great nation does not mock Heaven and its Powers, by pretending belief in a revelation which asserts the love of money to be the root of *all* evil, and declaring, at the same time, that it is actuated, and intends to be actuated, in all chief national deeds and measures, by no other love.

31. My friends, I do not know why any of us should talk about reading. We want some sharper discipline than that of reading; but, at all events, be assured, we cannot read. No reading is possible for a people with its mind in this state. No sentence of any great writer is intelligible to them. It is simply and sternly impossible for the English public, at this moment, to understand any thoughtful writing,—so incapable of thought has it become in its insanity of avarice. Happily, our disease is, as yet, little worse than this incapacity of thought; it is not corruption of the inner nature; we ring true still, when anything strikes home to us; and though the idea that everything should "pay" has infected our every purpose so deeply, that even when we would play the good Samaritan, we never take out our twopence and give them to the host without saying, "When I come again, thou shalt give me fourpence," there is a capacity of noble passion left in our hearts' core. We show it in our work,—in our war,—even in those unjust domestic affections which make us furious at a small private wrong, while we are polite to a boundless public one: we are still industrious to the last hour of the day, though we add the gambler's fury to the laborer's patience; we are still brave to the death, though incapable of discerning true cause for battle; and are still true in affection to our own flesh, to the death, as the sea-monsters are, and the rock-eagles. And there is hope for a nation while this can be still said of it. As long as it holds its life in its hand, ready to give it for its honor (though a foolish honor), for its love

(though a selfish love), and for its business (though a base business), there is hope for it. But hope only; for this instinctive, reckless virtue cannot last. No nation can last, which has made a mob of itself, however generous at heart. It must discipline its passions, and direct them, or they will discipline *it,* one day, with scorpion whips. Above all a nation cannot last as a money-making mob: it cannot with impunity,—it cannot with existence,—go on despising literature, despising science, despising art, despising nature, despising compassion, and concentrating its soul on Pence. Do you think these are harsh or wild words? Have patience with me but a little longer. I will prove their truth to you, clause by clause.

32. I.—I say first we have despised literature. What do we, as a nation, care about books? How much do you think we spend altogether on our libraries, public or private, as compared with what we spend on our horses? If a man spends lavishly on his library you call him mad—a bibliomaniac. But you never call any one a horse-maniac, though men ruin themselves every day by their horses, and you do not hear of people ruining themselves by their books. Or, to go lower still, how much do you think the contents of the book-shelves of the United Kingdom, public and private, would fetch, as compared with the contents of its wine-cellars? What position would its expenditure on literature take, as compared with its expenditure on luxurious eating? We talk of food for the mind, as of food for the body; now a good book contains such food inexhaustibly; it is a provision for life, and for the best part of us; yet how long most people would look at the best book before they would give the price of a large turbot for it! though there have been men who have pinched their stomachs and bared their backs, to buy a book, whose libraries were cheaper to them, I think, in the end, than most men's dinners are. We are few of us put to such trial, and more the pity; for, indeed, a precious thing is all the more precious to us if it has been won by work or economy; and if public libraries were half as costly as public dinners, or books cost the tenth part of what bracelets do, even foolish men and women might sometimes suspect there was good in

reading, as well as in munching and sparkling; whereas the very cheapness of literature is making even wise people forget that if a book is worth reading, it is worth buying. No book is worth anything which is not worth *much;* nor is it serviceable, until it has been read, and reread, and loved, and loved again; and marked, so that you can refer to the passages you want in it as a soldier can seize the weapon he needs in an armory, or a housewife bring the spice she needs from her store. Bread of flour is good: but there is bread, sweet as honey, if we would eat it, in a good book; and the family must be poor indeed which, once in their lives, cannot, for such multipliable barley-loaves, pay their baker's bill. We call ourselves a rich nation, and we are filthy and foolish enough to thumb each other's books out of circulating libraries!

33. II.—I say we have despised science. "What!" you exclaim, "are we not foremost in all discovery,[9] and is not the whole world giddy by reason, or unreason, of our inventions?" Yes; but do you suppose that is national work? That work is all done *in spite of* the nation; by private people's zeal and money. We are glad enough, indeed, to make our profit of science; we snap up anything in the way of a scientific bone that has meat on it, eagerly enough; but if the scientific man comes for a bone or a crust to *us,* that is another story. What have we publicly done for science? We are obliged to know what o'clock it is, for the safety of our ships, and therefore we pay for an observatory; and we allow ourselves, in the person of our Parliament, to be annually tormented into doing something, in a slovenly way, for the British Museum; sullenly apprehending that to be a place for keeping stuffed birds in, to amuse our children. If anybody will pay for his own telescope, and resolve another nebula, we cackle over the discernment as if it were our own; if one in ten thousand of our hunting squires suddenly perceives that the earth was indeed made to be something else than a portion for foxes, and burrows in it himself, and tells us where the gold is, and where the coals, we understand that there is some use

[9] Since this was written, the answer has become definitely—No; we have surrendered the field of Arctic discovery to the Continental nations, as being ourselves too poor to pay for ships.

in that; and very properly knight him; but is the accident of his having found out how to employ himself usefully any credit to *us?* (The negation of such discovery among his brother squires may perhaps be some *dis*credit to us, if we would consider of it.) But if you doubt these generalities, here is one fact for us all to meditate upon, illustrative of our love of science. Two years ago there was a collection of the fossils of Solenhofen to be sold in Bavaria; the best in existence, containing many specimens unique for perfectness, and one, unique as an example of a species (a whole kingdom of unknown living creatures being announced by that fossil). This collection, of which the mere market worth, among private buyers, would probably have been some thousand or twelve hundred pounds, was offered to the English nation for seven hundred; but we would not give seven hundred, and the whole series would have been in the Munich Museum at this moment, if Professor Owen[10] had not with loss of his own time, and patient tormenting of the British public in person of its representatives, got leave to give four hundred pounds at once, and himself become answerable for the other three! which the said public will doubtless pay him eventually, but sulkily, and caring nothing about the matter all the while; only always ready to cackle if any credit comes of it. Consider, I beg of you, arithmetically, what this fact means. Your annual expenditure for public purposes (a third of it for military apparatus), is at least fifty millions. Now 700*l.* is to 50,000,000*l.* roughly, as seven pence to two thousand pounds. Suppose then, a gentleman of unknown income, but whose wealth was to be conjectured from the fact that he spent two thousand a year on his park-walls and footmen only, professes himself fond of science; and that one of his servants comes eagerly to tell him that an unique collection of fossils, giving clue to a new era of creation, is to be had for the sum of seven pence sterling; and that the gentleman, who is fond of science, and spends two thousand a year on his park, answers, after keeping his servant waiting

[10] I state this fact without Professor Owen's permission: which of course he could not with propriety have granted, had I asked it; but I consider it so important that the public should be aware of the fact that I do what seems to be right though rude.

several months, "Well! I'll give you four pence for them, if you will be answerable for the extra three pence yourself, till next year!"

34. III.—I say you have despised Art! "What!" you again answer, "have we not Art exhibitions, miles long? and do we not pay thousands of pounds for single pictures? and have we not Art schools and institutions, more than ever nation had before?" Yes, truly, but all that is for the sake of the shop. You would fain sell canvas as well as coals, and crockery as well as iron; you would take every other nation's bread out of its mouth if you could;[11] not being able to do that, your ideal of life is to stand in the thoroughfares of the world, like Ludgate apprentices, screaming to every passer-by, "What d'ye lack?" You know nothing of your own faculties or circumstances; you fancy that, among your damp, flat fields of clay, you can have as quick art-fancy as the Frenchman among his bronzed vines, or the Italian under his volcanic cliffs;—that art may be learned as book-keeping is, and when learned, will give you more books to keep. You care for pictures, absolutely, no more than you do for the bills pasted on your dead walls. There is always room on the walls for the bills to be read,—never for the pictures to be seen. You do not know what pictures you have (by repute) in the country, nor whether they are false or true, nor whether they are taken care of or not; in foreign countries, you calmly see the noblest existing pictures in the world rotting in abandoned wreck—(in Venice you saw the Austrian guns deliberately pointed at the palaces containing them), and if you heard that all the fine pictures in Europe were made into sand-bags to-morrow on the Austrian forts, it would not trouble you so much as the chance of a brace or two of game less in your own bags, in a day's shooting. That is your national love of Art.

35. IV.—You have despised Nature; that is to say, all the deep and sacred sensations of natural scenery. The French revolutionists made stables of the cathedrals of France; you have made race-courses of the cathedrals of

[11] That was our real idea of "Free Trade"—"All the trade to myself." You find now that by "competition" other people can manage to sell something as well as you—and now we call for Protection again. Wretches!

the earth. Your *one* conception of pleasure is to drive in railroad carriages round their aisles, and eat off their altars.[12] You have put a railroad bridge over the fall of Schaffhausen. You have tunneled the cliffs of Lucerne by Tell's chapel; you have destroyed the Clarens shore of the Lake of Geneva; there is not a quiet valley in England that you have not filled with bellowing fire; there is no particle left of English land which you have not trampled coal ashes into[13]—nor any foreign city in which the spread of your presence is not marked among its fair old streets and happy gardens by a consuming white leprosy of new hotels and perfumers' shops: the Alps themselves, which your own poets used to love so reverently, you look upon as soaped poles in a bear-garden, which you set yourselves to climb, and slide down again with "shrieks of delight." When you are past shrieking, having no human articulate voice to say you are glad with, you fill the quietude of their valleys with gunpowder blasts, and rush home, red with cutaneous eruption of conceit, and voluble with convulsive hiccough of self-satisfaction. I think nearly the two sorrowfullest spectacles I have ever seen in humanity, taking the deep inner significance of them, are the English mobs in the valley of Chamouni, amusing themselves with firing rusty howitzers; and the Swiss vintagers of Zurich expressing their Christian thanks for the gift of the vine, by assembling in knots in the "towers of the vineyards," and slowly loading and firing horse-pistols from morning till evening. It is pitiful to have dim conceptions of duty; more pitiful, it seems to me, to have conceptions like these, of mirth.

36. Lastly. You despise compassion. There is no need of words of mine for proof of this. I will merely print one of the newspaper paragraphs which I am in the habit of cutting out and throwing into my store-drawer; here is one from a *Daily Telegraph* of an early date this year (1867)

[12] I meant that the beautiful places of the world—Switzerland, Italy, South Germany, and so on—are, indeed, the truest cathedrals—places to be reverent in, and to worship in; and that we only care to drive through them; and to eat and drink at their most sacred places.

[13] I was singularly struck, some years ago, by finding all the river shore at Richmond, in Yorkshire, black in its earth, from the mere drift of soot-laden air rom places many miles away.

(date which, though by me carelessly left unmarked, is easily discoverable; for on the back of the slip, there is the announcement that "yesterday the seventh of the special services of this year was performed by the Bishop of Ripon in St. Paul's"); it relates only one of such facts as happen now daily; this, by chance, having taken a form in which it came before the coroner. I will print the paragraph in red. Be sure, the facts themselves are written in that color in a book which we shall all of us, literate or illiterate, have to read our page of, some day.

"An inquiry was held on Friday by Mr. Richards, deputy coroner, at the White Horse Tavern, Christ Church, Spitalfields, respecting the death of Michael Collins, aged 58 years. Mary Collins, a miserable-looking woman, said that she lived with the deceased and his son in a room at 2, Cobb's Court, Christ Church. Deceased was a 'translator' of boots. Witness went out and bought old boots; deceased and his son made them into good ones, and then witness sold them for what she could get at the shops, which was very little indeed. Deceased and his son used to work night and day to try and get a little bread and tea, and pay for the room (2*s.* a week), so as to keep the home together. On Friday night week, deceased got up from his bench and began to shiver. He threw down the boots, saying, 'Somebody else must finish them when I am gone, for I can do no more.' There was no fire, and he said, 'I would be better if I was warm.' Witness therefore took two pairs of translated boots[14] to sell at the shop, but she could only get 14*d.* for the two pairs, for the people at the shop said, 'We must have our profit.' Witness got 14 lbs. of coal and a little tea and bread. Her son sat up the whole night to make the 'translations,' to get money, but deceased died on Saturday morning. The family never had enough to eat.—Coroner: 'It seems to me deplorable that you did not go into the workhouse.' Witness: 'We wanted the comforts of our little home.' A juror asked what the comforts were, for he only saw a little straw in the corner of the room, the windows of which were broken. The witness began to cry,

[14] One of the things which we must very resolutely enforce, for the good of all classes, in our future arrangements, must be that they wear no "translated" articles of dress.

and said that they had a quilt and other little things. The deceased said he never would go into the workhouse. In summer, when the season was good, they sometimes made as much as 10*s.* profit in a week. They then always saved towards the next week, which was generally a bad one. In winter they made not half so much. For three years they had been getting from bad to worse.—Cornelius Collins said that he had assisted his father since 1847. They used to work so far into the night that both nearly lost their eyesight. Witness now had a film over his eyes. Five years ago deceased applied to the parish for aid. The relieving officer gave him a 4-lb. loaf, and told him if he came again he should 'get the stones.'[15] That disgusted deceased, and he would have nothing to do with them since. They got worse and worse until last Friday week, when they had not even a halfpenny to buy a candle. Deceased then lay down on the straw, and said he could not live till morning.—A juror: 'You are dying of starvation yourself, and you ought to go into the house until the summer.' Witness: 'If we went in we should die. When we come out in the summer we should be like people dropped from the sky. No one would know us, and we would not have even a room. I could work now if I had food, for my sight would get better.' Dr. G. P. Walker said deceased died from syncope, from exhaustion, from want of food. The de-

[15] This abbreviation of the penalty of useless labor is curiously coincident in verbal form with a certain passage which some of us may remember. It may, perhaps, be well to preserve beside this paragraph another cutting out of my store-drawer, from the "Morning Post," of about a parallel date, Friday, March 10th, 1865:—"The *salons* of Mme. C——, who did the honors with clever imitative grace and elegance, were crowded with princes, dukes, marquises, and counts—in fact, with the same *male* company as one meets at the parties of the Princess Metternich and Madame Drouyn de Lhuys. Some English peers and members of Parliament were present, and appeared to enjoy the animated and dazzlingly improper scene. On the second floor the supper-tables were loaded with every delicacy of the season. That your readers may form some idea of the dainty fare of the Parisian demi-monde, I copy the menu of the supper, which was served to all the guests (about 200) seated at four o'clock. Choice Yquem, Johannisberg, Lafitte, Tokay, and Champagne of the finest vintages were served most lavishly throughout the morning. After supper dancing was resumed with increased animation, and the ball terminated with a *chaîne diabolique* and a *cancan d'enfer* at seven in the morning. (Morning-service—'Ere the fresh lawns appeared, under the opening eyelids of the Morn.—') Here is the menu:—'Consommé de volaille à la Bagration; 16 hors-d'œuvres variés. Bouchées à la Talleyrand. Saumons froids, sauce Ravigote. Filets de bœuf en Bellevue, timbales milanaises chaudfroid de gibier. Dindes truffées. Pâtés de foies gras, buissons d'écrevisses, salades vénétiennes, gelées blanches aux fruits, gateaux mancini, parisiens et parisiennes. Fromages glacés, Ananas. Dessert.'"

ceased had had no bed-clothes. For four months he had had nothing but bread to eat. There was not a particle of fat in the body. There was no disease, but if there had been medical attendance, he might have survived the syncope or fainting. The coroner having remarked upon the painful nature of the case, the jury returned the following verdict: 'That deceased died from exhaustion, from want of food and the common necessaries of life; also through want of medical aid.'"

37. "Why would witness not go into the workhouse?" you ask. Well, the poor seem to have a prejudice against the workhouse which the rich have not; for, of course, every one who takes a pension from Government goes into the workhouse on a grand scale;[16] only the workhouses for the rich do not involve the idea of work, and should be called play-houses. But the poor like to die independently, it appears; perhaps if we made the play-houses for them pretty and pleasant enough, or gave them their pensions at home, and allowed them a little introductory peculation with the public money, their minds might be reconciled to the conditions. Meantime, here are the facts: we make our relief either so insulting to them, or so painful, that they rather die than take it at our hands; or, for third alternative, we leave them so untaught and foolish that they starve like brute creatures, wild and dumb, not knowing what to do, or what to ask. I say, you despise compassion; if you did not, such a newspaper paragraph would be as impossible in a Christian country as a deliberate assassination permitted in its public streets.[17] "Christian" did I say? Alas,

[16] Please observe this statement, and think of it, and consider how it happens that a poor old woman will be ashamed to take a shilling a week from the country—but no one is ashamed to take a pension of a thousand a year.

[17] I am heartily glad to see such a paper as the "Pall Mall Gazette" established; for the power of the press in the hands of highly educated men, in independent position, and of honest purpose, may, indeed, become all that it has been hitherto vainly vaunted to be. Its editor will, therefore, I doubt not, pardon me, in that, by very reason of my respect for the journal, I do not let pass unnoticed an article in its third number, page 5, which was wrong in every word of it, with the intense wrongness which only an honest man can achieve who has taken a false turn of thought in the outset, and is following it, regardless of consequences. It contained at the end this notable passage:— "The bread of affliction, and the water of affliction—aye, and the bedsteads and blankets of affliction, are the very utmost that the law ought to give to *outcasts merely as outcasts.*" I merely put beside this expression of the gentlemanly mind of England in 1865, a part of the message which Isaiah was ordered to "lift up his voice like a trumpet" in declaring to the gentlemen of his day: "Ye fast for strife, and to smite with the fist

if we were but wholesomely *un*-Christian, it would be impossible; it is our imaginary Christianity that helps us to commit these crimes, for we revel and luxuriate in our faith, for the lewd sensation of it; dressing *it* up, like everything else, in fiction. The dramatic Christianity of the organ and aisle, of dawn-service and twilight-revival—the Christianity which we do not fear to mix the mockery of, pictorially, with our play about the devil, in our Satanellas,—Roberts,—Fausts; chanting hymns through traceried windows for back-ground effect, and artistically modulating the "Dio" through variation on variation of mimicked prayer (while we distribute tracts, next day, for the benefit of uncultivated swearers, upon what we suppose to be the signification of the Third Commandment);—this gas-lighted, and gas-inspired, Christianity, we are triumphant in, and draw back the hem of our robes from the touch of the heretics who dispute it. But to do a piece of common Christian righteousness in a plain English word or deed; to make Christian law any rule of life, and found one National act or hope thereon,—we know too well what our faith comes to for that! You might sooner get lightning out of incense smoke than true action or passion out of your modern English religion. You had better get rid of the smoke, and the organ-pipes, both; leave them, and the Gothic windows, and the painted glass, to the property-man; give up your carburetted hydrogen ghost in one healthy expiration, and look after Lazarus at the door-step. For there is a true Church wherever one hand meets another helpfully, and that is the only holy or Mother Church which ever was, or ever shall be.

of wickedness. Is not this the fast that I have chosen, to deal thy bread to the hungry, and that thou bring the poor *that are cast out* (margin 'afflicted') to *thy* house." The falsehood on which the writer had mentally founded himself, as previously stated by him, was this: "To confound the functions of the dispensers of the poor-rates with those of the dispensers of a charitable institution is a great and pernicious error." This sentence is so accurately and exquisitely wrong, that its substance must be thus reversed in our minds before we can deal with any existing problem of national distress. "To understand that the dispensers of the poor-rates are the almoners of the nation, and should distribute its alms with a gentleness and freedom of hand as much greater and franker than that possible to individual charity, as the collective national wisdom and power may be supposed greater than those of any single person, is the foundation of all law respecting pauperism." (Since this was written the "Pall Mall Gazette" has become a mere party paper—like the rest; but it writes well, and does more good than mischief on the whole.)

38. All these pleasures, then, and all these virtues, I repeat, you nationally despise. You have, indeed, men among you who do not; by whose work, by whose strength, by whose life, by whose death, you live, and never thank them. Your wealth, your amusement, your pride, would all be alike impossible, but for those whom you scorn or forget. The policeman, who is walking up and down the black lane all night to watch the guilt you have created there, and may have his brains beaten out, and be maimed for life, at any moment, and never be thanked; the sailor wrestling with the sea's rage; the quiet student poring over his book or his vial; the common worker, without praise, and nearly without bread, fulfilling his task as your horses drag your carts, hopeless, and spurned of all; these are the men by whom England lives; but they are not the nation; they are only the body and nervous force of it, acting still from old habit in a convulsive perseverance, while the mind is gone. Our National wish and purpose are to be amused; our National religion is the performance of church ceremonies, and preaching of soporific truths (or untruths) to keep the mob quietly at work, while we amuse ourselves; and the necessity for this amusement is fastening on us as a feverous disease of parched throat and wandering eyes—senseless, dissolute, merciless. How literally that word *Dis*-Ease; the Negation and impossibility of Ease, expresses the entire moral state of our English Industry and its Amusements!

39. When men are rightly occupied, their amusement grows out of their work, as the color-petals out of a fruitful flower;—when they are faithfully helpful and compassionate, all their emotions become steady, deep, perpetual, and vivifying to the soul as the natural pulse of the body. But now, having no true business, we pour our whole masculine energy into the false business of money-making; and having no true emotion, we must have false emotions dressed up for us to play with, not innocently, as children with dolls, but guiltily and darkly, as the idolatrous Jews with their pictures on cavern walls, which men had to dig to detect. The justice we do not execute, we mimic in the novel and on the stage; for the beauty we destroy in nature, we substitute the metamorphosis of the pantomime, and (the

human nature of us imperatively requiring awe and sorrow of *some* kind) for the noble grief we should have borne with our fellows, and the pure tears we should have wept with them, we gloat over the pathos of the police court, and gather the night-dew of the grave.

40. It is difficult to estimate the true significance of these things; the facts are frightful enough;—the measure of national fault involved in them is, perhaps, not as great as it would at first seem. We permit, or cause, thousands of deaths daily, but we mean no harm; we set fire to houses, and ravage peasants' fields; yet we should be sorry to find we had injured anybody. We are still kind at heart; still capable of virtue, but only as children are. Chalmers, at the end of his long life, having had much power with the public, being plagued in some serious matter by a reference to "public opinion," uttered the impatient exclamation, "The public is just a great baby!" And the reason that I have allowed all these graver subjects of thought to mix themselves up with an inquiry into methods of reading, is that, the more I see of our national faults and miseries, the more they resolve themselves into conditions of childish illiterateness, and want of education in the most ordinary habits of thought. It is, I repeat, not vice, not selfishness, not dullness of brain, which we have to lament; but an unreachable schoolboy's recklessness, only differing from the true schoolboy's in its incapacity of being helped, because it acknowledges no master.

41. There is a curious type of us given in one of the lovely, neglected works of the last of our great painters. It is a drawing of Kirkby Lonsdale churchyard, and of its brook, and valley, and hills, and folded morning sky beyond. And unmindful alike of these, and of the dead who have left these for other valleys and for other skies, a group of schoolboys have piled their little books upon a grave, to strike them off with stones. So, also, we play with the words of the dead that would teach us, and strike them far from us with our bitter, reckless will; little thinking that those leaves which the wind scatters had been piled, not only upon a gravestone, but upon the seal of an enchanted vault—nay, the gate of a great city of sleeping kings, who

would awake for us, and walk with us, if we knew but how to call them by their names. How often, even if we lift the marble entrance gate, do we but wander among those old kings in their repose, and finger the robes they lie in, and stir the crowns on their foreheads; and still they are silent to us, and seem but a dusty imagery; because we know not the incantation of the heart that would wake them;—which, if they once heard, they would start up to meet us in their power of long ago, narrowly to look upon us, and consider us; and, as the fallen kings of Hades meet the newly fallen, saying, "Art thou also become weak as we—art thou also become one of us?" so would these kings, with their undimmed, unshaken diadems, meet us, saying, "Art thou also become pure and mighty of heart as we? art thou also become one of us?"

42. Mighty of heart, mighty of mind—"magnanimous"—to be this, is, indeed, to be great in life; to become this increasingly, is, indeed, to "advance in life,"—in life itself—not in the trappings of it. My friends, do you remember that old Scythian custom, when the head of a house died? How he was dressed in his finest dress, and set in his chariot, and carried about to his friends' houses; and each of them placed him at his table's head, and all feasted in his presence? Suppose it were offered to you, in plain words, as it *is* offered to you in dire facts, that you should gain this Scythian honor, gradually, while you yet thought yourself alive. Suppose the offer were this: You shall die slowly; your blood shall daily grow cold, your flesh petrify, your heart beat at last only as a rusted group of iron valves. Your life shall fade from you, and sink through the earth into the ice of Caina; but, day by day, your body shall be dressed more gaily, and set in higher chariots, and have more orders on its breast—crowns on its head, if you will. Men shall bow before it, stare and shout round it, crowd after it up and down the streets; build palaces for it, feast with it at their tables' heads all the night long; your soul shall stay enough within it to know what they do, and feel the weight of the golden dress on its shoulders, and the furrow of the crown-edge on the skull;—no more. Would you take the offer, verbally made by the death-angel? Would

the meanest among us take it, think you? Yet practically and verily we grasp at it, every one of us, in a measure; many of us grasp at it in its fullness of horror. Every man accepts it, who desires to advance in life without knowing what life is; who means only that he is to get more horses, and more footmen, and more fortune, and more public honor, and—*not* more personal soul. He only is advancing in life, whose heart is getting softer, whose blood warmer, whose brain quicker, whose spirit is entering into Living peace. And the men who have this life in them are the true lords or kings of the earth—they, and they only. All other kingships, so far as they are true, are only the practical issue and expression of theirs; if less than this, they are either dramatic royalties,—costly shows, set off, indeed, with real jewels instead of tinsel,—but still only the toys of nations; or else, they are no royalties at all, but tyrannies, or the mere active and practical issue of national folly; for which reason I have said of them elsewhere, "Visible governments are the toys of some nations, the diseases of others, the harness of some, the burdens of more."

43. But I have no words for the wonder with which I hear Kinghood still spoken of, even among thoughtful men, as if governed nations were a personal property, and might be bought and sold, or otherwise acquired, as sheep, of whose flesh their king was to feed, and whose fleece he was to gather; as if Achilles' indignant epithet of base kings, "people-eating," were the constant and proper title of all monarchs; and enlargement of a king's dominion meant the same thing as the increase of a private man's estate! Kings who think so, however powerful, can no more be the true kings of the nation than gad-flies are the kings of a horse; they suck it, and may drive it wild, but do not guide it. They, and their courts, and their armies are, if one could see clearly, only a large species of marsh mosquito, with bayonet proboscis and melodious, band-mastered, trumpeting in the summer air; the twilight being, perhaps, sometimes fairer, but hardly more wholesome, for its glittering mists of midge companies. The true kings, meanwhile, rule quietly, if at all, and hate ruling; too many of them make "il gran

rifiúto"[18]; and if they do not, the mob, as soon as they are likely to become useful to it, is pretty sure to make *its* "gran rifiúto" of *them*.

44. Yet the visible king may also be a true one, some day, if ever day comes when he will estimate his dominion by the *force* of it,—not the geographical boundaries. It matters very little whether Trent cuts you a cantel out here, or Rhine rounds you a castle less there. But it does matter to you, king of men, whether you can verily say to this man, "Go," and he goeth; and to another, "Come," and he cometh. Whether you can turn your people, as you can Trent—and where it is that you bid them come, and where go. It matters to you, king of men, whether your people hate you, and die by you, or love you, and live by you. You may measure your dominion by multitudes better than by miles; and count degrees of love latitude, not from, but to a wonderfully warm and indefinite equator.

45. Measure! nay, you cannot measure. Who shall measure the difference between the power of those who "do and teach," and who are greatest in the kingdoms of earth, as of heaven—and the power of those who undo, and consume—whose power, at the fullest, is only the power of the moth and the rust? Strange! to think how the Moth-kings lay up treasures for the moth; and the Rust-kings, who are to their peoples' strength as rust to armor, lay up treasures for the rust; and the Robber-kings, treasures for the robber; but how few kings have ever laid up treasures that needed no guarding—treasures of which, the more thieves there were, the better! Broidered robe, only to be rent; helm and sword, only to be dimmed; jewel and gold, only to be scattered;—there have been three kinds of kings who have gathered these. Suppose there ever should arise a Fourth order of kings, who had read, in some obscure writing of long ago, that there was a Fourth kind of treasure, which the jewel and gold could not equal, neither should it be valued with pure gold. A web made fair in the weaving, by Athena's shuttle; an armor, forged in divine fire by Vulcanian force—a gold to be mined in the sun's red heart, where he sets over the Delphian cliffs;—deep-pictured tissue,

[18] The great renunciation.

impenetrable armor, potable gold!—the three great Angels of Conduct, Toil, and Thought, still calling to us, and waiting at the posts of our doors, to lead us, with their winged power, and guide us, with their unerring eyes, by the path which no fowl knoweth, and which the vulture's eye has not seen! Suppose kings should ever arise, who heard and believed this word, and at last gathered and brought forth treasures of—Wisdom—for their people?

46. Think what an amazing business *that* would be! How inconceivable, in the state of our present national wisdom! That we should bring up our peasants to a book exercise instead of a bayonet exercise!—organize, drill, maintain with pay, and good generalship, armies of thinkers, instead of armies of stabbers!—find national amusement in reading-rooms as well as rifle-grounds; give prizes for a fair shot at a fact, as well as for a leaden splash on a target. What an absurd idea it seems, put fairly in words, that the wealth of the capitalists of civilized nations should ever come to support literature instead of war!

47. Have yet patience with me, while I read you a single sentence out of the only book, properly to be called a book, that I have yet written myself, the one that will stand (if anything stand) surest and longest of all work of mine.

"It is one very awful form of the operation of wealth in Europe that it is entirely capitalists' wealth that supports unjust wars. Just wars do not need so much money to support them; for most of the men who wage such, wage them gratis; but for an unjust war, men's bodies and souls have both to be bought; and the best tools of war for them besides, which makes such war costly to the maximum; not to speak of the cost of base fear, and angry suspicion, between nations which have not grace nor honesty enough in all their multitudes to buy an hour's peace of mind with; as, at present, France and England, purchasing of each other ten millions' sterling worth of consternation, annually (a remarkably light crop, half thorns and half aspen leaves, sown, reaped, and granaried by the 'science' of the modern political economist, teaching covetousness instead of truth). And, all unjust war being supportable, if not by pillage of the enemy, only by loans from capitalists, these loans are repaid by subsequent taxation of the people, who appear to have no will in the matter, the capitalists' will being the primary root of the war; but its real root is the covetousness of the whole nation, rendering it incapable of faith, frankness, or justice, and bringing about, therefore, in due time, his own separate loss and punishment to each person."

48. France and England literally, observe, buy *panic* of each other; they pay, each of them, for ten thousand thousand pounds' worth of terror, a year. Now suppose, instead of buying these ten millions' worth of panic annually, they made up their minds to be at peace with each other, and buy ten millions' worth of knowledge annually; and that each nation spent its ten thousand thousand pounds a year in founding royal libraries, royal art galleries, royal museums, royal gardens, and places of rest. Might it not be better somewhat for both French and English?

49. It will be long, yet, before that comes to pass. Nevertheless, I hope it will not be long before royal or national libraries will be founded in every considerable city, with a royal series of books in them; the same series in every one of them, chosen books, the best in every kind, prepared for that national series in the most perfect way possible; their text printed all on leaves of equal size, broad of margin, and divided into pleasant volumes, light in the hand, beautiful, and strong, and thorough as examples of binders' work; and that these great libraries will be accessible to all clean and orderly persons at all times of the day and evening; strict law being enforced for this cleanliness and quietness.

I could shape for you other plans for art galleries, and for natural history galleries, and for many precious—many, it seems to me, needful—things; but this book plan is the easiest and needfullest, and would prove a considerable tonic to what we call our British constitution, which has fallen dropsical of late, and has an evil thirst, and evil hunger, and wants healthier feeding. You have got its corn laws repealed for it; try if you cannot get corn laws established for it dealing in a better bread;—bread made of that old enchanted Arabian grain, the Sesame, which opens doors;—doors not of robbers, but of Kings' Treasuries.

50. Note to ¶ 30.—Respecting the increase of rent by the deaths of the poor, for evidence of which, see the preface to the Medical officers' report to the Privy Council, just published, there are suggestions in its preface which will make some stir among us, I fancy, respecting which let me note these points following:—

There are two theories on the subject of land now abroad, and in contention; both false.

The first is that, by Heavenly law, there have always existed, and must continue to exist, a certain number of hereditarily sacred persons to whom the earth, air, and water of the world belong, as personal property; of which earth, air, and water, these persons may, at their pleasure, permit, or forbid, the rest of the human race to eat, breathe, or to drink. This theory is not for many years longer tenable. The adverse theory is that a division of the land of the world among the mob of the world would immediately elevate the said mob into sacred personages; that houses would then build themselves, and corn grow of itself; and that everybody would be able to live, without doing any work for his living. This theory would also be found highly untenable in practice.

It will, however, require some rough experiments, and rougher catastrophes, before the generality of persons will be convinced that no law concerning anything, least of all concerning land, for either holding or dividing it, or renting it high, or renting it low—would be of the smallest ultimate use to the people—so long as the general contest for life, and for the means of life, remains one of mere brutal competition. That contest, in an unprincipled nation, will take one deadly form or another, whatever laws you make against it. For instance, it would be an entirely wholesome law for England, if it could be carried, that maximum limits should be assigned to incomes according to classes; and that every nobleman's income should be paid to him as a fixed salary or pension by the nation; and not squeezed by him in variable sums, at discretion, out of the tenants of his land. But if you could get such a law passed to-morrow, and if, which would be farther necessary, you could fix the value of the assigned incomes by making a given weight of pure bread for a given sum, a twelvemonth would not pass before another currency would have been tacitly established, and the power of accumulative wealth would have reasserted itself in some other article, or some other imaginary sign. There is only one cure for public distress—and that is public education, directed to make men thoughtful, merciful, and just. There are, indeed, many laws conceivable which would gradually better and strengthen the national temper; but, for the most part, they are such as the national temper must be much bettered before it would bear. A nation in its youth may be helped by laws, as a weak child by backboards, but when it is old it cannot that way straighten its crooked spine.

And besides, the problem of land, at its worst, is a bye one; distribute the earth as you will, the principal question remains inexorable,—Who is to dig it? Which of us, in brief words, is to do the hard and dirty work for the rest—and for what pay? Who is to do the pleasant and clean work, and for what pay? Who is to do no work, and for what pay? And there are curious moral and religious questions connected with these. How far is it lawful to suck a portion of the soul out of a great many persons, in order to put the abstracted psychical quantities together and make one very beautiful or ideal soul? If we had to deal with mere blood, instead of spirit (and the thing might literally be done—as it has been done with infants before now)—so that it were possible by taking a certain quantity of blood from the arms of a given number of the mob, and putting it all into one person, to make a more azure-blooded gentleman of him, the thing would of course be managed; but secretly, I should conceive. But now, because it is brain and soul that we abstract, not visible blood, it can be done quite openly, and we live, we gentlemen, on delicatest prey, after the manner of weasels; that is to say, we keep a certain number of clowns digging and ditching, and generally stupefied, in order that we, being fed gratis, may have all the thinking and feeling to ourselves. Yet there is a great deal to be said for this. A highly-bred and trained English, French, Austrian, or Italian gentleman (much more a lady) is a great production,—a better production than most statues; being beautifully colored as well as shaped, and plus all the brains; a glorious thing to look at, a wonderful thing to talk to; and you cannot have it, any more than a pyramid or a church, but by sacrifice of much contributed life. And it is, perhaps, better to build a beautiful human creature than a beautiful dome or steeple—and more delightful to look up reverently to a creature far above us, than to a wall; only the beautiful human creature will have some duties to do in return—duties of living belfry and rampart—of which presently.

SESAME AND LILIES

LECTURE—II.—LILIES[1]

OF QUEENS' GARDENS.

"Be thou glad, oh thirsting Desert; let the desert be made cheerful, and bloom as the lily; and the barren places of Jordan shall run wild with wood."—ISAIAH xxxv, 1. (Septuagint.)

IT will, perhaps, be well, as this Lecture is the sequel of one previously given, that I should shortly state to you my general intention in both. The questions specially proposed to you in the first, namely, How and What to Read, rose out of a far deeper one, which it was my endeavor to make you propose earnestly to yourselves, namely, *Why* to Read. I want you to feel, with me, that whatever advantages we possess in the present day in the diffusion of education and of literature, can only be rightly used by any of us when we have apprehended clearly what education is to lead to, and literature to teach. I wish you to see that both well-directed moral training and well-chosen reading lead to the possession of a power over the ill-guided and illiterate, which is, according to the measure of it, in the truest sense, *kingly;* conferring indeed the purest kingship that can exist among men: too many other kingships (however distinguished by visible insignia or material power) being either spectral, or tyrannous;—Spectral—that is to say, aspects and shows only of royalty, hollow as death, and which only the "Likeness of a kingly crown have on"; or else tyrannous—that is to say, substituting their own will for the law of justice and love by which all true kings rule.

52. There is, then, I repeat—and as I want to leave this

[1] This lecture was given December 14, 1864, at the Town Hall, Manchester, in aid of the St. Andrew's Schools.

idea with you, I begin with it, and shall end with it—only one pure kind of kingship; an inevitable and external kind, crowned or not: the kingship, namely, which consists in a stronger moral state, and a truer thoughtful state, than that of others; enabling you, therefore, to guide, or to raise them. Observe that word "State"; we have got into a loose way of using it. It means literally the standing and stability of a thing; and you have the full force of it in the derived word "statue"—"the immovable thing." A king's majesty or "state," then, and the right of his kingdom to be called a state, depends on the movelessness of both:—without tremor, without quiver of balance; established and enthroned upon a foundation of eternal law which nothing can alter, nor overthrow.

53. Believing that all literature and all education are only useful so far as they tend to confirm this calm, beneficent, and *therefore* kingly, power—first, over ourselves, and, through ourselves, over all around us, I am now going to ask you to consider with me farther, what special portion or kind of this royal authority, arising out of noble education, may rightly be possessed by women; and how far they also are called to a true queenly power. Not in their households merely, but over all within their sphere. And in what sense, if they rightly understood and exercised this royal or gracious influence, the order and beauty induced by such benignant power would justify us in speaking of the territories over which each of them reigned, as "Queens' Gardens."

54. And here, in the very outset, we are met by a far deeper question, which—strange though this may seem—remains among many of us yet quite undecided, in spite of its infinite importance.

We cannot determine what the queenly power of women should be, until we are agreed what their ordinary power should be. We cannot consider how education may fit them for any widely extending duty, until we are agreed what is their true constant duty. And there never was a time when wilder words were spoken, or more vain imagination permitted, respecting this question—quite vital to all social happiness. The relations of the womanly to the manly nature, their different capacities of intellect or of virtue, seem never to have been yet estimated with entire consent. We hear of the "mission" and of the "rights" of Woman, as if these could ever be separate from the mission and the rights of Man;—as if she and her lord were creatures of independent kind, and of irreconcilable claim. This, at least, is wrong. And not less wrong—perhaps even more foolishly wrong (for I will anticipate thus far what I hope to prove) —is the idea that woman is only the shadow and attendant image of her lord, owing him a thoughtless and servile obedience, and supported altogether in her weakness, by the preëminence of his fortitude.

This, I say, is the most foolish of all errors respecting her who was made to be the helpmate of man. As if he could be helped effectively by a shadow, or worthily by a slave!

55. I.—Let us try, then, whether we cannot get at some clear and harmonious idea (it must be harmonious if it is true) of what womanly mind and virtue are in power and office, with respect to man's; and how their relations rightly accepted, aid, and increase, the vigor, and honor, and authority of both.

And now I must repeat one thing I said in the last lecture: namely, that the first use of education was to enable us to consult with the wisest and the greatest men on all points of earnest difficulty. That to use books rightly, was to go to them for help: to appeal to them, when our own knowledge and power of thought failed: to be led by them into wider sight—purer conception—than our own, and receive from them the united sentence of the judges and councils of all time, against our solitary and unstable opinion.

Let us do this now. Let us see whether the greatest, the wisest, the purest-hearted of all ages are agreed in any wise on this point: let us hear the testimony they have left respecting what they held to be the true dignity of woman, and her mode of help to man.

56. And first let us take Shakespeare.

Note broadly in the outset, Shakespeare has no heroes; —he has only heroines. There is not one entirely heroic figure in all his plays, except the slight sketch of Henry the Fifth, exaggerated for the purposes of the stage: and the still slighter Valentine in The Two Gentlemen of Verona. In his labored and perfect plays you have no hero. Othello would have been one, if his simplicity had not been so great as to leave him the prey of every base practice round him; but he is the only example even approximating to the heroic type. Coriolanus—Cæsar—Antony, stand in flawed strength, and fall by their vanities;—Hamlet is indolent, and drowsily speculative; Romeo an impatient boy; the Merchant of Venice languidly submissive to adverse fortune; Kent, in King Lear, is entirely noble at heart, but too rough and unpolished to be of true use at the critical time, and he sinks into the office of a servant only. Orlando, no less noble, is yet the despairing toy of chance, followed, comforted, saved, by Rosalind. Whereas there is hardly a play that has not a perfect woman in it, steadfast in grave hope and errorless purpose: Cordelia, Desdemona, Isabella, Hermione, Imogen, Queen Katherine, Perdita, Silvia, Viola, Rosalind, Helena, and last, and perhaps loveliest, Virgilia, are all faultless: conceived in the highest heroic type of humanity.

57. Then observe, secondly,

The catastrophe of every play is caused always by the folly or fault of a man; the redemption, if there be any, is by the wisdom and virtue of a woman, and failing that, there is none. The catastrophe of King Lear is owing to his own want of judgment, his impatient vanity, his misunderstanding of his children; the virtue of his one true daughter would have saved him from all the injuries of the others, unless he had cast her away from him; as it is, she all but saves him.

Of Othello I need not trace the tale;—nor the one weakness of his so mighty love; nor the inferiority of his perceptive intellect to that even of the second woman character in the play, the Emilia who dies in wild testimony against his error:—"Oh, murderous coxcomb! What should such a fool Do with so good a wife?"

In Romeo and Juliet, the wise and brave stratagem of the wife is brought to ruinous issue by the reckless impatience of her husband. In Winter's Tale and in Cymbeline, the happiness and existence of two princely households, lost through long years, and imperiled to the death by the folly and obstinacy of the husbands, are redeemed at last by the queenly patience and wisdom of the wives. In Measure for Measure, the foul injustice of the judge, and the foul cowardice of the brother, are opposed to the victorious truth and adamantine purity of a woman. In Coriolanus, the mother's counsel, acted upon in time, would have saved her son from all evil; his momentary forgetfulness of it is his ruin; her prayer at last granted, saves him—not, indeed, from death, but from the curse of living as the destroyer of his country.

And what shall I say of Julia, constant against the fickleness of a lover who is a mere wicked child?—of Helena, against the petulance and insult of a careless youth?—of the patience of Hero, the passion of Beatrice, and the calmly devoted wisdom of the "unlessoned girl," who appears among the helplessness, the blindness, and the vindictive passions of men, as a gentle angel, bringing courage and safety by her presence, and defeating the worst malignities of crime by what women are fancied most to fail in,—precision and accuracy of thought.

58. Observe, further, among all the principal figures in Shakespeare's plays, there is only one weak woman—Ophelia; and it is because she fails Hamlet at the critical moment, and is not, and cannot in her nature be, a guide to him when he needs her most, that all the bitter catastrophe follows. Finally, though there are three wicked women among the principal figures, Lady Macbeth, Regan, and Goneril, they are felt at once to be frightful exceptions to the ordinary laws of life; fatal in their influence also in proportion to the power for good which they have abandoned.

Such, in broad light, is Shakespeare's testimony to the position and character of women in human life. He represents them as infallibly faithful and wise counselors,—incorruptibly just and pure examples—strong always to sanctify, even when they cannot save.

59. Not as in any wise comparable in knowledge of the nature of man,—still less in his understanding of the causes and courses of fate,—but only as the writer who has given us the broadest view of the conditions and modes of ordi-

nary thought in modern society, I ask you next to receive the witness of Walter Scott.

I put aside his merely romantic prose writings as of no value; and though the early romantic poetry is very beautiful, its testimony is of no weight, other than that of a boy's ideal. But his true works, studied from Scottish life, bear a true witness; and, in the whole range of these, there are but three men who reach the heroic type[2]—Dandie Dinmont, Rob Roy, and Claverhouse; of these, one is a border farmer; another a freebooter; the third a soldier in a bad cause. And these touch the ideal of heroism only in their courage and faith, together with a strong, but uncultivated, or mistakenly applied, intellectual power; while his younger men are the gentlemanly playthings of fantastic fortune, and only by aid (or accident) of that fortune, survive, not vanquish, the trials they involuntarily sustain. Of any disciplined, or consistent character, earnest in a purpose wisely conceived, or dealing with forms of hostile evil, definitely challenged, and resolutely subdued, there is no trace in his conceptions of young men. Whereas in his imaginations of women,—in the characters of Ellen Douglas, of Flora MacIvor, Rose Bradwardine, Catherine Seyton, Diana Vernon, Lilias Redgauntlet, Alice Bridgenorth, Alice Lee, and Jeanie Deans,—with endless varieties of grace, tenderness, and intellectual power we find in all a quite infallible and inevitable sense of dignity and justice; a fearless, instant, and untiring self-sacrifice to even the appearance of duty, much more to its real claims; and, finally, a patient wisdom of deeply restrained affection, which does infinitely more than protect its objects from a momentary error; it gradually forms, animates, and exalts the characters of the unworthy lovers, until, at the close of the tale, we are just able, and no more, to take patience in hearing of their unmerited success.

So that in all cases, with Scott as with Shakespeare, it

[2] I ought, in order to make this assertion fully understood, to have noted the various weaknesses which lower the ideal of other great characters of men in the Waverley novels—the selfishness and narrowness of thought in Redgauntlet, the weak religious enthusiasm in Edward Glendinning, and the like; and I ought to have noticed that there are several quite perfect characters sketched sometimes in the backgrounds; three—let us accept joyously this courtesy to England and her soldiers—are English officers: Colonel Gardiner, Colonel Talbot, and Colonel Mannering.

is the woman who watches over, teaches, and guides the youth; it is never, by any chance, the youth who watches over or educates his mistress.

60. Next, take, though more briefly, graver testimony—that of the great Italians and Greeks. You know well the plan of Dante's great poem—that it is a love poem to his dead lady; a song of praise for her watch over his soul. Stooping only to pity, never to love, she yet saves him from destruction—saves him from hell. He is going eternally astray in despair; she comes down from heaven to his help, and throughout the ascents of Paradise is his teacher, interpreting for him the most difficult truths, divine and human, and leading him, with rebuke upon rebuke, from star to star.

I do not insist upon Dante's conception; if I began I could not cease; besides, you might think this a wild imagination of one poet's heart. So I will rather read to you a few verses of the deliberate writing of a knight of Pisa to his living lady, wholly characteristic of the feeling of all the noblest men of the thirteenth, or early fourteenth century, preserved among many other such records of knightly honor and love, which Dante Rossetti has gathered for us from among the early Italian poets.

"For lo! thy law is passed
That this my love should manifestly be
To serve and honor thee;
And so I do; and my delight is full,
Accepted for the servant of thy rule.

"Without almost, I am all rapturous,
Since thus my will was set
To serve, thou flower of joy, thine excellence;
Nor ever seems it anything could rouse
A pain or regret,
But on thee dwells mine every thought and sense;
Considering that from thee all virtues spread
As from a fountain head,—
That in thy gift is wisdom's best avail,
And honor without fail;
With whom each sovereign good dwells separate,
Fulfilling the perfection of thy state.

"Lady, since I conceived
That pleasurable aspect in my heart,

My life has been apart
In shining brightness and the place of truth;
Which till that time, good sooth,
Groped among shadows in a darken'd place,
Where many hours and days
It hardly ever had remember'd good.
But now my servitude
Is thine, and I am full of joy and rest.
A man from a wild beast
Thou madest me, since for thy love I lived."

61. You may think, perhaps, a Greek knight would have had a lower estimate of women than this Christian lover. His spiritual subjection to them was, indeed, not so absolute; but as regards their own personal character, it was only because you could not have followed me so easily, that I did not take the Greek women instead of Shakespeare's; and instance, for chief ideal types of human beauty and faith, the simple mother's and wife's heart of Andromache; the divine, yet rejected wisdom of Cassandra; the playful kindness and simple princess-life of happy Nausicaä; the housewifely calm of that of Penelope, with its watch upon the sea; the ever patient, fearless, hopelessly devoted piety of the sister and daughter, in Antigone; the bowing down of Iphigenia, lamb-like and silent; and, finally, the expectation of the resurrection, made clear to the soul of the Greeks in the return from her grave of that Alcestis, who, to save her husband, had passed calmly through the bitterness of death.

62. Now, I could multiply witness upon witness of this kind upon you if I had time. I would take Chaucer, and show you why he wrote a Legend of Good Women; but no Legend of Good Men. I would take Spenser, and show you how all his fairy knights are sometimes deceived and sometimes vanquished; but the soul of Una is never darkened, and the spear of Britomart is never broken. Nay, I could go back into the mythical teaching of the most ancient times, and show you how the great people,—by one of whose princesses it was appointed that the Lawgiver of all the earth should be educated, rather than by his own kindred;—how that great Egyptian people, wisest then of nations, gave to their Spirit of Wisdom the form of a

woman; and into her hand, for a symbol, the weaver's shuttle; and how the name and the form of that spirit, adopted, believed, and obeyed by the Greeks, became that Athena of the olive-helm, and cloudy shield, to faith in whom you owe, down to this date, whatever you hold most precious in art, in literature, or in types of national virtue.

63. But I will not wander into this distant and mythical element; I will only ask you to give its legitimate value to the testimony of these great poets and men of the world,—consistent, as you see it is, on this head. I will ask you whether it can be supposed that these men, in the main work of their lives, are amusing themselves with a fictitious and idle view of the relations between man and woman;—nay, worse than fictitious or idle; for a thing may be imaginary, yet desirable, if it were possible; but this, their ideal of woman, is, according to our common idea of the marriage relation, wholly undesirable. The woman, we say, is not to guide, nor even to think for herself. The man is always to be the wiser; he is to be the thinker, the ruler, the superior in knowledge and discretion, as in power.

64. Is it not somewhat important to make up our minds on this matter? Are all these great men mistaken, or are we? Are Shakespeare and Aeschylus, Dante and Homer, merely dressing dolls for us; or, worse than dolls, unnatural visions, the realization of which, were it possible, would bring anarchy into all households and ruin into all affections? Nay, if you could suppose this, take lastly the evidence of facts, given by the human heart itself. In all Christian ages which have been remarkable for their purity or progress, there has been absolute yielding of obedient devotion, by the lover, to his mistress. I say *obedient;*—not merely enthusiastic and worshiping in imagination, but entirely subject, receiving from the beloved woman, however young, not only the encouragement, the praise, and the reward of all toil, but so far as any choice is open, or any question difficult of decision, the *direction* of all toil. That chivalry, to the abuse and dishonor of which are attributable primarily whatever is cruel in war, unjust in peace, or corrupt and ignoble in domestic relations; and to the original purity and power of which we owe the defense

alike of faith, of law, and of love;—that chivalry, I say, in its very first conception of honorable life, assumes the subjection of the young knight to the command—should it even be the command in caprice—of his lady. It assumes this, because its masters knew that the first and necessary impulse of every truly taught and knightly heart is this of blind service to its lady; that where that true faith and captivity are not, all wayward and wicked passions must be; and that in this rapturous obedience to the single love of his youth, is the sanctification of all man's strength, and the continuance of all his purposes. And this, not because such obedience would be safe, or honorable, were it ever rendered to the unworthy; but because it ought to be impossible for every noble youth—it *is* impossible for every one rightly trained—to love any one whose gentle counsel he cannot trust, or whose prayerful command he can hesitate to obey.

65. I do not insist by any farther argument on this, for I think it should commend itself at once to your knowledge of what has been and to your feelings of what should be. You cannot think that the buckling on of the knight's armor by his lady's hand was a mere caprice of romantic fashion. It is the type of an eternal truth—that the soul's armor is never well set to the heart unless a woman's hand has braced it; and it is only when she braces it loosely that the honor of manhood fails. Know you not those lovely lines—I would they were learned by all youthful ladies of England.—

> "Ah, wasteful woman!—she who may
> On her sweet self set her own price,
> Knowing he cannot choose but pay—
> How has she cheapen'd Paradise!
> How given for nought her priceless gift,
> How spoiled the bread and spill'd the wine,
> Which, spent with due, respective thrift,
> Had made brutes men, and men divine!"[3]

66. Thus much, then, respecting the relations of lovers I believe you will accept. But what we too often doubt is the

[3] Coventry Patmore. You cannot read him too often or too carefully; as far as I know he is the only living poet who always strengthens and purifies; the others sometimes darken, and nearly always depress and discourage, the imagination they deeply seize.

fitness of the continuance of such a relation throughout the whole of human life. We think it right in the lover and mistress, not in the husband and wife. That is to say, we think that a reverent and tender duty is due to one whose affection we still doubt, and whose character we as yet do but partially and distantly discern; and that this reverence and duty are to be withdrawn, when the affection has become wholly and limitlessly our own, and the character has been so sifted and tried that we fear not to entrust it with the happiness of our lives. Do you not see how ignoble this is, as well as how unreasonable? Do you not feel that marriage,—when it is marriage at all,—is only the seal which marks the vowed transition of temporary into untiring service, and of fitful into eternal love?

67. But how, you will ask, is the idea of this guiding function of the woman reconcilable with a true wifely subjection? Simply in that it is a *guiding,* not a determining, function. Let me try to show you briefly how these powers seem to be rightly distinguishable.

We are foolish, and without excuse foolish, in speaking of the "superiority" of one sex to the other, as if they could be compared in similar things. Each has what the other has not: each completes the other, and is completed by the other: they are in nothing alike, and the happiness and perfection of both depends on each asking and receiving from the other what the other only can give.

68. Now their separate characters are briefly these: The man's power is active, progressive, defensive. He is eminently the doer, the creator, the discoverer, the defender. His intellect is for speculation and invention; his energy for adventure, for war, and for conquest, wherever war is just, wherever conquest necessary. But the woman's power is for rule, not for battle,—and her intellect is not for invention or creation, but for sweet ordering, arrangement, and decision. She sees the qualities of things, their claims, and their places. Her great function is Praise: she enters into no contest, but infallibly judges the crown of contest. By her office, and place, she is protected from all danger and temptation. The man, in his rough work in open world, must encounter all peril and trial: to him, therefore, must

be the failure, the offense, the inevitable error: often he must be wounded, or subdued; often misled; and *always* hardened. But he guards the woman from all this; within his house, as ruled by her, unless she herself has sought it, need enter no danger, no temptation, no cause of error or offense. This is the true nature of home—it is the place of Peace; the shelter, not only from all injury, but from all terror, doubt, and division. In so far as it is not this, it is not home: so far as the anxieties of the outer life penetrate into it, and the inconsistently-minded, unknown, unloved, or hostile society of the outer world is allowed by either husband or wife to cross the threshold, it ceases to be home; it is then only a part of that outer world which you have roofed over, and lighted fire in. But so far as it is a sacred place, a vestal temple, a temple of the hearth watched over by Household Gods, before whose faces none may come but those whom they can receive with love,—so far as it is this, and roof and fire are types only of a nobler shade and light,—shade as of the rock in a weary land, and light as of the Pharos in the stormy sea,—so far it vindicates the name, and fulfills the praise, of home.

And wherever a true wife comes, this home is always round her. The stars only may be over her head; the glow-worm in the night-cold grass may be the only fire at her foot: but home is yet wherever she is; and for a noble woman it stretches far round her, better than ceiled with cedar, or painted with vermilion, shedding its quiet light far, for those who else were homeless.

69. This, then, I believe to be,—will you not admit it to be,—the woman's true place and power? But do not you see that to fulfill this, she must—as far as one can use such terms of a human creature—be incapable of error? So far as she rules, all must be right, or nothing is. She must be enduringly, incorruptibly good; instinctively, infallibly wise—wise, not for self-development, but for self-renunciation: wise, not that she may set herself above her husband, but that she may never fail from his side: wise, not with the narrowness of insolent and loveless pride, but with the passionate gentleness of an infinitely variable, because infinitely applicable, modesty of service—the true changeful-

ness of woman. In that great sense—"La donna è mobile," not "Qual piúm' al vento"; no, nor yet "Variable as the shade, by the light quivering aspen made"; but variable as the *light,* manifold in fair and serene division, that it may take the color of all that it falls upon, and exalt it.

70. II.—I have been trying, thus far, to show you what should be the place, and what the power of woman. Now, secondly, we ask, What kind of education is to fit her for these?

And if you indeed think this is a true conception of her office and dignity, it will not be difficult to trace the course of education which would fit her for the one, and raise her to the other.

The first of our duties to her—no thoughtful persons now doubt this—is to secure for her such physical training and exercise as may confirm her health, and perfect her beauty, the highest refinement of that beauty being unattainable without splendor of activity and of delicate strength. To perfect her beauty, I say, and increase its power; it cannot be too powerful, nor shed its sacred light too far: only remember that all physical freedom is vain to produce beauty without a corresponding freedom of heart. There are two passages of that poet who is distinguished, it seems to me, from all others—not by power, but by exquisite *right*ness—which point you to the source, and describe to you, in a few syllables, the completion of womanly beauty. I will read the introductory stanzas, but the last is the one I wish you specially to notice:—

> "Three years she grew in sun and shower,
> Then Nature said, 'A lovelier flower
> On earth was never sown.
> This child I to myself will take;
> She shall be mine, and I will make
> A lady of my own.
>
> "'Myself will to my darling be
> Both law and impulse; and with me
> The girl, in rock and plain,
> In earth and heaven, in glade and bower,
> Shall feel an overseeing power
> To kindle, or restrain.

"'The floating clouds their state shall lend
To her; for her the willow bend;
Nor shall she fail to see
Even in the motions of the storm
Grace that shall mould the maiden's form
By silent sympathy.

"'And *vital feelings of delight*
Shall rear her form to stately height,
Her virgin bosom swell.
Such *thoughts* to Lucy I will give,
While she and I together live,
Here in this happy dell.'"[4]

"*Vital* feelings of delight," observe. There are deadly feelings of delight; but the natural ones are vital, necessary to very life.

And they must be feelings of delight, if they are to be vital. Do not think you can make a girl lovely, if you do not make her happy. There is not one restraint you put on a good girl's nature—there is not one check you give to her instincts of affection or of effort—which will not be indelibly written on her features, with a hardness which is all the more painful because it takes away the brightness from the eyes of innocence, and the charm from the brow of virtue.

71. This for the means: now note the end. Take from the same poet, in two lines, a perfect description of womanly beauty—

"A countenance in which did meet
Sweet records, promises as sweet."

The perfect loveliness of a woman's countenance can only consist in that majestic peace, which is founded in the memory of happy and useful years,—full of sweet records; and from the joining of this with that yet more majestic childishness, which is still full of change and promise;—opening always—modest at once, and bright, with hope of better things to be won, and to be bestowed. There is no old age where there is still that promise.

72. Thus, then, you have first to mould her physical frame, and then, as the strength she gains will permit you, to fill and temper her mind with all knowledge and thoughts which

[4] Observe, it is "Nature" who is speaking throughout, and who says, "While she and I together live."

tend to confirm its natural instincts of justice, and refine its natural tact of love.

All such knowledge should be given her as may enable her to understand, and even to aid, the work of men: and yet it should be given, not as knowledge,—not as if it were, or could be, for her an object to know; but only to feel, and to judge. It is of no moment, as a matter of pride or perfectness in herself, whether she knows many languages or one; but it is of the utmost, that she should be able to show kindness to a stranger, and to understand the sweetness of a stranger's tongue. It is of no moment to her own worth or dignity that she should be acquainted with this science or that; but it is of the highest that she should be trained in habits of accurate thought; that she should understand the meaning, the inevitableness, and the loveliness of natural laws; and follow at least some one path of scientific attainment, as far as to the threshold of that bitter Valley of Humiliation, into which only the wisest and bravest of men can descend, owning themselves forever children, gathering pebbles on a boundless shore. It is of little consequence how many positions of cities she knows, or how many dates of events, or names of celebrated persons —it is not the object of education to turn a woman into a dictionary; but it is deeply necessary that she should be taught to enter with her whole personality into the history she reads; to picture the passages of it vitally in her own bright imagination; to apprehend, with her fine instincts, the pathetic circumstances and dramatic relations, which the historian too often only eclipses by his reasoning, and disconnects by his arrangement: it is for her to trace the hidden equities of divine reward, and catch sight, through the darkness, of the fatal threads of woven fire that connect error with its retribution. But, chiefly of all, she is to be taught to extend the limits of her sympathy with respect to that history which is being for her determined as the moments pass in which she draws her peaceful breath: and to the contemporary calamity, which, were it but rightly mourned by her, would recur no more hereafter. She is to exercise herself in imagining what would be the effects upon her mind and conduct, if she were daily brought into the presence of the suffering which is not the less real because shut from her sight. She is to be taught somewhat to understand the nothingness of the proportion which that little world in which she lives and loves, bears to the world in which God lives and loves;—and solemnly she is to be taught to strive that her thoughts of piety may not be feeble in proportion to the number they embrace, nor her prayer more languid than it is for the momentary relief from pain of her husband or her child, when it is uttered for the multitudes of those who have none to love them,—and is, "for all who are desolate and oppressed."

73. Thus far, I think, I have had your concurrence; perhaps you will not be with me in what I believe is most needful for me to say. There *is* one dangerous science for women—one which they must indeed beware how they profanely touch—that of theology. Strange, and miserably strange, that while they are modest enough to doubt their powers, and pause at the threshold of sciences where every step is demonstrable and sure, they will plunge headlong, and without one thought of incompetency, into that science in which the greatest men have trembled, and the wisest erred. Strange, that they will complacently and pridefully bind up whatever vice or folly there is in them, whatever arrogance, petulance, or blind incomprehensiveness, into one bitter bundle of consecrated myrrh. Strange, in creatures born to be Love visible, that where they can know least, they will condemn first, and think to recommend themselves to their Master, by scrambling up the steps of His judgment throne, to divide it with Him. Strangest of all, that they should think they were led by the Spirit of the Comforter into habits of mind which have become in them the unmixed elements of home discomfort; and that they dare to turn the Household Gods of Christianity into ugly idols of their own;—spiritual dolls, for them to dress according to their caprice; and from which their husbands must turn away in grieved contempt, lest they should be shrieked at for breaking them.

74. I believe then, with this exception, that a girl's education should be nearly, in its course and material of study, the same as a boy's; but quite differently directed. A woman,

in any rank of life, ought to know whatever her husband is likely to know, but to know it in a different way. His command of it should be foundational and progressive; hers, general and accomplished for daily and helpful use. Not but that it would often be wiser in men to learn things in a womanly sort of way, for present use, and to seek for the discipline and training of their mental powers in such branches of study as will be afterwards fittest for social service; but, speaking broadly, a man ought to know any language or science he learns, thoroughly—while a woman ought to know the same language, or science, only so far as may enable her to sympathize in her husband's pleasures, and in those of his best friends.

75. Yet, observe, with exquisite accuracy as far as she reaches. There is a wide difference between elementary knowledge and superficial knowledge—between a firm beginning, and an infirm attempt at compassing. A woman may always help her husband by what she knows, however little; by what she half-knows, or mis-knows, she will only tease him.

And indeed, if there were to be any difference between a girl's education and a boy's, I should say that of the two the girl should be earlier led, as her intellect ripens faster, into deep and serious subjects: and that her range of literature should be, not more, but less frivolous; calculated to add the qualities of patience and seriousness to her natural poignancy of thought and quickness of wit; and also to keep her in a lofty and pure element of thought. I enter not now into any question of choice of books; only let us be sure that her books are not heaped up in her lap as they fall out of the package of the circulating library, wet with the last and lightest spray of the fountain of folly.

76. Or even of the fountain of wit; for with respect to that sore temptation of novel-reading, it is not the badness of a novel that we should dread, so much as its overwrought interest. The weakest romance is not so stupefying as the lower forms of religious exciting literature, and the worst romance is not so corrupting as false history, false philosophy, or false political essays. But the best romance becomes dangerous, if, by its excitement it renders the

ordinary course of life uninteresting, and increases the morbid thirst for useless acquaintance with scenes in which we shall never be called upon to act.

77. I speak therefore of good novels only; and our modern literature is particularly rich in types of such. Well read, indeed, these books have serious use, being nothing less than treatises on moral anatomy and chemistry; studies of human nature in the elements of it. But I attach little weight to this function: they are hardly ever read with earnestness enough to permit them to fulfill it. The utmost they usually do is to enlarge somewhat the charity of a kind reader, or the bitterness of a malicious one; for each will gather, from the novel, food for her own disposition. Those who are naturally proud and envious will learn from Thackeray to despise humanity; those who are naturally gentle, to pity it; those who are naturally shallow, to laugh at it. So also, there might be a serviceable power in novels to bring before us, in vividness, a human truth which we had before dimly conceived; but the temptation to picturesqueness of statement is so great, that often the best writers of fiction cannot resist it; and our views are rendered so violent and one-sided, that their vitality is rather a harm than good.

78. Without, however, venturing here on any attempt at decision of how much novel-reading should be allowed, let me at least clearly assert this, that whether novels, or poetry, or history be read, they should be chosen, not for their freedom from evil, but for their possession of good. The chance and scattered evil that may here and there haunt, or hide itself in, a powerful book, never does any harm to a noble girl; but the emptiness of an author oppresses her, and his amiable folly degrades her. And if she can have access to a good library of old and classical books, there need be no choosing at all. Keep the modern magazine and novel out of your girl's way; turn her loose into the old library every wet day, and let her alone. She will find what is good for her; you cannot; for there is just this difference between the making of a girl's character and a boy's—you may chisel a boy into shape, as you would a rock, or hammer him into it, if he be of a better kind, as

you would a piece of bronze. But you cannot hammer a girl into anything. She grows as a flower does,—she will wither without sun; she will decay in her sheath, as the narcissus will, if you do not give her air enough; she may fall, and defile her head in dust, if you leave her without help at some moments of her life; but you cannot fetter her; she must take her own fair form and way, if she take any, and in mind as in body, must have always—

> "Her household motions light and free
> And steps of virgin liberty."

Let her loose in the library, I say, as you do a fawn in a field. It knows the bad weeds twenty times better than you; and the good ones, too, and will eat some bitter and prickly ones, good for it, which you had not the slightest thought would have been so.

79. Then, in art, keep the finest models before her, and let her practice in all accomplishments to be accurate and thorough, so as to enable her to understand more than she accomplishes. I say the finest models—that is to say, the truest, simplest, usefullest. Note those epithets; they will range through all the arts. Try them in music, where you might think them the least applicable. I say the truest, that in which the notes most closely and faithfully express the meaning of the words, or the character of intended emotion; again, the simplest, that in which the meaning and melody are attained with the fewest and most significant notes possible; and, finally, the usefullest, that music which makes the best words most beautiful, which enchants them in our memories each with its own glory of sound, and which applies them closest to the heart at the moment we need them.

80. And not only in the material and in the course, but yet more earnestly in the spirit of it, let a girl's education be as serious as a boy's. You bring up your girls as if they were meant for sideboard ornament, and then complain of their frivolity. Give them the same advantages that you give their brothers—appeal to the same grand instincts of virtue in them; teach *them,* also, that courage and truth are the pillars of their being;—do you think that they would

not answer that appeal, brave and true as they are even now, when you know that there is hardly a girl's school in this Christian kingdom where the children's courage or sincerity would be thought of half so much importance as their way of coming in at a door; and when the whole system of society, as respects the mode of establishing them in life, is one rotten plague of cowardice and imposture—cowardice, in not daring to let them live, or love, except as their neighbors choose; and imposture, in bringing, for the purpose of our own pride, the full glow of the world's worst vanity upon a girl's eyes, at the very period when the whole happiness of her future existence depends upon her remaining undazzled?

81. And give them, lastly, not only noble teachings but noble teachers. You consider somewhat, before you send your boy to school, what kind of a man the master is;—whatsoever kind of a man he is, you at least give him full authority over your son, and show some respect for him yourself;—if he comes to dine with you, you do not put him at a side table; you know, also, that at his college, your child's immediate tutor will be under the direction of some still higher tutor, for whom you have absolute reverence. You do not treat the Dean of Christ Church or the Master of Trinity as your inferiors.

But what teachers do you give your girls, and what reverence do you show to the teachers you have chosen? Is a girl likely to think her own conduct, or her own intellect, of much importance, when you trust the entire formation of her character, moral and intellectual, to a person whom you let your servants treat with less respect than they do your housekeeper (as if the soul of your child were a less charge than jams and groceries), and whom you yourself think you confer an honor upon by letting her sometimes sit in the drawing-room in the evening?

82. Thus, then, of literature as her help, and thus of art. There is one more help which we cannot do without—one which, alone, has sometimes done more than all other influences besides,—the help of wild and fair nature. Hear this of the education of Joan of Arc:—

"The education of this poor girl was mean according to

the present standard; was ineffably grand, according to a purer philosophic standard; and only not good for our age, because for us it would be unattainable. . . .

"Next after her spiritual advantages, she owed most to the advantages of her situation. The fountain of Domrémy was on the brink of a boundless forest; and it was haunted to that degree by fairies, that the parish priest (*curé*) was obliged to read mass there once a year, in order to keep them in any decent bounds. . . .

"But the forest of Domrémy—those were the glories of the land; for in them abode mysterious powers and ancient secrets that towered into tragic strength. Abbeys there were, and abbey windows,'—'like Moorish temples of the Hindoos,' that exercised even princely power both in Touraine and in the German Diets. These had their sweet bells that pierced the forests for many a league at matins or vespers, and each its own dreamy legend. Few enough, and scattered enough, were these abbeys, so as in no degree to disturb the deep solitude of the region; yet many enough to spread a network or awning of Christian sanctity over what else might have seemed a heathen wilderness."[5]

Now you cannot, indeed, have here in England, woods eighteen miles deep to the centre; but you can, perhaps, keep a fairy or two for your children yet, if you wish to keep them. But *do* you wish it? Suppose you had each, at the back of your houses, a garden large enough for your children to play in, with just as much lawn as would give them room to run,—no more—and that you could not change your abode; but that, if you choose, you could double your income, or quadruple it, by digging a coal-shaft in the middle of the lawn, and turning the flower-beds into heaps of coke. Would you do it? I hope not. I can tell you, you would be wrong if you did, though it gave you income sixty-fold instead of four-fold.

83. Yet this is what you are doing with all England. The whole country is but a little garden, not more than enough for your children to run on the lawns of, if you would let them *all* run there. And this little garden you

[5] "Joan of Arc: in reference to M. Michelet's History of France." De Quincey's Works, Vol. III, page 217.

will turn into furnace-ground, and fill with heaps of cinders, if you can; and those children of yours, not you, will suffer for it. For the fairies will not be all banished; there are fairies of the furnace as of the wood, and their first gifts seem to be "sharp arrows of the mighty"; but their last gifts are "coals of juniper."

84. And yet I cannot—though there is no part of my subject that I feel more—press this upon you; for we made so little use of the power of nature while we had it, that we shall hardly feel what we have lost. Just on the other side of the Mersey you have your Snowdon, and your Menai Straits, and that mighty granite rock beyond the moors of Anglesea, splendid in its heatherly crest, and foot planted in the deep sea, once thought of as sacred—a divine promontory, looking westward; the Holy Head or Headland, still not without awe when its red light glares first through storm. These are the hills, and these the bays and blue inlets, which, among the Greeks, would have been always loved, always fateful in influence on the national mind. That Snowdon is your Parnassus; but where are its Muses? That Holyhead mountain is your Island of Ægina, but where is its Temple to Minerva?

85. Shall I read you what the Christian Minerva had achieved under the shadow of our Parnassus, up to the year 1848?—Here is a little account of a Welsh school, from page 261 of the report on Wales, published by the Committee of Council on Education. This is a school close to a town containing 5,000 persons:—

"I then called up a larger class, most of whom had recently come to the school. Three girls repeatedly declared that they had never heard of Christ, and two that they had never heard of God. Two out of six thought Christ was on earth now ('they might have had a worse thought, perhaps'); three knew nothing about the crucifixion. Four out of seven did not know the names of the months, nor the number of days in a year. They had no notion of addition beyond two and two, or three and three; their minds were perfect blanks."

Oh, ye women of England! from the Princess of that Wales to the simplest of you, do not think your own children can be brought into their true fold of rest while these are scattered on the hills, as sheep having no shepherd. And do not think your daughters can be trained to the truth of their own human beauty, while the pleasant places, which God made at once for their school-room and their playground, lie desolate and defiled. You cannot baptize them rightly in those inch-deep fonts of yours, unless you baptize them also in the sweet waters which the great Lawgiver strikes forth forever from the rocks of your native land—waters which a Pagan would have worshiped in their purity, and you only worship with pollution. You cannot lead your children faithfully to those narrow axe-hewn church altars of yours, while the dark azure altars in heaven—the mountains that sustain your island throne,—mountains on which a Pagan would have seen the powers of heaven rest in every wreathed cloud—remain for you without inscription; altars built, not to, but by, an Unknown God.

86. III.—Thus far, then, of the nature, thus far of the teaching, of women, and thus of her household office, and queenliness. We come now to our last, our widest question,—What is her queenly office with respect to the state?

Generally we are under an impression that a man's duties are public, and a woman's private. But this is not altogether so. A man has a personal work or duty, relating to his own home, and a public work or duty, which is the expansion of the other, relating to the state. So a woman has a personal work and duty, relating to her own home, and a public work and duty, which is also the expansion of that.

Now the man's work for his own home is, as has been said, to secure its maintenance, progress, and defence; the woman's to secure its order, comfort, and loveliness.

Expand both these functions. The man's duty, as a member of a commonwealth, is to assist in the maintenance, in the advance, in the defense of the state. The woman's duty, as a member of the commonwealth, is to assist in the ordering, in the comforting, and in the beautiful adornment of the state.

What the man is at his own gate, defending it, if need be, against insult and spoil, that also, not in a less, but in a more devoted measure, he is to be at the gate of his country, leaving his home, if need be, even to the spoiler, to do his more incumbent work there.

And, in like manner, what the woman is to be within her gates, as the center of order, the balm of distress, and the mirror of beauty; that she is also to be without her gates, where order is more difficult, distress more imminent, loveliness more rare.

And as within the human heart there is always set an instinct for all its real duties,—an instinct which you cannot quench, but only warp and corrupt if you withdraw it from its true purpose;—as there is the intense instinct of love, which, rightly disciplined, maintains all the sanctities of life, and, misdirected, undermines them; and *must* do either the one or the other;—so there is in the human heart an inextinguishable instinct, the love of power, which, rightly directed, maintains all the majesty of law and life, and, misdirected, wrecks them.

87. Deep rooted in the innermost life of the heart of man, and of the heart of woman, God set it there, and God keeps it there. Vainly, as falsely, you blame or rebuke the desire of power!—For Heaven's sake, and for Man's sake, desire it all you can. But *what* power? That is all the question. Power to destroy? the lion's limb, and the dragon's breath? Not so. Power to heal, to redeem, to guide, and to guard. Power of the scepter and shield; the power of the royal hand that heals in touching,—that binds the fiend and looses the captive; the throne that is founded on the rock of Justice, and descended from only by steps of mercy. Will you not covet such power as this, and seek such throne as this, and be no more housewives, but queens?

88. It is now long since the women of England arrogated, universally, a title which once belonged to nobility only, and, having once been in the habit of accepting the simple title of gentlewoman, as correspondent to that of gentleman, insisted on the privilege of assuming the title of "Lady,"[6] which properly corresponds only to the title of "Lord."

[6] I wish there were a true order of chivalry instituted for our English youth of certain ranks, in which both boy and girl should receive, at a

I do not blame them for this; but only for their narrow motive in this. I would have them desire and claim the title of Lady, provided they claim, not merely the title, but the office and duty signified by it. Lady means "bread-giver" or "loaf-giver," and Lord means "maintainer of laws," and both titles have reference, not to the law which is maintained in the house, nor to the bread which is given to the household, but to law maintained for the multitude, and to bread broken among the multitude. So that a Lord has legal claim only to his title in so far as he is the maintainer of the justice of the Lord of Lords; and a Lady has legal claim to her title only so far as she communicates that help to the poor representatives of her Master, which women once, ministering to Him of their substance, were permitted to extend to that Master Himself; and when she is known, as He Himself once was, in breaking of bread.

89. And this beneficent and legal dominion, this power of the Dominus, or House-Lord, and of the Domina, or House-Lady, is great and venerable, not in the number of those through whom it has lineally descended, but in the number of those whom it grasps within its sway; it is always regarded with reverent worship wherever its dynasty is founded on its duty, and its ambition co-relative with its beneficence. Your fancy is pleased with the thought of being noble ladies, with a train of vassals. Be it so: you cannot be too noble, and your train cannot be too great; but see to it that your train is of vassals whom you serve and feed, not merely of slaves who serve and feed *you;* and that the multitude which obeys you is of those whom you have comforted, not oppressed,—whom you have redeemed, not led into captivity.

90. And this, which is true of the lower or household dominion, is equally true of the queenly dominion;—that highest dignity is opened to you, if you will also accept that highest duty. Rex et Regina—Roi et Reine—"*Right*-doers"; they differ but from the Lady and Lord, in that their power is supreme over the mind as over the person—that they not

given age, their knighthood and ladyhood by true title; attainable only by certain probation and trial both of character and accomplishment; and to be forfeited, on conviction, by their peers, of any dishonorable act. Such an institution would be entirely, and with all noble results, possible, in a nation which loved honor. That it would not be possible among us is not to the discredit of the scheme.

only feed and clothe, but direct and teach. And whether consciously or not, you must be, in many a heart, enthroned: there is no putting by that crown; queens you must always be; queens to your lovers; queens to your husbands and your sons; queens of higher mystery to the world beyond, which bows itself, and will forever bow, before the myrtle crown, and the stainless scepter, of womanhood. But, alas! you are too often idle and careless queens, grasping at majesty in the least things, while you abdicate it in the greatest; and leaving misrule and violence to work their will among men, in defiance of the power, which, holding straight in gift from the Prince of all Peace, the wicked among you betray, and the good forget.

91. "Prince of Peace." Note that name. When kings rule in that name, and nobles, and the judges of the earth, they also, in their narrow place, and mortal measure, receive the power of it. There are no other rulers than they: other rule than theirs is but *mis*rule; they who govern verily "Dei gratiâ" are all princes, yes, or princesses, of peace. There is not a war in the world, no, nor an injustice, but you women are answerable for it; not in that you have provoked, but in that you have not hindered. Men, by their nature, are prone to fight; they will fight for any cause, or for none. It is for you to choose their cause for them, and to forbid them when there is no cause. There is no suffering, no injustice, no misery in the earth, but the guilt of it lies with you. Men can bear the sight of it, but you should not be able to bear it. Men may tread it down without sympathy in their own struggle; but men are feeble in sympathy, and contracted in hope; it is you only who can feel the depths of pain; and conceive the way of its healing. Instead of trying to do this, you turn away from it; you shut yourselves within your park walls and garden gates; and you are content to know that there is beyond them a whole world in wilderness —a world of secrets which you dare not penetrate; and of suffering which you dare not conceive.

92. I tell you that this is to me quite the most amazing among the phenomena of humanity. I am surprised at no depths to which, when once warped from its honor, that humanity can be degraded. I do not wonder at the miser's

death, with his hands, as they relax, dropping gold. I do not wonder at the sensualist's life, with the shroud wrapped about his feet. I do not wonder at the single-handed murder of a single victim, done by the assassin in the darkness of the railway, or reed-shadow of the marsh. I do not even wonder at the myriad-handed murder of multitudes, done boastfully in the daylight, by the frenzy of nations, and the immeasurable, unimaginable guilt, heaped up from hell to heaven, of their priests and kings. But this is wonderful to me—oh, how wonderful!—to see the tender and delicate woman among you, with her child at her breast, and a power, if she would wield it, over it, and over its father, purer than the air of heaven, and stronger than the seas of earth—nay a magnitude of blessing which her husband would not part with for all that earth itself, though it were made of one entire and perfect chrysolite:—to see her abdicate this majesty to play at precedence with her next-door neighbor! This is wonderful—oh, wonderful!—to see her, with every innocent feeling fresh within her, go out in the morning into her garden to play with the fringes of its guarded flowers, and lift their heads when they are drooping, with her happy smile upon her face, and no cloud upon her brow, because there is a little wall around her place of peace: and yet she knows, in her heart, if she would only look for its knowledge, that, outside of that little rose-covered wall, the wild grass, to the horizon, is torn up by the agony of men, and beat level by the drift of their life blood.

93. Have you ever considered what a deep under meaning there lies, or at least may be read, if we choose, in our custom of strewing flowers before those whom we think most happy? Do you suppose it is merely to deceive them into the hope that happiness is always to fall thus in showers at their feet?—that wherever they pass they will tread on the herbs of sweet scent, and that the rough ground will be made smooth for them by depth of roses? So surely as they believe that, they will have, instead, to walk on bitter herbs and thorns; and the only softness to their feet will be of snow. But it is not thus intended they should believe; there is a better meaning in that old custom. The path of a good woman is indeed strewn with

flowers: but they rise behind her steps not before them. "Her feet have touched the meadows, and left the daisies rosy."

94. You think that only a lover's fancy;—false and vain! How if it could be true? You think this also, perhaps, only a poet's fancy—

> "Even the light harebell raised its head
> Elastic from her airy tread."

But it is little to say of a woman, that she only does not destroy where she passes. She should revive; the harebells should bloom, not stoop, as she passes. You think I am rushing into wild hyperbole? Pardon me, not a whit —I mean what I say in calm English, spoken in resolute truth. You have heard it said—(and I believe there is more than fancy even in that saying, but let it pass for a fanciful one)—that flowers only flourish rightly in the garden of some one who loves them. I know you would like that to be true; you would think it a pleasant magic if you could flush your flowers into brighter bloom by a kind look upon them: nay, more, if your look had the power, not only to cheer but to guard them:—if you could bid the black blight turn away and the knotted caterpillar spare —if you could bid the dew fall upon them in the drought, and say to the south wind, in frost—"Come, thou south, and breathe upon my garden, that the spices of it may flow out." This you would think a great thing? And do you think it not a greater thing, that all this (and how much more than this!) you *can* do for fairer flowers than these—flowers that could bless you for having blessed them, and will love you for having loved them;—flowers that have thoughts like yours, and lives like yours; which, once saved, you save forever? Is this only a little power? Far among the moorlands and the rocks,—far in the darkness of the terrible streets,—these feeble florets are lying, with all their fresh leaves torn, and their stems broken—will you never go down to them, nor set them in order in their little fragrant beds, nor fence them in their trembling from the fierce wind? Shall morning follow morning, for you, but not for them; and the dawn rise to watch, far away, those frantic Dances of Death,[7] but no dawn rise to breathe upon these living banks of wild violet, and woodbine, and rose; nor call to you, through your casement,—call (not giving you the name of the English poet's lady, but the name of Dante's great Matilda, who on the edge of happy Lethe, stood wreathing flowers with flowers), saying:—

> "Come into the garden, Maud,
> For the black bat, night, has flown,
> And the woodbine spices are wafted abroad
> And the musk of the roses blown."

Will you not go down among them?—among those sweet living things, whose new courage, sprung from the earth with the deep color of heaven upon it, is starting up in strength of goodly spire; and whose purity, washed from the dust, is opening, bud by bud, into the flower of promise;—and still they turn to you and for you, "The Larkspur listens—I hear, I hear! And the Lily whispers—I wait."

95. Did you notice that I missed two lines when I read you that first stanza; and think that I had forgotten them? Hear them now:—

> "Come into the garden, Maud,
> For the black bat, night, has flown.
> Come into the garden, Maud,
> I am here at the gate, alone."

Who is it, think you, who stands at the gate of this sweeter garden, alone, waiting for you? Did you ever hear, not of a Maude but a Madeleine who went down to her garden in the dawn and found one waiting at the gate, whom she supposed to be the gardener? Have you not sought Him often;—sought Him in vain, all through the night;—sought Him in vain at the gate of that old garden where the fiery sword is set? He is never there; but at the gate of *this* garden He is waiting always—waiting to take your hand—ready to go down to see the fruits of the valley, to see whether the vine has flourished, and the pomegranate budded. There you shall see with Him the little tendrils of the vines that His hand is guiding—there

[7] See note, p. 124.

you shall see the pomegranate springing where His hand cast the sanguine seed;—more: you shall see the troops of the angel keepers, that, with their wings, wave away the hungry birds from the pathsides where He has sown, and call to each other between the vineyard rows, "Take us the foxes, the little foxes, that spoil the vines, for our vines have tender grapes." Oh—you queens—you queens; among the hills and happy greenwood of this land of yours, shall the foxes have holes, and the birds of the air have nests; and in your cities, shall the stones cry out against you, that they are the only pillows where the Son of Man can lay His head?

JOHN MILTON

BY

WALTER BAGEHOT

INTRODUCTORY NOTE

WALTER BAGEHOT, *economist, journalist, and critic, was born at Langport, Somersetshire, February 3, 1826. He was the son of a banker, and after graduating at University College, London, and being called to the bar, he joined his father in business. In 1851 he went to Paris, and was there during the* coup d'état *of Louis Napoleon, of which he gave a vivacious account in letters to an English journal. Soon after his return he began to contribute his first series of biographical studies to the "Prospective Review" and the "National Review," of which latter he was for some time joint-editor. From 1860 to 1877 he was editor of the "Economist," and during this period he published his notable work on "The English Constitution," his "Physics and Politics," and his "Lombard Street: a Description of the Money Market." He died March 24, 1877.*

It is chiefly as one of the most brilliant and original of recent writers on political philosophy that Bagehot is known, but he holds also a distinct place as a critic of literature. He did not write criticism like a professional man of letters, and his production in this field is at times less fine in workmanship than that of some men of much less ability. But, in compensation, he was free from the tendency to the use of a technical literary dialect and to the excessive self-consciousness in style which mars so much modern work in this department. He wrote as a man of affairs with a vigorous mind and a gift of picturesque speech, a robust taste and a genuine love of letters. He always had something definite to say, and no one can read his discussion of such a man as Milton without feeling braced and stimulated by contact with an intellect of uncommon strength and incisiveness.

JOHN MILTON[1]

(1859)

THE "Life of Milton," by Prof. Masson, is a difficulty for the critics. It is very laborious, very learned, and in the main, we believe, very accurate; it is exceedingly long,—there are 780 pages in this volume, and there are to be two volumes more; it touches on very many subjects, and each of these has been investigated to the very best of the author's ability. No one can wish to speak with censure of a book on which so much genuine labor has been expended; and yet we are bound, as true critics, to say that we think it has been composed upon a principle that is utterly erroneous. In justice to ourselves we must explain our meaning.

There are two methods on which biography may consistently be written. The first of these is what we may call the "exhaustive" method. Every fact which is known about the hero may be told us; everything which he did, everything which he would not do, everything which other people did to him, everything which other people would not do to him, may be narrated at full length. We may have a complete picture of all the events of his life; of all which he underwent, and all which he achieved. We may, as Mr. Carlyle expresses it, have a complete account "of his effect upon the universe, and of the effect of the universe upon him."[2] We admit that biographies of this species would be very long, and generally very tedious; we

[1] The Life of John Milton, narrated in connection with the Political, Ecclesiastical, and Literary History of his time. By David Masson, M. A., Professor of English Literature in University College, London, Cambridge: Macmillan.

An Account of the Life, Opinions, and Writings of John Milton. By Thomas Keightley; with an Introduction to "Paradise Lost." London: Chapman & Hall.

The Poems of Milton, with Notes by Thomas Keightley. London: Chapman & Hall.

[2] Review of Lockhart's Scott.

know that the world could not contain very many of them: but nevertheless, the principle on which they may be written is intelligible.

The second method on which the life of a man may be written is the selective. Instead of telling everything, we may choose what we will tell. We may select out of the numberless events, from among the innumerable actions of his life, those events and those actions which exemplify his true character, which prove to us what were the true limits of his talents, what was the degree of his deficiencies, which were his defects, which his vices; in a word, we may select the traits and the particulars which seem to give us the best idea of the man as he lived and as he was. On this side the Flood, as Sydney Smith would have said, we should have fancied that this was the only practicable principle on which biographies can be written about persons of whom many details are recorded. For ancient heroes the exhaustive method is possible: all that can be known of them is contained in a few short passages of Greek and Latin, and it is quite possible to say whatever can be said about every one of these; the result would not be unreasonably bulky, though it might be dull. But in the case of men who have lived in the thick of the crowded modern world, no such course is admissible; overmuch *may* be said, and we must choose what we will say. Biographers, however, are rarely bold enough to adopt the selective method consistently. They have, we suspect, the fear of the critics before their eyes. They do not like that it should be said that "the work of the learned gentleman contains serious omissions: the events of 1562 are not mentioned; those of October, 1579, are narrated but very cursorily"; and we fear that in any case such remarks will be made. Very learned people are pleased to show that they know what is *not* in the book; sometimes they may hint that perhaps the author did not know it, or surely he would have mentioned it. But a biographer who wishes to write what most people of cultivation will be pleased to read must be courageous enough to face the pain of such censures. He must choose, as we have explained, the characteristic parts of his subject: and all that he has to take care of besides is, so to narrate them that their characteristic elements shall be shown; to give such an account of the general career as may make it clear what these chosen events really were,—to show their respective bearings to one another; to delineate what is expressive in such a manner as to make it expressive.

This plan of biography is, however, by no means that of Mr. Masson: he has no dread of overgrown bulk and overwhelming copiousness. He finds indeed what we have called the "exhaustive method" insufficient: he not only wishes to narrate in full the life of Milton, but to add those of his contemporaries likewise; he seems to wish to tell us not only what Milton did, but also what every one else did in Great Britain during his lifetime. He intends his book to be not

"merely a biography of Milton, but also in some sort a continuous history of his time. . . . The suggestions of Milton's life have indeed determined the tracks of these historical researches and expositions, sometimes through the literature of the period, sometimes through its civil and ecclesiastical politics; but the extent to which I have pursued them, and the space which I have assigned to them, have been determined by my desire to present, by their combination, something like a connected historical view of British thought and British society in general prior to the great Revolution."

We need not do more than observe that this union of heterogeneous aims must always end, as it has in this case, in the production of a work at once overgrown and incomplete. A great deal which has only a slight bearing on the character of Milton is inserted; much that is necessary to a true history of "British thought and British society" is of necessity left out. The period of Milton's life which is included in the published volume makes the absurdity especially apparent. In middle life Milton was a great controversialist on contemporary topics; and though it would not be proper for a biographer to load his pages with a full account of all such controversies, yet some notice of the most characteristic of them would be expected from him. In this part of Milton's life some reference to public events would be necessary; and we should not severely censure a biographer if the great interest of those events induced him to stray a little from his topic. But the first thirty years of Milton's life require a very different treatment. He passed those years in the ordinary musings of a studious and meditative youth; it was the period of "Lycidas" and "Comus"; he then dreamed the

> "Sights which youthful poets dream
> On summer eve by haunted stream."[3]

We do not wish to have this part of his life disturbed, to a greater extent than may be necessary, with the harshness of public affairs. Nor is it necessary that it should be so disturbed: a life of poetic retirement requires but little reference to anything except itself; in a biography of Mr. Tennyson we should not expect to hear of the Reform Bill or the Corn Laws. Mr. Masson is, however, of a different opinion: he thinks it necessary to tell us, not only all which Milton did, but everything also that he might have heard of.

The biography of Mr. Keightley is on a very different scale: he tells the story of Milton's career in about half a small volume. Probably this is a little too concise, and the narrative is somewhat dry and bare. It is often, however, acute, and is always clear; and even were its defects greater than they are, we should think it unseemly to criticize the last work of one who has performed so many useful services to literature with extreme severity.

The bare outline of Milton's life is very well known. We have all heard that he was born in the latter years of King James, just when Puritanism was collecting its strength for the approaching struggle; that his father and mother were quiet good people, inclined, but not immoderately, to that persuasion; that he went up to Cambridge early, and had some kind of dissension with the authorities there; that the course of his youth was in a singular degree pure and staid; that in boyhood he was a devourer of books, and that he early became, and always remained, a severely studious man; that he married and had difficulties of a peculiar character with his first wife; that he wrote on divorce; that after the death of his first wife, he married a second time a lady who died very soon, and a third time a person who survived him more than fifty years; that he wrote early poems of singular beauty, which we still read; that

[3] "L'Allegro."

he travelled in Italy, and exhibited his learning in the academies there; that he plunged deep in the theological and political controversies of his time; that he kept a school, —or rather, in our more modern phrase, took pupils; that he was a republican of a peculiar kind, and of "no church," which Dr. Johnson thought dangerous;[4] that he was Secretary for Foreign Languages under the Long Parliament, and retained that office after the *coup d'état* of Cromwell; that he defended the death of Charles I., and became blind from writing a book in haste upon that subject; that after the Restoration he was naturally in a position of some danger and much difficulty; that in the midst of that difficulty he wrote "Paradise Lost"; that he did not fail in "heart or hope,"[5] but lived for fourteen years after the destruction of all for which he had labored, in serene retirement, "though fallen on evil days, though fallen on evil times,"[6] —all this we have heard from our boyhood. How much is wanting to complete the picture—how many traits both noble and painful, might be recovered from the past—we shall never know, till some biographer skilled in interpreting the details of human nature shall select this subject for his art. All that we can hope to do in an essay like this is, to throw together some miscellaneous remarks on the character of the Puritan poet, and on the peculiarities of his works; and if in any part of them we may seem to make unusual criticisms, and to be over-ready with depreciation or objection, our excuse must be, that we wish to paint a likeness and that the harsher features of the subject should have a prominence even in an outline.

There are two kinds of goodness conspicuous in the world, and often made the subject of contrast there; for which, however, we seem to want exact words, and which we are obliged to describe rather vaguely and incompletely. These characters may in one aspect be called the "sensuous" and the "ascetic." The character of the first is that which is almost personified in the poet-king of Israel, whose actions and whose history have been "improved" so often by

[4] "Life of Milton." [5] Sonnet xix.
[6] "Though fallen on evil days,
On evil days though fallen, and evil tongues."
—"Paradise Lost," Book vii.

various writers that it now seems trite even to allude to them. Nevertheless, the particular virtues and the particular career of David seem to embody the idea of what may be called "sensuous goodness" far more completely than a living being in general comes near to an abstract idea. There may have been shades in the actual man which would have modified the resemblance; but in the portrait which has been handed down to us, the traits are perfect and the approximation exact. The principle of this character is its sensibility to outward stimulus: it is moved by all which occurs, stirred by all which happens, open to the influences of whatever it sees, hears or meets with. The certain consequence of this mental constitution is a peculiar liability to temptation. Men are according to the divine, "put upon their trial through the senses." It is through the constant suggestions of the outer world that our minds are stimulated, that our will has the chance of a choice, that moral life becomes possible. The sensibility to this external stimulus brings with it, when men have it to excess, an unusual access of moral difficulty. Everything acts on them, and everything has a chance of turning them aside; the most tempting things act upon them very deeply and their influence, in consequence, is extreme. Naturally, therefore, the errors of such men are great. We need not point the moral:—

> "Dizzied faith and guilt and woe;
> Loftiest aims by earth defiled,
> Gleams of wisdom sin-beguiled,
> Sated power's tyrannic mood,
> Counsels shared with men of blood,
> Sad success, parental tears,
> And a dreary gift of years." [7]

But on the other hand, the excellence of such men has a charm, a kind of sensuous sweetness, that is its own. Being conscious of frailty, they are tender to the imperfect; being sensitive to this world, they sympathize with the world; being familiar with all the moral incidents of life, their goodness has a richness and a complication: they fascinate their own age, and in their deaths they are "not divided" from the love of others. Their peculiar sensibility gives

[7] John Henry Newman's "Call of David."

a depth to their religion: it is at once deeper and more human than that of other men. As their sympathetic knowledge of those whom they have seen is great, so it is with their knowledge of Him whom they have not seen; and as is their knowledge, so is their love, it is deep, from their nature; rich and intimate, from the variety of their experience; chastened by the ever-present sense of their weakness and of its consequences.

In extreme opposition to this is the ascetic species of goodness. This is not, as is sometimes believed, a self-produced ideal,—a simply voluntary result of discipline and restraint. Some men have by nature what others have to elaborate by effort. Some men have a repulsion from the world. All of us have, in some degree, a protective instinct; an impulse, that is to say, to start back from what may trouble us, to shun what may fascinate us, to avoid what may tempt us. On the moral side of human nature this preventive check is occasionally imperious: it holds the whole man under its control,—makes him recoil from the world, be offended at its amusements, be repelled by its occupations, be scared by its sins. The consequences of this tendency, when it is thus in excess, upon the character are very great and very singular. It secludes a man in a sort of natural monastery; he lives in a kind of moral solitude: and the effects of his isolation, for good and for evil, on his disposition are very many. The best result is a singular capacity for meditative religion. Being aloof from what is earthly, such persons are shut up with what is spiritual; being unstirred by the incidents of time, they are alone with the eternal; rejecting this life, they are alone with what is beyond. According to the measure of their minds, men of this removed and secluded excellence become eminent for a settled and brooding piety, for a strong and predominant religion. In human life, too, in a thousand ways, their isolated excellence is apparent. They walk through the whole of it with an abstinence from sense, a zeal of morality, a purity of ideal, which other men have not; their religion has an imaginative grandeur, and their life something of an unusual impeccability: and these are obviously singular excellences. But the deficiencies to which the same character tends are equally singular. In the first place, their isolation gives them a certain pride in themselves and an inevitable ignorance of others. They are secluded by their constitutional δαίμων from life; they are repelled from the pursuits which others care for; they are alarmed at the amusements which others enjoy. In consequence, they trust in their own thoughts; they come to magnify both them and themselves,—for being able to think and to retain them. The greater the nature of the man, the greater is this temptation. His thoughts are greater, and in consequence the greater is his tendency to prize them, the more extreme is his tendency to overrate them. This pride, too, goes side by side with a want of sympathy. Being aloof from others, such a mind is unlike others; and it feels, and sometimes it feels bitterly, its own unlikeness. Generally, however, it is too wrapped up in its own exalted thoughts to be sensible of the pain of moral isolation; it stands apart from others, unknowing and unknown. It is deprived of moral experience in two ways,—it is not tempted itself, and it does not comprehend the temptations of others. And this defect of moral experience is almost certain to produce two effects, one practical and the other speculative. When such a man is wrong, he will be apt to believe that he is right. If his own judgment err, he will not have the habit of checking it by the judgment of others: he will be accustomed to think most men wrong; differing from them would be no proof of error, agreeing with them would rather be a basis for suspicion. He may, too, be very wrong, for the conscience of no man is perfect on all sides. The strangeness of secluded excellence will be sometimes deeply shaded by very strange errors. To be commonly above others, still more to think yourself above others, is to be below them every now and then, and sometimes much below. Again, on the speculative side, this defect of moral experience penetrates into the distinguishing excellence of the character,—its brooding and meditative religion. Those who see life under only one aspect can see religion under only one likewise. This world is needful to interpret what is beyond; the seen must explain the unseen. It is from a tried and a varied and a troubled moral life that the deepest and truest idea of God arises. The ascetic character wants these; therefore in its religion there will be a harshness of outline,—a bareness, so to say,—as well as a grandeur. In life we may look for a singular purity; but also, and with equal probability, for singular self-confidence, a certain unsympathizing straitness, and perhaps a few singular errors.

The character of the ascetic or austere species of goodness is almost exactly embodied in Milton. Men, indeed, are formed on no ideal type: human nature has tendencies too various, and circumstances too complex; all men's characters have sides and aspects not to be comprehended in a single definition: but in this case, the extent to which the character of the man as we find it delineated approaches to the moral abstraction which we sketch from theory is remarkable. The whole being of Milton may, in some sort, be summed up in the great commandment of the austere character, "Reverence thyself." We find it expressed in almost every one of his singular descriptions of himself,—of those striking passages which are scattered through all his works, and which add to whatever interest may intrinsically belong to them one of the rarest of artistic charms, that of magnanimous autobiography. They have been quoted a thousand times, but one of them may perhaps be quoted again:

"I had my time, readers, as others have, who have good learning bestowed upon them, to be sent to those places where, the opinion was, it might be soonest attained; and as the manner is, was not unstudied in those authors which are most commended: whereof some were grave orators and historians, whose matter methought I loved indeed, but as my age then was, so I understood them; others were the smooth elegiac poets, whereof the schools are not scarce, whom both for the pleasing sound of their numerous writing, which in imitation I found most easy and most agreeable to nature's part in me, and for their matter, which what it is there be few who know not, I was so allured to read, that no recreation came to me better welcome. For that it was then those years with me which are excused, though they be least severe, I may be saved the labor to remember ye. Whence having observed them to account it the chief glory of their wit, in that they were ablest to judge, to praise, and by that could esteem themselves worthiest to love, those high perfections which under one or other name they took to celebrate, I thought with myself by every instinct and presage of nature, which is not wont to be false, that what emboldened them to this task might with such diligence as they used embolden me; and that what judgment, wit, or elegance was my share would herein best appear, and best value itself, by how much more wisely and with more love of virtue I should choose (let rude ears be absent) the object of not unlike praises. For albeit these thoughts to some will seem virtuous and commendable, to others only pardonable, to a third sort perhaps idle, yet the mentioning of them now will end in serious.

"Nor blame it, readers, in those years to propose to themselves such a reward, as the noblest dispositions above other things in this life have sometimes preferred; whereof not to be sensible when good and fair in one person meet, argues both a gross and shallow judgment, and withal an ungentle and swainish breast. For by the firm settling of these persuasions, I became, to my best memory, so much a proficient, that if I found those authors anywhere speaking unworthy things of themselves, or unchaste of those names which before they had extolled, this effect it wrought with me,—from that time forward their art I still applauded, but the men I deplored; and above them all, preferred the two famous renowners of *Beatrice* and *Laura*, who never write but honor of them to whom they devote their verse, displaying sublime and pure thoughts without transgression. And long it was not after, when I was confirmed in this opinion,—that he who would not be frustrate of his hope to write well hereafter in laudable things ought himself to be a true poem; that is, a composition and pattern of the best and honorablest things: not presuming to sing high praises of heroic men or famous cities, unless he have in himself the experience and the practice of all that which is praiseworthy." [8]

It may be fanciful to add, and we may be laughed at, but we believe that the self-reverencing propensity was a little aided by his singular personal beauty. All the describers of his youth concur in telling us that this was very remarkable. Mr. Masson has the following account of it:—

"When Milton left Cambridge in July, 1632, he was twenty-three years and eight months old. In stature, therefore, at least, he was already whatever he was to be. 'In stature,' he says himself at a later period, when driven to speak on the subject, 'I confess I am not tall, but still of what is nearer to middle height than to little; and what if I were of little, of which stature have often been very great men both in peace and war—though why should that be called little which is great enough for virtue?' ('Staturâ, fateor non sum procerâ, sed quæ mediocri tamen quàm parvæ propior sit; sed quid si parvâ, quâ et summi sæpe tum pace tum bello viri fuere—quanquam parva cur dicitur, quæ ad virtutem satis magna est?') This is precise enough; but we have Aubrey's words to the same effect. 'He was scarce so tall as I am,' says Aubrey; to which, to make it more intelligible, he appends this marginal note,—'*Qu. Quot* feet I am high? *Resp*. Of middle stature': *i. e.,* Milton was a little

[8] "Apology for Smectymnuus."

under middle height. 'He had light-brown hair,' continues Aubrey, —putting the word 'abrown' (auburn) in the margin by way of synonym for 'light brown';—'his complexion exceeding fair; oval face; his eye a dark gray.'"

We are far from accusing Milton of personal vanity: his character was too enormous, if we may be allowed so to say, for a fault so petty. But a little tinge of excessive self-respect will cling to those who can admire themselves. Ugly men are and ought to be ashamed of their existence; Milton was not so.

The peculiarities of the austere type of character stand out in Milton more remarkably than in other men who partake of it, because of the extreme strength of his nature. In reading him this is the first thing that strikes us. We seem to have left the little world of ordinary writers. The words of some authors are said to have "hands and feet"; they seem, that is, to have a vigor and animation which only belong to things which live and move. Milton's words have not this animal life,—there is no rude energy about them; but on the other hand, they have or seem to have a soul, a spirit which other words have not. He was early aware that what he wrote, "by certain vital signs it had," was such as the world would not "willingly let die."[9] After two centuries we feel the same. There is a solemn and firm music in the lines; a brooding sublimity haunts them; the spirit of the great writer moves over the face of the page. In life there seems to have been the same peculiar strength that his works suggest to us. His moral tenacity is amazing: he took his own course, and he kept his own course; and we may trace in his defects the same characteristics. "Energy and ill temper," some say, "are the same thing;" and though this is a strong exaggeration, yet there is a basis of truth in it. People who labor much will be cross if they do not obtain that for which they labor; those who desire vehemently will be vexed if they do not obtain that which they desire. As is the strength of the impelling tendency, so, other things being equal, is the pain which it will experience if it be baffled. Those, too, who are set on what is high will be proportionately offended by the

[9] "Reason of Church Government," introduction to Book iii.

intrusion of what is low. Accordingly, Milton is described by those who knew him as "a harsh and choleric man." "He had," we are told, "a gravity in his temper, not melancholy, or not till the latter part of his life, not sour, not morose or ill-natured, but a certain severity of mind; a mind not condescending to little things;"[10] and this although his daughter remembered that he was delightful company, the life of conversation, and that he was so "on account of a flow of subject, and an unaffected cheerfulness and civility." Doubtless this may have been so when he was at ease, and at home; but there are unmistakable traces of the harsher tendency in almost all his works.

Some of the peculiarities of the ascetic character were likewise augmented by his studious disposition. This began very early in life, and continued till the end. "My father," he says, "destined me . . . to the study of polite literature, which I embraced with such avidity, that from the twelfth year of my age I hardly ever retired to rest from my studies till midnight; which was the first source of injury to my eyes, to the natural weakness of which were added frequent headaches: all of which not retarding my eagerness after knowledge, he took care to have me instructed—" etc.[11] Every page of his works shows the result of this education. In spite of the occupations of manhood, and the blindness and melancholy of old age, he still continued to have his principal pleasure in that "studious and select" reading, which, though often curiously transmuted, is perpetually involved in the very texture of his works. We need not stay to observe how a habit in itself so austere conduces to the development of an austere character. Deep study, especially deep study which haunts and rules the imagination, necessarily removes men from life, absorbs them in themselves; purifies their conduct, with some risk of isolating their sympathies; develops that loftiness of mood which is gifted with deep inspirations and indulged with great ideas, but which tends in its excess to engender a contempt for others, and a self-appreciation which is even more displeasing to them.

These same tendencies were aggravated also by two de-

[10] Philips. [11] Translated by Keightley from "Defensio Secunda."

fects which are exceedingly rare in great English authors, and which perhaps Milton alone amongst those of the highest class is in a remarkable degree chargeable with; we mean a deficiency in humor, and a deficiency in a knowledge of plain human nature. Probably when, after the lapse of ages, English literature is looked at in its larger features only, and in comparison with other literatures which have preceded or which may follow it, the critics will lay down that its most striking characteristic as a whole is its involution, so to say, in life; the degree to which its book life resembles real life; the extent to which the motives, dispositions, and actions of common busy persons are represented in a medium which would seem likely to give us peculiarly the ideas of secluded and the tendencies of meditative men. It is but an aspect of this fact, that English literature abounds—some critics will say abounds excessively—with humor. This is in some sense the imaginative element of ordinary life,—the relieving charm, partaking at once of contrast and similitude, which gives a human and an intellectual interest to the world of clowns and cottages, of fields and farmers. The degree to which Milton is deficient in this element is conspicuous in every page of his writings where its occurrence could be looked for; and if we do not always look for it, this is because the subjects of his most remarkable works are on a removed elevation, where ordinary life, the world of "cakes and ale," is never thought of and never expected. It is in his dramas, as we should expect, that Milton shows this deficiency the most. "Citizens" never talk in his pages, as they do in Shakespeare. We feel instinctively that Milton's eye had never rested with the same easy pleasure on the easy, ordinary, shopkeeping world. Perhaps, such is the complication of art, it is on the most tragic occasions that we feel this want the most.

It may seem an odd theory, and yet we believe it to be a true principle, that catastrophes require a comic element. We appear to feel the same principle in life. We may read solemn descriptions of great events in history,—say of Lord Strafford's trial, and of his marvelous speech, and his appeal to his "saint in heaven"; but we comprehend the whole transaction much better when we learn from Mr. Baillie, the eye-witness, that people ate nuts and apples, and talked, and laughed, and betted on the great question of acquittal and condemnation. Nor is it difficult to understand why this should be so. It seems to be a law of the imagination, at least in most men, that it will not bear concentration. It is essentially a glancing faculty. It goes and comes, and comes and goes, and we hardly know whence or why. But we most of us know that when we try to fix it, in a moment it passes away. Accordingly, the proper procedure of art is to let it go in such a manner as to insure its coming back again. The force of artistic contrasts effects exactly this result: skillfully disposed opposites suggest the notion of each other. We realize more perfectly and easily the great idea, the tragic conception, when we are familiarized with its effects on the minds of little people, with the petty consequences which it causes as well as with the enormous forces from which it comes. The catastrophe of "Samson Agonistes" discloses Milton's imperfect mastery of this element of effect. If ever there was an occasion which admitted its perfect employment, it was this. The kind of catastrophe is exactly that which is sure to strike, and strike forcibly, the minds of common persons. If their observations on the occasion were really given to us, we could scarcely avoid something rather comic. The eccentricity, so to speak, of ordinary persons shows itself peculiarly at such times, and they say the queerest things. Shakespeare has exemplified this principle most skillfully on various occasions: it is the sort of art which is just in his way. His imagination always seems to be floating between the contrasts of things; and if his mind had a resting-place that it liked, it was this ordinary view of extraordinary events. Milton was under the great[est] obligation to use this relieving principle of art in the catastrophe of "Samson," because he has made every effort to heighten the strictly tragic element, which requires that relief. His art, always serious, was never more serious. His Samson is not the incarnation of physical strength which the popular fancy embodies in the character; nor is it the simple and romantic character of the Old Testament. On the contrary, Samson has become a Puritan the observations he makes would have done much credit to a religious pikeman in Cromwell's army. In consequence, his death requires some lightening touches to make it a properly artistic event. The pomp of seriousness becomes too oppressive.

> "At length for intermission sake they led him
> Between the pillars; he his guide requested
> (For so from such as nearer stood we heard),
> As over-tired, to let him lean awhile
> With both his arms on those two massy pillars
> That to the archèd roof gave main support.
> He unsuspicious led him; which when Samson
> Felt in his arms, with head awhile inclined,
> And eyes fast fixed, he stood, as one who prayed,
> Or some great matter in his mind revolved;
> At last with head erect thus cried aloud:
> 'Hitherto, lords, what your commands imposed
> I have performed, as reason was, obeying,
> Not without wonder or delight beheld;
> Now of my own accord such other trial
> I mean to show you of my strength, yet greater,
> As with amaze shall strike all who behold.'
> This uttered, straining all his nerves he bowed,
> As with the force of winds and waters pent
> When mountains tremble, those two massy pillars
> With horrible convulsion to and fro.
> He tugged, he shook, till down they came, and drew
> The whole roof after them, with burst of thunder,
> Upon the heads of all who sat beneath,—
> Lords, ladies, captains, counselors, or priests,
> Their choice nobility and flower, not only
> Of this, but each Philistian city round,
> Met from all parts to solemnize this feast.
> Samson with these immixed, inevitably
> Pulled down the same destruction on himself;
> The vulgar only 'scaped who stood without.
> *Chor.* O dearly bought revenge, yet glorious!
> Living or dying thou hast fulfilled
> The work for which thou wast foretold
> To Israel, and now liest victorious
> Among thy slain self-killed,
> Not willingly, but tangled in the fold
> Of dire necessity, whose law in death conjoined
> Thee with thy slaughtered foes, in number more
> Than all thy life had slain before."

This is grave and fine; but Shakespeare would have done it differently and better.

We need not pause to observe how certainly this deficiency in humor and in the delineation of ordinary human feeling is connected with a recluse, a solitary, and to some extent an unsympathizing life. If we combine a certain natural aloofness from common men with literary habits and an incessantly studious musing, we shall at once see how powerful a force is brought to bear on an instinctively austere character, and how sure it will be to develop the peculiar tendencies of it, both good and evil. It was to no purpose that Milton seems to have practiced a sort of professional study of life. No man could rank more highly the importance to a poet of an intellectual insight into all-important pursuits and "seemly arts." But it is not by the mere intellect that we can take in the daily occupations of mankind: we must sympathize with them, and see them in their human relations. A chimney-sweeper, *quâ* chimney-sweeper, is not very sentimental: it is in himself that he is so interesting.

Milton's austere character is in some sort the more evident because he possessed in large measure a certain relieving element, in which those who are eminent in that character are very deficient. Generally such persons have but obtuse senses: we are prone to attribute the purity of their conduct to the dullness of their sensations. Milton had no such obtuseness: he had every opportunity for knowing the "world of eye and ear";[12] you cannot open his works without seeing how much he did know of it. The austerity of his nature was not caused by the deficiency of his senses, but by an excess of the warning instinct. Even when he professed to delineate the world of sensuous delight, this instinct shows itself. Dr. Johnson thought he could discern melancholy in "L'Allegro";[13] if he had said "solitariness," it would have been correct.

The peculiar nature of Milton's character is very conspicuous in the events of his domestic life, and in the views which he took of the great public revolutions of his age. We can spare only a very brief space for the examination of either of these; but we will endeavor to say a few words upon each of them.

[12] Wordsworth, "Tintern Abbey." [13] "Life of Milton."

The circumstances of Milton's first marriage are as singular as any in the strange series of the loves of the poets. The scene opens with an affair of business. Milton's father, as is well known, was a scrivener,—a kind of professional money-lender, then well known in London; and having been early connected with the vicinity of Oxford, continued afterwards to have pecuniary transactions of a certain nature with country gentlemen of that neighborhood. In the course of these he advanced £500 to a certain Mr. Richard Powell, a squire of fair landed estate, residing at Forest Hill, which is about four miles from the city of Oxford. The money was lent on the 11th of June, 1627; and a few months afterwards Mr. Milton the elder gave £312 of it to his son the poet, who was then a youth at college, and made a formal memorandum of the same in the form then usual, which still exists. The debt was never wholly discharged; "for in 1650-1 we find Milton asserting on oath that he had received only about £180, 'in part satisfaction of my said just and principal debt, with damages for the same, and my costs of suit.'" Mr. Keightley supposes him to have taken "many a ride over to Forest Hill" after he left Cambridge and was living at Horton, which is not very far distant; but of course this is only conjecture. We only know that about 1643 "he took," as his nephew relates, "a journey into the country, nobody about him certainly knowing the reason, or that it was any more than a journey of recreation. After a month's stay, home he returns a married man, that went out a bachelor; his wife being Mary, the eldest daughter of Mr. Richard Powell, then a justice of the peace" for the county of Oxford. The suddenness of the event is rather striking; but Philips was at the time one of Milton's pupils, and it is possible that some pains may have been taken to conceal the love affair from the "young gentlemen." Still, as Philips was Milton's nephew, he was likely to hear such intelligence tolerably early; and as he does not seem to have done so, the *dénouement* was probably rather prompt. At any rate, he was certainly married at that time, and took his bride home to his house in Aldersgate Street; and there was feasting and gayety according to the usual custom of such events. A few weeks after, the lady went home to her friends, in which there was of course nothing remarkable; but it is singular that when the natural limit of her visit at home was come, she absolutely refused to return to her husband. The grounds of so strange a resolution are very difficult to ascertain. Political feeling ran very high; old Mr. Powell adhered to the side of the king, and Milton to that of the Parliament: and this might be fancied to have caused an estrangement. But on the other hand, these circumstances must have been well known three months before. Nothing had happened in that quarter of a year to change very materially the position of the two parties in the state. Some other cause for Mrs. Milton's conduct must be looked for. She herself is said to have stated that she did not like her husband's "spare diet and hard study."[14] No doubt, too, she found it dull in London: she had probably always lived in the country, and must have been quite unaccustomed to the not very pleasant scene in which she found herself. Still, many young ladies have married schoolmasters, and many young ladies have gone from Oxfordshire to London; and nevertheless, no such dissolution of matrimonial harmony is known to have occurred.

The fact we believe to be, that the bride took a dislike to her husband. We cannot but have a suspicion that she did not like him before marriage, and that pecuniary reasons had their influence. If, however, Mr. Powell exerted his paternal influence, it may be admitted that he had unusual considerations to advance in favor of the alliance he proposed. It is not every father whose creditors are handsome young gentlemen with fair incomes. Perhaps it seemed no extreme tyranny to press the young lady a little to do that which some others might have done without pressing. Still all this is but hypothesis: our evidence as to the love affairs of the time of King Charles I. is but meager. But whatever the feelings of Miss Powell may have been, those of Mrs. Milton are exceedingly certain. She would not return to her husband; she did not answer his letters; and a messenger whom he sent to bring her back was handled rather roughly. Unquestionably she was deeply to blame, by far

[14] Philips.

the most to blame of the two. Whatever may be alleged against him is as nothing compared with her offense in leaving him. To defend so startling a course, we must adopt views of divorce even more extreme than those which Milton was himself driven to inculcate; and whatever Mrs. Milton's practice may have been, it may be fairly conjectured that her principles were strictly orthodox. Yet if she could be examined by a commission to the ghosts, she would probably have some palliating circumstances to allege in mitigation of judgment. There were perhaps peculiarities in Milton's character which a young lady might not improperly dislike. The austere and ascetic character is of course far less agreeable to women than the sensuous and susceptible. The self-occupation, the pride, the abstraction of the former are to the female mind disagreeable; studious habits and unusual self-denial seem to it purposeless; lofty enthusiasm, public spirit, the solitary pursuit of an elevated ideal, are quite out of its way: they rest too little on the visible world to be intelligible, they are too little suggested by the daily occurrences of life to seem possible. The poet in search of an imaginary phantom has never been successful with women,—there are innumerable proofs of that; and the ascetic moralist is even less interesting. A character combined out of the two—and this to some extent was Milton's—is singularly likely to meet with painful failure; with a failure the more painful, that it could never anticipate or explain it. Possibly he was absorbed in an austere self-conscious excellence: it may never have occurred to him that a lady might prefer the trivial detail of daily happiness.

Milton's own view of the matter he has explained to us in his book on divorce; and it is a very odd one. His complaint was that his wife would not talk. What he wished in marriage was "an intimate and speaking help": he encountered "a mute and spiritless mate." One of his principal incitements to the "pious necessity of divorcing" was an unusual deficiency in household conversation. A certain loquacity in their wives has been the complaint of various eminent men; but his domestic affliction was a different one. The "ready and reviving associate," whom he had hoped to find, appeared to be a "coinhabiting mischief," who was sullen, and perhaps seemed bored and tired. And at times he is disposed to cast the blame of his misfortune on the uninstructive nature of youthful virtue. The "soberest and best governed men," he says, "are least practiced in these affairs," are not very well aware that "the bashful muteness" of a young lady "may ofttimes hide all the unliveliness and natural sloth which is really unfit for conversation," and are rather in too great haste to "light the nuptial torch": whereas those "who have lived most loosely, by reason of their bold accustoming, prove most successful in their matches; because their wild affections, unsettling at will have been as so many divorces to teach them experience." And he rather wishes to infer that the virtuous man should, in case of mischance, have his resource of divorce likewise.

In truth, Milton's book on divorce—though only containing principles which he continued to believe long after he had any personal reasons for wishing to do so—was clearly suggested at first by the unusual phenomena of his first marriage. His wife began by not speaking to him, and finished by running away from him. Accordingly, like most books which spring out of personal circumstances, his treatises on this subject have a frankness and a mastery of detail which others on the same topic sometimes want. He is remarkably free from one peculiarity of modern writers on such matters. Several considerate gentlemen are extremely anxious for the "rights of woman"; they think that women will benefit by removing the bulwarks which the misguided experience of ages has erected for their protection. A migratory system of domestic existence might suit Madame Dudevant, and a few cases of singular exception; but we cannot fancy that it would be, after all, so much to the taste of most ladies as the present more permanent system. We have some reminiscence of the stories of the wolf and the lamb, when we hear amiable men addressing a female auditory (in books, of course) on the advantages of a freer "development." We are perhaps wrong, but we cherish an indistinct suspicion that an indefinite extension of the power of selection would rather tend to the advantage of the sex which more usually chooses. But we have no occasion to avow such opinions now. Milton had no such modern views: he is frankly and honestly anxious for the rights of the man. Of the doctrine that divorce is only permitted for the help of wives, he exclaims, "Palpably uxorious! who can be ignorant that woman was created for man, and not man for woman? . . . What an injury is it after wedlock not to be beloved! what to be slighted! what to be contended with in point of house-rule who shall be the head; not for any parity of wisdom, for that were something reasonable, but out of female pride! 'I suffer not,' saith St. Paul, 'the woman to usurp authority over the man.' If the Apostle could not suffer it," he naturally remarks, "into what mold is he mortified that can?" He had a sincere desire to preserve men from the society of unsocial and unsympathizing women; and that was his principal idea.

His theory, to a certain extent, partakes of the same notion. The following passage contains a perspicuous exposition of it:—

"Moses, Deut. xxiv. 1, established a grave and prudent law, full of moral equity, full of due consideration towards nature, that cannot be resisted, a law consenting with the wisest men and civilest nations: that when a man hath married a wife, if it come to pass that he cannot love her by reason of some displeasing natural quality or unfitness in her, let him write her a bill of divorce. The intent of which law undoubtedly was this: that if any good and peaceable man should discover some helpless disagreement or dislike, either of mind or body, whereby he could not cheerfully perform the duty of a husband without the perpetual dissembling of offense and disturbance to his spirit,—rather than to live uncomfortably and unhappy both to himself and to his wife, rather than to continue undertaking a duty which he could not possibly discharge, he might dismiss her whom he could not tolerably, and so not conscionably, retain. And this law the Spirit of God by the mouth of Solomon, Prov. xxx. 21, 23, testifies to be a good and a necessary law, by granting it that 'a hated woman' (for so the Hebrew word signifies, rather than 'odious,' though it come all to one),—that 'a hated woman, when she is married, is a thing that the earth cannot bear.'"

And he complains that the civil law of modern states interferes with the "domestical prerogative of the husband."

His notion would seem to have been that a husband was bound not to dismiss his wife, except for a reason really sufficient; such as a thoroughly incompatible temper, an incorrigible "muteness," and a desertion like that of Mrs.

Milton. But he scarcely liked to admit that in the use of this power he should be subject to the correction of human tribunals. He thought that the circumstances of each case depended upon "utterless facts"; and that it was practically impossible for a civil court to decide on a subject so delicate in its essence, and so imperceptible in its data. But though amiable men doubtless suffer much from the deficiencies of their wives, we should hardly like to intrust them, in their own cases, with a jurisdiction so prompt and summary.

We are far from being concerned, however, just now, with the doctrine of divorce on its intrinsic merits: we were only intending to give such an account of Milton's opinions upon it as might serve to illustrate his character. We think we have shown that it is possible there may have been in his domestic relations, a little overweening pride; a tendency to overrate the true extent of masculine rights, and to dwell on his wife's duty to be social towards him rather than on his duty to be social towards her,—to be rather sullen whenever she was not quite cheerful. Still, we are not defending a lady for leaving her husband for defects of such inferior magnitude. Few households would be kept together, if the right of transition were exercised on such trifling occasions. We are but suggesting that she may share the excuse which our great satirist has suggested for another unreliable lady: "My mother was an angel; but angels are not always *commodes à vivre.*"

This is not a pleasant part of our subject, and we must leave it. It is more agreeable to relate that on no occasion of his life was the substantial excellence of Milton's character more conclusively shown than in his conduct at the last stage of this curious transaction. After a very considerable interval, and after the publication of his book on divorce, Mrs. Milton showed a disposition to return to her husband; and in spite of his theories, he received her with open arms. With great Christian patience, he received her relations too. The Parliamentary party was then victorious; and old Mr. Powell, who had suffered very much in the cause of the king, lived until his death untroubled, and "wholly to his devotion," as we are informed, in the house of his son-in-law.

Of the other occurrences of Milton's domestic life we have left ourselves no room to speak; we must turn to our second source of illustration for his character,—his opinions on the great public events of his time. It may seem odd, but we believe that a man of austere character naturally tends *both* to an excessive party spirit and to an extreme isolation. Of course the circumstances which develop the one must be different from those which are necessary to call out the other: party spirit requires companionship; isolation, if we may be pardoned so original a remark, excludes it. But though, as we have shown, this species of character is prone to mental solitude, tends to an ntellectual isolation where it is possible and as soon as it can, yet when invincible circumstances throw it into mental companionship, when it is driven into earnest association with earnest men on interesting topics, its zeal becomes excessive. Such a man's mind is at home only with its own enthusiasm; it is cooped up within the narrow limits of its own ideas, and it can make no allowance for those who differ from or oppose them. We may see something of this excessive party zeal in Burke. No one's reasons are more philosophical; yet no one who acted with a party went farther in aid of it or was more violent in support of it. He forgot what could be said for the tenets of the enemy; his imagination made that enemy an abstract incarnation of his tenets. A man, too, who knows that he formed his opinions originally by a genuine and intellectual process is but little aware of the undue energy those ideas may obtain from the concurrence of those around. Persons who first acquired their ideas at second hand are more open to a knowledge of their own weakness, and better acquainted with the strange force which there is in the sympathy of others. The isolated mind, when it acts with the popular feeling, is apt to exaggerate that feeling for the most part by an almost inevitable consequence of the feelings which render it isolated. Milton is an example of this remark. In the commencement of the struggle between Charles I. and the Parliament, he sympathized strongly with the popular movement, and carried to what seems now a strange extreme his partisanship. No one could imagine that the first literary

Englishman of his time could write the following passage on Charles I.:—

"Who can with patience hear this filthy, rascally fool speak so irreverently of persons eminent both in greatness and piety? Dare you compare King *David* with King *Charles:* a most religious king and prophet with a superstitious prince, and who was but a novice in the Christian religion; a most prudent, wise prince with a weak one; a valiant prince with a cowardly one; finally, a most just prince with a most unjust one? Have you the impudence to commend his chastity and sobriety, who is known to have committed all manner of lewdness in company with his confidant the Duke of *Buckingham?* It were to no purpose to inquire into the private actions of his life, who publicly at plays would embrace and kiss the ladies." [15]

Whatever may be the faults of that ill-fated monarch,—and they assuredly were not small,—no one would now think this absurd invective to be even an excusable exaggeration. It misses the true mark altogether, and is the expression of a strongly imaginative mind, which has seen something that it did not like, and is unable in consequence to see anything that has any relation to it distinctly or correctly. But with the supremacy of the Long Parliament Milton's attachment to their cause ceased. No one has drawn a more unfavorable picture of the rule which they established. Years after their supremacy had passed away, and the restoration of the monarchy had covered with a new and strange scene the old actors and the old world, he thrust into a most unlikely part of his "History of England" [Book iii.] the following attack on them:—

"But when once the superficial zeal and popular fumes that acted their New Magistracy were cooled and spent in them, straight every one betook himself (setting the Commonwealth behind, his private ends before) to do as his own profit or ambition led him. Then was justice delayed, and soon after denied; spite and favor determined all: hence faction, thence treachery, both at home and in the field; everywhere wrong and oppression; foul and horrid deeds committed daily, or maintained, in secret or in open. Some who had been called from shops and warehouses, without other merit, to sit in supreme councils and committees (as their breeding was), fell to huckster the Commonwealth. Others did thereafter as men could soothe and humor them best; so he who would give most, or under covert of hypocritical zeal insinuate basest, enjoyed unworthily the rewards of learning and fidelity, or escaped the punishment of his

[15] "Defense of the People of England," Chap. iv.

crimes and misdeeds. Their votes and ordinances, which men looked should have contained the repealing of bad laws, and the immediate constitution of better, resounded with nothing else but new impositions, taxes, excises,—yearly, monthly, weekly; not to reckon the offices, gifts, and preferments bestowed and shared among themselves."

His dislike of this system of committees, and of the generally dull and unemphatic administration of the Commonwealth, attached him to the Puritan army and to Cromwell; but in the continuation of the passage we have referred to, he expresses—with something, let it be said, of a schoolmaster's feeling—an unfavorable judgment on their career:—

"For *Britain*, to speak a truth not often spoken, as it is a land fruitful enough of men stout and courageous in war, so it is naturally not over-fertile of men able to govern justly and prudently in peace, trusting only in their mother-wit; who consider not justly that civility, prudence, love of the public good more than of money or vain honor, are to this soil in a manner outlandish,—grow not here, but in minds well implanted with solid and elaborate breeding; too impolitic else and rude, if not headstrong and intractable to the industry and virtue either of executing or understanding true civil government. Valiant indeed, and prosperous to win a field; but to know the end and reason of winning, unjudicious and unwise: in good or bad success, alike unteachable. For the sun, which we want, ripens wits as well as fruits; and as wine and oil are imported to us from abroad, so must ripe understanding and many civil virtues be imported into our minds from foreign writings and examples of best ages; we shall else miscarry still, and come short in the attempts of any great enterprise. Hence did their victories prove as fruitless as their losses dangerous, and left them still, conquering, under the same grievances that men suffer conquered: which was indeed unlikely to go otherwise, unless men more than vulgar—bred up, as few of them were, in the knowledge of ancient and illustrious deeds, invincible against many and vain titles, impartial to friendships and relations—had conducted their affairs; but then, from the chapman to the retailer, many whose ignorance was more audacious than the rest were admitted with all their sordid rudiments to bear no mean sway among them, both in church and state."

We need not speak of Milton's disapprobation of the Restoration. Between him and the world of Charles II. the opposition was inevitable and infinite. Therefore the general fact remains, that except in the early struggles, when he exaggerated the popular feeling, he remained solitary in opinion, and had very little sympathy with any of the prevailing parties of his time.

Milton's own theory of government is to be learned from his works. He advocated a free commonwealth, without rule of a single person or House of Lords; but the form of his projected commonwealth was peculiar. He thought that a certain perpetual council, which should be elected by the nation once for all, and the number of which should be filled up as vacancies might occur, was the best possible machine of government. He did not confine his advocacy to abstract theory, but proposed the immediate establishment of such a council in this country. We need not go into an elaborate discussion to show the errors of this conclusion. Hardly any one, then or since, has probably adopted it. The interest of the theoretical parts of Milton's political works is entirely historical. The tenets advocated are not of great value, and the arguments by which he supports them are perhaps of less; but their relation to the times in which they were written gives them a very singular interest. The time of the Commonwealth was the only period in English history in which the fundamental questions of government have been thrown open for popular discussion in this country. We read in French literature, discussions on the advisability of establishing a monarchy, on the advisability of establishing a republic, on the advisability of establishing an empire; and before we proceed to examine the arguments, we cannot help being struck at the strange contrast which this multiplicity of open questions presents to our own uninquiring acquiescence in the hereditary polity which has descended to us. "Kings, Lords, and Commons" are, we think, ordinances of nature. Yet Milton's political writings embody the reflections of a period when, for a few years, the government of England was nearly as much a subject of fundamental discussion as that of France was in 1851. An "invitation to thinkers," to borrow the phrase of Necker, was given by the circumstances of the time; and with the habitual facility of philosophical speculation, it was accepted, and used to the utmost.

Such are not the kind of speculations in which we expect assistance from Milton. It is not in its transactions with others, in its dealings with the manifold world, that the isolated and austere mind shows itself to the most advantage. Its strength lies in itself. It has "a calm and pleasing solitariness." It hears thoughts which others cannot hear. It enjoys the quiet and still air of delightful studies; and is ever conscious of such musing and poetry "as is not to be obtained by the invocation of Dame Memory and her twin daughters, but by devout prayer to that Eternal Spirit, who can enrich with all utterance and knowledge, and sends out his seraphim with the hallowed fire of his altar."

"Descend from heaven, Urania, by that name
If rightly thou art called, whose voice divine
Following, above th' Olympian hill I soar.
Above the flight of Pegaséan wing.
The meaning, not the name, I call; for thou
Nor of the Muses nine, nor on the top
Of old Olympus dwell'st, but heavenly born:
Before the hills appeared, or fountain flowed,
Thou with eternal Wisdom didst converse,
Wisdom thy sister, and with her didst play
In presence of th' Almighty Father, pleased
With thy celestial song. Up led by thee,
Into the heaven of heavens I have presumed,
An earthly guest, and drawn empyreal air,
Thy tempering. With like safety guided down,
Return me to my native element;
Lest from this flying steed unreined (as once
Bellerophon, though from a lower clime),
Dismounted, on th' Aleian field I fall,
Erroneous there to wander, and forlorn.
Half yet remains unsung, but narrower bound
Within the visible diurnal sphere:
Standing on earth, not rapt above the pole,
More safe I sing with mortal voice, unchanged
To hoarse or mute, though fallen on evil days,
On evil days though fallen, and evil tongues;
In darkness, and with dangers compassed round,
And solitude: yet not alone, while thou
Visit'st my slumbers nightly, or when morn
Purples the east. Still govern thou my song,
Urania, and fit audience find, though few;
But drive far off the barbarous dissonance
Of Bacchus and his revelers, the race
Of that wild rout that tore the Thracian bard
In Rhodope, where woods and rocks had ears
To rapture, till the savage clamor drowned

> Both harp and voice, nor could the Muse defend
> Her son. So fail not thou, who thee implores;
> For thou art heavenly, she an empty dream." [16]

"An ancient clergyman of Dorsetshire, Dr. Wright, found John Milton in a small chamber hung with rusty green, sitting in an elbow-chair, and dressed neatly in black; pale, but not cadaverous. . . . He used also to sit in a gray coarse-cloth coat at the door of his house near Bunhill Fields, in warm sunny weather;" [17] and the common people said he was inspired.

If from the man we turn to his works, we are struck at once with two singular contrasts. The first of them is this:—The distinction between ancient and modern art is sometimes said, and perhaps truly, to consist in the simple bareness of the imaginative conceptions which we find in ancient art, and the comparatively complex clothing in which all modern creations are embodied. If we adopt this distinction, Milton seems in some sort ancient, and in some sort modern. Nothing is so simple as the subject-matter of his works. The two greatest of his creations, the character of Satan and the character of Eve, are two of the simplest —the latter probably the very simplest—in the whole field of literature. On this side Milton's art is classical. On the other hand, in no writer is the imagery more profuse, the illustrations more various, the dress altogether more splendid; and in this respect the style of his art seems romantic and modern. In real truth, however, it is only ancient art in a modern disguise: the dress is a mere dress, and can be stripped off when we will,—we all of us do perhaps in memory strip it off for ourselves. Notwithstanding the lavish adornments with which her image is presented, the character of Eve is still the simplest sort of feminine essence,—the pure embodiment of that inner nature which we believe and hope that women have. The character of Satan, though it is not so easily described, has nearly as few elements in it. The most purely modern conceptions will not bear to be unclothed in this manner: their romantic garment clings inseparably to them. Hamlet and Lear are not to be thought of ex-

[16] "Paradise Lost," Book vii. [17] Richardson.

cept as complex characters, with very involved and complicated embodiments. They are as difficult to draw out in words as the common characters of life are: that of Hamlet, perhaps, is more so. If we make it, as perhaps we should, the characteristic of modern and romantic art that it presents us with creations which we cannot think of or delineate except as very varied and so to say circumstantial, we must not rank Milton among the masters of romantic art. And without involving the subject in the troubled sea of an old controversy, we may say that the most striking of the poetical peculiarities of Milton is the bare simplicity of his ideas and the rich abundance of his illustrations.

Another of his peculiarities is equally striking. There seems to be such a thing as second-hand poetry: some poets, musing on the poetry of other men, have unconsciously shaped it into something of their own. The new conception is like the original, it would never probably have existed had not the original existed previously: still, it is sufficiently different from the original to be a new thing, not a copy or a plagiarism; it is a creation, though so to say, a suggested creation.

Gray is as good an example as can be found of a poet whose works abound in this species of semi-original conceptions. Industrious critics track his best lines back, and find others like them which doubtless lingered near his fancy while he was writing them. The same critics have been equally busy with the works of Milton, and equally successful. They find traces of his reading in half his works; not, which any reader could do, in overt similes and distinct illustrations, but also in the very texture of the thought and the expression. In many cases doubtless, they discover more than he himself knew. A mind like his, which has an immense store of imaginative recollections, can never know which of his own imaginations is exactly suggested by which recollection. Men awake with their best ideas; it is seldom worth while to investigate very curiously whence they came. Our proper business is to adapt and mold and act upon them. Of poets perhaps this is true even more remarkably than of other men: their ideas are suggested in modes, and according to laws, which are even more impossible to specify than the ideas of the rest of the world. Second-hand poetry, so to say, often seems quite original to the poet himself; he frequently does not know that he derived it from an old memory: years afterwards it may strike him as it does others. Still, in general, such inferior species of creation is not so likely to be found in minds of singular originality as in those of less. A brooding, placid, cultivated mind, like that of Gray, is the place where we should expect to meet with it. Great originality disturbs the adaptive process, removes the mind of the poet from the thoughts of other men, and occupies it with its own heated and flashing thoughts. Poetry of the second degree is like the secondary rocks of modern geology,—a still, gentle, alluvial formation; the igneous glow of primary genius brings forth ideas like the primeval granite, simple, astounding, and alone. Milton's case is an exception to this rule. His mind has marked originality, probably as much of it as any in literature; but it has as much of molded recollection as any mind, too. His poetry in consequence is like an artificial park, green and soft and beautiful, yet with outlines bold, distinct, and firm, and the eternal rock ever jutting out; or better still, it is like our own lake scenery where nature has herself the same combination, where we have Rydal Water side by side with the everlasting upheaved mountain. Milton has the same union of softened beauty with unimpaired grandeur; and it is his peculiarity.

These are the two contrasts which puzzle us at first in Milton, and which distinguish him from other poets in our remembrance afterwards. We have a superficial complexity in illustration and imagery and metaphor; and in contrast with it we observe a latent simplicity of idea, an almost rude strength of conception. The underlying thoughts are few, though the flowers on the surface are so many. We have likewise the perpetual contrast of the soft poetry of the memory, and the firm—as it were, fused—and glowing poetry of the imagination. His words, we may half fancifully say, are like his character: there is the same austerity in the real essence, the same exquisiteness of sense, the same delicacy of form which we know that he had, the same music which we imagine there was in his voice. In both his character and his poetry there was an ascetic nature in a sheath of beauty.

No book, perhaps, which has ever been written is more difficult to criticize than "Paradise Lost." The only way to criticize a work of the imagination is, to describe its effect upon the mind of the reader,—at any rate, of the critic; and this can only be adequately delineated by strong illustrations, apt similes, and perhaps a little exaggeration. The task is in its very nature not an easy one: the poet paints a picture on the fancy of the critic, and the critic has in some sort to copy it on the paper; he must say what it is before he can make remarks upon it. But in the case of "Paradise Lost" we hardly like to use illustrations. The subject is one which the imagination rather shrinks from. At any rate, it requires courage and an effort to compel the mind to view such a subject as distinctly and vividly as it views other subjects. Another peculiarity of "Paradise Lost" makes the difficulty even greater. It does not profess to be a mere work of art; or rather, it claims to be by no means that and that only. It starts with a dogmatic aim: it avowedly intends to

> "assert eternal Providence,
> And justify the ways of God to men."

In this point of view we have always had a sympathy with the Cambridge mathematician who has been so much abused. He said, "After all, 'Paradise Lost' *proves* nothing"; and various persons of poetical tastes and temperament have been very severe on the prosaic observation. Yet, "after all," he was right: Milton professed to prove something; he was too profound a critic—rather, he had too profound an instinct of those eternal principles of art which criticism tries to state—not to know that on such a subject he must prove something. He professed to deal with the great problem of human destiny: to show why man was created, in what kind of universe he lives, whence he came and whither he goes. He dealt of necessity with the greatest of subjects; he had to sketch the greatest of objects. He was concerned with infinity and eternity even more than with time and sense: he undertook to delineate the ways and consequently the character of Providence, as well as the conduct and the tendencies of man. The essence of success in such an attempt is to satisfy the religious sense of man; to bring home to our hearts what we know to be true; to teach us what we have not seen; to awaken us to what we have forgotten; to remove the "covering" from all people, and the "veil" that is spread over all nations: to give us, in a word, such a conception of things divine and human as we can accept, believe, and trust. The true doctrine of criticism demands what Milton invites,—an examination of the degree in which the great epic attains this aim. And if, in examining it, we find it necessary to use unusual illustrations, and plainer words than are customary, it must be our excuse that we do not think the subject can be made clear without them.

The defect of "Paradise Lost" is that, after all, it is founded on a *political* transaction. The scene is in heaven very early in the history of the universe, before the creation of man or the fall of Satan. We have a description of a court [Book v.] The angels,

"by imperial summons called,"

appear:—

"Under their hierarchs in orders bright
Ten thousand thousand ensigns high advanced;
Standards and gonfalons 'twixt van and rear
Stream in the air, and for distinction serve
Of hierarchies, or orders, and degrees."

To this assemblage "th' Omnipotent" speaks:—

"Hear, all ye angels, progeny of light,
Thrones, dominations, princedoms, virtues, powers,
Hear my decree, which unrevoked shall stand:
This day I have begot whom I declare
My only Son, and on this holy hill
Him have anointed, whom ye now behold
At my right hand; your Head I him appoint:
And by myself have sworn, to him shall bow
All knees in heaven, and shall confess him Lord;
Under his great vicegerent reign abide
United as one individual soul,
Forever happy. Him who disobeys,
Me disobeys, breaks union, and that day,
Cast out from God and blessed vision, falls

> Int' utter darkness, deep ingulfed, his place
> Ordained without redemption, without end."

This act of patronage was not popular at court; and why should it have been? The religious sense is against it. The worship which sinful men owe to God is not transferable to lieutenants and vicegerents. The whole scene of the court jars upon a true feeling; we seem to be reading about some emperor of history, who admits his son to a share in the empire, who confers on him a considerable jurisdiction, and requires officials, with "standards and gonfalons," to bow before him. The orthodoxy of Milton is quite as questionable as his accuracy; the old Athanasian creed was not made by persons who would allow such a picture as that of Milton to stand before their imaginations. The generation of the Son was to them a fact "before all time," an eternal fact. There was no question in their minds of patronage or promotion: the Son was the Son before all time, just as the Father was the Father before all time. Milton had in such matters a bold but not very sensitive imagination. He accepted the inevitable materialism of Biblical (and to some extent of all religious) language as distinct revelation. He certainly believed, in contradiction to the old creed, that God had both "parts and passions." He imagined that earth is

> "but the shadow of heaven, and things therein
> Each to other like more than on earth is thought." [18]

From some passages it would seem that he actually thought of God as having "the members and form" of a man. Naturally, therefore, he would have no toleration for the mysterious notions of time and eternity which are involved in the traditional doctrine. We are not, however, now concerned with Milton's belief, but with his representation of his creed,—his picture, so to say, of it in "Paradise Lost"; still, as we cannot but think, that picture is almost irreligious, and certainly different from that which has been generally accepted in Christendom. Such phrases as "before all time," "eternal generation," are doubtless very vaguely interpreted by the mass of men; nevertheless, no

[18] Book v., Raphael to Adam.

sensitively orthodox man *could* have drawn the picture of a generation, not to say an exaltation, *in* time.

We shall see this more clearly by reading what follows in the poem.

> "All seemed well pleased; all seemed, but were not all."

One of the archangels, whose name can be guessed, decidedly disapproved, and calls a meeting, at which he explains that

> "orders and degrees
> Jar not with liberty, but well consist;"

but still, that the promotion of a new person, on grounds of relationship merely, above—even infinitely above—the old angels, with imperial titles, was a "new law," and rather tyrannical. Abdiel,

> "than whom none with more zeal adored
> The Deity, and divine commands obeyed,"

attempts a defense:—

> "Grant it thee unjust,
> That equal over equals monarch reign:
> Thyself, though great and glorious, dost thou count,
> Or all angelic nature joined in one,
> Equal to him begotten Son? by whom
> As by his word the mighty Father made
> All things, even thee, and all the spirits of heaven
> By him created in their bright degrees,
> Crowned them with glory, and to their glory named
> Thrones, dominations, princedoms, virtues, powers,
> Essential Powers; nor by his reign obscured,
> But more illustrious made, since he the Head
> One of our number thus reduced becomes,
> His laws our laws, all honor to him done
> Returns our own. Cease then this impious rage,
> And tempt not these; but hasten to appease
> Th' incensèd Father and th' incensèd Son,
> While pardon may be found, in time besought."

Yet though Abdiel's intentions were undeniably good, his argument is rather specious. Acting as an instrument in the process of creation would scarcely give a valid claim to the obedience of the created being. Power may be shown in the act, no doubt; but mere power gives no true claim to the obedience of moral beings. It is a kind of principle of all manner of idolatries and false religions to believe that it does so. Satan, besides, takes issue on the fact:—

> "That we were formed then, say'st thou? and the work
> Of secondary hands, by task transferred
> From Father to his Son? Strange point and new!
> Doctrine which we would know whence learned."

And we must say that the speech in which the new ruler is introduced to the "Thrones, dominations, princedoms, virtues, powers," is hard to reconcile with Abdiel's exposition. "*This day*" he seems to have come into existence, and could hardly have assisted at the creation of the angels, who are not young, and who converse with one another like old acquaintances.

We have gone into this part of the subject at length, because it is the source of the great error which pervades "Paradise Lost": Satan is made *interesting*. This has been the charge of a thousand orthodox and even heterodox writers against Milton. Shelley, on the other hand, has gloried in it; and fancied, if we remember rightly, that Milton intentionally ranged himself on the Satanic side of the universe, just as Shelley himself would have done, and that he wished to show the falsity of the ordinary theology. But Milton was born an age too early for such aims, and was far too sincere to have advocated any doctrine in a form so indirect. He believed every word he said. He was not conscious of the effect his teaching would produce in an age like this, when skepticism is in the air, and when it is not possible to help looking coolly on his delineations. Probably in our boyhood we can recollect a period when any solemn description of celestial events would have commanded our respect; we should not have dared to read it intelligently, to canvass its details and see what it meant: it was a religious book; it sounded reverential, and that would have sufficed. Something like this was the state of mind of the seventeenth century. Even Milton probably shared in a vague reverence for religious language; he hardly felt the moral effect of the pictures he was drawing. His artistic instinct, too, often hurries him away. His Satan was to him, as to us, the hero of his poem: having commenced by making him resist on an occasion which in an earthly kingdom would have been excusable and proper, he probably a little sympathized with him, just as his readers do.

The interest of Satan's character is at its height in the first two books. Coleridge justly compared it to that of Napoleon. There is the same pride, the same Satanic ability, the same will, the same egotism. His character seems to grow with his position. He is far finer after his fall, in misery and suffering, with scarcely any resource except in himself, than he was originally in heaven; at least, if Raphael's description of him can be trusted. No portrait which imagination or history has drawn of a revolutionary anarch is nearly so perfect; there is all the grandeur of the greatest human mind, and a certain infinitude in his circumstances which humanity must ever want. Few Englishmen feel a profound reverence for Napoleon I.; there was no French alliance in *his* time; we have most of us some tradition of antipathy to him. Yet hardly any Englishman can read the account of the campaign of 1814 without feeling his interest in the Emperor to be strong, and without perhaps being conscious of a latent wish that he may succeed. Our opinion is against him, our serious wish is of course for England; but the imagination has a sympathy of its own, and will not give place. We read about the great general,—never greater than in that last emergency,—showing resources of genius that seem almost infinite, and that assuredly have never been surpassed, yet vanquished, yielding to the power of circumstances, to the combined force of adversaries each of whom singly he outmatches in strength, and all of whom together he surpasses in majesty and in mind. Something of the same sort of interest belongs to the Satan of the first two books of "Paradise Lost." We know that he will be vanquished; his name is not a recommendation. Still, we do not imagine distinctly the minds by which he is to be vanquished; we do not take the same interest in them that we do in him; our sympathies, our fancy, are on his side.

Perhaps much of this was inevitable; yet what a defect it is! especially what a defect in Milton's own view, and looked at with the stern realism with which he regarded it! Suppose that the author of evil in the universe were the most attractive being in it; suppose that the source of all sin were the origin of all interest to us! We need not dwell upon this.

As we have said, much of this was difficult to avoid, if indeed it could be avoided in dealing with such a theme. Even Milton shrank, in some measure, from delineating the Divine character. His imagination evidently halts when it is required to perform that task. The more delicate imagination of our modern world would shrink still more. Any person who will consider what such an attempt must end in, will find his nerves quiver. But by a curiously fatal error, Milton has selected for delineation exactly that part of the Divine nature which is most beyond the reach of the human faculties, and which is also, when we try to describe our fancy of it, the least effective to our minds. He has made God *argue*. Now, the procedure of the Divine mind from truth to truth must ever be incomprehensible to us; the notion, indeed, of his proceeding at all is a contradiction: to some extent, at least, it is inevitable that we should use such language, but we know it is in reality inapplicable. A long train of reasoning in such a connection is so out of place as to be painful; and yet Milton has many. He relates a series of family prayers in heaven, with sermons afterwards, which are very tedious. Even Pope was shocked at the notion of Providence talking like a "school-divine."[19] And there is the still worse error, that if you once attribute reasoning to him, subsequent logicians may discover that he does not reason very well.

Another way in which Milton has contrived to strengthen our interest in Satan is the number and insipidity of the good angels. There are old rules as to the necessity of a supernatural machinery for an epic poem, worth some fraction of the paper on which they are written, and derived from the practice of Homer, who believed his gods and goddesses to be real beings, and would have been rather harsh with a critic who called them machinery. These rules had probably an influence with Milton, and induced him to manipulate these serious angels more than he would have done otherwise. They appear to be excellent administrators with

[19] Imitation of Horace's Epistle to Augustus, Book ii., Ep. i.

very little to do; a kind of grand chamberlains with wings, who fly down to earth and communicate information to Adam and Eve. They have no character: they are essentially messengers,—merely conductors, so to say, of the Providential will; no one fancies that they have an independent power of action; they seem scarcely to have minds of their own. No effect can be more unfortunate. If the struggle of Satan had been with Deity directly, the natural instincts of religion would have been awakened; but when an angel possessed of mind is contrasted with angels possessed only of wings, we sympathize with the former.

In the first two books, therefore, our sympathy with Milton's Satan is great; we had almost said unqualified. The speeches he delivers are of well-known excellence. Lord Brougham, no contemptible judge of emphatic oratory, has laid down that if a person had not an opportunity of access to the great Attic masterpieces, he had better choose these for a model. What is to be regretted about the orator is, that he scarcely acts up to his sentiments. "Better to reign in hell than serve in heaven," is at any rate an audacious declaration; but he has no room for exhibiting similar audacity in action. His offensive career is limited; in the nature of the subject, there was scarcely any opportunity for the fallen archangel to display in the detail of his operations the surpassing intellect with which Milton has endowed him. He goes across chaos, gets into a few physical difficulties; but these are not much. His grand aim is the conquest of our first parents; and we are at once struck with the enormous inequality of the conflict. Two beings just created, without experience, without guile, without knowledge of good and evil, are expected to contend with a being on the delineation of whose powers every resource of art and imagination, every subtle suggestion, every emphatic simile has been lavished. The idea in every reader's mind is, and must be, not surprise that our first parents should yield, but wonder that Satan should not think it beneath him to attack them. It is as if an army should invest a cottage.

We have spoken more of theology than we intended; and we need not say how much the monstrous inequalities attributed to the combatants affect our estimate of the results of the conflict. The state of man is what it is, because the defenseless Adam and Eve of Milton's imagination yielded to the nearly all-powerful Satan whom he has delineated. Milton has in some sense invented this difficulty; for in the book of Genesis there is no such inequality. The serpent may be subtler than any beast of the field; but he is not necessarily subtler or cleverer than man. So far from Milton having justified the ways of God to man, he has loaded the common theology with a new incumbrance.

We may need refreshment after this discussion; and we cannot find it better than in reading a few remarks of Eve:—

> "That day I oft remember, when from sleep
> I first awaked, and found myself reposed
> Under a shade on flowers, much wondering where
> And what I was, whence hither brought, and how.
> Not distant far from thence a murmuring sound
> Of waters issued from a cave, and spread
> Into a liquid plain, then stood unmoved
> Pure as th' expanse of heaven; I thither went
> With unexperienced thought, and laid me down
> On the green bank, to look into the clear
> Smooth lake, that to me seemed another sky.
> As I bent down to look, just opposite
> A shape within the watery gleam appeared,
> Bending to look on me. I started back,
> It started back: but pleased I soon returned;
> Pleased it returned, as soon with answering looks
> Of sympathy and love. There I had fixed
> Mine eyes till now, and pined with vain desire,
> Had not a voice thus warned me:—'What thou seest,
> What there thou seest, fair creature, is thyself;
> With thee it came and goes: but follow me,
> And I will bring thee where no shadow stays
> Thy coming, and thy soft embraces; he
> Whose image thou art, him thou shalt enjoy
> Inseparably thine; to him shalt bear
> Multitudes like thyself, and thence be called
> Mother of human race.' What could I do
> But follow straight, invisibly thus led?
> Till I espied thee, fair indeed and tall,
> Under a platan; yet methought less fair,
> Less winning soft, less amiably mild,
> Than that smooth watery image. Back I turned;
> Thou following criedst aloud, 'Return, fair Eve;
> Whom fly'st thou?'"[20]

[20] Book iv.

Eve's character, indeed, is one of the most wonderful efforts of the human imagination. She is a kind of abstract woman; essentially a typical being; an official "mother of all living." Yet she is a real interesting woman, not only full of delicacy and sweetness, but with all the undefinable fascination, the charm of personality, which such typical characters hardly ever have. By what consummate miracle of wit this charm of individuality is preserved, without impairing the general idea which is ever present to us, we cannot explain, for we do not know.

Adam is far less successful. He has good hair,—"hyacinthine locks" that "from his parted forelock manly hung"; a "fair large front" and "eye sublime": but he has little else that we care for. There is, in truth, no opportunity of displaying manly virtues, even if he possessed them. He has only to yield to his wife's solicitations, which he does. Nor are we sure that he does it well: he is very tedious. He indulges in sermons which are good; but most men cannot but fear that so delightful a being as Eve must have found him tiresome. She steps away, however, and goes to sleep at some of the worst points.

Dr. Johnson remarked that after all, "Paradise Lost" was one of the books which no one wished longer: we fear, in this irreverent generation, some wish it shorter. Hardly any reader would be sorry if some portions of the latter books had been spared him. Coleridge, indeed, discovered profound mysteries in the last; but in what could not Coleridge find a mystery if he wished? Dryden more wisely remarked that Milton became tedious when he entered upon a "track of Scripture."[21] Nor is it surprising that such is the case. The style of many parts of Scripture is such that it will not bear addition or subtraction. A word less or an idea more, and the effect upon the mind is the same no longer. Nothing can be more tiresome than a sermonic amplification of such passages. It is almost too much when, as from the pulpit, a paraphrastic commentary is prepared for our spiritual improvement. In deference to the intention, we bear it, but we bear it unwillingly; and we cannot endure it at all when, as in poems, the object is to awaken our fancy

[21] "Essay on Satire."

rather than to improve our conduct. The account of the creation in the book of Genesis is one of the compositions from which no sensitive imagination would subtract an iota, to which it could not bear to add a word. Milton's paraphrase is alike copious and ineffective. The universe is, in railway phrase, "opened," but not created; no green earth springs in a moment from the indefinite void. Instead, too, of the simple loneliness of the Old Testament, several angelic officials are in attendance, who help in nothing, but indicate that heaven must be plentifully supplied with tame creatures.

There is no difficulty in writing such criticisms and indeed other unfavorable criticisms, on "Paradise Lost." There is scarcely any book in the world which is open to a greater number, or which a reader who allows plain words to produce a due effect will be less satisfied with. Yet what book is really greater? In the best parts the words have a magic in them; even in the inferior passages you are hardly sensible of their inferiority till you translate them into your own language. Perhaps no style ever written by man expressed so adequately the conceptions of a mind so strong and so peculiar; a manly strength, a haunting atmosphere of enhancing suggestions, a firm continuous music, are only some of its excellences. To comprehend the whole of the others, you must take the volume down and read it,—the best defense of Milton, as has been said most truly, against all objections.

Probably no book shows the transition which our theology has made since the middle of the seventeenth century, at once so plainly and so fully. We do not now compose long narratives to "justify the ways of God to men." The more orthodox we are, the more we shrink from it, the more we hesitate at such a task, the more we allege that we have no powers for it. Our most celebrated defenses of established tenets are in the style of Butler, not in that of Milton. They do not profess to show a satisfactory explanation of human destiny: on the contrary, they hint that probably we could not understand such an explanation if it were given us; at any rate, they allow that it is not given us. Their course is palliative: they suggest an "analogy of difficulties"; if our minds were greater, so they reason, we should comprehend these doctrines,—now we cannot explain analogous facts which we see and know. No style can be more opposite to the bold argument, the boastful exposition of Milton. The teaching of the eighteenth century is in the very atmosphere we breathe: we read it in the teachings of Oxford; we hear it from the missionaries of the Vatican. The air of the theology is clarified. We know our difficulties, at least: we are rather prone to exaggerate the weight of some than to deny the reality of any.

We cannot continue a line of thought which would draw us on too far for the patience of our readers. We must, however, make one more remark, and we shall have finished our criticism on "Paradise Lost." It is analogous to that which we have just made. The scheme of the poem is based on an offense against positive morality. The offense of Adam was not against nature or conscience, nor against anything of which we can see the reason or conceive the obligation, but against an unexplained injunction of the Supreme Will. The rebellion in heaven, as Milton describes it, was a rebellion not against known ethics or immutable spiritual laws, but against an arbitrary selection and an unexplained edict. We do not say that there is no such thing as positive morality,—we do not think so; even if we did, we should not insert a proposition so startling at the conclusion of a literary criticism. But we are sure that wherever a positive moral edict is promulgated, it is no subject, except perhaps under a very peculiar treatment, for literary art. By the very nature of it, it cannot satisfy the heart and conscience. It is a difficulty; we need not attempt to explain it away,—there are mysteries enough which will never be explained away. But it is contrary to every principle of criticism to state the difficulty as if it were not one; to bring forward the puzzle, yet leave it to itself; to publish so strange a problem, and give only an untrue solution of it: and yet such, in its bare statement, is all that Milton has done.

Of Milton's other writings we have left ourselves no room to speak; and though every one of them, or almost every one of them, would well repay a careful criticism, yet few of them seem to throw much additional light on his character, or add much to our essential notion of his genius, though they may exemplify and enhance it. "Comus" is the poem which does so the most. Literature has become so much lighter than it used to be, that we can scarcely realize the position it occupied in the light literature of our forefathers. We have now in our own language many poems that are pleasanter in their subject, more graceful in their execution, more flowing in their outline, more easy to read. Dr. Johnson, though perhaps no very excellent authority on the more intangible graces of literature, was disposed to deny to Milton the capacity of creating the lighter literature: "Milton, madam, was a genius that could cut a colossus from a rock, but could not carve heads upon cherry-stones." And it would not be surprising if this generation, which has access to the almost infinite quantity of lighter compositions which have been produced since Johnson's time, were to echo his sentence. In some degree, perhaps, the popular taste does so. "Comus" has no longer the peculiar exceptional popularity which it used to have: we can talk without general odium of its defects; its characters are nothing, its sentiments are tedious, its story is not interesting. But it is only when we have realized the magnitude of its deficiencies that we comprehend the peculiarity of its greatness. Its power is in its style. A grave and firm music pervades it; it is soft, without a thought of weakness; harmonious and yet strong; impressive as few such poems are, yet covered with a bloom of beauty and a complexity of charm that few poems have either. We have perhaps light literature in itself better, that we read oftener and more easily, that lingers more in our memories; but we have not any, we question if there ever will be any, which gives so true a conception of the capacity and the dignity of the mind by which it was produced. The breath of solemnity which hovers round the music attaches us to the writer. Every line, here as elsewhere, in Milton excites the idea of indefinite power.

And so we must draw to a close. The subject is an infinite one, and if we pursued it, we should lose ourselves in miscellaneous commentary, and run on far beyond the patience of our readers. What we have said has at least a defined intention: we have wished to state the impression which the character of Milton and the greatest of Milton's works are likely to produce on readers of the present generation,—a generation different from his own almost more than any other.

SCIENCE AND CULTURE

BY

THOMAS HENRY HUXLEY

INTRODUCTORY NOTE

THOMAS HENRY HUXLEY *(1825-95) was born at Ealing, near London, and having studied medicine went to sea as assistant surgeon in the navy. After leaving the Government service, he became Professor of Natural History at the Royal School of Mines and Fullerian Professor of Physiology at the Royal Institution, and later held many commissions and received many distinctions in the scientific world. His special field was morphology, and in it he produced a large number of monographs and several comprehensive manuals.*

It is not, however, by his original contributions to knowledge that Huxley's name is best known to readers outside of technical science, but rather by his labors in popularization and in polemics. He was one of the foremost and most effective champions of Darwinism, and no scientist has been more conspicuous in the battle between the doctrine of evolution and the older religious orthodoxy. Outside of this particular issue, he was a vigorous opponent of supernaturalism in all its forms, and a supporter of the agnosticism which demands that nothing shall be believed "with greater assurance than the evidence warrants"—the evidence intended being, of course, of the same kind as that admitted in natural science.

Huxley's interests thus extended from pure science into many adjoining fields, such as those of theology, philosophy (where he wrote an admirable book on Hume), and education. Of his attitude toward this last, a clear idea may be gained from the following address on "Science and Culture," a singularly forcible plea for the importance of natural science in general education.

In all his writings Huxley commands a style excellently adapted to his purpose: clear, forcible, free from mannerism, yet telling and often memorable in phrase. Whatever may be the exact magnitude of his services to pure science, he was a master in the writing of English for the purposes of exposition and controversy, and a powerful intellectual influence on almost all classes in his generation.

SCIENCE AND CULTURE[1]

SIX years ago, as some of my present hearers may remember, I had the privilege of addressing a large assemblage of the inhabitants of this city, who had gathered together to do honor to the memory of their famous townsman, Joseph Priestley; and, if any satisfaction attaches to posthumous glory, we may hope that the manes of the burnt-out philosopher were then finally appeased.

No man, however, who is endowed with a fair share of common-sense, and not more than a fair share of vanity, will identify either contemporary or posthumous fame with the highest good; and Priestley's life leaves no doubt that he, at any rate, set a much higher value upon the advancement of knowledge, and the promotion of that freedom of thought which is at once the cause and the consequence of intellectual progress.

Hence I am disposed to think that, if Priestley could be amongst us to-day, the occasion of our meeting would afford him even greater pleasure than the proceedings which celebrated the centenary of his chief discovery. The kindly heart would be moved, the high sense of social duty would be satisfied, by the spectacle of well-earned wealth, neither squandered in tawdry luxury and vainglorious show, nor scattered with the careless charity which blesses neither him that gives nor him that takes, but expended in the execution of a well-considered plan for the aid of present and future generations of those who are willing to help themselves.

We shall all be of one mind thus far. But it is needful to share Priestley's keen interest in physical science; and to have learned, as he had learned, the value of scientific training in fields of inquiry apparently far remote from physical

[1] Originally delivered as an address, in 1880, at the opening of Mason College, Birmingham, England, now the University of Birmingham.

science; in order to appreciate, as he would have appreciated, the value of the noble gift which Sir Josiah Mason has bestowed upon the inhabitants of the Midland district.

For us children of the nineteenth century, however, the establishment of a college under the conditions of Sir Josiah Mason's trust has a significance apart from any which it could have possessed a hundred years ago. It appears to be an indication that we are reaching the crisis of the battle, or rather of the long series of battles, which have been fought over education in a campaign which began long before Priestley's time, and will probably not be finished just yet.

In the last century, the combatants were the champions of ancient literature, on the one side, and those of modern literature on the other; but, some thirty years[2] ago, the contest became complicated by the appearance of a third army, ranged round the banner of physical science.

I am not aware that any one has au hority to speak in the name of this new host. For it must be admitted to be somewhat of a guerilla force, composed largely of irregulars, each of whom fights pretty much for his own hand. But the impressions of a full private, who has seen a good deal of service in the ranks, respecting the present position of affairs and the conditions of a permanent peace, may not be devoid of interest; and I do not know that I could make a better use of the present opportunity than by laying them before you.

From the time that the first suggestion to introduce physical science into ordinary education was timidly whispered, until now, the advocates of scientific education have met with opposition of two kinds. On the one hand, they have been poohpoohed by the men of business who pride themselves on being the representatives of practicality; while, on the other hand, they have been excommunicated by the classical scholars, in their capacity of Levites in charge of the ark of culture and monopolists of liberal education.

The practical men believed that the idol whom they worship—rule of thumb—has been the source of the past prosperity, and will suffice for the future welfare of the arts and

[2] The advocacy of the introduction of physical science into general education by George Combe and others commenced a good deal earlier; but the movement had acquired hardly any practical force before the time to which I refer.

manufactures. They were of opinion that science is speculative rubbish; that theory and practice have nothing to do with one another; and that the scientific habit of mind is an impediment, rather than an aid, in the conduct of ordinary affairs.

I have used the past tense in speaking of the practical men—for although they were very formidable thirty years ago, I am not sure that the pure species has not been extirpated. In fact, so far as mere argument goes, they have been subjected to such a *feu d'enfer* that it is a miracle if any have escaped. But I have remarked that your typical practical man has an unexpected resemblance to one of Milton's angels. His spiritual wounds, such as are inflicted by logical weapons, may be as deep as a well and as wide as a church door, but beyond shedding a few drops of ichor, celestial or otherwise, he is no whit the worse. So, if any of these opponents be left, I will not waste time in vain repetition of the demonstrative evidence of the practical value of science; but knowing that a parable will sometimes penetrate where syllogisms fail to effect an entrance, I will offer a story for their consideration.

Once upon a time, a boy, with nothing to depend upon but his own vigorous nature, was thrown into the thick of the struggle for existence in the midst of a great manufacturing population. He seems to have had a hard fight, inasmuch as, by the time he was thirty years of age, his total disposable funds amounted to twenty pounds. Nevertheless, middle life found him giving proof of his comprehension of the practical problems he had been roughly called upon to solve, by a career of remarkable prosperity.

Finally, having reached old age with its well-earned surroundings of "honor, troops of friends," the hero of my story bethought himself of those who were making a like start in life, and how he could stretch out a helping hand to them.

After long and anxious reflection this successful practical man of business could devise nothing better than to provide them with the means of obtaining "sound, extensive, and practical scientific knowledge." And he devoted a large part of his wealth and five years of incessant work to this end.

I need not point the moral of a tale which, as the solid and spacious fabric of the Scientific College assures us, is no fable, nor can anything which I could say intensify the force of this practical answer to practical objections.

We may take it for granted then, that, in the opinion of those best qualified to judge, the diffusion of thorough scientific education is an absolutely essential condition of industrial progress; and that the college which has been opened to-day will confer an inestimable boon upon those whose livelihood is to be gained by the practice of the arts and manufactures of the district.

The only question worth discussion is, whether the conditions, under which the work of the college is to be carried out, are such as to give it the best possible chance of achieving permanent success.

Sir Josiah Mason, without doubt most wisely, has left very large freedom of action to the trustees, to whom he proposes ultimately to commit the administration of the college, so that they may be able to adjust its arrangements in accordance with the changing conditions of the future. But, with respect to three points, he has laid most explicit injunctions upon both administrators and teachers.

Party politics are forbidden to enter into the minds of either, so far as the work of the college is concerned; theology is as sternly banished from its precincts; and finally, it is especially declared that the college shall make no provision for "mere literary instruction and education."

It does not concern me at present to dwell upon the first two injunctions any longer than may be needful to express my full conviction of their wisdom. But the third prohibition brings us face to face with those other opponents of scientific education, who are by no means in the moribund condition of the practical man, but alive, alert, and formidable.

It is not impossible that we shall hear this express exclusion of "literary instruction and education" from a college which, nevertheless, professes to give a high and efficient education, sharply criticised. Certainly the time was that the Levites of culture would have sounded their trumpets against its walls as against an educational Jericho.

How often have we not been told that the study of physical

science is incompetent to confer culture; that it touches none of the higher problems of life; and, what is worse, that the continual devotion to scientific studies tends to generate a narrow and bigoted belief in the applicability of scientific methods to the search after truth of all kinds. How frequently one has reason to observe that no reply to a troublesome argument tells so well as calling its author a "mere scientific specialist." And, as I am afraid it is not permissible to speak of this form of opposition to scientific education in the past tense; may we not expect to be told that this, not only omission, but prohibition, of "mere literary instruction and education" is a patent example of scientific narrow-mindedness?

I am not acquainted with Sir Josiah Mason's reasons for the action which he has taken; but if, as I apprehend is the case, he refers to the ordinary classical course of our schools and universities by the name of "mere literary instruction and education," I venture to offer sundry reasons of my own in support of that action.

For I hold very strongly by two convictions. The first is, that neither the discipline nor the subject-matter of classical education is of such direct value to the student of physical science as to justify the expenditure of valuable time upon either; and the second is, that for the purpose of attaining real culture, an exclusively scientific education is at least as effectual as an exclusively literary education.

I need hardly point out to you that these opinions, especially the latter, are diametrically opposed to those of the great majority of educated Englishmen, influenced as they are by school and university traditions. In their belief, culture is obtainable only by a liberal education; and a liberal education is synonymous, not merely with education and instruction in literature, but in one particular form of literture, namely, that of Greek and Roman antiquity. They hold that the man who has learned Latin and Greek, however little, is educated; while he who is versed in other branches of knowledge, however deeply, is a more or less respectable specialist, not admissible into cultured caste. The stamp of the educated man, the university degree, is not for him.

I am too well acquainted with the generous catholicity of

spirit, the true sympathy with scientific thought, which pervades the writings of our chief apostle of culture to identify him with these opinions; and yet one may cull from one and another of those epistles to the Philistines, which so much delight all who do not answer to that name, sentences which lend them some support.

Mr. Arnold tells us that the meaning of culture is "to know the best that has been thought and said in the world." It is the criticism of life contained in literature. That criticism regards "Europe as being, for intellectual and spiritual purposes, one great confederation, bound to a joint action and working to a common result; and whose members have, for their common outfit, a knowledge of Greek, Roman, and Eastern antiquity, and of one another. Special, local, and temporary advantages being put out of account, that modern nation will in the intellectual and spiritual sphere make most progress, which most thoroughly carries out this programme. And what is that but saying that we too, all of us, as individuals, the more thoroughly we carry it out, shall make the more progress?"

We have here to deal with two distinct propositions. The first, that a criticism of life is the essence of culture; the second, that literature contains the materials which suffice for the construction of such a criticism.

I think that we must all assent to the first proposition. For culture certainly means something quite different from learning or technical skill. It implies the possession of an ideal, and the habit of critically estimating the value of things by comparison with a theoretic standard. Perfect culture should apply a complete theory of life, based upon a clear knowledge alike of its possibilities and of its limitations.

But we may agree to all this, and yet strongly dissent from the assumption that literature alone is competent to supply this knowledge. After having learnt all that Greek, Roman, and Eastern antiquity have thought and said, and all that modern literatures have to tell us, it is not self-evident that we have laid a sufficiently broad and deep foundation for that criticism of life which constitutes culture.

Indeed, to any one acquainted with the scope of physical science, it is not at all evident. Considering progress only in the "intellectual and spiritual sphere," I find myself wholly unable to admit that either nations or individuals will really advance, if their common outfit draws nothing from the stores of physical science. I should say that an army, without weapons of precision, and with no particular base of operations, might more hopefully enter upon a campaign on the Rhine, than a man, devoid of a knowledge of what physical science has done in the last century, upon a criticism of life.

When a biologist meets with an anomaly, he instinctively turns to the study of development to clear it up. The rationale of contradictory opinions may with equal confidence be sought in history.

It is, happily, no new thing that Englishmen should employ their wealth in building and endowing institutions for educational purposes. But, five or six hundred years ago, deeds of foundation expressed or implied conditions as nearly as possible contrary to those which have been thought expedient by Sir Josiah Mason. That is to say, physical science was practically ignored, while a certain literary training was enjoined as a means to the acquirement of knowledge which was essentially theological.

The reason of this singular contradiction between the actions of men alike animated by a strong and disinterested desire to promote the welfare of their fellows, is easily discovered.

At that time, in fact, if any one desired knowledge beyond such as could be obtained by his own observation, or by common conversation, his first necessity was to learn the Latin language, inasmuch as all the higher knowledge of the western world was contained in works written in that language. Hence, Latin grammar, with logic and rhetoric, studied through Latin, were the fundamentals of education. With respect to the substance of the knowledge imparted through this channel, the Jewish and Christian Scriptures, as interpreted and supplemented by the Romish Church, were held to contain a complete and infallibly true body of information.

Theological dicta were, to the thinkers of those days, that which the axioms and definitions of Euclid are to the geometers of these. The business of the philosophers of the Middle Ages was to deduce from the data furnished by the theologians, conclusions in accordance with ecclesiastical decrees. They were allowed the high privilege of showing, by logical process, how and why that which the Church said was true, must be true. And if their demonstrations fell short of or exceeded this limit, the Church was maternally ready to check their aberrations, if need be, by the help of the secular arm.

Between the two, our ancestors were furnished with a compact and complete criticism of life. They were told how the world began, and how it would end; they learned that all material existence was but a base and insignificant blot upon the fair face of the spiritual world, and that nature was, to all intents and purposes, the play-ground of the devil; they learned that the earth is the centre of the visible universe, and that man is the cynosure of things terrestrial; and more especially is it inculcated that the course of nature had no fixed order, but that it could be, and constantly was, altered by the agency of innumerable spiritual beings, good and bad, according as they were moved by the deeds and prayers of men. The sum and substance of the whole doctrine was to produce the conviction that the only thing really worth knowing in this world was how to secure that place in a better, which, under certain conditions, the Church promised.

Our ancestors had a living belief in this theory of life, and acted upon it in their dealings with education, as in all other matters. Culture meant saintliness—after the fashion of the saints of those days; the education that led to it was, of necessity, theological; and the way to theology lay through Latin.

That the study of nature—further than was requisite for the satisfaction of everyday wants—should have any bearing on human life was far from the thoughts of men thus trained. Indeed, as nature had been cursed for man's sake, it was an obvious conclusion that those who meddled with nature were likely to come into pretty close contact with Satan. And, if any born scientific investigator followed his instincts, he might safely reckon upon earning the reputation, and probably upon suffering the fate, of a sorcerer.

Had the western world been left to itself in Chinese isolation, there is no saying how long this state of things might have endured. But, happily, it was not left to itself. Even earlier than the thirteenth century, the development of Moorish civilization in Spain and the great movement of the Crusades had introduced the leaven which, from that day to this, has never ceased to work. At first, through the intermediation of Arabic translations, afterwards by the study of the originals, the western nations of Europe became acquainted with the writings of the ancient philosophers and poets, and, in time, with the whole of the vast literature of antiquity.

Whatever there was of high intellectual aspiration or dominant capacity in Italy, France, Germany, and England, spent itself for centuries in taking possession of the rich inheritance left by the dead civilization of Greece and Rome. Marvelously aided by the invention of printing, classical learning spread and flourished. Those who possessed it prided themselves on having attained the highest culture then within the reach of mankind.

And justly. For, saving Dante on his solitary pinnacle, there was no figure in modern literature at the time of the Renaissance to compare with the men of antiquity; there was no art to compete with their sculpture; there was no physical science but that which Greece had created. Above all, there was no other example of perfect intellectual freedom—of the unhesitating acceptance of reason as the sole guide to truth and the supreme arbiter of conduct.

The new learning necessarily soon exerted a profound influence upon education. The language of the monks and schoolmen seemed little better than gibberish to scholars fresh from Vergil and Cicero, and the study of Latin was placed upon a new foundation. Moreover, Latin itself ceased to afford the sole key to knowledge. The student who sought the highest thought of antiquity found only a second-hand reflection of it in Roman literature, and turned his face to the full light of the Greeks. And after a battle, not altogether dissimilar to that which is at present being fought over the teaching of physical science, the study of Greek was recognized as an essential element of all higher education.

Thus the humanists, as they were called, won the day; and the great reform which they effected was of incalculable service to mankind. But the Nemesis of all reformers is finality; and the reformers of education, like those of religion, fell into the profound, however common, error of mistaking the beginning for the end of the work of reformation.

The representatives of the humanists in the nineteenth century take their stand upon classical education as the sole avenue to culture, as firmly as if we were still in the age of Renaissance. Yet, surely, the present intellectual relations of the modern and the ancient worlds are profoundly different from those which obtained three centuries ago. Leaving aside the existence of a great and characteristically modern literature, of modern painting, and, especially, of modern music, there is one feature of the present state of the civilized world which separates it more widely from the Renaissance than the Renaissance was separated from the Middle Ages.

This distinctive character of our own times lies in the vast and constantly increasing part which is played by natural knowledge. Not only is our daily life shaped by it, not only does the prosperity of millions of men depend upon it, but our whole theory of life has long been influenced, consciously or unconsciously, by the general conceptions of the universe, which have been forced upon us by physical science.

In fact, the most elementary acquaintance with the results of scientific investigation shows us that they offer a broad and striking contradiction to the opinions so implicitly credited and taught in the Middle Ages.

The notions of the beginning and the end of the world entertained by our forefathers are no longer credible. It is very certain that the earth is not the chief body in the material universe, and that the world is not subordinated to man's use. It is even more certain that nature is the expression of a definite order with which nothing interferes, and that the chief business of mankind is to learn that order and govern themselves accordingly. Moreover this scientific "criticism of life" presents itself to us with different credentials from any other. It appeals not to authority, nor to what anybody may have thought or said, but to nature. It admits that all our interpretations of natural fact are more or less imperfect and symbolic, and bids the learner seek for truth not among words but among things. It warns us that the assertion which outstrips evidence is not only a blunder but a crime.

The purely classical education advocated by the representatives of the humanists in our day gives no inkling of all this. A man may be a better scholar than Erasmus, and know no more of the chief causes of the present intellectual fermentation than Erasmus did. Scholarly and pious persons, worthy of all respect, favor us with allocutions upon the sadness of the antagonism of science to their mediæval way of thinking, which betray an ignorance of the first principles of scientific investigation, an incapacity for understanding what a man of science means by veracity, and an unconsciousness of the weight of established scientific truths, which is almost comical.

There is no great force in the *tu quoque* argument, or else the advocates of scientific education might fairly enough retort upon the modern humanists that they may be learned specialists, but that they possess no such sound foundation for a criticism of life as deserves the name of culture. And, indeed, if we were disposed to be cruel, we might urge that the humanists have brought this reproach upon themselves, not because they are too full of the spirit of the ancient Greek, but because they lack it.

The period of the Renaissance is commonly called that of the "Revival of Letters," as if the influences then brought to bear upon the mind of Western Europe had been wholly exhausted in the field of literature. I think it is very commonly forgotten that the revival of science, effected by the same agency, although less conspicuous, was not less momentous.

In fact, the few and scattered students of nature of that day picked up the clew to her secrets exactly as it fell from the hands of the Greeks a thousand years before. The foundations of mathematics were so well laid by them that our children learn their geometry from a book written for the schools of Alexandria two thousand years ago. Modern astronomy is the natural continuation and development of the work of Hipparchus and of Ptolemy; modern physics of that of Democritus and of Archimedes; it was long before modern biological science outgrew the knowledge bequeathed to us by Aristotle, by Theophrastus, and by Galen.

We cannot know all the best thoughts and sayings of the Greeks unless we know what they thought about natural phenomena. We cannot fully apprehend their criticism of life unless we understand the extent to which that criticism was affected by scientific conceptions. We falsely pretend to be the inheritors of their culture, unless we are penetrated, as the best minds among them were, with an unhesitating faith that the free employment of reason, in accordance with scientific method, is the sole method of reaching truth.

Thus I venture to think that the pretensions of our modern humanists to the possession of the monopoly of culture and to the exclusive inheritance of the spirit of antiquity must be abated, if not abandoned. But I should be very sorry that anything I have said should be taken to imply a desire on my part to depreciate the value of classical education, as it might be and as it sometimes is. The native capacities of mankind vary no less than their opportunities; and while culture is one, the road by which one man may best reach it is widely different from that which is most advantageous to another. Again, while scientific education is yet inchoate and tentative, classical education is thoroughly well organized upon the practical experience of generations of teachers. So that, given ample time for learning and destination for ordinary life, or for a literary career, I do not think that a young Englishman in search of culture can do better than follow the course usually marked out for him, supplementing its deficiencies by his own efforts.

But for those who mean to make science their serious occupation; or who intend to follow the profession of medicine; or who have to enter early upon the business of life; for all these, in my opinion, classical education is a mistake; and it is for this reason that I am glad to see "mere literary education and instruction" shut out from the curriculum of Sir Josiah Mason's college, seeing that its inclusion would probably lead to the introduction of the ordinary smattering of Latin and Greek.

Nevertheless, I am the last person to question the importance of genuine literary education, or to suppose that intellectual culture can be complete without it. An exclusively scientific training will bring about a mental twist as surely as an exclusive literary training. The value of the cargo does not compensate for a ship's being out of trim; and I should be very sorry to think that the Scientific College would turn out none but lop-sided men.

There is no need, however, that such a catastrophe should happen. Instruction in English, French, and German is provided, and thus the three greatest literatures of the modern world are made accessible to the student.

French and German, and especially the latter language, are absolutely indispensable to those who desire full knowledge in any department of science. But even supposing that the knowledge of these languages acquired is not more than sufficient for purely scientific purposes, every Englishman has, in his native tongue, an almost perfect instrument of literary expression; and, in his own literature, models of every kind of literary excellence. If an Englishman cannot get literary culture out of his Bible, his Shakespeare, his Milton, neither, in my belief, will the profoundest study of Homer and Sophocles, Vergil and Horace, give it to him.

Thus, since the constitution of the college makes sufficient provision for literary as well as for scientific education, and since artistic instruction is also contemplated, it seems to me that a fairly complete culture is offered to all who are willing to take advantage of it.

But I am not sure that at this point the "practical" man, scotched but not slain, may ask what all this talk about culture has to do with an institution, the object of which is defined to be "to promote the prosperity of the manufactures and the industry of the country." He may suggest that what is wanted for this end is not culture, nor even a purely scientific discipline, but simply a knowledge of applied science.

I often wish that this phrase, "applied science," had never been invented. For it suggests that there is a sort of scientific knowledge of direct practical use, which can be studied apart from another sort of scientific knowledge, which is of no practical utility, and which is termed "pure science." But there is no more complete fallacy than this. What people call applied science is nothing but the application of pure science to particular classes of problems. It consists of deductions from those general principles, established by reasoning and observation, which constitute pure science. No one can safely make these deductions until he has a firm grasp of the principles; and he can obtain that grasp only by personal experience of the operations of observation and of reasoning on which they are founded.

Almost all the processes employed in the arts and manufactures fall within the range either of physics or of chemistry. In order to improve them one must thoroughly understand them; and no one has a chance of really understanding them, unless he has obtained that mastery of principles and that habit of dealing with facts which is given by long-continued and well-directed purely scientific training in the physical and chemical laboratory. So that there really is no question as to the necessity of purely scientific discipline, even if the work of the college were limited by the narrowest interpretation of its stated aims.

And, as to the desirableness of a wider culture than that yielded by science alone, it is to be recollected that the improvement of manufacturing processes is only one of the conditions which contribute to the prosperity of industry. Industry is a means and not an end; and mankind work only to get something which they want. What that something is depends partly on their innate, and partly on their acquired, desires.

If the wealth resulting from prosperous industry is to be spent upon the gratification of unworthy desires, if the increasing perfection of manufacturing processes is to be accompanied by an increasing debasement of those who carry them on, I do not see the good of industry and prosperity.

Now it is perfectly true that men's views of what is desirable depend upon their characters; and that the innate proclivities to which we give that name are not touched by any amount of instruction. But it does not follow that even mere intellectual education may not, to an indefinite extent, modify the practical manifestation of the characters of men in their actions, by supplying them with motives unknown to the ignorant. A pleasure-loving character will have pleasure of some sort; but, if you give him the choice, he may prefer pleasures which do not degrade him to those which do. And this choice is offered to every man who possesses in literary or artistic culture a never-failing source of pleasures, which are neither withered by age, nor staled by custom, nor embittered in the recollection by the pangs of self-reproach.

If the institution opened to-day fulfils the intention of its founder, the picked intelligences among all classes of the population of this district will pass through it. No child born in Birmingham, henceforward, if he have the capacity to profit by the oportunities offered to him, first in the primary and other schools, and afterward in the Scientific College, need fail to obtain, not merely the instruction, but the culture most appropriate to the conditions of his life.

Within these walls the future employer and the future artisan may sojourn together for awhile, and carry, through all their lives, the stamp of the influences then brought to bear upon them. Hence, it is not beside the mark to remind you that the prosperity of industry depends not merely upon the improvement of manufacturing processes, not merely upon the ennobling of the individual character, but upon a third condition, namely, a clear understanding of the conditions of social life on the part of both the capitalist and the operative, and their agreement upon common principles of social action. They must learn that social phenomena are as much the expression of natural laws as any others; that no social arrangements can be permanent unless they harmonize with the requirements of social statics and dynamics; and that, in the nature of things, there is an arbiter whose decisions execute themselves.

But this knowledge is only to be obtained by the application of the methods of investigation adopted in physical researches to the investigation of the phenomena of society. Hence, I confess I should like to see one addition made to the excellent scheme of education propounded for the college, in the shape of provision for the teaching of sociology. For though we are all agreed that party politics are to have no place in the instruction of the college; yet in this country, practically governed as it is now by universal suffrage, every man who does his duty must exercise political functions. And, if the evils which are inseparable from the good of political liberty are to be checked, if the perpetual oscillation of nations between anarchy and despotism is to be replaced by the steady march of self-restraining freedom; it will be because men will gradually bring themselves to deal with political, as they now deal with scientifical questions; to be as ashamed of undue haste and partisan prejudice in the one case as in the other; and to believe that the machinery of society is at least as delicate as that of a spinning-jenny, and as little likely to be improved by the meddling of those who have not taken the trouble to master the principles of its action.

In conclusion, I am sure that I make myself the mouthpiece of all present in offering to the venerable founder of the institution, which now commences its beneficent career, our congratulations on the completion of his work; and in expressing the conviction that the remotest posterity will point to it as a crucial instance of the wisdom which natural piety leads all men to ascribe to their ancestors.

RACE AND LANGUAGE

BY

EDWARD AUGUSTUS FREEMAN

INTRODUCTORY NOTE

EDWARD AUGUSTUS FREEMAN *(1823-92), one of the most distinguished of recent English historians, was born at Harborne, in Staffordshire, and educated at Oxford, where he was a Fellow of Trinity College, and later Regius Professor of Modern History. His earlier writings show great interest in architecture, and it was one of his distinctions to be the first historian to make extensive use in his subject of the evidences and illustrations supplied by the study of that art. His most famous and most elaborate work was his "History of the Norman Conquest" (1867-79), a monument which is likely long to remain the great authority on its period.*

Freeman believed in the unity of the study of history, and in the wide range of his own writings he went far toward realizing the universality he preached. Outside of the field just mentioned he wrote on ancient Greece, on Sicily, on the Ottoman Empire, on the United States, on the methods of historical study, and on many other subjects. His interests were primarily political, and he took an active part in the politics of his own day, writing for many years for the "Saturday Review." As a teacher he influenced profoundly the scientific study of history in England.

Of few terms in general use has the average man a less exact or less accurate comprehension than of the word "race." The speculative philologists of last century, with their attempts to classify the peoples of the earth according to linguistic evidences, succeeded, as far as the layman is concerned, chiefly in adding to the confusion by popularizing prematurely facts whose signification was improperly understood. The anthropologists of a more recent time, with their study of skull-shapes and complexions, have sought to correct misapprehensions; but the popular mind is still in a mist about the whole matter. In the following essay Freeman brings his knowledge of modern scientific results and his enormous historical information to the rescue of the bewildered student, and does much to clear up the perplexing relations of race with language, custom, and blood.

RACE AND LANGUAGE[1]

IT IS no very great time since the readers of the English newspapers were, perhaps a little amused, perhaps a little startled, at the story of a deputation of Hungarian students going to Constantinople to present a sword of honor to an Ottoman general. The address and the answer enlarged on the ancient kindred of Turks and Magyars, on the long alienation of the dissevered kinsfolk, on the return of both in these later times to a remembrance of the ancient kindred and to the friendly feelings to which such kindred gave birth. The discourse has a strange sound when we remember the reigns of Sigismund and Wladislaus, when we think of the dark days of Nikopolis and Varna, when we think of Huniades encamped at the foot of Hæmus, and of Belgrade beating back Mahomet the Conqueror from her gates. The Magyar and the Ottoman embracing with the joy of reunited kinsfolk is a sight which certainly no man would have looked forward to in the fourteenth or fifteenth century. At an earlier time the ceremony might have seemed a degree less wonderful. If a man whose ideas are drawn wholly from the modern map should sit down to study the writings of Constantine Porphyrogennêtos, he would perhaps be startled at finding Turks and Franks spoken of as neighbors, at finding *Turcia* and *Francia*—we must not translate *Τουρκία* and *Φραγγία* by *Turkey* and *France*—spoken of as border-lands. A little study will perhaps show him that the change lies almost wholly in the names and not in the boundaries. The lands are there still, and the frontier between them has shifted much less than one might have looked for in nine hundred years. Nor has there been any great change in the population of the two countries. The Turks and the Franks of the Imperial geographer are there still, in the lands which

[1] From "Historical Essays," Third Series, 1879.

he calls Turcia and Francia; only we no longer speak of them as Turks and Franks. The Turks of Constantine are Magyars; the Franks of Constantine are Germans. The Magyar students may not unlikely have turned over the Imperial pages, and they may have seen how their forefathers stand described there. We can hardly fancy that the Ottoman general is likely to have given much time to lore of such a kind. Yet the Ottoman answer was as brimful of ethnological and antiquarian sympathy as the Magyar address. It is hardly to be believed that a Turk, left to himself, would by his own efforts have found out the primeval kindred between Turk and Magyar. He might remember that Magyar exiles had found a safe shelter on Ottoman territory; he might look deep enough into the politics of the present moment to see that the rule of Turk and Magyar alike is threatened by the growth of Slavonic national life. But the idea that Magyar and Turk owe each other any love or any duty, directly on the ground of primeval kindred, is certainly not likely to have presented itself to the untutored Ottoman mind. In short, it sounds, as some one said at the time, rather like the dream of a professor who has run wild with an ethnological craze, than like the serious thought of a practical man of any nation. Yet the Magyar students seem to have meant their address quite seriously. And the Turkish general, if he did not take it seriously, at least thought it wise to shape his answer as if he did. As a piece of practical politics, it sounds like Frederick Barbarossa threatening to avenge the defeat of Crassus upon Saladin, or like the French of the revolutionary wars making the Pope Pius of those days answerable for the wrongs of Vercingetorix. The thing sounds like comedy, almost like conscious comedy. But it is a kind of comedy which may become tragedy, if the idea from which it springs get so deeply rooted in men's minds as to lead to any practical consequences. As long as talk of this kind does not get beyond the world of hot-headed students, it may pass for a craze. It would be more than a craze, if it should be so widely taken up on either side that the statesmen on either side find it expedient to profess to take it up also.

To allege the real or supposed primeval kindred between

Magyars and Ottomans as a ground for political action, or at least for political sympathy, in the affairs of the present moment, is an extreme case—some may be inclined to call it a *reductio ad absurdum*—of a whole range of doctrines and sentiments which have in modern days gained a great power over men's minds. They have gained so great a power that those who may regret their influence cannot afford to despise it. To make any practical inference from the primeval kindred of Magyar and Turk is indeed pushing the doctrine of race, and of sympathies arising from race, as far as it well can be pushed. Without plunging into any very deep mysteries, without committing ourselves to any dangerous theories in the darker regions of ethnological inquiry, we may perhaps be allowed at starting to doubt whether there is any real primeval kindred between the Ottoman and the Finnish Magyar. It is for those who have gone specially deep into the antiquities of the non-Aryan races to say whether there is or is not. At all events, as far as the great facts of history go, the kindred is of the vaguest and most shadowy kind. It comes to little more than the fact that Magyars and Ottomans are alike non-Aryan invaders who have made their way into Europe within recorded times, and that both have, rightly or wrongly, been called by the name of Turks. These do seem rather slender grounds on which to build up a fabric of national sympathy between two nations, when several centuries of living practical history all pull the other way. It is hard to believe that the kindred of Turk and Magyar was thought of when a Turkish pacha ruled at Buda. Doubtless Hungarian Protestants often deemed, and not unreasonably deemed, that the contemptuous toleration of the Moslem sultan was a lighter yoke than the persecution of the Catholic emperor. But it was hardly on grounds of primeval kindred that they made the choice. The ethnological dialogue held at Constantinople does indeed sound like ethnological theory run mad. But it is the very wildness of the thing which gives it its importance. The doctrine of race, and of sympathies springing from race, must have taken very firm hold indeed of men's minds before it could be carried out in a shape which we are tempted to call so grotesque as this.

The plain fact is that the new lines of scientific and historical inquiry which have been opened in modern times have had a distinct and deep effect upon the politics of the age. The fact may be estimated in many ways, but its existence as a fact cannot be denied. Not in a merely scientific or literary point of view, but in one strictly practical, the world is not the same world as it was when men had not yet dreamed of the kindred between Sanscrit, Greek, and English, when it was looked on as something of a paradox to him that there was a distinction between Celtic and Teutonic tongues and nations. Ethnological and philological researches—I do not forget the distinction between the two, but for the present I must group them together—have opened the way for new national sympathies, new national antipathies, such as would have been unintelligible a hundred years ago. A hundred years ago a man's political likes and dislikes seldom went beyond the range which was suggested by the place of his birth or immediate descent. Such birth or descent made him a member of this or that political community, a subject of this or that prince, a citizen—perhaps a subject—of this or that commonwealth. The political community of which he was a member had its traditional alliances and traditional enmities, and by those alliances and enmities the likes and dislikes of the members of that community were guided. But those traditional alliances and enmities were seldom determined by theories about language or race. The people of this or that place might be discontented under a foreign government; but, as a rule, they were discontented only if subjection to that foreign government brought with it personal oppression or at least political degradation. Regard or disregard of some purely local privilege or local feeling went for more than the fact of a government being native or foreign. What we now call the sentiment of nationality did not go for much; what we call the sentiment of race went for nothing at all. Only a few men here and there would have understood the feelings which have led to those two great events of our own time, the political reunion of the German and Italian nations after their long political dissolution. Not a soul would have understood the feelings which have allowed Panslavism to be a great practical agent in the affairs of Europe, and which have made talk about "the Latin race," if not practical, at least possible. Least of all, would it have been possible to give any touch of political importance to what would have then seemed so wild a dream as a primeval kindred between Magyar and Ottoman.

That feelings such as these, and the practical consequences which have flowed from them, are distinctly due to scientific and historical teaching there can, I think, be no doubt. Religious sympathy and purely national sympathy are both feelings of much simpler growth, which need no deep knowledge nor any special teaching. The cry which resounded through Christendom when the Holy City was taken by the Mussulmans, the cry which resounded through Islam when the same city was taken by the Christians, the spirit which armed England to support French Huguenots and which armed Spain to support French Leaguers, all spring from motives which lie on the surface. Nor need we seek for any explanation but such as lies on the surface for the natural wish for closer union which arose among Germans or Italians who found themselves parted off by purely dynastic arrangements from men who were their countrymen in everything else. Such a feeling has to strive with the counter-feeling which springs from local jealousies and local dislikes; but it is a perfectly simple feeling, which needs no subtle research either to arouse or to understand it. So, if we draw our illustrations from the events of our own time, there is nothing but what is perfectly simple in the feeling which calls Russia, as the most powerful of Orthodox states, to the help of her Orthodox brethren everywhere, and which calls the members of the Orthodox Church everywhere to look to Russia as their protector. The feeling may have to strive against a crowd of purely political considerations, and by those purely political considerations it may be outweighed. But the feeling is in itself altogether simple and natural. So again, the people of Montenegro and of the neighboring lands in Herzegovina and by the *Bocche* of Cattaro feel themselves countrymen in every sense but the political accident which keeps them asunder. They are drawn together by a tie which everyone can understand, by the same tie which would draw together the people of three adjoining English counties, if any strange political action should part them asunder in like manner. The feeling here is that of nationality in the strictest sense, nationality in a purely local or geographical sense. It would exist all the same if Panslavism had never been heard of; it might exist though those who feel it had never heard of the Slavonic race at all. It is altogether another thing when we come to the doctrine of race, and of sympathies founded on race, in the wider sense. Here we have a feeling which professes to bind together, and which as a matter of fact has had a real effect in binding together, men whose kindred to one another is not so obvious at first sight as the kindred of Germans, Italians, or Serbs who are kept asunder by nothing but a purely artificial political boundary. It is a feeling at whose bidding the call to union goes forth to men whose dwellings are geographically far apart, to men who may have had no direct dealings with one another for years or for ages, to men whose languages, though the scholar may at once see that they are closely akin, may not be so closely akin as to be mutually intelligible for common purposes. A hundred years back the Servian might have cried for help to the Russian on the ground of common Orthodox faith; he would hardly have called for help on the ground of common Slavonic speech and origin. If he had done so, it would have been rather by way of grasping at any chance, however desperate or far-fetched, than as putting forward a serious and well understood claim which he might expect to find accepted and acted on by large masses of men. He might have received help, either out of genuine sympathy springing from community of faith or from the baser thought that he could be made use of as a convenient political tool. He would have got but little help purely on the ground of a community of blood and speech which had had no practical result for ages. When Russia in earlier days interfered between the Turk and his Christian subjects, there is no sign of any sympathy felt or possessed for Slaves as Slaves. Russia dealt with Montenegro, not, as far as one can see, out of any Slavonic brotherhood, but because an independent Orthodox State at enmity with the Turk could not fail to be a useful ally. The earlier dealings of Russia with the subject nations were far more busy among the Greeks than among the Slaves. In fact, till quite lately all the Orthodox subjects of the Turk were in most European eyes looked on as alike Greeks. The Orthodox Church has been commonly known as the Greek Church; and it has often been very hard to make people understand that the vast mass of the members of that so-called Greek Church are not Greek in any other sense. In truth we may doubt whether, till comparatively lately, the subject nations themselves were fully alive to the differences of race and speech among them. A man must in all times and places know whether he speaks the same language as another man; but he does not always go on to put his consciousness of difference into the shape of a sharply drawn formula. Still less does he always make the difference the ground of any practical course of action. The Englishman in the first days of the Norman Conquest felt the hardships of foreign rule, and he knew that those hardships were owing to foreign rule. But he had not learned to put his sense of hardship into any formula about an oppressed nationality. So, when the policy of the Turk found that the subtle intellect of the Greek could be made use of as an instrument of dominion over the other subject nations, the Bulgarian felt the hardship of the state of things in which, as it was proverbially said, his body was in bondage to the Turk and his soul in bondage to the Greek. But we may suspect that this neatly turned proverb dates only from the awakening of a distinctly national Bulgarian feeling in modern times. The Turk was felt to be an intruder and an enemy, because his rule was that of an open oppressor belonging to another creed. The Greek, on the other hand, though his spiritual dominion brought undoubted practical evils with it, was not felt to be an intruder and an enemy in the same sense. His quicker intellect and superior refinement made him a model. The Bulgarian imitated the Greek tongue and Greek manners; he was willing in other lands to be himself looked on as a Greek. It is only in quite modern times, under the direct influence of the preaching of the doctrine of race, that a hard and fast line has been drawn between Greeks and Bulgarians. That doctrine has cut two ways. It has given both nations, Greek and Bulgarian alike, a renewed national life, national strength, national hopes, such as neither of them had felt for ages. In so doing, it has done one of the best and most hopeful works of the age. But in so doing, it has created one of the most dangerous of immediate political difficulties. In calling two nations into a renewed being, it has arrayed them in enmity against each other, and that in the face of a common enemy in whose presence all lesser differences and jealousies ought to be hushed into silence.

There is then a distinct doctrine of race, and of sympathies founded on race, distinct from the feeling of community of religion, and distinct from the feeling of nationality in the narrower sense. It is not so simple or easy a feeling as either of those two. It does not in the same way lie on the surface; it is not in the same way grounded on obvious facts which are plain to every man's understanding. The doctrine of race is essentially an artificial doctrine, a learned doctrine. It is an inference from facts which the mass of mankind could never have found out for themselves; facts which, without a distinctly learned teaching, could never be brought home to them in any intelligible shape. Now what is the value of such a doctrine? Does it follow that, because it is confessedly artificial, because it springs, not from a spontaneous impulse, but from a learned teaching, it is therefore necessarily foolish, mischievous, perhaps unnatural? It may perhaps be safer to hold that like many other doctrines, many other sentiments, it is neither universally good nor universally bad, neither inherently wise nor inherently foolish. It may be safer to hold that it may, like other doctrines and sentiments, have a range within which it may work for good, while in some other range it may work for evil. It may in short be a doctrine which is neither to be rashly accepted, nor rashly cast aside, but one which may need to be guided, regulated, modified, according to time, place, and circumstance. I am not now called on so much to estimate the practical good and evil of the doctrine as to work out what the doctrine itself is, and to try to explain some difficulties about it, but I must emphatically say that nothing can be more shallow, nothing more foolish, nothing more purely sentimental, than the talk of those who think that they can simply laugh down or shriek down any doctrine or sentiment which they themselves do not understand. A belief or a feeling which has a practical effect on the conduct of great masses of men, sometimes on the conduct of whole nations, may be very false and very mischievous; but it is in every case a great and serious fact, to be looked gravely in the face. Men who sit at their ease and think that all wisdom is confined to themselves and their own clique may think themselves vastly superior to the great emotions which stir our times, as they would doubtless have thought themselves vastly superior to the emotions which stirred the first Saracens or the first Crusaders. But the emotions are there all the same, and they do their work all the same. The most highly educated man in the most highly educated society cannot sneer them out of being.

But it is time to pass to the more strictly scientific aspect of the subject. The doctrine of race, in its popular form, is the direct offspring of the study of scientific philology; and yet it is just now, in its popular form at least, somewhat under the ban of scientific philologers. There is nothing very wonderful in this. It is in fact the natural course of things which might almost have been reckoned on beforehand. When the popular mind gets hold of a truth it seldom gets hold of it with strict scientific precision. It commonly gets hold of one side of the truth; it puts forth that side of the truth only. It puts that side forth in a form which may not be in itself distorted or exaggerated, but which practically becomes distorted and exaggerated, because other sides of the same truth are not brought into their due relation with it. The popular idea thus takes a shape which is naturally offensive to men of strict precision, and which men of strict scientific precision have naturally, and from their own point of view quite rightly, risen up to rebuke. Yet it may often happen that, while the scientific statement is the only true one for scientific purposes, the popular version may also have a kind of practical truth for the somewhat rough and ready purposes of a popular version. In our present case scientific philologers are beginning to complain, with perfect truth and perfect justice from their own point of view, that the popular doctrine of race confounds race and language. They tell us, and they do right to tell us, that language is no certain test of race, that men who speak the same tongue are not therefore necessarily men of the same blood. And they tell us further, that from whatever quarter the alleged popular confusion came, it certainly did not come from any teaching of scientific philologers.

The truth of all this cannot be called in question. We have too many instances in recorded history of nations laying aside the use of one language and taking to the use of another, for anyone who cares for accuracy to set down language as any sure test of race. In fact, the studies of the philologer and those of the ethnologer strictly so called are quite distinct, and they deal with two wholly different sets of phenomena. The science of the ethnologer is strictly a physical science. He has to deal with purely physical phenomena; his business lies with the different varieties of the human body, and specially, to take that branch of his inquiries which most impresses the unlearned, with the various conformations of the human skull. His researches differ in nothing from those of the zoölogist or the paleontologist, except that he has to deal with the physical phenomena of man, while they deal with the physical phenomena of other animals. He groups the different races of men, exactly as the others group the genera and species of living or extinct mammals or reptiles. The student of ethnology as a physical science may indeed strengthen his conclusions by evidence of other kinds, evidence from arms, ornaments, pottery, modes of burial. But all these are secondary; the primary ground of classification is the physical conformation of man himself. As to language, the ethnological method, left to itself, can find out nothing whatever. The science of the ethnologer then is primarily physical; it is historical only in that secondary sense in which paleontology, and geology itself, may fairly be called historical. It arranges the varieties of mankind according to a strictly physical classification; what the language of each variety may have been, it leaves to the professors of another branch of study to find out.

The science of the philologer, on the other hand, is strictly historical. There is doubtless a secondary sense in which purely philological science may be fairly called physical, just as there is a secondary sense in which pure ethnology may be called historical. That is to say, philology has to deal with physical phenomena, so far as it has to deal with the physical aspect of the sounds of which human language is made up. Its primary business, like the primary business of any other historical science, is to deal with phenomena which do not depend on physical laws, but which do depend on the human will. The science of language is, in this respect, like the science of human institutions or of human beliefs. Its subject-matter is not, like that of pure ethnology, what man is, but, like that of any other historical science, what man does. It is plain that no man's will can have any direct influence on the shape of his skull. I say no direct influence, because it is not for me to rule how far habits, places of abode, modes of life, a thousand things which do come under the control of the human will, may indirectly affect the physical conformation of a man himself or of his descendants. Some observers have made the remark that men of civilized nations who live in a degraded social state do actually approach to the physical type of inferior races. However this may be, it is quite certain, that as no man can by taking thought add a cubit to his stature, so no man can by taking thought make his skull brachycephalic or dolichocephalic. But the language which a man speaks does depend upon his will; he can by taking thought make his speech Romance or Teutonic. No doubt he has in most cases practically no choice in the matter. The language which he speaks is practically determined for him by fashion, habit, early teaching, a crowd of things over which he has practically no control. But still the control is not physical and inevitable, as it is in the case of the shape of his skull. If we say that he cannot help speaking in a particular way; that is, that he cannot help speaking a particular language, this simply means that his circumstances are such that no other way of speaking presents itself to his mind. And in many cases, he has a real choice between two or more ways of speaking; that is, between two or more languages. Every word that a man speaks is the result of a real, though doubtless unconscious, act of his free will. We are apt to speak of gradual changes in languages, as in institutions or anything else, as if they were the result of a physical law, acting upon beings who had no choice in the matter. Yet every change of the kind is simply the aggregate of various acts of the will on the part of all concerned. Every change in speech, every introduction of a new sound or a new word, was really the result of an act of the will of some one or other. The choice may have been unconscious; circumstances may have been such as practically to give him but one choice; still he did choose; he spoke in one way, when there was no physical hinderance to his speaking in another way, when there was no physical compulsion to speak at all. The Gauls need not have changed their own language for Latin; the change was not the result of a physical necessity, but of a number of acts of the will on the part of this and that Gaul. Moral causes directed their choice, and determined that Gaul should become a Latin-speaking land. But whether the skulls of the Gauls should be long or short, whether their hair should be black or yellow, those were points over which the Gauls themselves had no direct control whatever.

The study of men's skulls then is a study which is strictly physical, a study of facts over which the will of man has no direct control. The study of men's languages is strictly an historical study, a study of facts over which the will of man has a direct control. It follows therefore from the very nature of the two studies that language cannot be an absolutely certain test of physical descent. A man cannot, under any circumstances, choose his own skull; he may, under some circumstances, choose his own language. He must keep the skull which has been given him by his parents; he cannot, by any process of taking thought, determine what kind of skull he will hand on to his own children. But he may give up the use of the language which he has learned from his parents, and he may determine what language he will teach to his children. The physical characteristics of a race are unchangeable, or are changed only by influences over which the race itself has no direct control. The language which the race speaks may be changed, either by a conscious act of the will or by that power of fashion which is in truth the aggregate of countless unconscious acts of the will. And, as the very nature of the case thus shows that language is no sure test of race, so the facts of recorded history equally prove the same truth. Both individuals and whole nations do in fact often exchange the language of their forefathers for some other language. A man settles in a foreign country. He learns the language of that country; sometimes he forgets the use of his own language. His children may perhaps speak both tongues; if they speak one tongue only, it will be the tongue of the country where they live. In a generation or two all trace of foreign origin will have passed away. Here then language is no test of race. If the great-grandchildren speak the language of their great-grandfathers, it will simply be as they may speak any other foreign language. Here are men who by speech belong to one nation, by actual descent to another. If they lose the physical characteristics of the race to which the original settler belonged, it will be due to inter-marriage, to climate, to some cause altogether independent of language. Every nation will have some adopted children of this kind, more or fewer; men who belong to it by speech, but who do not belong to it by race. And what happens in the case of individuals happens in the case of whole nations. The pages of history are crowded with cases in which nations have cast aside the tongue of their forefathers, and have taken instead the tongue of some other people. Greek in the East, Latin in the West, became the familiar speech of millions who had not a drop of Greek or Italian blood in their veins. The same has been the case in later times with Arabic, Persian, Spanish, German, English. Each of those tongues has become the familiar speech of vast regions where the mass of the people are not Arabian, Spanish, or English, otherwise than by adoption. The Briton of Cornwall has, slowly but in the end thoroughly, adopted the speech of England. In the American continent full-blooded Indians preside over commonwealths which speak the tongue of Cortes and Pizarro. In the lands to which all eyes are now turned, the Greek, who has been busily assimilating strangers ever since he first planted his colonies in Asia and Sicily, goes on busily assimilating his Albanian neighbors. And between renegades, janizaries, and mothers of all nations, the blood of many a Turk must be physically anything rather than Turkish. The inherent nature of the case, and the witness of recorded history, join together to prove that language is no certain test of race, and that the scientific philologers are doing good service to accuracy of expression and accuracy of thought by emphatically calling attention to the fact that language is no such test.

But on the other hand, it is quite possible that the truth to which our attention is just now most fittingly called may, if put forth too broadly and without certain qualifications, lead to error quite as great as the error at which it is aimed. I do not suppose that anyone ever thought that language was, necessarily and in all cases, an absolute and certain test. If anybody does think so, he has put himself altogether out of court by shutting his eyes to the most manifest facts of the case. But there can be no doubt that many people have given too much importance to language as a test of race. Though they have not wholly forgotten the facts which tell the other way, they have not brought them out with enough prominence. But I can also believe that many people have written and spoken on the subject in a way which cannot be justified from a strictly scientific point of view, but which may have been fully justified from the point of view of the writers and speakers themselves. It may often happen that a way of speaking may not be scientifically accurate, but may yet be quite near enough to the truth for the purposes of the matter in hand. It may, for some practical or even historical purpose, be really more true than the statement which is scientifically more exact. Language is no certain test of race; but if a man, struck by this wholesome warning, should run off into the belief that language and race have absolutely nothing to do with one another, he had better have gone without the warning. For in such a case the last error would be worse than the first. The natural instinct of mankind connects race and language. It does not assume that language is an infallible test of race; but it does assume that language and race have something to do with one another. It assumes, that though language is not an accurately scientific test of race, yet it is a rough and ready test which does for many practical purposes. To make something more of an exact definition, one might say, that though language is not a test of race, it is, in the absence of evidence to the contrary, a presumption of race; that though it is not a test of race, yet it is a test of something which, for many practical purposes, is the same as race. Professor Max Müller warned us long ago that we must not speak of a Celtic skull. Mr. Sayce has more lately warned us that we must not infer from community of Aryan speech that there is any kindred in blood between this or that Englishman and this or that Hindoo. And both warnings are scientifically true. Yet anyone who begins his studies on these matters with Professor Müller's famous Oxford Essay will practically come to another way of looking at things. He will fill his mind with a vivid picture of the great Aryan family, as yet one, dwelling in one place, speaking one tongue, having already taken the first steps towards settled society, recognizing the domestic relations, possessing the first rudiments of government and religion, and calling all these first elements of culture by names of which traces still abide here and there among the many nations of the common stock. He will go on to draw pictures equally vivid of the several branches of the family parting off from the primeval home. One great branch he will see going to the southeast, to become the forefathers of the vast, yet isolated colony in the Asiatic lands of Persia and India. He watches the remaining mass sending off wave after wave, to become the forefathers of the nations of historical Europe. He traces out how each branch starts with its own share of the common stock—how the language, the creed, the institutions, once common to all, grow up into different, yet kindred, shapes, among the many parted branches which grew up, each with an independent life and strength of its own. This is what our instructors set before us as the true origin of nations and their languages. And, in drawing out the picture, we cannot avoid, our teachers themselves do not avoid, the use of words which imply that the strictly family relation, the relation of community of blood, is at the root of the whole matter. We cannot help talking about the family and its branches, about parents, children, brothers, sisters, cousins. The nomenclature of natural kindred exactly fits the case; it fits it so exactly that no other nomenclature could enable us to set forth the case with any clearness. Yet we cannot be absolutely certain that there was any real community of blood in the whole story. We really know nothing of the origin of language or the origin of society. We may make a thousand ingenious guesses; but we cannot prove any of them. It may be that the group which came together, and which formed the primeval society which spoke the primeval Aryan tongue, were not brought together by community of blood, but by some other cause which threw them in one another's way. If we accept the Hebrew genealogies, they need not have had any community of blood nearer than common descent from Adam and Noah. That is, they need not have been all children of Shem, of Ham, or of Japheth; some children of Shem, some of Ham, and some of Japheth may have been led by some cause to settle together. Or if we believe in independent creations of men, or in the development of men out of mollusks, the whole of the original society need not have been descendants of the same man or the same mollusk. In short, there is no theory of the origin of man which requires us to believe that the primeval Aryans were a natural family; they may have been more like an accidental party of fellow-travelers. And if we accept them as a natural family, it does not follow that the various branches which grew into separate races and nations, speaking separate though kindred languages, were necessarily marked off by more immediate kindred. It may be that there is no nearer kindred in blood between this or that Persian, this or that Greek, this or that Teuton, than the general kindred of all Aryans. For, when this or that party marched off from the common home, it does not follow that those who marched off together were necessarily immediate brothers or cousins. The party which grew into Hindoos or Teutons may not have been made up exclusively of one set of near kinsfolk. Some of the children of the same parents or forefathers may have marched one way, while others marched another way, or stayed behind. We may, if we please, indulge our fancy by conceiving that there may actually be family distinctions older than distinctions of nation and race. It may be that the Gothic *Amali* and the Roman *Æmilii*—I throw out the idea as a mere illustration—were branches of a family which had taken a name before the division of Teuton and Italian. Some of the members of that family may have joined the band of which came the Goths, while other members joined the band of which came the Romans. There is no difference but the length of time to distinguish such a supposed case from the case of an English family, one branch of which settled in the seventeenth century at Boston in Massachusetts, while another branch stayed behind at Boston in Holland. Mr. Sayce says truly that the use of a kindred language does not prove that the Englishman and the Hindoo are really akin in race; for, as he adds, many Hindoos are men of non-Aryan race who have simply learned to speak tongues of Sanscrit origin. He might have gone on to say, with equal truth, that there is no positive certainty that there was any community in blood among the original Aryan group itself, and that if we admit such community of blood in the original Aryan group, it does not follow that there is any further special kindred between Hindoo and Hindoo or between Englishman and Englishman. The original group may not have been a family, but an artificial union. And if it was a family, those of its members who marched together east or west or north or south may have had no tie of kindred beyond the common cousinship of all.

Now the tendency of this kind of argument is to lead to something a good deal more startling than the doctrine that language is no certain test of race. Its tendency is to go on further, and to show that race is no certain test of community of blood. And this comes pretty nearly to saying that there is no such thing as race at all. For our whole conception of race starts from the idea of community of blood If the word "race" does not mean community of blood, it is hard to see what it does mean. Yet it is certain that there can be no positive proof of real community of blood, even among those groups of mankind which we instinctively speak of as families and races. It is not merely that the blood has been mingled in after-times; there is no positive proof that there was any community of blood in the beginning. No living Englishman can prove with absolute certainty that he comes in the male line of any of the Teutonic settlers in Britain in the fifth or sixth centuries. I say in the male line, because anyone who is descended from any English king can prove such descent, though he can prove it only through a long and complicated web of female successions. But we may be sure that in no other case can such a pedigree be proved by the kind of proof which lawyers would require to make out the title to an estate or a peerage. The actual forefathers of the modern Englishman may chance to have been, not true-born Angles or Saxons, but Britons, Scots, in later days Frenchmen, Flemings, men of any other nation who learned to speak English and took to themselves English names. But supposing that a man could make out such a pedigree, supposing that he could prove that he came in the male line of some follower of Hengest or Cerdic, he would be no nearer to proving original community of blood either in the particular Teutonic race or in the general Aryan family. If direct evidence is demanded, we must give up the whole doctrine of families and races, as far as we take language, manners, institutions, anything but physical conformation, as the distinguishing marks of races and families. That is to say, if we wish never to use any word of whose accuracy we cannot be perfectly certain, we must leave off speaking of races and families at all from any but the purely physical side. We must content ourselves with saying that certain groups of mankind have a common history, that they have languages, creeds, and institutions in common, but that we have no evidence whatever to show how they came to have languages, creeds, and institutions in common. We cannot say for certain what was the tie which brought the members of the original group together, any more than we can name the exact time and the exact place when and where they came together.

We may thus seem to be landed in a howling wilderness of scientific uncertainty. The result of pushing our inquiries so far may seem to be to show that we really know nothing at all. But in truth the uncertainty is no greater than the uncertainty which attends all inquiries in the historical sciences. Though a historical fact may be recorded in the most trustworthy documents, though it may have happened in our own times, though we may have seen it happen with our own eyes, yet we cannot have the same certainty about it as the mathematician has about the proposition which he proves to absolute demonstration. We cannot have even that lower degree of certainty which the geologist has with regard to the order of succession between this and that stratum. For in all historical inquiries we are dealing with facts which themselves come within the control of human will and human caprice, and the evidence for which depends on the trustworthiness of human informants, who may either purposely deceive or unwittingly mislead. A man may lie; he may err. The triangles and the rocks can neither lie nor err. I may with my own eyes see a certain man do a certain act; he may tell me himself, or some one else may tell me, that he is the same man who did some other act; but as to his statement I cannot have absolute certainty, and no one but myself can have absolute certainty as to the statement which I make as to the facts which I saw with my own eyes. Historical evidence may range through every degree, from the barest likelihood to that undoubted moral certainty on which every man acts without hesitation in practical affairs. But it cannot get beyond this last standard. If, then, we are ever to use words like race, family, or even nation, to denote groups of mankind marked off by any kind of historical, as distinguished from physical, characteristics, we must be content to use those words, as we use many other words, without being able to prove that our use of them is accurate, as mathematicians judge of accuracy. I cannot be quite sure that William the Conqueror landed at Pevensey, though I have strong reasons for believing that he did so. And I have strong reasons for believing many facts about race and language about which I am much further from being quite sure than I am about William's landing at Pevensey. In short, in all these matters, we must be satisfied to let presumption very largely take the place of actual proof; and, if we only let presumption in, most of our difficulties at once fly away. Language is no certain test of race; but it is a presumption of race. Community of race, as we commonly understand race, is no certain proof of original community of blood; but it is a presumption of original community of blood. The presumption amounts to moral proof, if only we do not insist on proving such physical community of blood as would satisfy a genealogist. It amounts to moral proof, if all that we seek is to establish a relation in which the community of blood is the leading idea, and in which where natural community of blood does not exist, its place is supplied by something which by a legal fiction is looked upon as its equivalent.

If, then, we do not ask for scientific, for what we may call physical, accuracy, but if we are satisfied with the kind of proof which is all that we can ever get in the historical sciences—if we are satisfied to speak in a way which is true for popular and practical purposes—then we may say that language has a great deal to do with race, as race is commonly understood, and that race has a great deal to do with community of blood. If we once admit the Roman doctrine of adoption, our whole course is clear. The natural family is the starting-point of everything; but we must give the natural family the power of artificially enlarging itself by admitting adoptive members. A group of mankind is thus formed, in which it does not follow that all the members have any natural community of blood, but in which community of blood is the starting-point, in which those who are connected by natural community of blood form the original body within whose circle the artificial members are admitted. A group of mankind thus formed is something quite different from a fortuitous concurrence of atoms. Three or four brothers by blood, with a fourth or fifth man whom they agree to look on as filling in everything the same place as a brother by blood, form a group which is quite unlike a union of four or five men, none of whom is bound by any tie of blood to any of the others. In the latter kind of union the notion of kindred does not come in at all. In the former kind the notion of kindred is the groundwork of everything; it determines the character of every relation and every action, even though the kindred between some members of the society and others may be owing to a legal fiction and not to natural descent. All that we know of the growth of tribes, races, nations, leads us to believe that they grew in this way. Natural kindred was the groundwork, the leading and determining idea; but, by one of those legal fictions which have such an influence on all institutions, adoption was in certain cases allowed to count as natural kindred.[2]

The usage of all language shows that community of blood was the leading idea in forming the greater and smaller groups of mankind. Words like φῦλον, γένος, *gens, natio, kin,* all point to the natural family as the origin of all society. The family in the narrower sense, the children of one father in one house, grew into a more extended family, the *gens.* Such were the Alkmaiônidai, the Julii, or the Scyldingas, the real or artificial descendants of a real or supposed forefather. The nature of the *gens* has been set forth often enough. If it is a mistake to fancy that every Julius or Cornelius was the natural kinsman of every other Julius or Cornelius, it is equally a mistake to think that the *gens Julia* or *Cornelia* was in its origin a mere artificial association, into which the idea of natural kindred did not enter. It is indeed possible that really artificial *gentes,* groups of men of whom it might chance that none were natural kinsmen, were formed in later times after the model of the original *gentes.* Still such imitation would bear witness to the original conception of the *gens.* It would be the doctrine of adoption turned the other way; instead of a father adopting a son, a number of men would agree to adopt a common father. The family then grew into the *gens;* the union of *gentes* formed the State, the political community, which in its first form was commonly a tribe. Then came the nation, formed of a union of tribes. Kindred, real or artificial, is the one basis on which all society and all government have grown up.

Now it is plain, that as soon as we admit the doctrine of artificial kindred—that is, as soon as we allow the exercise

[2] I am here applying to this particular purpose a line of thought which both myself and others have often applied to other purposes. See, above all, Sir Henry Maine's lecture "On Kinship as the Basis of Society" in the lectures on the "Early History of Institutions"; I would refer also to my own lecture on "The State" in "Comparative Politics."

of the law of adoption—physical purity of race is at an end. Adoption treats a man as if he were the son of a certain father; it cannot really make him the son of that father. If a brachycephalic father adopts a dolichocephalic son, the legal act cannot change the shape of the adopted son's skull. I will not undertake to say whether, not indeed the rite of adoption, but the influences and circumstances which would spring from it, might not, in the course of generations, affect even the skull of the man who entered a certain *gens,* tribe, or nation by artificial adoption only. If by any chance the adopted son spoke a different language from the adopted father, the rite of adoption itself would not of itself change his language. But it would bring him under influences which would make him adopt the language of his new *gens* by a conscious act of the will, and which would make his children adopt it by the same unconscious act of the will by which each child adopts the language of his parents. The adopted son, still more the son of the adopted son, became, in speech, in feelings, in worship, in everything but physical descent, one with the *gens* into which he was adopted. He became one of that *gens* for all practical, political, historical purposes. It is only the physiologist who could deny his right to his new position. The nature of the process is well expressed by a phrase of our own law. When the nation—the word itself keeps about it the remembrance of birth as the groundwork of everything—adopts a new citizen, that is, a new child of the State, he is said to be naturalized. That is, a legal process puts him in the same position, and gives him the same rights, as a man who is a citizen and a son by birth. It is assumed that the rights of citizenship come by nature—that is, by birth. The stranger is admitted to them only by a kind of artificial birth; he is naturalized by law; his children are in a generation or two naturalized in fact. There is now no practical distinction between the Englishman whose forefathers landed with William, or even between the Englishman whose forefathers sought shelter from Alva or from Louis XIV, and the Englishman whose forefathers landed with Hengest. It is for the physiologist to say whether any difference can be traced in their several skulls; for all practical purposes, historical or political, all distinction between these several classes has passed away.

We may, in short, say that the law of adoption runs through everything, and that it may be practised on every scale. What adoption is at the hands of the family, naturalization is at the hands of the State. And the same process extends itself from adopted or naturalized individuals to large classes of men, indeed to whole nations. When the process takes place on this scale, we may best call it assimilation. Thus Rome assimilated the continental nations of western Europe to that degree that, allowing for a few survivals here and there, not only Italy, but Gaul and Spain, became Roman. The people of those lands, admitted step by step to the Roman franchise, adopted the name and tongue of Romans. It must soon have been hard to distinguish the Roman colonist in Gaul or Spain from the native Gaul or Spaniard who had, as far as in him lay, put on the guise of a Roman. This process of assimilation has gone on everywhere and at all times. When two nations come in this way into close contact with one another, it depends on a crowd of circumstances which shall assimilate the other, or whether they shall remain distinct without assimilation either way. Sometimes the conquerors assimilate their subjects; sometimes they are assimilated by their subjects; sometimes conquerors and subjects remain distinct forever. When assimilation either way does take place, the direction which it takes in each particular case will depend, partly on their respective numbers, partly on their degrees of civilization. A small number of less civilized conquerors will easily be lost among a greater number of more civilized subjects, and that even though they give their name to the land and people which they conquer. The modern Frenchman represents, not the conquering Frank, but the conquered Gaul, or, as he called himself, the conquered Roman. The modern Bulgarian represents, not the Finnish conqueror, but the conquered Slave. The modern Russian represents, not the Scandinavian ruler, but the Slave who sent for the Scandinavian to rule over him. And so we might go on with endless other cases. The point is that the process of adoption, naturalization, assimilation, has gone on everywhere. No nation can boast of absolute purity of blood, though no doubt some nations come much nearer to it than others. When I speak of purity of blood, I leave out of sight the darker questions which I have already raised with regard to the groups of mankind in days before recorded history. I assume great groups like Celtic, Teutonic, Slavonic, as having what we may call a real corporate existence, however we may hold that that corporate existence began. My present point is that no existing nation is, in the physiologist's sense of purity, purely Celtic, Teutonic, Slavonic, or anything else. All races have assimilated a greater or less amount of foreign elements. Taking this standard, one which comes more nearly within the range of our actual knowledge than the possibilities of unrecorded times, we may again say that, from the purely scientific or physiological point of view, not only is language no test of race, but that, at all events among the great nations of the world, there is no such thing as purity of race at all.

But, while we admit this truth, while we even insist upon it from the strictly scientific point of view, we must be allowed to look at it with different eyes from a more practical standing point. This is the standing point, whether of history which is the politics of the past, or of politics which are the history of the present. From this point of view, we may say unhesitatingly that there are such things as races and nations, and that to the grouping of those races and nations language is the best guide. We cannot undertake to define with any philosophical precision the exact distinction between race and race, between nation and nation. Nor can we undertake to define with the like precision in what way the distinctions between race and race, between nation and nation, began. But all analogy leads us to believe that tribes, nations, races, were all formed according to the original model of the family, the family which starts from the idea of the community of blood, but which allows artificial adoption to be its legal equivalent. In all cases of adoption, naturalization, assimilation, whether of individuals or of large classes of men, the adopted person or class is adopted into an existing community. Their adoption undoubtedly influences the community into which they are adopted. It at once destroys any claim on the part of that community to purity of blood, and it influences the adopting community in many ways, physical and moral. A family, a tribe, or a nation, which has largely recruited itself by adopted members, cannot be the same as one which has never practised adoption at all, but all whose members come of the original stock. But the influence which the adopting community exercises upon its adopted members is far greater than any influence which they exercise upon it. It cannot change their blood; it cannot give them new natural forefathers; but it may do everything short of this; it may make them, in speech, in feeling, in thought, and in habit, genuine members of the community which has artificially made them its own. While there is not in any nation, in any race, any such thing as strict purity of blood, yet there is in each nation, in each race, a dominant element—or rather something more than an element—something which is the true essence of the race or nation, something which sets its standard and determines its character, something which draws to itself and assimilates to itself all other elements. It so works that all other elements are not coequal elements with itself, but mere infusions poured into an already existing body. Doubtless these infusions do in some measure influence the body which assimilates them; but the influence which they exercise is as nothing compared to the influence which they undergo. We may say that they modify the character of the body into which they are assimilated; they do not effect its personality. Thus, assuming the great groups of mankind as primary facts, the origin of which lies beyond our certain knowledge, we may speak of families and races, of the great Aryan family and of the races into which it parted, as groups which have a real, practical existence, as groups founded on the ruling primeval idea of kindred, even though in many cases the kindred may not be by natural descent, but only by law of adoption. The Celtic, Teutonic, Slavonic races of man are real living and abiding groups, the distinction between which we must accept among the primary facts of history. And they go on as living and abiding groups, even though we know that each of them has assimilated many adopted members, sometimes from other branches of the Aryan family, sometimes from races of men alien to the whole

Aryan stock. These races which, in a strictly physiological point of view, have no existence at all, have a real existence from the more practical point of view of history and politics. The Bulgarian calls to the Russian for help, and the Russian answers to his call for help, on the ground of their being alike members of the one Slavonic race. It may be that, if we could trace out the actual pedigree of this or that Bulgarian, of this or that Russian, we might either find that there was no real kindred between them, or we might find that there was a real kindred, but a kindred which must be traced up to another stock than that of the Slaves. In point of actual blood, instead of both being Slaves, it may be that one of them comes, it may be that both of them come of a stock which is not Slavonic or even Aryan. The Bulgarian may chance to be a Bulgarian in a truer sense than he thinks for; he may come of the blood of those original Finnish conquerors who gave the Bulgarian name to the Slaves among whom they were merged. And if this or that Bulgarian may chance to come of the stock of Finnish conquerors assimilated by their Slavonic subjects, this or that Russian may chance to come of the stock of Finnish subjects assimilated by their Slavonic conquerors. It may then so happen that the cry for help goes up, and is answered on a ground of kindred which in the eye of the physiologist has no existence. Or it may happen that the kindred is real in a way which neither the suppliant nor his helper thinks of. But in either case, for the practical purposes of human life, the plea is a good plea; the kindred on which it is founded is a real kindred. It is good by the law of adoption. It is good by the law the force of which we all admit whenever we count a man as an Englishman whose forefathers, two generations or twenty generations back, came to our shores as strangers. For all practical purposes, for all the purposes which guide men's actions, public or private, the Russian and the Bulgarian, kinsmen so long parted, perhaps in very truth no natural kinsmen at all, are members of the same race, bound together by the common sentiment of race. They belong to the same race, exactly as an Englishman whose forefathers came into Britain fourteen hundred years back, and an Englishman whose forefathers came only one or two hundred years back, are like members of the same nation, bound together by a tie of common nationality.

And now, having ruled that races and nations, though largely formed by the workings of an artificial law, are still real and living things, groups in which the idea of kindred is the idea around which everything has grown, how are we to define our races and our nations? How are we to mark them off one from the other? Bearing in mind the cautions and qualifications which have been already given, bearing in mind large classes of exceptions which will presently be spoken of, I say unhesitatingly that for practical purposes there is one test, and one only, and that that test is language. It is hardly needful to show that races and nations cannot be defined by the merely political arrangements which group men under various governments. For some purposes of ordinary language, for some purposes of ordinary politics, we are tempted, sometimes driven, to take this standard. And in some parts of the world, in our own western Europe for instance, nations and governments do, in a rough way, fairly answer to one another. And, in any case, political divisions are not without their influence on the formation of national divisions, while national divisions ought to have the greatest influence on political divisions. That is to say, *primâ facie* a nation and government should coincide. I say only *primâ facie;* for this is assuredly no inflexible rule; there are often good reasons why it should be otherwise; only, whenever it is otherwise, there should be some good reason forthcoming. It might even be true that in no case did a government and a nation exactly coincide, and yet it would none the less be the rule that a government and a nation should coincide. That is to say, so far as a nation and a government coincide, we accept it as the natural state of things, and ask no question as to the cause. So far as they do not coincide, we mark the case as exceptional, by asking what is the cause. And by saying that a government and a nation should coincide we mean that, as far as possible, the boundaries of governments should be so laid out as to agree with the boundaries of nations. That is, we assume the nation as something already existing, something primary, to which the secondary arrangements of government should, as far as possible, conform. How then do we define the nation, which is, if there is no especial reason to the contrary, to fix the limits of a government? Primarily, I say, as a rule, but a rule subject to exception—as a *primâ facie* standard, subject to special reasons to the contrary—we define the nation by language. We may at least apply the test negatively. It would be unsafe to rule that all speakers of the same language must have a common nationality; but we may safely say that where there is not community of language, there is no common nationality in the highest sense. It is true that without community of language there may be an artificial nationality, a nationality which may be good for all political purposes, and which may engender a common national feeling. Still this is not quite the same thing as that fuller national unity which is felt where there is community of language. In fact, mankind instinctively takes language as the badge of nationality. We so far take it as the badge, that we instinctively assume community of language in a nation as the rule, and we set down anything that departs from that rule as an exception. The first idea suggested by the word Frenchman or German or any other national name, is that he is a man who speaks French or German as his mother-tongue. We take for granted, in the absence of anything to make us think otherwise, that a Frenchman is a speaker of French, and that a speaker of French is a Frenchman. Where in any case it is otherwise, we mark that case as an exception, and we ask the special cause. Again, the rule is none the less the rule, nor the exceptions the exceptions, because the exceptions may easily outnumber the instances which conform to the rule. The rule is still the rule, because we take the instances which conform to it as a matter of course, while in every case which does not conform to it we ask for the explanation. All the larger countries of Europe provide us with exceptions; but we treat them all as exceptions. We do not ask why a native of France speaks French. But when a native of France speaks as his mother-tongue some other tongue than French, when French, or something which popularly passes for French, is spoken as his mother-tongue by someone who is not a native of France, we at once ask the reason. And the reason will be found in each case in some special historical cause which withdraws that case from the operation of the general law. A very good reason can be given why French, or something which popularly passes for French, is spoken in parts of Belgium and Switzerland, whose inhabitants are certainly not Frenchmen. But the reason has to be given, and it may fairly be asked.

In the like sort, if we turn to our own country, whenever within the bounds of Great Britain we find any tongue spoken other than English, we at once ask the reason, and we learn the special historic cause. In a part of France and a part of Great Britain we find tongues spoken which differ alike from English and from French, but which are strongly akin to one another. We find that these are the survivals of a group of tongues once common to Gaul and Britain, but which the settlement of other nations, the introduction and the growth of other tongues, have brought down to the level of survivals. So again we find islands which both speech and geographical position seem to mark as French, but which are dependencies, and loyal dependencies, of the English crown. We soon learn the cause of the phenomenon which seems so strange. Those islands are the remains of a State and a people which adopted the French tongue, but which, while it remained one, did not become a part of the French State. That people brought England by force of arms under the rule of their own sovereigns. The greater part of that people were afterward conquered by France, and gradually became French in feeling as well as in language. But a remnant clave to their connection with the land which their forefathers had conquered, and that remnant, while keeping the French tongue, never became French in feeling. This last case, that of the Norman islands, is a specially instructive one. Normandy and England were politically connected, while language and geography pointed rather to a union between Normandy and France. In the case of continental Normandy, where the geographical tie was strongest, language and geography together could carry the day, and the continental Norman became a Frenchman.

In the islands, where the geographical tie was less strong, political traditions and manifest interest carried the day against language and a weaker geographical tie. The insular Norman did not become a Frenchman. But neither did he become an Englishman. He alone remained Norman, keeping his own tongue and his own laws, but attached to the English crown by a tie at once of tradition and of advantage. Between States of the relative size of England and the Norman islands, the relation naturally becomes a relation of dependence on the part of the smaller members of the union. But it is well to remember that our forefathers never conquered the forefathers of the men of the Norman islands, but that their forefathers did once conquer ours.

These instances, and countless others, bear out the position that, while community of language is the most obvious sign of common nationality, while it is the main element, or something more than an element, in the formation of nationality, the rule is open to exceptions of all kinds, and that the influence of language is at all times liable to be overruled by other influences. But all the exceptions confirm the rule, because we specially remark those cases which contradict the rule, and we do not specially remark those cases which do not conform to it.

In the cases which we have just spoken of, the growth of the nation as marked out by language, and the growth of the exceptions to the rule of language, have both come through the gradual, unconscious working of historical causes. Union under the same government, or separation under separate governments, has been among the foremost of those historical causes. The French nation consists of the people of all that extent of continuous territory which has been brought under the rule of the French kings. But the working of the cause has been gradual and unconscious. There was no moment when anyone deliberately proposed to form a French nation by joining together all the separate duchies and countries which spoke the French tongue. Since the French nation has been formed, men have proposed to annex this or that land on the ground that its people spoke the French tongue, or perhaps only some tongue akin to the

French tongue. But the formation of the French nation itself was the work of historical causes, the work doubtless of a settled policy acting through many generations, but not the work of any conscious theory about races and languages. It is a special mark of our time, a special mark of the influence which doctrines about race and language have had on men's minds, that we have seen great nations united by processes in which theories of race and language really have had much to do with bringing about their union. If statesmen have not been themselves moved by such theories, they have at least found that it suited their purpose to make use of such theories as a means of working on the minds of others. In the reunion of the severed German and Italian nations the conscious feeling of nationality, and the acceptance of a common language as the outward badge of nationality, had no small share. Poets sang of language as the badge of national union; statesmen made it the badge, so far as political considerations did not lead them to do anything else. The revivified kingdom of Italy is very far from taking in all the speakers of the Italian tongue. Lugano, Trent, Aquileia—to take places which are clearly Italian, and not to bring in places of more doubtful nationality, like the cities of Istria and Dalmatia—form no part of the Italian political body, and Corsica is not under the same rule as the other two great neighboring islands. But the fact that all these places do not belong to the Italian body at once suggests the twofold question, why they do not belong to it, and whether they ought not to belong to it. History easily answers the first question; it may perhaps also answer the second question in a way which will say Yes as regards one place and No as regards another. Ticino must not lose her higher freedom; Trieste must remain the needful mouth for southern Germany; Dalmatia must not be cut off from the Slavonic mainland; Corsica would seem to have sacrificed national feeling to personal hero-worship. But it is certainly hard to see why Trent and Aquileia should be kept apart from the Italian body. On the other hand, the revivified Italian kingdom contains very little which is not Italian in speech. It is perhaps by a somewhat elastic view of language that the dialect of Piedmont and the dialect of Sicily are classed under one head; still, as a matter of fact, they have a single classical standard, and they are universally accepted as varieties of the same tongue. But it is only in a few Alpine valleys that languages are spoken which, whether Romance or Teutonic, are in any case not Italian. The reunion of Italy, in short, took in all that was Italian, save when some political cause hindered the rule of language from being followed. Of anything not Italian by speech so little has been taken in that the non-Italian parts of Italy, Burgundian Aosta and the Seven German Communes—if these last still keep their Teutonic language—fall under the rule that there are some things too small for laws to pay heed to.

But it must not be forgotten that all this simply means that in the lands of which we have just been speaking the process of adoption has been carried out on the largest scale. Nations, with languages as their rough practical test, have been formed; but they have been formed with very little regard to physical purity of blood. In short, throughout western Europe assimilation has been the rule. That is to say, in any of the great divisions of Western Europe, though the land may have been settled and conquered over and over again, yet the mass of the people of the land have been drawn to some one national type. Either some one among the races inhabiting the land has taught the others to put on its likeness, or else a new national type has arisen which has elements drawn from several of those races. Thus the modern Frenchman may be defined as produced by the union of blood which is mainly Celtic with a speech which is mainly Latin, and with an historical polity which is mainly Teutonic. That is, he is neither Gaul, Roman, nor Frank, but a fourth type, which has drawn important elements from all three. Within modern France this new national type has so far assimilated all others as to make everything else merely exceptional. The Fleming of one corner, the Basque of another, even the far more important Breton of a third corner, have all in this way become mere exceptions to the general type of the country. If we pass into our own islands we shall find that the same process has been at work. If we look to Great Britain only, we shall find that, though the means have not been the same, yet the end has been gained hardly less thoroughly than in France. For all real political purposes, for everything which concerns a nation in the face of other nations, Great Britain is as thoroughly united as France is. Englishmen, Scotchmen, Welshmen feel themselves one people in the general affairs of the world. A secession of Scotland or Wales is as unlikely as a secession of Normandy or Languedoc. The part of the island which is not thoroughly assimilated in langauge, that part which still speaks Welsh or Gaelic, is larger in proportion than the non-French part of modern France. But however much either the northern or the western Briton may, in a fit of antiquarian politics, declaim against the Saxon, for all practical political purposes he and the Saxon are one. The distinction between the southern and the northern English—for the men of Lothian and Fife must allow me to call them by this last name—is, speaking politically and without ethnological or linguistic precision, much as if France and Aquitaine had been two kingdoms united on equal terms, instead of Aquitaine being merged in France. When we cross into Ireland, we indeed find another state of things, and one which comes nearer to some of the phenomena which we shall come to in other parts of the world. Ireland is, most unhappily, not so firmly united to Great Britain as the different parts of Great Britain are to one another. Still even here the division arises quite as much from geographical and historical causes as from distinctions of race strictly so called. If Ireland had had no wrongs, still two great islands can never be so thoroughly united as a continuous territory can be. On the other hand, in point of language, the discontented part of the United Kingdom is much less strongly marked off than that fraction of the contented part which is not thoroughly assimilated. Irish is certainly not the language of Ireland in at all the same degree in which Welsh is the language of Wales. The Saxon has commonly to be denounced in the Saxon tongue.

In some other parts of Western Europe, as in the Spanish and Scandinavian peninsulas, the coincidence of language and nationality is stronger than it is in France, Britain, or even Italy. No one speaks Spanish except in Spain or in the colonies of Spain. And within Spain the proportion of those who do not speak Spanish, namely the Basque remnant, is smaller than the non-assimilated element in Britain and France. Here two things are to be marked: First, the modern Spanish nation has been formed, like the French, by a great process of assimilation; secondly, the actual national arrangements of the Spanish peninsula are wholly due to historical causes, we might almost say historical accidents, and those of very recent date. Spain and Portugal are separate kingdoms, and we look on their inhabitants as forming separate nations. But this is simply because a queen of Castile in the fifteenth century married a king of Aragon. Had Isabella married a king of Portugal we should now talk of Spain and Aragon as we now talk of Spain and Portugal, and we should count Portugal for part of Spain. In language, in history, in everything else, Aragon was really more distinct from Castile than Portugal was. The king of Castile was already spoken of as king of Spain, and Portugal would have merged in the Spanish kingdom at last as easily as Aragon did. In Scandinavia, on the other hand, there must have been less assimilation than anywhere else. In the present kingdoms of Norway and Sweden there must be a nearer approach to actual purity of blood than in any other part of Europe. One cannot fancy that much Finnish blood has been assimilated, and there have been no conquests or settlements later than that of the Northmen themselves.

When we pass into central Europe we shall find a somewhat different state of things. The distinctions of race seem to be more lasting. While the national unity of the German Empire is greater than that of either France or Great Britain, it has not only subjects of other languages, but actually discontented subjects, in three corners, on its French, its Danish, and its Polish frontiers. We ask the reason, and it will be at once answered that the discontent of all three is the result of recent conquest, in two cases of very recent conquest indeed. But this is one of the very points to be marked; the strong national unity of the German Empire has been largely the result of assimilation; and these three parts, where recent conquest has not yet been followed by assimilation, are chiefly important because in all three cases, the discontented territory is geographically continuous with a territory of its own speech outside the Empire. This does not prove that assimilation can never take place, but it will undoubtedly make the process longer and harder.

So again, wherever German-speaking people dwell outside the bounds of the revived German State, as well as when that revived German State contains other than German-speaking people, we ask the reason and we can find it. Political reasons forbade the immediate annexation of Austria, Tyrol, and Salzburg. Combined political and geographical reasons, and, if we look a little deeper, ethnological reasons too, forbade the annexation of Courland, Livonia, and Esthonia. Some reason or other will, it may be hoped, always be found to hinder the annexation of lands which, like Zürich and Berne, have reached a higher political level. Outlying brethren in Transsilvania or at Saratof again come under the rule "*De minimis non curat lex.*" In all these cases the rule that nationality and language should go together yields to unavoidable circumstances. But, on the other hand, where French or Danish or Slavonic or Lithuanian is spoken within the bounds of the new empire, the principle that language is the badge of nationality, that without community of language nationality is imperfect, shows itself in another shape. One main object of modern policy is to bring these exceptional districts under the general rule by spreading the German language in them. Everywhere, in short, wherever a power is supposed to be founded on nationality, the common feeling of mankind instinctively takes language as the test of nationality. We assume language as the test of a nation, without going into any minute questions as to the physical purity of blood in that nation. A continuous territory, living under the same government and speaking the same tongue, forms a nation for all practical purposes. If some of its inhabitants do not belong to the original stock of blood, they at least belong to it by adoption.

The question may now fairly be asked, What is the case in those parts of the world where people who are confessedly of different races and languages inhabit a continuous territory and live under the same government? How do we define nationality in such cases as these? The answer will be very different in different cases, according to the means by which the different national elements in such a territory have been brought together. They may form what I have already called an artificial nation, united by an act of its own free will. Or it may be simply a case where distinct nations, distinct in everything which can be looked on as forming a nation, except the possession of an independent government, are brought together, by whatever causes, under a common ruler. The former case is very distinctly an exception which proves the rule, and the latter is, though in quite another way, an exception which proves the rule also. Both cases may need somewhat more in the way of definition. We will begin with the first, the case of a nation which has been formed out of elements which differ in language, but which still have been brought together so as to form an artificial nation. In the growth of the chief nations of western Europe the principle which was consciously or unconsciously followed has been that the nation should be marked out by language, and the use of any tongue other than the dominant tongue of the nation should be at least exceptional. But there is one nation in Europe, one which has a full right to be called a nation in a political sense, which has been formed on the directly opposite principle. The Swiss Confederation has been formed by the union of certain detached fragments of the German, Italian, and Burgundian nations. It may indeed be said that the process has been in some sort a process of adoption, that the Italian and Burgundian elements have been incorporated into an already existing German body; that, as those elements were once subjects or dependents or protected allies, the case is one of clients or freedmen who have been admitted to the full privileges of the *gens*. This is undoubtedly true, and it is equally true of a large part of the German element itself. Throughout the Confederation allies and subjects have been raised to the rank of confederates. But the former position of the component elements does not matter for our purpose. As a matter of fact, the foreign dependencies have all been admitted into the Confederation on equal terms. German is undoubtedly the language of a great majority of the Confederation; but the two recognized Romance languages are each the speech, not of a mere fragment or survival, like Welsh in Britain or Breton in France, but of a large minority forming a visible element in the general body. The three languages are all of them alike recognized as national languages, though, as if to keep up the universal rule that there should be some exceptions to all rules, a fourth language still lives on within the bounds of the Confederation, which is not admitted to the rights of the other three, but is left in the state of a fragment or a survival.[3] Is such an artificial body as this to be called a nation? It is plainly not a nation by blood or by speech. It can hardly be called a nation by adoption. For, if we chose to say that the three elements have all agreed to adopt one another as brethren, yet it has been adoption without assimilation. Yet surely the Swiss Confederation is a nation. It is not a mere power, in which various nations are brought together, whether willingly, or unwillingly, under a common ruler, but without any further tie of union. For all political purposes the Swiss Confederation is a nation, a nation capable of as strong and true national feeling as any other nation. Yet it is a nation purely artificial, one in no way defined by blood or speech. It thus proves the rule in two ways. We at once feel that this artificially formed nation, which has no common language, but each of whose elements speaks a language common to itself with some other nation, is something different from those nations which are defined by a universal or at least a predominant language. We mark it as an exception, as something different from other cases. And when we see how nearly this artificial nation comes, in every point but that of language, to the likeness of those nations which are defined by language, we see that it is a nation defined by language which sets the standard, and after the model of

[3] While the Swiss Confederation recognizes German, French, and Italian as all alike national languages, the independent Romance language, which is still used in some parts of the Canton of Graubünden, that which is known specially as *Romansch,* is not recognized. It is left in the same position in which Welsh and Gaelic are left in Great Britain, in which Basque, Breton, Provençal, Walloon, and Flemish are left within the borders of that French kingdom which has grown so as to take them all in.

which the artificial nation forms itself. The case of the Swiss Confederation and its claim to rank as a nation would be like the case of those *gentes,* if any such there were, which did not spring even from the expansion of an original family, but which were artificially formed in imitation of those which did, and which, instead of a real or traditional forefather, chose for themselves an adopted one.

In the Swiss Confederation, then, we have a case of a nation formed by an artificial process, but which still is undoubtedly a nation in the face of other nations. We now come to the other class, in which nationality and language keep the connection which they have elsewhere, but in which nations do not even in the roughest way answer to governments. We have only to go into the Eastern lands of Europe to find a state of things in which the notion of nationality, as marked out by language and national feeling, has altogether parted company from the notion of political government. It must be remembered that this state of things is not confined to the nations which are or have lately been under the yoke of the Turk. It extends also to the nations or fragments of nations which make up the Austro-Hungarian monarchy. In all the lands held by these two powers we come across phenomena of geography, race, and language, which stand out in marked contrast with anything to which we are used in western Europe. We may perhaps better understand what these phenomena are if we suppose a state of things which sounds absurd in the West, but which has its exact parallel in many parts of the East. Let us suppose that in a journey through England we came successively to districts, towns, or villages, where we found, one after another, first, Britons speaking Welsh; then Romans speaking Latin; then Saxons or Angles, speaking an older form of our own tongue; then Scandinavians speaking Danish; then Normans speaking Old-French; lastly, perhaps a settlement of Flemings, Huguenots, or Palatines, still remaining a distinct people and speaking their own tongue. Or let us suppose a journey through northern France, in which we found at different stages, the original Gaul, the Roman, the Frank, the Saxon of Bayeux, the Dane of Coutances, each remaining a distinct people, each of them keeping the tongue which they first brought with them into the land. Let us suppose further that, in many of these cases, a religious distinction was added to a national distinction. Let us conceive one village Roman Catholic, another Anglican, others Nonconformist of various types, even if we do not call up any remnants of the worshippers of Jupiter or of Woden. All this seems absurd in any Western country, and absurd enough it is. But the absurdity of the West is the living reality of the East. There we may still find all the chief races which have ever occupied the country, still remaining distinct, still keeping separate tongues, and those for the most part, their own original tongues. Within the present and late European dominions of the Turk, the original races, those whom we find there at the first beginnings of history, are all there still, and two of them keep their original tongues. They form three distinct nations. First of all there are the Greeks. We have not here to deal with them as the representatives of that branch of the Roman Empire which adopted their speech, but simply as one of the original elements in the population of the Eastern peninsula. Known almost down to our own day by their historical name of Romans, they have now fallen back on the name of Hellênes. And to that name they have a perfectly good claim. If the modern Greeks are not all true Hellênes, they are an aggregate of adopted Hellênes gathered round and assimilated to a true Hellenic kernel. Here we see the oldest recorded inhabitants of a large part of the land abiding, and abiding in a very different case from the remnants of the Celt and the Iberian in Western Europe. The Greeks are no survival of a nation; they are a true and living nation—a nation whose importance is quite out of proportion to its extent in mere numbers. They still abide, the predominant race in their own ancient and again independent land, the predominant race in those provinces of the continental Turkish dominion which formed part of their ancient land, the predominant race through all the shores and islands of the Ægæan and of part of the Euxine also. In near neighborhood to the Greeks still live another race of equal antiquity, the Skipetar or Albanians. These, as I believe is no longer doubted, represent the ancient Illyrians. The exact degree of their ethnical kindred with the Greeks is a scientific question which need not here be considered; but the facts that they are more largely intermingled with the Greeks than any of the other neighboring nations, that they show a special power of identifying themselves with the Greeks—a power, so to speak, of becoming Greeks and making part of the artificial Greek nation, are matters of practical history. It must never be forgotten that, among the worthies of the Greek War of Independence, some of the noblest were not of Hellenic but Albanian blood. The Orthodox Albanian easily turns into a Greek; and the Mahometan Albanian is something which is broadly distinguished from a Turk. He has, as he well may have, a strong national feeling, and that national feeling has sometimes got the better of religious divisions. If Albania is among the most backward parts of the peninsula, still it is, by all accounts, the part where there is most hope of men of different religions joining together against the common enemy.

Here then are two ancient races, the Greeks and another race, not indeed so advanced, so important, or so widely spread, but a race which equally keeps a real national being. There is also a third ancient race which survives as a distinct people, though they have for ages adopted a foreign language. These are the Vlachs or Roumans, the surviving representatives of the great race, call it Thracian or any other, which at the beginning of history held the great inland mass of the Eastern peninsula, with the Illyrians to the west of them and the Greeks to the south. Every one knows that in the modern principality of Roumania and in the adjoining parts of the Austro-Hungarian monarchy, there is to be seen that phenomenon so unique in the East, a people who not only, as the Greeks did till lately, still keep the Roman name, but who speak neither Greek nor Turkish, neither Slave nor Skipetar, but a dialect of Latin, a tongue akin, not to the tongues of any of their neighbors, but to the tongues of Gaul, Italy, and Spain. And any one who has given any real attention to this matter knows that the same race is to be found, scattered here and there, if in some parts only as wandering shepherds, in the Slavonic, Albanian, and Greek lands south of the Danube. The assumption has commonly been that this outlying Romance people owe their Romance character to the Roman colonization of Dacia under Trajan. In this view, the modern Roumans would be the descendants of Trajan's colonists and of Dacians who had learned of them to adopt the speech and manners of Rome. But when we remember that Dacia was the first Roman province to be given up—that the modern Roumania was for ages the highway of every barbarian tribe on its way from the East to the West—that the land has been conquered and settled and forsaken over and over again—it would be passing strange if this should be the one land, and its people the one race, to keep the Latin tongue when it has been forgotten in all the neighboring countries. In fact, this idea has been completely dispersed by modern research. The establishment of the Roumans in Dacia is of comparatively recent date, beginning only in the thirteenth century. The Roumans of Wallachia, Moldavia, and Transsilvania, are isolated from the scattered Rouman remnant on Pindos and elsewhere. They represent that part of the inhabitants of the peninsula which became Latin, while the Greeks remained Greek, and the Illyrians remained barbarian. Their lands, Mœsia, Thrace specially so called, and Dacia, were added to the empire at various times from Augustus to Trajan. That they should gradually adopt the Latin language is in no sort wonderful. Their position with regard to Rome was exactly the same as that of Gaul and Spain. Where Greek civilization had been firmly established, Latin could nowhere displace it. Where Greek civilization was unknown, Latin overcame the barbarian tongue. It would naturally do so in this part of the East exactly as it did in the West.[4]

Here then we have in the southeastern peninsula three nations which have all lived on to all appearances from the very beginnings of European history, three distinct nations, speaking three distinct languages. We have nothing answering to this in the West. It needs no proof that the speakers of Celtic and Basque in Gaul and in Spain do not hold the same position in western Europe which the Greeks, Albanians, and Roumans do in eastern Europe. In the

[4] On Rouman history I have followed Roesler's "Romanische Studien" and Jirecek's "Geschichte der Bulgaren."

East the most ancient inhabitants of the land are still there, not as scraps or survivals, not as fragments of nations lingering on in corners, but as nations in the strictest sense, nations whose national being forms an element in every modern and political question. They all have their memories, their grievances, and their hopes; and their memories, their grievances, and their hopes are all of a practical and political kind. Highlanders, Welshmen, Bretons, French Basques, whatever we say of the Spanish brethren, have doubtless memories, but they have hardly political grievances or hopes. Ireland may have political grievances; it certainly has political hopes; but they are not exactly of the same kind as the grievances or hopes of the Greek, the Albanian, and the Rouman. Let Home Rule succeed to the extent of setting up an independent king and parliament of Ireland, yet the language and civilization of that king and parliament would still be English. Ireland would form an English State, politically hostile, it may be, to Great Britain, but still an English State. No Greek, Albanian or Rouman State would be in the same way either Turkish or Austrian.

On these primitive and abiding races came, as on other parts of Europe, the Roman conquest. That conquest planted Latin colonies on the Dalmatian coast, where the Latin tongue still remains in its Italian variety as the speech of literature and city life; it Romanized one great part of the earlier inhabitants: it had the great political effect of all, that of planting the Roman power in a Greek city, and thereby creating a State, and in the end a nation, which was Roman on one side, and Greek on the other. Then came the wandering of the nations, on which, as regards men of our own race, we need not dwell. The Goths marched at will through the Eastern Empire; but no Teutonic settlement was ever made within its bounds, no lasting Teutonic settlement was ever made even on its border. The part of the Teuton in the West was played, far less perfectly indeed, by the Slave in the East. He is there what the Teuton is here, the great representative of what we may call the modern European races, those whose part in history began after the establishment of the Rouman power. The differences between the position of the two races are chiefly these. The

Slave in the East has pre-Roman races standing alongside of him in a way in which the Teuton has not in the West. On the Greeks and Albanians he has had but little influence; on the Rouman and his language his influence has been far greater, but hardly so great as the influence of the Teuton on the Romance nations and languages of western Europe. The Slave too stands alongside of races which have come in since his own coming, in a way in which the Teuton in the West is still further from doing. That is to say, besides Greeks, Albanians, and Roumans, he stands alongside of Bulgarians, Magyars, and Turks, who have nothing to answer to them in the West. The Slave, in the time of his coming, in the nature of his settlement, answers roughly to the Teuton; his position is what that of the Teuton would be if western Europe had been brought under the power of an alien race at some time later than his own settlement. The Slaves undoubtedly form the greatest element in the population of the Eastern peninsula, and they once reached more widely still. Taking the Slavonic name in its widest meaning, they occupy all the lands from the Danube and its great tributaries southward to the strictly Greek border. The exceptions are where earlier races remain, Greek or Italian on the coast-line, Albanian in the mountains. The Slaves hold the heart of the peninsula, and they hold more than the peninsula itself. The Slave lives equally on both sides of what is or was the frontier of the Austrian and Ottoman empires; indeed, but for another set of causes which have affected eastern Europe, the Slave might have reached uninterruptedly from the Baltic to the Ægæan.

This last set of causes are those which specially distinguish the histories of eastern and of western Europe; a set of causes which, though exactly twelve hundred years old,[5] are still fresh and living, and which are the special causes which have aggravated the special difficulties of the last five hundred years. In Western Europe, though we have had plenty of political conquests, we have had no national migrations since the days of the Teutonic settlements—at least, if we may extend these last so as to take in the Scandinavian set-

[5] It should be remembered that, as the year 1879 saw the beginning of the liberated Bulgarian State, the year 679 saw the beginning of the first Bulgarian kingdom south of the Danube.

tlements in Britain and Gaul. The Teuton has pressed to the East at the expense of the Slave and the Old-Prussian: the borders between the Romance and the Teutonic nations in the West have fluctuated; but no third set of nations has come in, strange alike to the Roman and the Teuton and to the whole Aryan family. As the Huns of Attila showed themselves in western Europe as passing ravagers, so did the Magyars at a later day; so did the Ottoman Turks in a day later still, when they besieged Vienna and laid waste the Venetian mainland. But all these Turanian invaders appeared in western Europe simply as passing invaders; in eastern Europe their part has been widely different. Besides the temporary dominion of Avars, Patzinaks, Chazars, Cumans, and a crowd of others, three bodies of more abiding settlers, the Bulgarians, the Magyars, and the Mongol conquerors of Russia, have come in by one path; a fourth, the Ottoman Turks, have come in by another path. Among all these invasions we have one case of thorough assimilation, and only one. The original Finnish Bulgarians have, like Western conquerors, been lost among Slavonic subjects and neighbors. The geographical function of the Magyar has been to keep the two great groups of Slavonic nations apart. To his coming, more than to any other cause, we may attribute the great historical gap which separates the Slave of the Baltic from his southern kinsfolk. The work of the Ottoman Turk we all know. These latter settlers remain alongside of the Slave, just as the Slave remains alongside of the earlier settlers. The Slavonized Bulgarians are the only instance of assimilation such as we are used to in the West. All the other races, old and new, from the Albanian to the Ottoman, are still there, each keeping its national being and its national speech. And in one part of the ancient Dacia we must add quite a distinct element, the element of Teutonic occupation in a form unlike any in which we see it in the West, in the shape of the Saxons of Transsilvania.

We have thus worked out our point in detail. While in each Western country some one of the various races which have settled in it has, speaking roughly, assimilated the others, in the lands which are left under the rule of the Turk, or which have been lately delivered from his rule, all the races that have ever settled in the country still abide side by side. So when we pass into the lands which form the Austro-Hungarian monarchy, we find that that composite dominion is just as much opposed as the dominion of the Turk is to those ideas of nationality towards which Western Europe has been long feeling its way. We have seen by the example of Switzerland that it is possible to make an artificial nation out of fragments which have split off from three several nations. But the Austro-Hungarian monarchy is not a nation, not even an artificial nation of this kind. Its elements are not bound together in the same way as the three elements of the Swiss Confederation. It does indeed contain one whole nation in the form of the Magyars; we might say that it contains two, if we reckon the Czechs for a distinct nation. Of its other elements, we may for the moment set aside those parts of Germany which are so strangely united with the crowns of Hungary and Dalmatia. In those parts of the monarchy which come within the more strictly Eastern lands—the *Roman* and the *Rouman*—we may so distinguish the Romance-speaking inhabitants of Dalmatia and the Romance-speaking inhabitants of Transsilvania. The Slave of the north and of the south, the Magyar conqueror, the Saxon immigrant, all abide as distinct races. That the Ottoman is not to be added to our list in Hungary, while he is to be added in lands farther south, is simply because he has been driven out of Hungary, while he is allowed to abide in lands farther south. No point is more important to insist on now than the fact that the Ottoman once held the greater part of Hungary by exactly the same right, the right of the strongest, as that by which he still holds Macedonia and Epeiros. It is simply the result of a century of warfare, from Sobieski to Joseph II, which fixed the boundary which only yesterday seemed eternal to diplomatists, but which now seems to have vanished. The boundary has advanced and gone back over and over again. As Buda once was Turkish, Belgrade has more than once been Austrian. The whole of the southeastern lands, Austrian, Turkish, and independent, from the Carpathian Mountains southward, present the same characteristic of permanence and distinctness among the several races which occupy them. The several races may lie, here in large continuous masses, there in small detached settlements; but there they all are in their distinctness. There is among them plenty of living and active national feeling; but while in the West political arrangements for the most part follow the great lines of national feeling, in the East the only way in which national feeling can show itself is by protesting, whether in arms or otherwise, against existing political arrangements. Save the Magyars alone, the ruling race in the Hungarian kingdom, there is no case in those lands in which the whole continuous territory inhabited by speakers of the same tongue is placed under a separate national government of its own. And, even in this case, the identity between nation and government is imperfect in two ways. It is imperfect, because, after all, though Hungary has a separate national government in internal matters, yet it is not the Hungarian kingdom, but the Austro-Hungarian monarchy of which it forms a part, which counts as a power among the other powers of Europe. And the national character of the Hungarian government is equally imperfect from the other side. It is national as regards the Magyar; it is not national as regards the Slave, the Saxon, and the Rouman. Since the liberation of part of Bulgaria, no whole European nation is under the rule of the Turk. No one nation of the southeast peninsula forms a single national government. One fragment of a nation is free under a national government, another fragment is ruled by civilized strangers, a third is trampled down by barbarians. The existing States of Greece, Roumania, and Servia are far from taking in the whole of the Greek, Rouman, and Servian nations. In all these lands, Austrian, Turkish, and independent, there is no difficulty in marking off the several nations; only in no case do the nations answer to any existing political power.

In all these cases, where nationality and government are altogether divorced, language becomes yet more distinctly the test of nationality than it is in Western lands where nationality and government do to some extent coincide. And when nationality and language do not coincide in the East, it is owing to another cause, of which also we know nothing in the West. In many cases religion takes the place of nationality; or rather the ideas of religion and nationality can hardly be distinguished. In the West a man's nationality is in no way affected by the religion which he professes, or even by his change from one religion to another. In the East it is otherwise. The Christian renegade who embraces Islam becomes for most practical purposes a Turk. Even if, as in Crete and Bosnia, he keeps his Greek or Slavonic language, he remains Greek or Slave only in a secondary sense. For the first principle of the Mahometan religion, the lordship of the true believer over the infidel, cuts off the possibility of any true national fellowship between the true believer and the infidel. Even the Greek or Armenian who embraces the Latin creed goes far toward parting with his nationality as well as with his religion. For the adoption of the Latin creed implies what is in some sort the adoption of a new allegiance, the accepting of the authority of the Roman bishop. In the Armenian indeed we are come very near to the phenomena of the further East, where names like Parsee and Hindoo, names in themselves as strictly ethnical as Englishman or Frenchman, have come to express distinctions in which religion and nationality are absolutely the same thing. Of this whole class of phenomena the Jew is of course the crowning example. But we speak of these matters here only as bringing in an element in the definition of nationality to which we are unused in the West. But it quite comes within our present subject to give one definition from the southeastern lands. What is the Greek? Clearly he who is at once a Greek in speech and Orthodox in faith. The Hellenic Mussulmans in Crete, even the Hellenic Latins in some of the other islands, are at the most imperfect members of the Hellenic body. The utmost that can be said is that they keep the power of again entering that body, either by their own return to the national faith, or by such a change in the state of things as shall make difference in religion no longer inconsistent with true national fellowship.

Thus, wherever we go, we find language to be the rough practical test of nationality. The exceptions are many; they may perhaps outnumber the instances which conform to the rule. Still they are exceptions. Community of language does not imply community of blood; it might be added that diversity of language does not imply diversity of blood. But community of language is, in the absence of any evidence to the contrary, a presumption of the community of blood, and it is proof of something which for practical purposes is the same as community of blood. To talk of "the Latin race" is in strictness absurd. We know that the so-called race is simply made up of those nations which adopted the Latin language. The Celtic, Teutonic, and Slavonic races may conceivably have been formed by a like artificial process. But the presumption is the other way; and if such a process ever took place, it took place long before history began. The Celtic, Teutonic, and Slavonic races come before us as groups of mankind marked out by the test of language. Within those races separate nations are again marked out by a stricter application of the test of language. Within the race we may have languages which are clearly akin to each other, but which need not be mutually intelligible. Within the nation we have only dialects which are mutually intelligible, or which, at all events, gather round some one central dialect which is intelligible to all. We take this standard of races and nations, fully aware that it will not stand a physiological test, but holding that for all practical purposes adoption must pass as equivalent to natural descent. And, among the practical purposes which are affected by the facts of race and nationality, we must, as long as a man is what he is, as long as he has not been created afresh according to some new scientific pattern, not shrink from reckoning those generous emotions which, in the present state of European feeling, are beginning to bind together the greater as well as the lesser groups of mankind. The sympathies of men are beginning to reach wider than could have been dreamed of a century ago. The feeling which was once confined to the mere household extended itself to the tribe or city. From the tribe or city it extended itself to the nation; from the nation it is beginning to extend itself to the whole race. In some cases it can extend itself to the whole race far more easily than in others. In some cases historical causes have made nations of the same race bitter enemies, while they have made nations of different races friendly allies. The same thing happened in earlier days between tribes and cities of the same nation. But, when hindrances of this kind do not exist, the feeling of race, as something beyond the narrower feeling of nationality, is beginning to be a powerful agent in the feelings and actions of men and of nations. A long series of mutual wrongs, conquest, and oppression on one side, avenged by conquest and oppression on the other side, have made the Slave of Poland and the Slave of Russia the bitterest of enemies. No such hindrance exists to stop the flow of natural and generous feeling between the Slave of Russia and the Slave of the southeastern lands. Those whose statesmanship consists in some hand-to-mouth shift for the moment, whose wisdom consists in refusing to look either back to the past or onward to the future, cannot understand this great fact of our times; and what they cannot understand they mock at. But the fact exists, and does its work in spite of them. And it does its work none the less because in some cases the feeling of sympathy is awakened by a claim of kindred, where, in the sense of the physiologist or the genealogist, there is no kindred at all. The practical view, historical or political, will accept as members of this or that race or nation many members whom the physiologist would shut out, whom the English lawyer would shut out, but whom the Roman lawyer would gladly welcome to every privilege of the stock on which they were grafted. The line of the Scipios, of the Cæsars, and of the Antonines was continued by adoption; and for all practical purposes the nations of the earth have agreed to follow the examples set them by their masters.

TRUTH OF INTERCOURSE
SAMUEL PEPYS

BY

ROBERT LOUIS STEVENSON

INTRODUCTORY NOTE

Robert Louis Balfour Stevenson *(1850-94), novelist, essayist, and poet, was descended from a famous family of lighthouse builders. He was born at Edinburgh, Scotland, and was intended for the ancestral profession of engineer. Abandoning this, he tried law with no better success, and finally devoted himself to his destined vocation of letters.*

Stevenson began his career with the writing of essays, then issued two charming volumes of humorous and contemplative travel, "An Inland Voyage" and "Travels with a Donkey in the Cevennes"; then collected in his "New Arabian Nights" a number of fanciful short stories he had been publishing in a magazine. In 1883 he first caught the attention of the larger public with "Treasure Island," one of the best, and probably the best written, boys' story in the language. His most sensational success was "The Strange Case of Dr. Jekyll and Mr. Hyde"; but a much higher literary quality appears in such novels as "The Master of Ballantrae," "Kidnapped," and "Catriona," in which he to some extent follows the tradition of Scott, with far greater finish of style, but without Scott's fine spontaneity and unconsciousness. He published also three small volumes of verse, some of it of great charm and delicacy.

Stevenson was essentially an artist in words. The modern desire for subtlety of cadence and for the rendering of fine shades of expression is seen in a high degree in all he wrote, and his work has the merits and defects that accompany this extreme preoccupation with style. But he had also great virtues of matter. He was a superb story-teller, an acute and sensitive critic, a genial and whole-hearted lover of life. In the essay on "Truth of Intercourse" will be found an example of his gracious and tactful moralizing; in "Samuel Pepys," a penetrating interpretation of one of the most amazing pieces of self-revelation in the annals of literature.

TRUTH OF INTERCOURSE

AMONG sayings that have a currency in spite of being wholly false upon the face of them for the sake of a half-truth upon another subject which is accidentally combined with error, one of the grossest and broadest conveys the monstrous proposition that it is easy to tell the truth and hard to tell a lie. I wish heartily it were. But the truth is one; it has first to be discovered, then justly and exactly uttered. Even with instruments specially contrived for such a purpose—with a foot rule, a level, or a theodolite—it is not easy to be exact; it is easier, alas! to be inexact. From those who mark the divisions on a scale to those who measure the boundaries of empires or the distance of the heavenly stars, it is by careful method and minute, unwearying attention that men rise even to material exactness or to sure knowledge even of external and constant things. But it is easier to draw the outline of a mountain than the changing appearance of a face; and truth in human relations is of this more intangible and dubious order: hard to seize, harder to communicate. Veracity to facts in a loose, colloquial sense—not to say that I have been in Malabar when as a matter of fact I was never out of England, not to say that I have read Cervantes in the original when as a matter of fact I know not one syllable of Spanish—this, indeed, is easy and to the same degree unimportant in itself. Lies of this sort, according to circumstances, may or may not be important; in a certain sense even they may or may not be false. The habitual liar may be a very honest fellow, and live truly with his wife and friends; while another man who never told a formal falsehood in his life may yet be himself one lie—heart and face, from top to bottom. This is the kind of lie which poisons intimacy. And, *vice versâ,* veracity to sentiment, truth in a relation, truth to your own heart and your friends, never to feign or falsify emotion—that is the truth which makes love possible and mankind happy.

L'art de bien dire is but a drawing-room accomplishment unless it be pressed into the service of the truth. The difficulty of literature is not to write, but to write what you mean; not to affect your reader, but to affect him precisely as you wish. This is commonly understood in the case of books or set orations; even in making your will, or writing an explicit letter, some difficulty is admitted by the world. But one thing you can never make Philistine natures understand; one thing, which yet lies on the surface, remains as unseizable to their wits as a high flight of metaphysics—namely, that the business of life is mainly carried on by means of this difficult art of literature, and according to a man's proficiency in that art shall be the freedom and the fulness of his intercourse with other men. Anybody, it is supposed, can say what he means; and, in spite of their notorious experience to the contrary, people so continue to suppose. Now, I simply open the last book I have been reading—Mr. Leland's captivating *English Gipsies.* "It is said," I find on p. 7, "that those who can converse with Irish peasants in their own native tongue form far higher opinions of their appreciation of the beautiful, and of *the elements of humour and pathos in their hearts,* than to those who know their thoughts only through the medium of English. I know from my own observations that this is quite the case with the Indians of North America, and it is unquestionably so with the gipsy." In short, where a man has not a full possession of the language, the most important, because the most amiable, qualities of his nature have to lie buried and fallow; for the pleasure of comradeship, and the intellectual part of love, rest upon these very "elements of humour and pathos." Here is a man opulent in both, and for lack of a medium he can put none of it out to interest in the market of affection! But what is thus made plain to our apprehensions in the case of a foreign language is partially true even with the tongue we learned in childhood. Indeed, we all speak different dialects; one shall be copious and exact, another loose and meagre; but the speech of the ideal talker shall correspond and fit upon the truth of fact—not clumsily, obscuring lineaments, like a mantle, but cleanly adhering, like an athlete's skin. And what is the result? That the one can open himself more clearly to his friends, and can enjoy more of what makes life truly valuable—intimacy with those he loves. An orator makes a false step; he employs some trivial, some absurd, some vulgar phrase; in the turn of a sentence he insults by a side wind, those whom he is labouring to charm; in speaking to one sentiment he unconsciously ruffles another in parenthesis; and you are not surprised, for you know his task to be delicate and filled with perils. "O frivolous mind of man, light ignorance!" As if yourself, when you seek to explain some misunderstanding or excuse some apparent fault, speaking swiftly and addressing a mind still recently incensed, were not harnessing for a more perilous adventure; as if yourself required less tact and eloquence; as if an angry friend or a suspicious lover were not more easy to offend than a meeting of indifferent politicians! Nay, and the orator treads in a beaten round; the matters he discusses have been discussed a thousand times before; language is ready-shaped to his purpose; he speaks out of a cut and dry vocabulary. But you—may it not be that your defence reposes on some subtlety of feeling, not so much as touched upon in Shakespeare, to express which, like a pioneer, you must venture forth into zones of thought still unsurveyed, and become yourself a literary innovator? For even in love there are unlovely humours; ambiguous acts, unpardonable words, may yet have sprung from a kind sentiment. If the injured one could read your heart, you may be sure that he would understand and pardon; but, alas! the heart cannot be shown—it has to be demonstrated in words. Do you think it is a hard thing to write poetry? Why, that is to write poetry, and of a high, if not the highest, order.

I should even more admire "the lifelong and heroic literary labours" of my fellow-men, patiently clearing up in words their loves and their contentions, and speaking their autobiography daily to their wives, were it not for a circumstance which lessens their difficulty and my admiration by equal parts. For life, though largely, is not entirely carried on by literature. We are subject to physical passions and contortions; the voice breaks and changes, and speaks by unconscious and winning inflections; we have legible countenances, like an open book; things that cannot be said look eloquently through the eye; and the soul, not locked into the body as a dungeon, dwells ever on the threshold with appealing signals. Groans and tears, looks and gestures, a flush or a paleness, are often the most clear reporters of the heart, and speak more directly to the hearts of others. The message flies by these interpreters in the least space of time, and the misunderstanding is averted in the moment of its birth. To explain in words takes time and a just and patient hearing; and in the critical epochs of a close relation, patience and justice are not qualities on which we can rely. But the look or the gesture explains things in a breath; they tell their message without ambiguity; unlike speech, they cannot stumble, by the way, on a reproach or an allusion that should steel your friend against the truth; and then they have a higher authority, for they are the direct expression of the heart, not yet transmitted through the unfaithful and sophisticating brain. Not long ago I wrote a letter to a friend which came near involving us in quarrel; but we met, and in personal talk I repeated the worst of what I had written, and added worse to that; and with the commentary of the body it seemed not unfriendly either to hear or say. Indeed, letters are in vain for the purposes of intimacy; an absence is a dead break in the relation; yet two who know each other fully and are bent on perpetuity in love, may so preserve the attitude of their affections that they may meet on the same terms as they had parted.

Pitiful is the case of the blind, who cannot read the face; pitiful that of the deaf, who cannot follow the changes of the voice. And there are others also to be pitied; for there are some of an inert, uneloquent nature, who have been denied all the symbols of communication, who have neither a lively play of facial expression, nor speaking gestures, nor a responsive voice, nor yet the gift of frank, explanatory speech: people truly made of clay, people tied for life into a bag which no one can undo. They are poorer than the gipsy, for their heart can speak no language under heaven. Such people we must learn slowly by the tenor of their acts, or through yea and nay communications; or we take them on trust on the strength of a general air, and now and again, when we see the spirit breaking through in a flash, correct or change our estimate. But these will be uphill intimacies, without charm or freedom, to the end; and freedom is the chief ingredient in confidence. Some minds, romantically dull, despise physical endowments. That is a doctrine for a misanthrope; to those who like their fellow-creatures it must always be meaningless; and, for my part, I can see few things more desirable, after the possession of such radical qualities as honour and humour and pathos, than to have a lively and not a stolid countenance; to have looks to correspond with every feeling; to be elegant and delightful in person, so that we shall please even in the intervals of active pleasing, and may never discredit speech with uncouth manners or become unconsciously our own burlesques. But of all unfortunates there is one creature (for I will not call him man) conspicuous in misfortune. This is he who has forfeited his birthright of expression, who has cultivated artful intonations, who has taught his face tricks, like a pet monkey, and on every side perverted or cut off his means of communication with his fellow-men. The body is a house of many windows: there we all sit, showing ourselves and crying on the passers-by to come and love us. But this fellow has filled his windows with opaque glass, elegantly coloured. His house may be admired for its design, the crowd may pause before the stained windows, but meanwhile the poor proprietor must lie languishing within, uncomforted, unchangeably alone.

Truth of intercourse is something more difficult than to refrain from open lies. It is possible to avoid falsehood and yet not tell the truth. It is not enough to answer formal questions. To reach the truth by yea and nay communications implies a questioner with a share of inspiration such as is often found in mutual love. *Yea* and *nay* mean nothing; the meaning must have been related in the question. Many words are often necessary to convey a very simple statement; for in this sort of exercise we never hit the gold; the most that we can hope is by many arrows, more or less far off on different sides, to indicate, in the course of time, for what target we are aiming, and after an hour's talk, back and forward, to convey the purport of a single principle or a single thought. And yet while the curt, pithy speaker misses the point entirely, a wordy, prolegomenous babbler will often add three new offences in the process of excusing one. It is really a most delicate affair. The world was made before the English language, and seemingly upon a different design. Suppose we held our converse, not in words, but in music; those who have a bad ear would find themselves cut off from all near commerce, and no better than foreigners in this big world. But we do not consider how many have "a bad ear" for words, nor how often the most eloquent find nothing to reply. I hate questioners and questions; there are so few that can be spoken to without a lie. "*Do you forgive me?*" Madam and sweetheart, so far as I have gone in life I have never yet been able to discover what forgiveness means. "*Is it still the same between us?*" Why, how can it be? It is eternally different; and yet you are still the friend of my heart. "Do you understand me?" God knows; I should think it highly improbable.

The cruelest lies are often told in silence. A man may have sat in a room for hours and not opened his teeth, and yet come out of that room a disloyal friend or a vile calumniator. And how many loves have perished because, from pride, or spite, or diffidence, or that unmanly shame which withholds a man from daring to betray emotion, a lover, at the critical point of the relation, has but hung his head and held his tongue? And, again, a lie may be told by a truth, or a truth conveyed through a lie. Truth to facts is not always truth to sentiment; and part of the truth, as often happens in answer to a question, may be the foulest calumny. A fact may be an exception; but the feeling is the law, and it is that which you must neither garble nor belie. The whole tenor of a conversation is a part of the meaning of each separate statement; the beginning and the end define and travesty the intermediate conversation. You never speak to God; you address a fellow-man, full of his own tempers; and to tell truth, rightly understood, is not to state the true facts, but to convey a true impression; truth in spirit, not truth to letter, is the true veracity. To reconcile averted friends a Jesuitical discretion is often needful, not so much to gain a kind hearing as to communicate sober truth. Women have an ill name in this connection; yet they live in as true relations; the lie of a good woman is the true index of her heart.

"It takes," says Thoreau, in the noblest and most useful passage I remember to have read in any modern author,[1] "two to speak truth—one to speak and another to hear." He must be very little experienced, or have no great zeal for truth, who does not recognise the fact. A grain of anger or a grain of suspicion produces strange acoustical effects, and makes the ear greedy to remark offence. Hence we find those who have once quarrelled carry themselves distantly, and are ever ready to break the truce. To speak truth there must be moral equality or else no respect; and hence between parent and child intercourse is apt to degenerate into a verbal fencing bout, and misapprehensions to become ingrained. And there is another side to this, for the parent begins with an imperfect notion of the child's character, formed in early years or during the equinoctial gales of youth; to this he adheres, noting only the facts which suit with his preconception; and wherever a person fancies himself unjustly judged, he at once and finally gives up the effort to speak truth. With our chosen friends, on the other hand, and still more between lovers (for mutual understanding is love's essence), the truth is easily indicated by the one and aptly comprehended by the other. A hint taken, a look understood, conveys the gist of long and delicate explanations; and where the life is known even *yea* and *nay* become luminous. In the closest of all relations—that of a love well founded and equally shared—speech is half discarded, like a roundabout, infantile process or a ceremony of formal etiquette; and the two communicate directly by their presences, and with few looks and fewer words contrive to share their good and evil and uphold each other's

[1] "A Week on the Concord and Merrimack Rivers," Wednesday, p. 283.

hearts in joy. For love rests upon a physical basis; it is a familiarity of nature's making and apart from voluntary choice. Understanding has in some sort outrun knowledge, for the affection perhaps began with the acquaintance; and as it was not made like other relations, so it is not, like them, to be perturbed or clouded. Each knows more than can be uttered; each lives by faith, and believes by a natural compulsion; and between man and wife the language of the body is largely developed and grown strangely eloquent. The thought that prompted and was conveyed in a caress would only lose to be set down in words—ay, although Shakespeare himself should be the scribe.

Yet it is in these dear intimacies, beyond all others, that we must strive and do battle for the truth. Let but a doubt arise, and alas! all the previous intimacy and confidence is but another charge against the person doubted. "*What a monstrous dishonesty is this if I have been deceived so long and so completely!*" Let but that thought gain entrance, and you plead before a deaf tribunal. Appeal to the past; why, that is your crime! Make all clear, convince the reason; alas! speciousness is but a proof against you. "*If you can abuse me now, the more likely that you have abused me from the first.*"

For a strong affection such moments are worth supporting, and they will end well; for your advocate is in your lover's heart and speaks her own language; it is not you but she herself who can defend and clear you of the charge. But in slighter intimacies, and for a less stringent union? Indeed, is it worth while? We are all *incompris,* only more or less concerned for the mischance; all trying wrongly to do right; all fawning at each other's feet like dumb, neglected lap-dogs. Sometimes we catch an eye—this is our opportunity in the ages—and we wag our tail with a poor smile. "*Is that all?*" All? If you only knew! But how can they know? They do not love us; the more fools we to squander life on the indifferent.

But the morality of the thing, you will be glad to hear, is excellent; for it is only by trying to understand others that we can get our own hearts understood; and in matters of human feeling the clement judge is the most successful pleader.

SAMUEL PEPYS

IN two books a fresh light has recently been thrown on the character and position of Samuel Pepys. Mr. Mynors Bright has given us a new transcription of the Diary, increasing it in bulk by near a third, correcting many errors, and completing our knowledge of the man in some curious and important points. We can only regret that he has taken liberties with the author and the public. It is no part of the duties of the editor of an established classic to decide what may or may not be "tedious to the reader." The book is either an historical document or not, and in condemning Lord Braybrooke Mr. Bright condemns himself. As for the time-honored phrase, "unfit for publication," without being cynical, we may regard it as the sign of a precaution more or less commercial; and we may think, without being sordid, that when we purchase six huge and distressingly expensive volumes, we are entitled to be treated rather more like scholars and rather less like children. But Mr. Bright may rest assured: while we complain, we are still grateful. Mr. Wheatley, to divide our obligation, brings together, clearly and with no lost words, a body of illustrative material. Sometimes we might ask a little more; never, I think, less. And as a matter of fact, a great part of Mr. Wheatley's volume might be transferred, by a good editor of Pepys, to the margin of the text, for it is precisely what the reader wants.

In the light of these two books, at least, we have now to read our author. Between them they contain all we can expect to learn for, it may be, many years. Now, if ever, we should be able to form some notion of that unparalleled figure in the annals of mankind—unparalleled for three good reasons: first, because he was a man known to his contemporaries in a halo of almost historical pomp, and to his remote descendants with an indecent familiarity, like a tap-room comrade; second, because he has outstripped all competitors in the art or virtue of a conscious honesty about oneself; and, third, because, being in many ways a very ordinary person, he has yet placed himself before the public eye with such a fulness and such an intimacy of detail as might be envied by a genius like Montaigne. Not then for his own sake only, but as a character in a unique position, endowed with a unique talent, and shedding a unique light upon the lives of the mass of mankind, he is surely worthy of prolonged and patient study.

The Diary

That there should be such a book as Pepys's Diary is incomparably strange. Pepys, in a corrupt and idle period, played the man in public employments, toiling hard and keeping his honor bright. Much of the little good that is set down to James the Second comes by right to Pepys; and if it were little for a king, it is much for a subordinate. To his clear, capable head was owing somewhat of the greatness of England on the seas. In the exploits of Hawke, Rodney, or Nelson, this dead Mr. Pepys of the Navy Office had some considerable share. He stood well by his business in the appalling plague of 1666. He was loved and respected by some of the best and wisest men in England. He was President of the Royal Society; and when he came to die, people said of his conduct in that solemn hour—thinking it needless to say more—that it was answerable to the greatness of his life. Thus he walked in dignity, guards of soldiers sometimes attending him in his walks, subalterns bowing before his periwig; and when he uttered his thoughts they were suitable to his state and services. On February 8, 1668, we find him writing to Evelyn, his mind bitterly occupied with the late Dutch war, and some thoughts of the different story of the repulse of the great Armada: "Sir, you will not wonder at the backwardness of my thanks for the present you made me, so many days since, of the Prospect of the Medway, while the Hollander rode master in it, when I have told you that the sight of it hath led me to such reflections on my particular interest, by my employment, in the reproach due to that miscarriage, as have given me little less disquiet than he is fancied to have who found his face in Michael Angelo's hell. The same should serve me also in excuse for my silence in celebrating your mastery shown in the design and draught, did not indignation rather than courtship urge me so far to commend them, as to wish the furniture of our House of Lords changed from the story of '88 to that of '67 (of Evelyn's designing), till the pravity of this were reformed to the temper of that age, wherein God Almighty found his blessings more operative than, I fear, he doth in ours his judgments."

This is a letter honorable to the writer, where the meaning rather than the words is eloquent. Such was the account he gave of himself to his contemporaries; such thoughts he chose to utter, and in such language: giving himself out for a grave and patriotic public servant. We turn to the same date in the Diary by which he is known, after two centuries, to his descendants. The entry begins in the same key with the letter, blaming the "madness of the House of Commons" and "the base proceedings, just the epitome of all our public proceedings in this age, of the House of Lords;" and then, without the least transition, this is how our diarist proceeds: "To the Strand, to my bookseller's, and there bought an idle, rogueish French book, *L'escholle des Filles,* which I have bought in plain binding, avoiding the buying of it better bound, because I resolve, as soon as I have read it, to burn it, that it may not stand in the list of books, nor among them, to disgrace them, if it should be found." Even in our day, when responsibility is so much more clearly apprehended, the man who wrote the letter would be notable; but what about the man, I do not say who bought a roguish book, but who was ashamed of doing so, yet did it, and recorded both the doing and the shame in the pages of his daily journal?

We all, whether we write or speak, must somewhat drape ourselves when we address our fellows; at a given moment we apprehend our character and acts by some particular side; we are merry with one, grave with another, as befits the nature and demands of the relation. Pepys's letter to Evelyn would have little in common with that other one to Mrs. Knipp which he signed by the pseudonym of *Dapper Dicky;* yet each would be suitable to the character of his correspondent. There is no untruth in this, for man, being a Protean animal, swiftly shares and changes with his company and surroundings; and these changes are the better part of his education in the world. To strike a posture once for all, and to march through life like a drum-major, is to be highly disagreeable to others and a fool for oneself into the bargain. To Evelyn and to Knipp we understand the double facing; but to whom was he posing in the Diary, and what, in the name of astonishment, was the nature of the pose? Had he suppressed all mention of the book, or had he bought it, gloried in the act, and cheerfully recorded his glorification, in either case we should have made him out. But no; he is full of precautions to conceal the "disgrace" of the purchase, and yet speeds to chronicle the whole affair in pen and ink. It is a sort of anomaly in human action, which we can exactly parallel from another part of the Diary.

Mrs. Pepys had written a paper of her too just complaints against her husband, and written it in plain and very pungent English. Pepys, in an agony lest the world should come to see it, brutally seizes and destroys the tell-tale document; and then—you disbelieve your eyes—down goes the whole story with unsparing truth and in the cruellest detail. It seems he has no design but to appear respectable, and here he keeps a private book to prove he was not. You are at first faintly reminded of some of the vagaries of the morbid religious diarist; but at a moment's thought the resemblance disappears. The design of Pepys is not at all to edify; it is not from repentance that he chronicles his peccadilloes, for he tells us when he does repent, and, to be just to him, there often follows some improvement. Again, the sins of the religious diarist are of a very formal pattern, and are told with an elaborate whine. But in Pepys you come upon good, substantive misdemeanors; beams in his eye of which he alone remains unconscious; healthy outbreaks of the animal nature, and laughable subterfuges to himself that always command belief and often engage the sympathies.

Pepys was a young man for his age, came slowly to himself in the world, sowed his wild oats late, took late to industry, and preserved till nearly forty the headlong gusto of a boy. So, to come rightly at the spirit in which the Diary was written, we must recall a class of sentiments which with most of us are over and done before the age of twelve. In our tender years we still preserve a freshness of surprise at our prolonged existence; events make an impression out of all proportion to their consequence; we are unspeakably touched by our own past adventures, and look forward to our future personality with sentimental interest. It was something of this, I think, that clung to Pepys. Although not sentimental in the abstract, he was sweetly sentimental about himself. His own past clung about his heart, an evergreen. He was the slave of an association. He could not pass by Islington, where his father used to carry him to cakes and ale, but he must light at the "King's Head" and eat and drink "for remembrance of the old house sake." He counted it good fortune to lie a night at Epsom to renew his old walks, "where Mrs. Hely and I did use to walk and talk, with whom I had the first sentiments of love and pleasure in a woman's company, discourse and taking her by the hand, she being a pretty woman." He goes about weighing up the *Assurance,* which lay near Woolwich under water, and cries in a parenthesis, "Poor ship, that I have been twice merry in, in Captain Holland's time;" and after revisiting the *Naseby,* now changed into the *Charles,* he confesses "it was a great pleasure to myself to see the ship that I began my good fortune in." The stone that he was cut for he preserved in a case; and to the Turners he kept alive such gratitude for their assistance that for years, and after he had begun to mount himself into higher zones, he continued to have that family to dinner on the anniversary of the operation. Not Hazlitt nor Rousseau had a more romantic passion for their past, although at times they might express it more romantically; and if Pepys shared with them this childish fondness, did not Rousseau, who left behind him the *Confessions,* or Hazlitt, who wrote the *Liber Amoris,* and loaded his essays with loving personal detail, share with Pepys in his unwearied egotism? For the two things go hand in hand; or, to be more exact, it is the first that makes the second either possible or pleasing.

But, to be quite in sympathy with Pepys, we must return once more to the experience of children. I can remember to have written, in the fly-leaf of more than one book, the date and the place where I then was—if, for instance, I was ill in bed or sitting in a certain garden; these were jottings for my future self; if I should chance on such a note in after years, I thought it would cause me a particular thrill to recognize myself across the intervening distance. Indeed, I might come upon them now, and not be moved one tittle—which shows that I have comparatively failed in life, and grown older than Samuel Pepys. For in the Diary we can find more than one such note of perfect childish egotism; as when he explains that his candle is going out, "which makes me write thus slobberingly;" or as in this incredible particularity, "To my study, where I only wrote thus much of this day's passages to this, and so out again;" or lastly, as here, with more of circumstance: "I staid up till the bellman came by with his bell under my window, *as I was writing of this very line,* and cried, 'Past one of the clock, and a cold, frosty, windy morning.'" Such passages are not to be misunderstood. The appeal to Samuel Pepys years hence is unmistakable. He desires that dear, though unknown, gentleman keenly to realize his predecessor; to remember why a passage was uncleanly written; to recall (let us fancy, with a sigh) the tones of the bellman, the chill of the early, windy morning, and the very line his own romantic self was scribing at the moment. The man, you will perceive was making reminiscences—a sort of pleasure by ricochet, which comforts many in distress, and turns some others into sentimental libertines: and the whole book, if you will but look at it in that way, is seen to be a work of art to Pepys's own address.

Here, then, we have the key to that remarkable attitude preserved by him throughout his Diary, to that unflinching —I had almost said, that unintelligent—sincerity which makes it a miracle among human books. He was not unconscious of his errors—far from it; he was often startled into shame, often reformed, often made and broke his vows of change. But whether he did ill or well, he was still his own unequalled self; still that entrancing *ego* of whom alone he cared to write; and still sure of his own affectionate indulgence, when the parts should be changed, and the writer come to read what he had written. Whatever he did, or said, or thought, or suffered, it was still a trait of Pepys, a character of his career; and as, to himself, he was more interesting than Moses or than Alexander, so all should be faithfully set down. I have called his Diary a work of art. Now when the artist has found something, word or deed, exactly proper to a favorite character in play or novel, he will neither suppress nor diminish it, though the remark be silly or the act mean. The hesitation of Hamlet, the credulity of Othello, the baseness of Emma Bovary, or the irregularities of Mr. Swiveller, caused neither disappointment nor disgust to their creators. And so with Pepys and his adored protagonist: adored not blindly, but with trenchant insight and enduring, human toleration. I have gone over and over the greater part of the Diary; and the points where, to the most suspicious scrutiny, he has seemed not perfectly sincere, are so few, so doubtful, and so petty, that I am ashamed to name them. It may be said that we all of us write such a diary in airy characters upon our brain; but I fear there is a distinction to be made; I fear that as we render to our consciousness an account of our daily fortunes and behavior, we too often weave a tissue of romantic compliments and dull excuses; and even if Pepys were the ass and coward that men call him, we must take rank as sillier and more cowardly than he. The bald truth about oneself, what we are all too timid to admit when we are not too dull to see it, that was what he saw clearly and set down unsparingly.

It is improbable that the Diary can have been carried on in the same single spirit in which it was begun. Pepys was not such an ass, but he must have perceived, as he went on, the extraordinary nature of the work he was producing. He was a great reader, and he knew what other books were like. It must, at least, have crossed his mind that some one might ultimately decipher the manuscript, and he himself, with all his pains and pleasures, be resuscitated in some later day; and the thought, although discouraged, must have warmed his heart. He was not such an ass, besides, but he must have been conscious of the deadly explosives, the gun-cotton and the giant powder, he was hoarding in his drawer. Let some contemporary light upon the Journal, and Pepys was plunged forever in social and political disgrace. We can trace the growth of his terrors by two facts. In 1660, while the Diary was still in its youth, he tells about it, as a matter of course, to a lieutenant in the navy; but in 1669, when it was already near an end, he could have bitten his tongue out, as the saying is, because he had let slip his secret to one so grave and friendly as Sir William Coventry. And from two other facts I think we may infer that he had entertained, even if he had not acquiesced in, the thought of a far-distant publicity. The first is of capital importance: the Diary was not destroyed. The second—that he took unusual precautions to confound the cipher in "rogueish" passages—proves, beyond question, that he was thinking of some other reader besides himself. Perhaps while his friends were admiring the "greatness of his behavior" at the approach of death, he may have had a twinkling hope of immortality. *Mens cujusque is est quisque,* said his chosen motto; and, as he had stamped his mind with every crook and foible in the pages of the Diary, he might feel that what he left behind him was indeed himself. There is perhaps no other instance so remarkable of the desire of man for publicity and an enduring name. The greatness of his life was open, yet he longed to communicate its smallness also; and, while contemporaries bowed before him, he must buttonhole posterity with the news that his periwig was once alive with nits. But this thought, although I cannot doubt he had it, was neither his first nor his deepest; it did not color one word that he wrote; the Diary, for as long as he kept it, remained what it was when he began, a private pleasure for himself. It was his bosom secret; it added a zest to all his pleasures; he lived in and for it, and might well write these solemn words, when he closed that confidant forever: "And so I betake myself to that course which is almost as much as to see myself go into the grave; for which, and all the discomforts that will accompany my being blind, the good God prepare me."

A Liberal Genius

Pepys spent part of a certain winter Sunday, when he had taken physic, composing "a song in praise of a liberal genius (such as I take my own to be) to all studies and pleasures." The song was unsuccessful, but the Diary is, in a sense, the very song that he was seeking; and his portrait by Hales, so admirably reproduced in Mynors Bright's edition, is a confirmation of the Diary. Hales it would appear, had known his business; and though he put his sitter to a deal of trouble, almost breaking his neck "to have the portrait full of shadows," and draping him in an Indian gown hired expressly for the purpose, he was preoccupied about no merely picturesque effects, but to portray the essence of the man. Whether we read the picture by the Diary or the Diary by the picture, we shall at least agree that Hales was among the number of those who can "surprise the manners in the face." Here we have a mouth pouting, moist with desires; eyes greedy, protuberant, and yet apt for weeping too; a nose great alike in character and dimensions; and altogether a most fleshly, melting countenance. The face is attractive by its promise of reciprocity. I have used the word *greedy,* but the reader must not suppose that he can change it for that closely kindred one of *hungry;* for there is here no aspiration, no waiting for better things, but an animal joy in all that comes. It could never be the face of an artist; it is the face of a *viveur*—kindly, pleased and pleasing, protected from excess and upheld in contentment by the shifting versatility of his desires. For a single desire is more rightly to be called a lust; but there is health in a variety, where one may balance and control another.

The whole world, town or country, was to Pepys a garden of Armida. Wherever he went, his steps were winged with the most eager expectation; whatever he did, it was done with the most lively pleasure. An insatiable curiosity in all the shows of the world and all the secrets of knowledge, filled him brimful of the longing to travel, and supported him in the toils of study. Rome was the dream of his life; he was never happier than when he read or talked of the Eternal City. When he was in Holland, he was "with child" to see any strange thing. Meeting some friends and singing with them in a palace near The Hague, his pen fails him to express his passion of delight, "the more so because in a heaven of pleasure and in a strange country." He must go to see all famous executions. He must needs visit the body of a murdered man, defaced "with a broad wound," he says, "that makes my hand now shake to write of it." He learned to dance, and was "like to make a dancer." He learned to sing, and walked about Gray's Inn Fields "humming to myself (which is now my constant practice) the trillo." He learned to play the lute, the flute, the flageolet, and the theorbo, and it was not the fault of his intention if he did not learn the harpsichord or the spinet. He learned to compose songs, and burned to give forth "a scheme and theory of music not yet ever made in the world." When he heard "a fellow whistle like a bird exceeding well," he promised to return another day and give an angel for a lesson in the art. Once, he writes, "I took the Bezan back with me, and with a brave gale and tide reached up that night to the Hope, taking great pleasure in learning the seamen's manner of singing when they sound the depths." If he found himself rusty in his Latin grammar, he must fall to it like a schoolboy. He was a member of Harrington's Club till its dissolution, and of the Royal Society before it had received the name. Boyle's *Hydrostatics* was "of infinite delight" to him, walking in Barnes Elms. We find him comparing Bible concordances, a captious judge of sermons, deep in Descartes and Aristotle. We find him, in a single year, studying timber and the measurement of timber; tar and oil, hemp, and the process of preparing cordage; mathematics and accounting; the hull and the rigging of ships from a model; and "looking and improving himself of the (naval) stores with"—hark to the fellow!—"great delight." His familiar spirit of delight was not the same with Shelley's; but how true it was to him through life! He is only copying something, and behold, he "takes great pleasure to rule the lines, and have the capital words wrote with red ink;" he has only had his coal-cellar emptied and cleaned, and behold, "it do please him exceedingly." A hog's harslett is "a piece of meat he loves." He cannot ride home in my Lord Sandwich's coach, but he must exclaim, with breathless gusto, "his noble, rich coach!" When he is bound for a supper party, he anticipates a "glut of pleasure." When he has a new watch, "to see my childishness," says he, "I could not forbear carrying it in my hand and seeing what o'clock it was an hundred times." To go to Vauxhall, he says, and "to hear the nightingales and other birds, hear fiddles, and there a harp and here a Jew's trump, and here laughing, and there fine people walking, is mighty divertising." And the nightingales, I take it, were particularly dear to him; and it was again "with great pleasure" that he paused to hear them as he walked to Woolwich, while the fog was rising and the April sun broke through.

He must always be doing something agreeable, and, by preference, two agreeable things at once. In his house he had a box of carpenter's tools, two dogs, an eagle, a canary, and a blackbird that whistled tunes, lest, even in that full life, he should chance upon an empty moment. If he had to wait for a dish of poached eggs, he must put in the time by playing on the flageolet; if a sermon were dull, he must read in the book of Tobit or divert his mind with sly advances on the nearest women. When he walked, it must be with a book in his pocket to beguile the way in case the nightingales were silent; and even along the streets of London, with so many pretty faces to be spied for and dignitaries to be saluted, his trail was marked by little debts "for wine, pictures, etc.," the true headmark of a life intolerant of any joyless passage. He had a kind of idealism in pleasure; like the princess in the fairy story, he was conscious of a rose-leaf out of place. Dearly as he loved to talk, he could not enjoy nor shine in a conversation when he thought himself unsuitably dressed. Dearly as he loved eating, he "knew not how to eat alone;" pleasure for him must heighten pleasure; and the eye and ear must be flattered like the palate ere he avow himself content. He had no zest in a good dinner when it fell to be eaten "in a bad street and in a periwig-maker's house;" and a collation was spoiled for him by indifferent music. His body was indefatigable, doing him yeoman service in this breathless chase of pleasures. On April 11, 1662, he mentions that he went to bed "weary, *which I seldom am;*" and already over thirty, he would sit up all night cheerfully to see a comet. But it is never pleasure that exhausts the pleasure-seeker; for in that career, as in all others, it is failure that kills. The man who enjoys so wholly and bears so impatiently the slightest widowhood from joy, is just the man to lose a night's rest over some paltry question of his right to fiddle on the leads, or to be "vexed to the blood" by a solecism in his wife's attire; and we find in consequence that he was always peevish when he was hungry, and that his head "aked mightily" after a dispute. But nothing could divert him from his aim in life; his remedy in care was the same as his delight in prosperity; it was with pleasure, and with pleasure only, that he sought to drive out sorrow; and, whether he was jealous of his wife or skulking from a bailiff, he would equally take refuge in the theatre. There, if the house be full and the company noble, if the songs be tunable, the actors perfect, and the play diverting, this old hero of the secret Diary, this private self-adorer, will speedily be healed of his distresses.

Equally pleased with a watch, a coach, a piece of meat, a tune upon the fiddle, or a fact in hydrostatics, Pepys was pleased yet more by the beauty, the worth, the mirth, or the mere scenic attitude in life of his fellow-creatures. He shows himself throughout a sterling humanist. Indeed, he who loves himself, not in idle vanity, but with a plenitude of knowledge, is the best equipped of all to love his neighbors. And perhaps it is in this sense that charity may be most properly said to begin at home. It does not matter what quality a person has: Pepys can appreciate and love him for it. He "fills his eyes" with the beauty of Lady Castlemaine; indeed, he may be said to dote upon the thought of her for years; if a woman be good-looking and not painted, he will walk miles to have another sight of her; and even when a lady by a mischance spat upon his clothes, he was immediately consoled when he had observed that she was pretty. But, on the other hand, he is delighted to see Mrs. Pett upon her knees, and speaks thus of his Aunt James: "a poor, religious, well-meaning, good soul, talking of nothing but God Almighty, and that with so much innocence that mightily pleased me." He is taken with Pen's merriment and loose songs, but not less taken with the sterling worth of Coventry. He is jolly with a drunken sailor, but listens with interest and patience, as he rides the Essex roads, to the story of a Quaker's spiritual trials and convictions. He lends a critical ear to the discourse of kings and royal dukes. He spends an evening at Vauxhall with "Killigrew and young Newport—loose company," says he, "but worth a man's being in for once, to know the nature of it, and their manner of talk and lives." And when a rag-boy lights him home, he examines him about his business and other ways of livelihood for destitute children. This is almost half-way to the beginning of philanthropy; had it only been the fashion, as it is at present, Pepys had perhaps been a man famous for good deeds. And it is through this quality that he rises, at times, superior to his surprising egotism; his interest in the love affairs of others is, indeed, impersonal; he is filled with concern for my Lady Castlemaine, whom he only knows by sight, shares in her very jealousies, joys with her in her successes; and it is not untrue, however strange it seems in his abrupt presentment, that he loved his maid Jane because she was in love with his man Tom.

Let us hear him, for once, at length: "So the women and W. Hewer and I walked upon the Downes, where a flock of sheep was; and the most pleasant and innocent sight that ever I saw in my life. We found a shepherd and his little boy reading, far from any houses or sight of people, the Bible to him; so I make the boy to read to me, which he did with the forced tone that children do usually read, that was mighty pretty; and then I did give him something, and went to the father, and talked with him. He did content himself mightily in my liking his boy's reading, and did bless God for him, the most like one of the old patriarchs that ever I saw in my life, and it brought those thoughts of the old age of the world in my mind for two or three days after. We took notice of his woollen knit stockings of two colors mixed, and of his shoes shod with iron, both at the toe and heels, and with great nails in the soles of his feet, which was mighty pretty; and taking notice of them, 'Why,' says the poor man, 'the downes, you see, are full of stones, and we are faine to shoe ourselves thus; and these,' says he, 'will make the stones fly till they ring before me.' I did give the poor man something, for which he was mighty thankful, and I tried to cast stones with his horne crooke. He values his dog mightily, that would turn a sheep any way which he would have him, when he goes to fold them; told me there was about eighteen score sheep in his flock, and that he hath four shillings a week the year round for keeping of them; and Mrs. Turner, in the common fields here, did gather one of the prettiest nosegays that ever I saw in my life."

And so the story rambles on to the end of that day's pleasuring; with cups of milk, and glow-worms, and people walking at sundown with their wives and children, and all the way home Pepys still dreaming "of the old age of the world" and the early innocence of man. This was how he walked through life, his eyes and ears wide open, and his hand, you will observe, not shut; and thus he observed the lives, the speech, and the manners of his fellow-men, with prose fidelity of detail and yet a lingering glamour of romance.

It was "two or three days after" that he extended this passage in the pages of his Journal, and the style has thus the benefit of some reflection. It is generally supposed that, as a writer, Pepys must rank at the bottom of the scale of merit. But a style which is indefatigably lively, telling, and picturesque through six large volumes of everyday experience, which deals with the whole matter of a life, and yet is rarely wearisome, which condescends to the most fastidious particulars, and yet sweeps all away in the forthright current of the narrative,—such a style may be ungrammatical, it may be inelegant, it may be one tissue of mistakes, but it can never be devoid of merit. The first and the true function of the writer has been thoroughly performed throughout; and though the manner of his utterance may be childishly awkward, the matter has been transformed and assimilated by his unfeigned interest and delight. The gusto of the man speaks out fierily after all these years. For the difference between Pepys and Shelly, to return to that half whimsical approximation, is one of quality but not one of degree; in his sphere, Pepys felt as keenly, and his is the true prose of poetry—prose because the spirit of the man was narrow and earthly, but poetry because he was delightedly alive. Hence, in such a passage as this about the Epsom shepherd, the result upon the reader's mind is entire conviction and unmingled pleasure. So, you feel, the thing fell out, not otherwise; and you would no more change it than you would change a sublimity of Shakespeare's, a homely touch of Bunyan's, or a favored reminiscence of your own.

There never was a man nearer being an artist, who yet was not one. The tang was in the family; while he was writing the journal for our enjoyment in his comely house in Navy Gardens, no fewer than two of his cousins were tramping the fens, kit under arm, to make music to the country girls. But he himself, though he could play so many instruments and pass judgment in so many fields of art, remained an amateur. It is not given to any one so keenly to enjoy, without some greater power to understand. That he did not like Shakespeare as an artist for the stage may be a fault, but it is not without either parallel or excuse. He certainly admired him as a poet; he was the first beyond mere actors on the rolls of that innumerable army who have got "To be or not to be" by heart. Nor was he content with that; it haunted his mind; he quoted it to himself in the pages of the Diary, and, rushing in where angels fear to tread, he set it to music. Nothing, indeed, is more notable than the heroic quality of the verses that our little sensualist in a periwig chose out to marry with his own mortal strains. Some gust from brave Elizabethan times must have warmed his spirit, as he sat tuning his sublime theorbo. "To be or not to be. Whether 'tis nobler"—"Beauty retire, thou dost my pity move"—"It is decreed, nor shall thy fate, O Rome;"—open and dignified in the sound, various and majestic in the sentiment, it was no inapt, as it was certainly no timid, spirit that selected such a range of themes. Of "Gaze not on Swans," I know no more than these four words; yet that also seems to promise well. It was, however, not a probable suspicion, the work of his master, Mr. Berkenshaw—as the drawings that figure at the breaking up of a young ladies' seminary are the work of the professor attached to the establishment. Mr. Berkenshaw was not altogether happy in his pupil. The amateur cannot usually rise into the artist, some leaven of the world still clogging him; and we find Pepys behaving like a pickthank to the man who taught him composition. In relation to the stage, which he so warmly loved and understood, he was not only more hearty, but more generous to others. Thus he encounters Colonel Reames, "a man," says he, "who understands and loves a play as well as I, and I love him for it." And again, when he and his wife had seen a most ridiculous insipid piece, "Glad we were," he writes, "that Betterton had no part in it." It is by such a zeal and loyalty to those who labor for his delight that the amateur grows worthy of the artist. And it should be kept in mind that, not only in art, but in morals, Pepys rejoiced to recognize his betters. There was not one speck of envy in the whole human-hearted egotist.

Respectability

When writers inveigh against respectability, in the present degraded meaning of the word, they are usually suspected of a taste for clay pipes and beer cellars; and their performances are thought to hail from the *Owl's Nest* of the comedy. They have something more, however, in their eye than the dulness of a round million dinner parties that sit down yearly in old England. For to do anything because others do it, and not because the thing is good, or kind, or honest in its own right, is to resign all moral control and captaincy upon yourself, and go post-haste to the devil with the greater number. We smile over the ascendency of priests; but I had rather follow a priest than what they call the leaders of society. No life can better than that of Pepys illustrate the dangers of this respectable theory of living. For what can be more untoward than the occurrence, at a critical period and while the habits are still pliable, of such sweeping transformation as the return of Charles the Second? Round went the whole fleet of England on the other tack; and while a few tall pintas, Milton or Pen, still sailed a lonely course by the stars and their own private compass, the cock-boat, Pepys, must go about with the majority among "the stupid starers and the loud huzzas."

The respectable are not led so much by any desire of

applause as by a positive need for countenance. The weaker and the tamer the man, the more will he require this support; and any positive quality relieves him, by just so much, of this dependence. In a dozen ways, Pepys was quite strong enough to please himself without regard for others; but his positive qualities were not co-extensive with the field of conduct; and in many parts of life he followed, with gleeful precision, in the footprints of the contemporary Mrs. Grundy. In morals, particularly, he lived by the countenance of others; felt a slight from another more keenly than a meanness in himself, and then first repented when he was found out. You could talk of religion or morality to such a man; and by the artist side of him, by his lively sympathy and apprehension, he could rise, as it were dramatically, to the significance of what you said. All that matter in religion which has been nicknamed other-worldliness was strictly in his gamut; but a rule of life that should make a man rudely virtuous, following right in good report and ill report, was foolishness and a stumbling-block to Pepys. He was much thrown across the Friends; and nothing can be more instructive than his attitude toward these most interesting people of that age. I have mentioned how he conversed with one as he rode; when he saw some brought from a meeting under arrest, "I would to God," said he, "they would either conform, or be more wise and not be catched;" and to a Quaker in his own office he extended a timid though effectual protection. Meanwhile there was growing up next door to him that beautiful nature, William Pen. It is odd that Pepys condemned him for a fop; odd, though natural enough when you see Pen's portrait, that Pepys was jealous of him with his wife. But the cream of the story is when Pen publishes his *Sandy Foundation Shaken,* and Pepys has it read aloud by his wife. "I find it," he says, "so well writ as, I think, it is too good for him ever to have writ it; and it is a serious sort of book, and *not fit for everybody to read.*" Nothing is more galling to the merely respectable than to be brought in contact with religious ardor. Pepys had his own foundations, sandy enough, but dear to him from practical considerations, and he would read the book with true uneasiness of spirit; for conceive the blow if, by some plaguy accident, this Pen were to convert him! It was a different kind of doctrine that he judged profitable for himself and others. "A good sermon of Mr. Gifford's at our church, upon 'Seek ye first the kingdom of heaven.' A very excellent and persuasive, good and moral sermon. He showed, like a wise man, that righteousness is a surer moral way of being rich than sin and villainy." It is thus that respectable people desire to have their Greathearts address them, telling, in mild accents, how you may make the best of both worlds, and be a moral hero without courage, kindness, or troublesome reflection; and thus the Gospel, cleared of Eastern metaphor, becomes a manual of worldly prudence, and a handybook for Pepys and the successful merchant.

The respectability of Pepys was deeply grained. He has no idea of truth except for the Diary. He has no care that a thing shall be, if it but appear; gives out that he has inherited a good estate, when he has seemingly got nothing but a lawsuit; and is pleased to be thought liberal when he knows he has been mean. He is conscientiously ostentatious. I say conscientiously, with reason. He could never have been taken for a fop, like Pen, but arrayed himself in a manner nicely suitable to his position. For long he hesitated to assume the famous periwig; for a public man should travel gravely with his fashions, not foppishly before, nor dowdily behind, the central movement of his age. For long he durst not keep a carriage; that, in his circumstances, would have been improper; but a time comes, with the growth of his fortune, when the impropriety has shifted to the other side, and he is "ashamed to be seen in a hackney." Pepys talked about being "a Quaker or some very melancholy thing;" for my part, I can imagine nothing so melancholy, because nothing half so silly, as to be concerned about such problems. But so respectability and the duties of society haunt and burden their poor devotees; and what seems at first the very primrose path of life, proves difficult and thorny like the rest. And the time comes to Pepys, as to all the merely respectable, when he must not only order his pleasures, but even clip his virtuous movements, to the public patter of the age. There was some juggling among officials to avoid direct taxation; and Pepys, with a noble impulse, growing ashamed of this dishonesty, designed to charge himself with £1000; but finding none to set him an example, "nobody of our ablest merchants" with this moderate liking for clean hands, he judged it "not decent;" he feared it would "be thought vain glory;" and, rather than appear singular, cheerfully remained a thief. One able merchant's countenance, and Pepys had dared to do an honest act! Had he found one brave spirit, properly recognized by society, he might have gone far as a disciple. Mrs. Turner, it is true, can fill him full of sordid scandal, and make him believe, against the testimony of his senses, that Pen's venison pasty stank like the devil; but, on the other hand, Sir William Coventry can raise him by a word into another being. Pepys, when he is with Coventry, talks in the vein of an old Roman. What does he care for office or emolument? "Thank God, I have enough of my own," says he, "to buy me a good book and a good fiddle, and I have a good wife." And again, we find this pair projecting an old age when an ungrateful country shall have dismissed them from the field of public service; Coventry living retired in a fine house, and Pepys dropping in, "it may be, to read a chapter of Seneca."

Under this influence, the only good one in his life, Pepys continued zealous and, for the period, pure in his employment. He would not be "bribed to be unjust," he says, though he was "not so squeamish as to refuse a present after," suppose the king to have received no wrong. His new arrangement for the victualling of Tangier, he tells us with honest complacency, will save the king a thousand and gain Pepys three hundred pounds a year,—a statement which exactly fixes the degree of the age's enlightenment. But for his industry and capacity no praise can be too high. It was an unending struggle for the man to stick to his business in such a garden of Armida as he found this life; and the story of his oaths, so often broken, so courageously renewed, is worthy rather of admiration than the contempt it has received.

Elsewhere, and beyond the sphere of Coventry's influence, we find him losing scruples and daily complying further with the age. When he began the Journal, he was a trifle prim and puritanic; merry enough, to be sure, over his private cups, and still remembering Magdalene ale and his acquaintance with Mrs. Ainsworth of Cambridge. But youth is a hot season with all; when a man smells April and May he is apt at times to stumble; and in spite of a disordered practice, Pepy's theory, the better things that he approved and followed after, we may even say were strict. Where there was "tag, rag, and bobtail, dancing, singing, and drinking," he felt "ashamed, and went away;" and when he slept in church he prayed God forgive him. In but a little while we find him with some ladies keeping each other awake "from spite," as though not to sleep in church were an obvious hardship; and yet later he calmly passes the time of service, looking about him, with a perspective glass, on all the pretty women. His favorite ejaculation, "Lord!" occurs but once that I have observed in 1660, never in '61, twice in '62, and at least five times in '63; after which the "Lords" may be said to pullulate like herrings, with here and there a solitary "damned," as it were a whale among the shoal. He and his wife, once filled with dudgeon by some innocent freedoms at a marriage, are soon content to go pleasuring with my Lord Brouncker's mistress, who was not even, by his own account, the most discreet of mistresses. Tag, rag, and bobtail, dancing, singing, and drinking become his natural element; actors and actresses and drunken, roaring courtiers are to be found in his society; until the man grew so involved with Saturnalian manners and companions that he was shot almost unconsciously into the grand domestic crash of 1668.

That was the legitimate issue and punishment of years of staggering walk and conversation. The man who has smoked his pipe for half a century in a powder magazine finds himself at last the author and the victim of a hideous disaster. So with our pleasant-minded Pepys and his peccadilloes. All of a sudden, as he still trips dexterously enough among the dangers of a double-faced career, thinking no great evil, humming to himself the trillo, Fate takes the further conduct of that matter from his hands, and brings him face to face with the consequences of his acts. For a man still, after so many years, the lover, although not the constant lover, of his wife,—for a man, besides, who was so greatly careful of appearances,—the revelation of his infidelities was a crushing blow. The tears that he shed, the indignities that he endured, are not to be measured. A vulgar woman, and now justly incensed, Mrs. Pepys spared him no detail of suffering. She was violent, threatening him with the tongs; she was careless of his honor, driving him to insult the mistress whom she had driven him to betray and to discard; worst of all, she was hopelessly inconsequent in word and thought and deed, now lulling him with reconciliations, and anon flaming forth again with the original anger. Pepys had not used his wife well; he had wearied her with jealousies, even while himself unfaithful; he had grudged her clothes and pleasures, while lavishing both upon himself; he had abused her in words; he had bent his fist at her in anger; he had once blacked her eye; and it is one of the oddest particulars in that odd Diary of his, that, while the injury is referred to once in passing, there is no hint as to the occasion or the manner of the blow. But now, when he is in the wrong, nothing can exceed the long-suffering affection of this impatient husband. While he was still sinning and still undiscovered, he seems not to have known a touch of penitence stronger than what might lead him to take his wife to the theatre, or for an airing, or to give her a new dress, by way of compensation. Once found out, however, and he seems to himself to have lost all claim to decent usage. It is perhaps the strongest instance of his externality. His wife may do what she pleases, and though he may groan, it will never occur to him to blame her; he has no weapon left but tears and the most abject submission. We should perhaps have respected him more had he not given away so utterly,—above all, had he refused to write, under his wife's dictation, an insulting letter to his unhappy fellow-culprit, Miss Willet; but somehow I believe we like him better as he was.

The death of his wife, following so shortly after, must have stamped the impression of this episode upon his mind. For the remaining years of his long life we have no Diary to help us, and we have seen already how little stress is to be laid upon the tenor of his correspondence; but what with the recollection of the catastrophe of his married life, what with the natural influence of his advancing years and reputation, it seems not unlikely that the period of gallantry was at an end for Pepys; and it is beyond a doubt that he sat down at last to an honored and agreeable old age among his books and music, the correspondent of Sir Isaac Newton, and in one instance at least, the poetical counsellor of Dryden. Through all this period, that Diary which contained the secret memoirs of his life, with all its inconsistencies and escapades, had been religiously preserved; nor when he came to die, does he appear to have provided for its destruction. So we may conceive him faithful to the end to all his dear and early memories; still mindful of Mrs. Hely in the woods at Epsom; still lighting at Islington for a cup of kindness to the dead; still, if he heard again that air that once so much disturbed him, thrilling at the recollection of the love that bound him to his wife.

ON THE ELEVATION OF THE LABORING CLASSES

BY

WILLIAM ELLERY CHANNING

INTRODUCTORY NOTE

WILLIAM ELLERY CHANNING, *the chief apostle of New England Unitarianism, was born at Newport, Rhode Island, April 7, 1780. He graduated from Harvard in 1798, and five years later became minister of the Federal Street Church in Boston, where he remained for thirty-seven years. He died October 2, 1842.*

Channing was still a child when, in 1785, King's Chapel in Boston, in revising its liturgy, eliminated the doctrine of the Trinity. For the next fifty years the movement went on, separating the Congregational churches in New England into Trinitarian and Unitarian. A sermon preached by Channing in Baltimore in 1819, at the ordination of Jared Sparks, is generally regarded as the formulation of the Unitarian creed, and throughout his life Channing continued a leader in the denomination.

To the tolerance, the culture, and the high civic and private virtue that characterized the typical Unitarian of that time, Channing added an emotional and spiritual quality, and an interest in philosophy, that make him not merely the greatest of the Unitarian leaders, but in important respects the first of the Transcendentalists. "The Calvinists," it has been said, "believed that human nature is totally depraved; the Unitarians denied this, their denial carrying with it the positive implication that human nature is essentially good; the Transcendentalists believed that human nature is divine" (Goddard). Judged by this test, Channing belongs to the third group, for it is in his passionate faith in the divinity of human nature, apparent in the following lectures "On the Elevation of the Laboring Classes," as in his writing and preaching in general, that one finds the characteristic mark of his spirit and the main secret of his power.

INTRODUCTORY REMARKS

THE following lectures were prepared for two meetings of mechanics, one of them consisting of apprentices, the other of adults. For want of strength they were delivered only to the former, though, in preparing them, I had kept the latter also in view. "The Mechanic Apprentices' Library Association," at whose request the lectures are published, is an institution of much promise, not only furnishing a considerable means of intellectual improvement, but increasing the self-respect and conducing to the moral safety of the members.

When I entered on this task, I thought of preparing only one lecture of the usual length. But I soon found that I could not do justice to my views in so narrow a compass. I therefore determined to write at large, and to communicate through the press the results of my labor, if they should be thought worthy of publication. With this purpose, I introduced topics which I did not deliver, and which I thought might be usefully presented to some who might not hear me. I make this statement to prevent the objection, that the lectures are not, in all things, adapted to those to whom they were delivered. Whilst written chiefly for a class, they were also intended for the community.

As the same general subject is discussed in these lectures as in the "Lecture on Self-Culture," published last winter, there will, of course, be found in them that coincidence of thoughts which always takes place in the writings of a man who has the inculcation of certain great principles much at heart. Still, the point of view, the mode of discussion, and the choice of topics, differ much in the two productions; so that my state of mind would be given very imperfectly were the present lectures withheld.

This is, probably, the last opportunity I shall have for communicating with the laboring classes through the press. I may, therefore, be allowed to express my earnest wishes for their happiness, and my strong hope that they will justify the confidence of their friends, and will prove by their example the possibility of joining with labor all the improvements which do honor to our nature.—*W. E. C., Boston, February 11, 1840.*

ON THE ELEVATION OF THE LABORING CLASSES

IT is with no common pleasure that I take part in the present course of lectures. Such a course is a sign of the times, and very interesting to all who are interested in the progress of their fellow-creatures. We hear much of the improvements of our age. The wonders achieved by machinery are the common talk of every circle; but I confess that, to me, this gathering of mechanics' apprentices, whose chief bond of union is a library, and who come together weekly to refresh and improve themselves by the best instruction which the state of society places within their reach, is more encouraging than all the miracles of the machinist. In this meeting I see, what I desire most to see, that the mass of the people are beginning to comprehend themselves and their true happiness, that they are catching glimpses of the great work and vocation of human beings, and are rising to their true place in the social state. The present meeting indicates a far more radical, more important change in the world than the steam-engine, or the navigation of the Atlantic in a fortnight. That members of the laboring class, at the close of a day's work, should assemble in such a hall as this, to hear lectures on science, history, ethics, and the most stirring topics of the day, from men whose education is thought to fit them for the highest offices, is a proof of a social revolution to which no bounds can be set, and from which too much cannot be hoped. I see in it a repeal of the sentence of degradation passed by ages on the mass of mankind. I see in it the dawn of a new era, in which it will be understood that the first object of society is to give incitements and means of progress to all its members. I see in it the sign of the approaching triumph of men's spiritual over their outward and material interests. In the hunger and thirst for knowledge and for refined pleasures which this course of lectures indicates in those who labor, I see that the spirit of man is not always to be weighed down by toils for animal life and by the appetite for animal indulgences. I do attach great importance to this meeting, not for its own sake or its immediate benefits, but as a token and pledge of a new impulse given to society through all its conditions. On this account, I take more pleasure in speaking here than I should feel in being summoned to pronounce a show-oration before all the kings and nobles on earth. In truth, it is time to have done with shows. The age is too stirring, we are pressed on by too solemn interests, to be justified in making speeches for self-display or mere amusement. He who cannot say something in sympathy with, or in aid of, the great movements of humanity, might as well hold his peace.

With these feelings and convictions, I am naturally, almost necessarily, led to address you on a topic which must insure the attention of such an audience: namely, the elevation of that portion of the community who subsist by the labor of the hands. This work, I have said, is going on. I may add, that it is advancing nowhere so rapidly as in this city. I do not believe that, on the face of the earth, the spirit of improvement has anywhere seized so strongly on those who live by the sweat of the brow as among ourselves. Here it is nothing rare to meet the union of intellectual culture and self-respect with hard work. Here the prejudice against labor as degrading has very much given way. This, then, is the place where the subject which I have proposed should be discussed. We ought to consider in what the true elevation of the laboring portion consists, how far it is practicable, and how it may be helped onward. The subject, I am aware, is surrounded with much prejudice and error. Great principles need to be brought out, and their application plainly stated. There are serious objections to be met, fears to be disarmed, and rash hopes to be crushed. I do not profess to have mastered the topic. But I can claim one merit, that of coming to the discussion with a feeling of its importance, and with a deep interest in the class of people whom it concerns. I trust that this expression of interest will not be set down as mere words, or as meant to answer any selfish purpose. A politician who professes attachment to the people is suspected to love them for their votes. But a man who neither seeks nor would accept any place within their gift may hope to be listened to as their friend. As a friend, I would speak plainly. I cannot flatter. I see defects in the laboring classes. I think that, as yet, the greater part of them have made little progress; that the prejudices and passions, the sensuality and selfishness of multitudes among them, are formidable barriers to improvement; that multitudes have not waked as yet to a dim conception of the end for which they are to struggle. My hopes do not blind me to what exists; and with this clear sense of the deficiencies of the multitude of men, I cannot, without guilt, minister to their vanity. Not that they alone are to be charged with deficiencies. Look where we may, we shall discern in all classes ground for condemnation; and whoever would do good ought to speak the truth of all, only remembering that he is to speak with sympathy, and with a consciousness of his own fallibleness and infirmity.

In giving my views of the elevation of the laboring multitude, I wish that it may be understood that I shall often speak prospectively, or of changes and improvements which are not to be expected immediately, or soon; and this I say, that I may not be set down as a dreamer, expecting to regenerate the world in a day. I fear, however, that this explanation will not shield me from this and like reproaches. There are men who, in the face of all history, of the great changes wrought in men's condition, and of the new principles which are now acting on society, maintain that the future is to be a copy of the past, and probably a faded rather than bright copy. From such I differ, and did I not differ I would not stand here. Did I expect nothing better from human nature than I see, I should have no heart for the present effort, poor as it may be. I see the signs of a better futurity, and especially signs that the large class by whose toil we all live are rising from the dust; and this faith is my only motive to what I now offer.

The elevation of the laboring portion of society: this is our subject. I shall first consider in what this consists. I shall then consider some objections to its practicableness, and to this point shall devote no small part of the discussion; and shall close the subject with giving some grounds of my faith and hope in regard to the most numerous class of our fellow-beings.

I. What is to be understood by the elevation of the laboring class? This is our first topic. To prevent misapprehension, I will begin with stating what is *not* meant by it, in what it does not consist.—I say, then, that by the elevation of the laborer, I do not understand that he is to be raised above the need of labor. I do not expect a series of improvements, by which he is to be released from his daily work. Still more, I have no desire to dismiss him from his workshop and farm, to take the spade and axe from his hand, and to make his life a long holiday. I have faith in labor, and I see the goodness of God in placing us in a world where labor alone can keep us alive. I would not change, if I could, our subjection to physical laws, our exposure to hunger and cold, and the necessity of constant conflicts with the material world. I would not, if I could, so temper the elements that they should infuse into us only grateful sensations, that they should make vegetation so exuberant as to anticipate every want, and the minerals so ductile as to offer no resistance to our strength and skill. Such a world would make a contemptible race. Man owes his growth, his energy, chiefly to that striving of the will, that conflict with difficulty, which we call effort. Easy, pleasant work does not make robust minds, does not give men a consciousness of their powers, does not train them to endurance, to perseverance, to steady force of will, that force without which all other acquisitions avail nothing. Manual labor is a school in which men are placed to get energy of purpose and character,—a vastly more important endowment than all the learning of all other schools. They are placed, indeed, under hard masters, physical sufferings and wants, the power of fearful elements, and the vicissitudes of all human things; but these stern teachers do a work which no compassionate, indulgent friend could do for us; and true wisdom will bless Providence for their sharp ministry. I have great faith in hard work. The material world does much for the mind by its beauty and order; but it does more for our minds by the pains it inflicts; by its obstinate resistance, which nothing but patient toil can overcome; by its vast forces, which nothing but unremitting skill and effort can turn to our use; by its perils, which demand continual vigilance; and by its tendencies to decay. I believe that difficulties are more important to the human mind than what we call assistances. Work we all must, if we mean to bring out and perfect our nature. Even if we do not work with the hands, we must undergo equivalent toil in some other direction. No business or study which does not present obstacles, tasking to the full the intellect and the will, is worthy of a man. In science, he who does not grapple with hard questions, who does not concentrate his whole intellect in vigorous attention, who does not aim to penetrate what at first repels him, will never attain to mental force. The uses of toil reach beyond the present world. The capacity of steady, earnest labor is, I apprehend, one of our great preparations for another state of being. When I see the vast amount of toil required of men, I feel that it must have important connection with their future existence; and that he who has met this discipline manfully has laid one essential foundation of improvement, exertion, and happiness in the world to come. You will here see that to me labor has great dignity. It is not merely the grand instrument by which the earth is overspread with fruitfulness and beauty, and the ocean subdued, and matter wrought into innumerable forms for comfort and ornament. It has a far higher function, which is to give force to the will, efficiency, courage, the capacity of endurance, and of persevering devotion to far-reaching plans. Alas, for the man who has not learned to work! He is a poor creature. He does not know himself. He depends on others, with no capacity of making returns for the support they give; and let him not fancy that he has a monopoly of enjoyment. Ease, rest, owes its deliciousness to toil; and no toil is so burdensome as the rest of him who has nothing to task and quicken his powers.

I do not, then, desire to release the laborer from toil. This is not the elevation to be sought for him. Manual labor is a great good; but, in so saying, I must be understood to speak of labor in its just proportions. In excess it does great harm. It is not a good, when made the sole work of life. It must be joined with higher means of improvement, or it degrades instead of exalting. Man has a various nature, which requires a variety of occupation and discipline for its growth. Study, meditation, society, and relaxation should be mixed up with his physical toils. He has intellect, heart, imagination, taste, as well as bones and muscles; and he is grievously wronged when compelled to exclusive drudgery for bodily subsistence. Life should be an alternation of employments, so diversified as to call the whole man into action. Unhappily our present civilization is far from realizing this idea. It tends to increase the amount of manual toil, at the very time that it renders this toil less favorable to the culture of the mind. The division of labor, which distinguishes civilized from savage life, and to which we owe chiefly the perfection of the arts, tends to dwarf the intellectual powers, by confining the activity of the individual to a narrow range, to a few details, perhaps to the heading of pins, the pointing of nails, or the tying together of broken strings; so that while the savage has his faculties sharpened by various occupations, and by exposure to various perils, the civilized man treads a monotonous, stupefying round of unthinking toil. This cannot, must not, always be. Variety of action, corresponding to the variety of human powers, and fitted to develop all, is the most important element of human civilization. It should be the aim of philanthropists. In proportion as Christianity shall spread the spirit of brotherhood, there will and must be a more equal distribution of toils and means of improvement. That system of labor which saps the health, and shortens life, and famishes intellect, needs, and must receive, great modification. Still, labor in due proportion is an important part of our present lot. It is the condition of all outward comforts and improvements, whilst, at the same time, it conspires with higher means and influences in ministering to the vigor and growth of the soul. Let us not fight against it. We need this admonition, because at the present moment there is a general disposition to shun labor; and this ought to be regarded as a bad sign of our times. The city is thronged with adventurers from the country, and the liberal professions are overstocked, in the hope of escaping the primeval sentence of living by the sweat of the brow; and to this crowding of men into trade we owe not only the neglect of agriculture, but, what is far worse, the demoralization of the community. It generates excessive competition, which of necessity generates fraud. Trade is turned to gambling; and a spirit of mad speculation exposes public and private interests to a disastrous instability. It is, then, no part of the philanthropy which would elevate the laboring body, to exempt them from manual toil. In truth, a wise philanthropy would, if possible, persuade all men of all conditions to mix up a measure of this toil with their other pursuits. The body as well as the mind needs vigorous exertion, and even the studious would be happier were they trained to labor as well as thought. Let us learn to regard manual toil as the true discipline of a man. Not a few of the wisest, grandest spirits have toiled at the work-bench and the plough.

I have said that, by the elevation of the laboring mass, I do not mean that they are to be released from labor. I add, in the next place, that this elevation is not to be gained by efforts to force themselves into what are called the upper ranks of society. I wish them to rise, but I have no desire to transform them into gentlemen or ladies, according to the common acceptation of these terms. I desire for them not an outward and showy, but an inward and real change; not to give them new titles and an artificial rank, but substantial improvements and real claims to respect. I have no wish to dress them from a Parisian tailor's shop, or to teach them manners from a dancing-school. I have no desire to see them, at the end of the day, doff their working dress, that they may play a part in richly attired circles. I have no desire that they should be admitted to luxurious feasts, or should get a taste for gorgeous upholstery. There is nothing cruel in the necessity which sentences the multitude of men to eat, dress, and lodge plainly and simply, especially where the sentence is executed so mildly as in this country. In this country, where the demand for labor is seldom interrupted, and the openings for enterprise are numerous beyond precedent, the laboring class, with few exceptions, may well be satisfied with their accommodations. Very many of them need nothing but a higher taste for beauty, order, and neatness, to give an air of refinement and grace as well as comfort to their establishments. In this country, the mass of laborers have their share of outward good. Their food, abundant and healthful, seasoned with the appetite which labor gives, is, on the whole, sweeter as well as healthier than the elaborate luxuries of the prosperous; and their sleep is sounder and more refreshing than falls to the lot of the less employed. Were it a possible thing, I should be sorry to see them turned into men and women of fashion. Fashion is a poor vocation. Its creed, that idleness is a privilege, and work a disgrace, is among the deadliest errors. Without depth of thought, or earnestness of feeling, or strength of purpose, living an unreal life, sacrificing substance to show, substituting the factitious for the natural, mistaking a crowd for society, finding its chief pleasure in ridicule, and exhausting its ingenuity in expedients for killing time, fashion is among the last influences under which a human being, who respects himself or who comprehends the great end of life, would desire to be placed. I use strong language, because I would combat the disposition, too common in the laboring mass, to regard what is called the upper class with envy or admiration. This disposition manifests itself among them in various forms. Thus, when one of their number prospers he is apt to forget his old acquaintance, and to work his way, if possible, into a more fashionable caste. As far, indeed, as he extends his acquaintance among the intelligent, refined, generous, and truly honorable, he makes a substantial improvement of his condition; but if, as is too often the case, he is admitted by way of favor into a circle which has few claims beyond those of greater luxury and show, and which bestows on him a patronizing, condescending notice, in exchange for his old, honorable influence among his original associates, he does any thing but rise. Such is not the elevation I desire for the laborer. I do not desire him to struggle into another rank. Let him not be a servile copyist of other classes, but aim at something higher than has yet been realized in any body of men. Let him not associate the idea of dignity or honor with certain modes of living, or certain outward connections. I would have every man stand on his own ground, and take his place among men according to personal endowments and worth, and not according to outward appendages; and I would have every member of the community furnished with such means of improvement, that, if faithful to himself, he may need no outward appendage to attract the respect of all around him.

I have said, that the people are not to be elevated by escaping labor, or by pressing into a different rank. Once more, I do not mean by the elevation of the people, that they should become self-important politicians; that, as individuals or a class, they should seize on political power; that by uniting their votes they should triumph over the more prosperous; or that they should succeed in bending the administration of government to their particular interests. An individual is not elevated by figuring in public affairs, or even by getting into office. He needs previous elevation to save him from disgrace in his public relations. To govern one's self, not others, is true glory. To serve through love, not to rule, is Christian greatness. Office is not dignity. The lowest men, because most faithless in principle, most servile to opinion, are to be found in office. I am sorry to say it, but the truth should be spoken, that, at the present moment, political action in this country does little to lift up any who are concerned in it. It stands in opposition to a high morality. Politics, indeed, regarded as the study and pursuit of the true, enduring good of a community, as the application of great unchangeable principles to public affairs, is a noble sphere of thought and action; but politics, in its common sense, or considered as the invention of temporary shifts, as the playing of a subtile game, as the tactics of party for gaining power and the spoils of office, and for elevating one set of men above another, is a paltry and debasing concern. The laboring class are sometimes stimulated to seek power as a class, and this it is thought will raise them. But no class, as such, should bear rule among us. All conditions of society should be represented in the government, and alike protected by it; nor can any thing be expected but disgrace to the individual and the country from the success of any class in grasping at a monopoly of political power. I would by no means discourage the attention of the people to politics. They ought to study in earnest the interests of the country, the principles of our institutions, the tendencies of public measures. But the unhappiness is, they do not *study;* and, until they do, they cannot rise by political action. A great amount of time, which, if well used, would form an enlightened population, is now wasted on newspapers and conversations, which inflame the passions, which unscrupulously distort the truth, which denounce moral independence as treachery to one's party, which agitate the country for no higher end than a triumph over opponents; and thus multitudes are degraded into men-worshippers or men-haters, into the dupes of the ambitious, or the slaves of a faction. To rise, the people must substitute reflection for passion. There is no other way. By these remarks, I do not mean to charge on the laboring class all the passionateness of the country. All classes partake of the madness, and all are debased by it. The fiery spirits are not confined to one portion of the community. The men, whose ravings resound through the halls of Congress, and are then circulated through the country as eloquence, are not taken from among those who toil. Party prejudices break out as fiercely on the exchange, and even in the saloon, as in the workshop. The disease has spread everywhere. Yet it does not dishearten me, for I see that it admits of mitigation, if not of cure. I trust that these lectures, and other sources of intellectual enjoyment now opening to the public, will abate the fever of political excitement, by giving better occupation to the mind. Much, too, may be hoped from the growing self-respect of the people, which will make them shrink indignantly from the disgrace of being used as blinded partisans and unreflecting tools. Much also is to be hoped from the discovery, which must sooner or later be made, that the importance of government is enormously overrated, that it does not deserve all this stir, that there are vastly more effectual means of human happiness. Political institutions are to be less and less deified, and to shrink into a narrower space; and just in proportion as a wiser estimate of government prevails, the present frenzy of political excitement will be discovered and put to shame.

I have now said what I do not mean by the elevation of the laboring classes. It is not an outward change of condition. It is not release from labor. It is not struggling for another rank. It is not political power. I understand something deeper. I know but one elevation of a human being, and that is elevation of soul. Without this, it matters nothing where a man stands or what he possesses; and with it, he towers, he is one of God's nobility, no matter what place he holds in the social scale. There is but one elevation for a laborer, and for all other men. There are not different kinds of dignity for different orders of men, but one and the same to all. The only elevation of a human being consists in the exercise, growth, energy of the higher principles and powers of his soul. A bird may be shot upward to the skies by a foreign force; but it rises, in the true sense of the word, only when it spreads its own wings and soars by its own living power. So a man may be thrust upward into a conspicuous place by outward accidents; but he rises, only in so far as he exerts himself, and expands his best faculties, and ascends by a free effort to a nobler region of thought and action. Such is the elevation I desire for the laborer, and I desire no other. This elevation is indeed to be aided by an improvement of his outward condition, and in turn it greatly improves his outward lot; and thus connected, outward good is real and great; but supposing it to exist in separation from inward growth and life, it would be nothing worth, nor would I raise a finger to promote it.

I know it will be said, that such elevation as I have spoken of is not and cannot be within the reach of the laboring multitude, and of consequence they ought not to be tantalized with dreams of its attainment. It will be said that the principal part of men are plainly designed to work on matter for the acquisition of material and corporeal good, and that, in such, the spirit is of necessity too wedded to matter to rise above it. This objection will be considered by and by; but I would just observe, in passing, that the objector must have studied very carelessly the material world, if he suppose that it is meant to be the grave of the minds of most of those who occupy it. Matter was made for spirit, body for mind. The mind, the spirit, is the end of this living organization of flesh and bones, of nerves and muscles; and the end of this vast system of sea and land, and air and skies. This unbounded creation of sun, and moon, and stars, and clouds, and seasons, was not ordained merely to feed and clothe the body, but first and supremely to awaken, nourish, and expand the soul, to be the school of the intellect, the nurse of thought and imagination, the field for the active powers, a revelation of the Creator, and a bond of social union. We were placed in the material creation, not to be its slaves, but to master it, and to make it a minister to our highest powers. It is interesting to observe how much the material world does for the mind. Most of the sciences, arts, professions, and occupations of life, grow out of our connection with matter. The natural philosopher, the physician, the lawyer, the artist, and the legislator, find the objects or occasions of their researches in matter. The poet borrows his beautiful imagery from matter. The sculptor and painter express their noble conceptions through matter. Material wants rouse the world to activity. The material organs of sense, especially the eye, wake up infinite thoughts in the mind. To maintain, then, that the mass of men are and must be so immersed in matter, that their souls cannot rise, is to contradict the great end of their connection with matter. I maintain that the philosophy which does not see, in the laws and phenomena of outward nature, the means of awakening mind, is lamentably short-sighted; and that a state of society which leaves the mass of men to be crushed and famished in soul by excessive toils on matter is at war with God's designs, and turns into means of bondage what was meant to free and expand the soul.

Elevation of soul, this is to be desired for the laborer as for every human being; and what does this mean? The phrase, I am aware, is vague, and often serves for mere declamation. Let me strive to convey some precise ideas of it; and in doing this, I can use no language which will save the hearer from the necessity of thought. The subject is a spiritual one. It carries us into the depths of our own nature, and I can say nothing about it worth saying, without tasking your powers of attention, without demanding some mental toil. I know that these lectures are meant for entertainment rather than mental labor; but, as I have told you, I have great faith in labor, and I feel that I cannot be more useful than in exciting the hearer to some vigorous action of mind.

Elevation of soul, in what does this consist? Without aiming at philosophical exactness, I shall convey a sufficiently precise idea of it, by saying that it consists, first, in force of thought exerted for the acquisition of truth; secondly, in force of pure and generous feeling; thirdly, in force of moral purpose. Each of these topics needs a lecture for its development. I must confine myself to the first; from which, however, you may learn in a measure my views of the other two.—Before entering on this topic, let me offer one preliminary remark. To every man who would rise in dignity as a man, be he rich or poor, ignorant or instructed, there is one essential condition, one effort, one purpose, without which not a step can be taken. He must resolutely purpose and labor to free himself from whatever he knows to be wrong in his motives and life. He who habitually allows himself in any known crime or wrong-doing, effectually bars his progress towards a higher intellectual and moral life. On this point every man should deal honestly with himself. If he will not listen to his conscience, rebuking him for violations of plain duty, let him not dream of self-elevation. The foundation is wanting. He will build, if at all, in sand.

I now proceed to my main subject. I have said that the elevation of a man is to be sought, or rather consists, first, in force of thought exerted for the acquisition of truth; and to this I ask your serious attention. Thought, thought, is the fundamental distinction of mind, and the great work of life. All that a man does outwardly is but the expression and completion of his inward thought. To work effectually, he must think clearly. To act nobly, he must think nobly. Intellectual force is a principal element of the soul's life, and should be proposed by every man as a principal end of his being. It is common to distinguish between the intellect and the conscience, between the power of thought and virtue, and to say that virtuous action is worth more than strong thinking. But we mutilate our nature by thus drawing lines between actions or energies of the soul, which are intimately, indissolubly bound together. The head and the heart are not more vitally connected than thought and virtue. Does not conscience include, as a part of itself, the noblest action of the intellect or reason? Do we not degrade it by making it a mere feeling? Is it not something more? Is it not a wise discernment of the right, the holy, the good? Take away thought from virtue, and what remains worthy of a man? Is not high virtue more than blind instinct? Is it not founded on, and does it not include clear, bright perceptions of what is lovely and grand in character and action? Without power of thought, what we call conscientiousness, or a desire to do right, shoots out into illusion, exaggeration, pernicious excess. The most cruel deeds on earth have been perpetrated in the name of conscience. Men have hated and murdered one another from a sense of duty. The worst frauds have taken the name of pious. Thought, intelligence, is the dignity of a man, and no man is rising but in proportion as he is learning to think clearly and forcibly, or directing the energy of his mind to the acquisition of truth. Every man, in whatsoever condition, is to be a student. No matter what other vocation he may have, his chief vocation is to Think.

I say every man is to be a student, a thinker. This does not mean that he is to shut himself within four walls, and bend his body and mind over books. Men thought before books were written, and some of the greatest thinkers never entered what we call a study. Nature, Scripture, society, and life, present perpetual subjects for thought; and the man who collects, concentrates, employs his faculties on any of these subjects for the purpose of getting the truth, is so far a student, a thinker, a philosopher, and is rising to the dignity of a man. It is time that we should cease to limit to professed scholars the titles of thinkers, philosophers. Whoever seeks truth with an earnest mind, no matter when or how, belongs to the school of intellectual men.

In a loose sense of the word, all men may be said to think; that is, a succession of ideas, notions, passes through their minds from morning to night; but in as far as this succession is passive, undirected, or governed only by accident and outward impulse, it has little more claim to dignity than the experience of the brute, who receives, with like passiveness, sensations from abroad through his waking hours. Such thought, if thought it may be called, having no aim, is as useless as the vision of an eye which rests on nothing, which flies without pause over earth and sky, and of consequence receives no distinct image. Thought, in its true sense, is an energy of intellect. In thought, the mind not only receives impressions or suggestions from without or within, but reacts upon them, collects its attention, concentrates its forces upon them, breaks them up and analyzes them like a living laboratory, and then combines them anew, traces their connections, and thus impresses itself on all the objects which engage it.

The universe in which we live was plainly meant by God to stir up such thought as has now been described. It is full of difficulty and mystery, and can only be penetrated and unravelled by the concentration of the intellect. Every object, even the simplest in nature and society, every event of life, is made up of various elements subtly bound together; so that, to understand anything, we must reduce it from its complexity to its parts and principles, and examine their relations to one another. Nor is this all. Every thing which enters the mind not only contains a depth of mystery in itself, but is connected by a thousand ties with all other things. The universe is not a disorderly, disconnected heap, but a beautiful whole, stamped throughout with unity, so as to be an image of the One Infinite Spirit. Nothing stands alone. All things are knit together, each existing for all and all for each. The humblest object has infinite connections. The vegetable, which you saw on your table to-day, came to you from the first plant which God made to grow on the earth, and was the product of the rains and sunshine of six thousand years. Such a universe demands thought to be understood; and we are placed in it to think, to put forth the power within, to look beneath the surface of things, to look beyond particular facts and events to their causes and effects, to their reasons and ends, their mutual influences, their diversities and resemblances, their proportions and harmonies, and the general laws which bind them together. This is what I mean by thinking; and by such thought the mind rises to a dignity which humbly represents the greatness of the Divine intellect; that is, it rises more and more to consistency of views, to broad general principles, to universal truths, to glimpses of the order and harmony and infinity of the Divine system, and thus to a deep, enlightened veneration of the Infinite Father. Do not be startled, as if I were holding out an elevation of mind utterly to be despaired of; for all thinking, which aims honestly and earnestly to see things as they are, to see them in their connections, and to bring the loose, conflicting ideas of the mind into consistency and harmony, all such thinking, no matter in what sphere, is an approach to the dignity of which I speak. You are all capable of the thinking which I recommend. You have all practised it in a degree. The child, who casts an inquiring eye on a new toy, and breaks it to pieces that he may discover the mysterious cause of its movements, has begun the work of which I speak, has begun to be a philosopher, has begun to penetrate the unknown, to seek consistency and harmony of thought; and let him go on as he has begun, and make it one great business of life to inquire into the elements, connections, and reasons of whatever he witnesses in his own breast, or in society, or in outward nature, and, be his condition what it may, he will rise by degrees to a freedom and force of thought, to a breadth and unity of views, which will be to him an inward revelation and promise of the intellectual greatness for which he was created.

You will observe, that in speaking of force of thought as the elevation of the laborer and of every human being,

I have continually supposed this force to be exerted for the purpose of acquiring truth. I beg you never to lose sight of this motive, for it is essential to intellectual dignity. Force of thought may be put forth for other purposes,—to amass wealth for selfish gratification, to give the individual power over others, to blind others, to weave a web of sophistry, to cast a deceitful lustre on vice, to make the worse appear the better cause. But energy of thought so employed, is suicidal. The intellect, in becoming a pander to vice, a tool of the passions, an advocate of lies, becomes not only degraded, but diseased. It loses the capacity of distinguishing truth from falsehood, good from evil, right from wrong; it becomes as worthless as an eye which cannot distinguish between colors or forms. Woe to that mind which wants the love of truth! For want of this, genius has become a scourge to the world, its breath a poisonous exhalation, its brightness a seducer into paths of pestilence and death. Truth is the light of the Infinite Mind, and the image of God in his creatures. Nothing endures but truth. The dreams, fictions, theories, which men would substitute for it, soon die. Without its guidance effort is vain, and hope baseless. Accordingly, the love of truth, a deep thirst for it, a deliberate purpose to seek it and hold it fast, may be considered as the very foundation of human culture and dignity. Precious as thought is, the love of truth is still more precious; for without it, thought—thought wanders and wastes itself, and precipitates men into guilt and misery. There is no greater defect in education and the pulpit than that they inculcate so little an impartial, earnest, reverential love of truth, a readiness to toil, to live and die for it. Let the laboring man be imbued in a measure with this spirit; let him learn to regard himself as endowed with the power of thought, for the very end of acquiring truth; let him learn to regard truth as more precious than his daily bread; and the spring of true and perpetual elevation is touched within him. He has begun to be a man; he becomes one of the elect of his race. Nor do I despair of this elevation of the laborer. Unhappily little, almost nothing, has been done as yet to inspire either rich or poor with the love of truth for its own sake, or for the life, and inspiration, and dignity it gives to the soul. The prosperous have as little of this principle as the laboring mass. I think, indeed, that the spirit of luxurious, fashionable life, is more hostile to it than the hardships of the poor. Under a wise culture, this principle may be awakened in all classes, and wherever awakened, it will form philosophers, successful and noble thinkers. These remarks seem to me particularly important, as showing how intimate a union subsists between the moral and intellectual nature, and how both must work together from the beginning. All human culture rests on a moral foundation, on an impartial, disinterested spirit, on a willingness to make sacrifices to the truth. Without this moral power, mere force of thought avails nothing towards our elevation.

I am aware that I shall be told that the work of thought which I have insisted on is difficult,—that to collect and concentrate the mind for the truth is harder than to toil with the hands. Be it so. But are we weak enough to hope to rise without toil? Does any man, laborer or not, expect to invigorate body or mind without strenuous effort? Does not the child grow and get strength by throwing a degree of hardship and vehemence and conflict into his very sports? Does not life without difficulty become insipid and joyless? Cannot a strong interest turn difficulty into pleasure? Let the love of truth, of which I have spoken, be awakened, and obstacles in the way to it will whet, not discourage, the mind, and inspire a new delight into its acquisition.

I have hitherto spoken of force of thought in general. My views will be given more completely and distinctly, by considering, next, the objects on which this force is to be exerted. These may be reduced to two classes, matter and mind—the physical world which falls under our eyes, and the spiritual world. The working man is particularly called to make matter his study, because his business is to work on it, and he works more wisely, effectually, cheerfully, and honorably, in proportion as he knows what he acts upon, knows the laws and forces of which he avails himself, understands the reason of what he does, and can explain the changes which fall under his eye. Labor becomes a new thing when thought is thrown into it, when the mind keeps pace with the hands. Every farmer should study chemistry, so as to understand the elements or ingredients which enter into soils, vegetation, and manures, and the laws according to which they combine with and are loosened from one another. So, the mechanic should understand the mechanical powers, the laws of motion, and the history and composition of the various substances which he works on. Let me add, that the farmer and the mechanic should cultivate the perception of beauty. What a charm and new value might the farmer add to his grounds and cottage, were he a man of taste! The product of the mechanic, be it great or small, a house or a shoe, is worth more, sometimes much more, if he can succeed in giving it the grace of proportion. In France, it is not uncommon to teach drawing to mechanics, that they may get a quick eye and a sure hand, and may communicate to their works the attraction of beauty. Every man should aim to impart this perfection to his labors. The more of mind we carry into toil, the better. Without a habit of thought, a man works more like a brute or machine than like a man. With it, his soul is kept alive amidst his toils. He learns to fix an observing eye on the processes of his trade, catches hints which abridge labor, gets glimpses of important discoveries, and is sometimes able to perfect his art. Even now, after all the miracles of invention which honor our age, we little suspect what improvements of machinery are to spring from spreading intelligence and natural science among workmen.

But I do not stop here. Nature is to engage our force of thought, not simply for the aid which the knowledge of it gives in working, but for a higher end. Nature should be studied for its own sake, because so wonderful a work of God, because impressed with his perfection, because radiant with beauty, and grandeur, and wisdom, and beneficence. A laborer, like every other man, is to be liberally educated, that is, he is to get knowledge, not only for his bodily subsistence, but for the life, and growth, and elevation of his mind. Am I asked, whether I expect the laborer to traverse the whole circle of the physical sciences? Certainly not; nor do I expect the merchant, or the lawyer, or preacher to do it. Nor is this at all necessary to elevation of soul. The truths of physical science, which give greatest dignity to the mind, are those general laws of the creation which it has required ages to unfold, but which an active mind, bent on self-enlargement, may so far study and comprehend, as to interpret the changes of nature perpetually taking place around us, as to see in all the forces of the universe the workings of one Infinite Power, and in all its arrangements the manifestation of one unsearchable wisdom.

And this leads me to observe the second great object on which force of thought is to be exerted, and that is mind, spirit, comprehending under this word God and all his intelligent offspring. This is the subject of what are called the metaphysical and moral sciences. This is the grand field for thought; for the outward, material world is the shadow of the spiritual, and made to minister to it. This study is of vast extent. It comprehends theology, metaphysics, moral philosophy, political science, history, literature. This is a formidable list, and it may seem to include a vast amount of knowledge which is necessarily placed beyond the reach of the laborer. But it is an interesting thought, that the key to these various sciences is given to every human being in his own nature, so that they are peculiarly accessible to him. How is it that I get my ideas of God, of my fellow-creatures, of the deeds, suffering, motives, which make up universal history? I comprehend all these from the consciousness of what passes in my own soul. The mind within me is a type representative of all others, and therefore I can understand all. Whence come my conceptions of the intelligence, and justice, and goodness, and power of God? It is because my own spirit contains the germs of these attributes. The ideas of them are first derived from my own nature, and therefore I comprehend them in other beings. Thus the foundation of all the sciences which treat of mind is laid in every man's breast. The good man is exercising in his business and family faculties and affections which bear a likeness to the attributes of the Divinity, and to the energies which have made the greatest men illustrious; so that in studying himself, in learning the highest principles and laws of his own soul, he is in truth studying God, studying all human history, studying the philosophy which has immortalized the sages of ancient and modern times. In every man's mind and life all other minds and lives are more or less represented and wrapped up. To study other things, I must go into the outward world, and perhaps go far. To study the science of spirit, I must come home and enter my own soul. The profoundest books that have ever been written do nothing more than bring out, place in clear light, what is passing in each of your minds. So near you, so within you, is the grandest truth.

I have, indeed, no expectation that the laborer is to understand in detail the various sciences which relate to mind. Few men in any vocation do so understand them. Nor is it necessary; though, where time can be commanded, the thorough study of some particular branch, in which the individual has a special interest, will be found of great utility. What is needed to elevate the soul is, not that a man should know all that has been thought and written in regard to the spiritual nature, not that a man should become an encyclopædia, but that the great ideas, in which all discoveries terminate, which sum up all sciences, which the philosopher extracts from infinite details, may be comprehended and felt. It is not the quantity but the quality of knowledge which determines the mind's dignity. A man of immense information may, through the want of large and comprehensive ideas, be far inferior in intellect to a laborer, who, with little knowledge, has yet seized on great truths. For example, I do not expect the laborer to study theology in the ancient languages, in the writings of the Fathers, in the history of sects, &c., &c.; nor is this needful. All theology, scattered as it is through countless volumes, is summed up in the idea of God; and let this idea shine bright and clear in the laborer's soul and he has the essence of theological libraries, and a far higher light than has visited thousands of renowned divines. A great mind is formed by a few great ideas, not by an infinity of loose details. I have known very learned men who seemed to me very poor in intellect, because they had no grand thoughts. What avails it that a man has studied ever so minutely the histories of Greece and Rome, if the great ideas of freedom, and beauty, and valor, and spiritual energy, have not been kindled by these records into living fires in his soul? The illumination of an age does not consist in the amount of its knowledge, but in the broad and noble principles of which that knowledge is the foundation and inspirer. The truth is, that the most laborious and successful student is confined in his researches to a very few of God's works; but this limited knowledge of things may still suggest universal laws, broad principles, grand ideas, and these elevate the mind. There are certain thoughts, principles, ideas, which by their nature rule over all knowledge, which are intrinsically glorious, quickening, all-comprehending, eternal, and with these I desire to enrich the mind of the laborer and of every human being.

To illustrate my meaning, let me give a few examples of the great ideas which belong to the study or science of mind. Of course, the first of these, the grandest, the most comprehensive, is the idea of God, the Parent Mind, the Primitive and Infinite Intelligence. Every man's elevation is to be measured first and chiefly by his conception of this Great Being; and to attain a just, and bright, and quickening knowledge of Him, is the highest aim of thought. In truth, the great end of the universe, of revelation, of life, is to develop in us the idea of God. Much earnest, patient, laborious thought is required to see this Infinite Being as He is, to rise above the low, gross notions of the Divinity, which rush in upon us from our passions, from our selfish partialities, and from the low-minded world around us. There is one view of God particularly suited to elevate us. I mean the view of Him as the "Father of our spirits;" as having created us with great powers to grow up to perfection; as having ordained all outward things to minister to the progress of the soul; as always present to inspire and strengthen us, to wake us up to inward life, and to judge and rebuke our wrong-doing; as looking with parental joy on our resistance of evil; as desiring to communicate himself to our minds for ever. This one idea, expanded in the breast of the laborer, is a germ of elevation more fruitful than all science, no matter how extensive or profound, which treats only of outward finite things. It places him in the first rank of human beings. You hear of great theologians. He only deserves the name, be his condition what it may, who has, by thought and obedience, purified and enlarged his conception of God.

From the idea of God, I proceed to another grand one, that of man, of human nature; and this should be the object of serious, intense thought. Few men know, as yet, what a man is. They know his clothes, his complexion, his property, his rank, his follies, and his outward life. But the thought of his inward being, his proper humanity, has hardly dawned on multitudes; and yet, who can live a man's life that does not know what is the distinctive worth of a human being? It is interesting to observe how faithful men generally are to their idea of a man; how they act up to it. Spread the notion that courage is true manhood, and how many will die rather than fall short of that standard; and hence, the true idea of a man, brought out in the laborer's mind, elevates him above every other class who may want it. Am I asked for my conception of the dignity of a human being? I should say, that it consists, first, in that spiritual principle, called sometimes the reason, sometimes the conscience, which, rising above what is local and temporary, discerns immutable truth and everlasting right; which, in the midst of imperfect things, conceives of perfection; which is universal and impartial, standing in direct opposition to the partial, selfish principles of human nature; which says to me with authority, that my neighbor is as precious as myself, and his rights as sacred as my own; which commands me to receive all truth, however it may war with my pride, and to do all justice, however it may conflict with my interest; and which calls me to rejoice with love in all that is beautiful, good, holy, happy, in whatever being these attributes may be found. This principle is a ray of Divinity in man. We do not know what man is, still something of the celestial grandeur of this principle in the soul may be discerned. There is another grand view of man, included indeed in the former, yet deserving distinct notice. He is a free being; created to act from a spring in his own breast, to form himself and to decide his own destiny; connected intimately with nature, but not enslaved to it; connected still more strongly with God, yet not enslaved even to the Divinity, but having power to render or withhold the service due to his Creator; encompassed by a thousand warring forces, by physical elements which inflict pleasure and pain, by dangers seen and unseen, by the influences of a tempting, sinful world, yet endued by God with power to contend with all, to perfect himself by conflict with the very forces which threaten to overwhelm him. Such is the idea of a man. Happy he in whom it is unfolded by earnest thought!

Had I time, I should be glad to speak of other great ideas belonging to the science of mind, and which sum up and give us, in one bright expression, the speculations of ages. The idea of human life, of its true end and greatness; the idea of virtue, as the absolute and ultimate good; the idea of liberty, which is the highest thought of political science, and which, by its intimate presence to the minds of the people, is the chief spring of our country's life and greatness,—all these might be enlarged on; and I might show how these may be awakened in the laborer, and may give him an elevation which many who are above labor want. But, leaving all these, I will only refer to another, one of the most important results of the science of mind, and which the laborer, in common with every man, may and should receive, and should strengthen by patient thought. It is the idea of his importance as an individual. He is to understand that he has a value, not as belonging to a community, and contributing to a general good which is distinct from himself, but on his own account. He is not a mere part of a machine. In a machine the parts are useless, but as conducing to the end of the whole, for which alone they subsist. Not so a man. He is not simply a means, but an end, and exists for his own sake, for the unfolding of his nature, for his own virtue and happiness. True, he is to work for others, but not servilely, not with a broken spirit, not so as to degrade himself: he is to work for others from a wise self-regard, from principles of justice and benevolence, and in the exercise of a free will and intelligence, by which his own character is perfected. His individual dignity, not derived from birth, from success, from wealth, from outward show, but consisting in the indestructible principles of his soul,—this ought to enter into his habitual consciousness. I do not speak rhetorically or use the cant of rhapsodists, but I utter my calm, deliberate conviction, when I say that the laborer ought to regard himself with a self-respect unknown to the proudest monarch who rests on outward rank.

I have now illustrated what I mean by the great ideas which exalt the mind. Their worth and power cannot be exaggerated. They are the mightiest influences on earth. One great thought breathed into a man may regenerate him. The idea of freedom in ancient and modern republics, the idea of inspiration in various religious sects, the idea of immortality, how have these triumphed over worldly interests! How many heroes and martyrs have they formed! Great ideas are mightier than the passions. To awaken them is the highest office of education. As yet it has been little thought of. The education of the mass of the people has consisted in giving them mechanical habits, in breaking them to current usages and modes of thinking, in teaching religion and morality as traditions. It is time that a rational culture should take the place of mechanical; that men should learn to act more from ideas and principles, and less from blind impulse and undiscerning imitation.

Am I met here by the constantly recurring objection, that such great thoughts as have now been treated of are not to be expected in the multitude of men whose means of culture are so confined? To this difficulty I shall reply in the next lecture; but I wish to state a fact, or law of our nature, very cheering to those who, with few means, still pant for generous improvement. It is this, that great ideas come to us less from outward, direct, laborious teaching, than from indirect influences, and from the native working of our own minds; so that those who want the outward apparatus for extensive learning are not cut off from them. Thus, laborious teachers may instruct us for years in God, and virtue, and the soul, and we may remain nearly as ignorant of them as at the beginning; whilst a look, a tone, an act of a fellow-creature, who is kindled by a grand thought, and who is thrown in our path at some susceptible season of life, will do much to awaken and expand this thought within us. It is a matter of experience that the greatest ideas often come to us, when right-minded, we know not how. They flash on us as lights from heaven. A man seriously given to the culture of his mind in virtue and truth finds himself under better teaching than that of man. Revelations of his own soul, of God's intimate presence, of the grandeur of the creation, of the glory of disinterestedness, of the deformity of wrong-doing, of the dignity of universal justice, of the might of moral principle, of the immutableness of truth, of immortality, and of the inward sources of happiness; these revelations, awakening a thirst for something higher than he is or has, come of themselves to an humble, self-improving man. Sometimes a common scene in nature, one of the common relations of life, will open itself to us with a brightness and pregnancy of meaning unknown before. Sometimes a thought of this kind forms an era in life. It changes the whole future course. It is a new creation. And these great ideas are not confined to men of any class. They are communications of the Infinite Mind to all minds which are open to their reception; and labor is a far better condition for their reception than luxurious or fashionable life. It is even better than a studious life, when this fosters vanity, pride, and the spirit of jealous competition. A childlike simplicity attracts these revelations more than a selfish culture of intellect, however far extended.—Perhaps a caution should be added to these suggestions. In speaking of great ideas, as sometimes springing up of themselves, as sudden illuminations, I have no thought of teaching that we are to wait for them passively, or to give up our minds unthinkingly to their control. We must prepare ourselves for them by faithfulness to our own powers, by availing ourselves of all means of culture within our reach; and, what is more, these illuminations, if they come, are not distinct, complete, perfect views, but glimpses, suggestions, flashes, given us, like all notices and impressions from the outward world, to be thought upon, to be made subjects of patient reflection, to be brought by our own intellect and activity into their true connection with all our other thoughts. A great idea, without reflection, may dazzle and bewilder, may destroy the balance and proportion of the mind, and impel to dangerous excess. It is to awaken the free, earnest exertion of our powers, to rouse us from passiveness to activity and life, that inward inspirations, and the teachings of outward nature, are accorded to the mind.

I have thus spoken at large of that force of thought which the laborer is to seek as his true elevation; and I will close the subject with observing, that on whatever objects or for whatever purposes this force may be exerted, one purpose should be habitually predominant, and that is, to gain a larger, clearer comprehension of all the duties of life. Thought cannot take too wide a range; but its chief aim should be to acquire juster and brighter perceptions of the right and the good, in every relation and condition in which we may be placed. Do not imagine that I am here talking professionally, or sliding unconsciously, by the force of habit, into the tone of the pulpit. The subject of duty belongs equally to all professions and all conditions. It were as wise to think of living without breath, or of seeing without light, as to exclude moral and religious principle from the work of self-elevation. And I say this, because you are in danger of mistaking mere knowledge for improvement. Knowledge fails of its best end when it does not minister to a high virtue. I do not say that we are never to think, read, or study, but for the express purpose of learning our duties. The mind must not be tied down by rigid rules. Curiosity, amusement, natural tastes, may innocently direct reading and study to a certain extent. Even in these cases, however, we are bound to improve ourselves morally as well as intellectually, by seeking truth and rejecting falsehood, and by watching against the taint which inheres in almost all human productions. What avails intellectual without moral power? How little does it avail us to study the outward world, if its greatness inspire no reverence of its Author, if its beneficence awaken no kindred love towards our fellow-creatures! How little does it avail us to study history, if the past do not help us to comprehend the dangers and duties of the present; if from the sufferings of those who have gone before us, we do not learn how to suffer, and from their great and good deeds how to act nobly; if the development of the human heart, in different ages and countries, do not give us a better knowledge of ourselves! How little does literature benefit us, if the sketches of life and character, the generous sentiments, the testimonies to disinterestedness and rectitude, with which it abounds, do not incite and guide us to wiser, purer, and more graceful action! How little substantial good do we derive from poetry and the fine arts, if the beauty, which delights the imagination, do not warm and refine the heart, and raise us to the love and admiration of what is fair, and perfect, and lofty, in character and life! Let our studies be as wide as our condition will allow; but let this be their highest aim, to instruct us in our duty and happiness, in the perfection of our nature, in the true use of life, in the best direction of our powers. Then is the culture of intellect an unmixed good, when it is sacredly used to enlighten the conscience, to feed the flame of generous sentiment, to perfect us in our common employments, to throw a grace over our common actions, to make us sources of innocent cheerfulness and centres of holy influence, and to give us courage, strength, stability, amidst the sudden changes and sore temptations and trials of life.

LECTURE II

IN my last lecture I invited your attention to a subject of great interest,—the elevation of the laboring portion of the community. I proposed to consider, first, in what this elevation consists; secondly the objections which may be made to its practicableness; thirdly, the circumstances which now favor it, and gives us hope that it will be more and more accomplished. In considering the first head, I began with stating in what the elevation of the laboring class does not consist, and then proceeded to show positively what it is, what it does consist in. I want time to retrace the ground over which we then travelled. I must trust to your memories. I was obliged by my narrow limits to confine myself chiefly to the consideration of the intellectual elevation which the laborer is to propose; though, in treating this topic, I showed the moral, religious, social improvements which enter into his true dignity. I observed that the laborer was to be a student, a thinker, an intellectual man, as well as a laborer; and suggested the qualifications of this truth which are required by this peculiar employment, by his daily engagement in manual toil. I now come to consider the objections which spring up in many minds, when such views of the laborer's destiny are given. This is our second head.

First, it will be objected, that the laboring multitude cannot command a variety of books, or spend much time in reading; and how, then, can they gain the force of thought, and the great ideas, which were treated of in the former lecture? This objection grows out of the prevalent disposition to confound intellectual improvement with book-learning. Some seem to think that there is a kind of magic in a printed page, that types give a higher knowledge than can be gained from other sources. Reading is considered as the royal road to intellectual eminence. This prejudice I have virtually set aside in my previous remarks; but it has taken so strong a hold of many as to need some consideration. I shall not attempt to repel the objection by decrying books. Truly good books are more than mines to those who can understand them. They are the breathings of the great souls of past times. Genius is not embalmed in them, as is sometimes said, but *lives* in them perpetually. But we need not many books to answer the great ends of reading. A few are better than many, and a little time given to a faithful study of the few will be enough to quicken thought and enrich the mind. The greatest men have not been book-men. Washington, it has often been said, was no great reader. The learning commonly gathered from books is of less worth than the truths we gain from experience and reflection. Indeed, most of the knowledge from reading, in these days, being acquired with little mental action, and seldom or never reflected on and turned to use, is very much a vain show. Events stirring the mind to earnest thought and vigorous application of its resources, do vastly more to elevate the mind than most of our studies at the present time. Few of the books read among us deserve to be read. Most of them have no principle of life, as is proved by the fact that they die the year of their birth. They do not come from thinkers, and how can they awaken thought? A great proportion of the reading of this city is useless, I had almost said pernicious. I should be sorry to see our laborers exchanging their toils for the reading of many of our young ladies and young gentlemen, who look on the intellect as given them for amusement; who read, as they visit, for amusement, who discuss no great truths and put forth no energy of thought on the topics which fly through their minds. With this insensibility to the dignity of the intellect, and this frittering away of the mind on superficial reading, I see not with what face they can claim superiority to the laboring mass, who certainly understand one thing thoroughly, that is, their own business, and who are doing something useful for themselves and their fellow-creatures. The great use of books is to rouse us to thought; to turn us to questions which great men have been working on for ages; to furnish us with materials for the exercise of judgment, imagination, and moral feeling; to breathe into us a moral life from higher spirits than our own; and this benefit of books may be enjoyed by those who have not much time for retired study.

It must not be forgotten, by those who despair of the laboring classes because they cannot live in libraries, that the highest sources of truth, light, and elevation of mind, are not libraries, but our inward and outward experience. Human life, with its joys and sorrows, its burdens and alleviations, its crimes and virtues, its deep wants, its solemn changes, and its retributions, always pressing on us; what a library is this! and who may not study it? Every human being is a volume worthy to be studied. The books which circulate most freely through the community are those which give us pictures of human life. How much more improving is the original, did we know how to read it? The laborer has this page always open before him; and, still more, the laborer is every day writing a volume more full of instruction than all human productions,—I mean his own life. No work of the most exalted genius can teach us so much as the revelation of human nature in the secrets of our own souls, in the workings of our own passions, in the operations of our own intelligence, in the retributions which follow our own good and evil deeds, in the dissatisfaction with the present, in the spontaneous thoughts and aspirations which form part of every man's biography. The study of our own history from childhood, of all the stages of our development, of the good and bad influences which have beset us, of our mutations of feeling and purpose, and of the great current which is setting us towards future happiness or woe,—this is a study to make us nobly wise; and who of us has not access to this fountain of eternal truth? May not the laborer study and understand the pages which he is writing in his own breast?

In these remarks, I have aimed to remove the false notion into which the laborers themselves fall, that they can do little towards acquiring force and fulness of thought, because in want of books. I shall next turn to prejudices more confined to other classes. A very common one is, that the many are not to be called to think, study, improve their minds, because a privileged few are intended by God to do their thinking for them. "Providence," it is said, "raises up superior minds, whose office it is to discover truth for the rest of the race. Thinking and manual toil are not meant to go together. The division of labor is a great law of nature. One man is to serve society by his head, another by his hands. Let each class keep to its proper work." These doctrines I protest against. I deny to any individual or class this monopoly of thought. Who among men can show God's commission to think for his brethren, to shape passively the intellect of the mass, to stamp his own image on them as if they were wax? As well might a few claim a monopoly of light and air, of seeing and breathing, as of thought. Is not the intellect as universal a gift as the organs of sight and respiration? Is not truth as freely spread abroad as the atmosphere or the sun's rays? Can we imagine that God's highest gifts of intelligence, imagination, and moral power were bestowed to provide only for animal wants? to be denied the natural means of growth, which is action? to be starved by drudgery? Were the mass of men made to be monsters? to grow only in a few organs and faculties, and to pine away and shrivel in others? or were they made to put forth all the powers of men, especially the best and most distinguishing? No man, not the lowest, is all hands, all bones and muscles. The mind is more essential to human nature, and more enduring, than the limbs; and was this made to lie dead? Is not thought the right and duty of all? Is not truth alike precious to all? Is not truth the natural ailment of the mind, as plainly as the wholesome grain is of the body? Is not the mind adapted to thought, as plainly as the eye to light, the ear to sound? Who dares to withhold it from its natural action, its natural element and joy? Undoubtedly some men are more gifted than others, and are marked out for more studious lives. But the work of such men is not to do others' thinking for them, but to help them to think more vigorously and effectually. Great minds are to make others great. Their superiority is to be used, not to break the multitude to intellectual vassalage, not to establish over them a spiritual tyranny, but to rouse them from lethargy, and to aid them to judge for themselves. The light and life which spring up in one soul are to be spread far and wide. Of all treasons against humanity, there is no one worse than his who employs great intellectual force to keep down the intellect of his less favored brother.

It is sometimes surged by those who consider the multitude as not intended to think, that at best they can learn but little, and that this is likely to harm rather than to do them good. "A little learning," we are told, "is a dangerous thing." "Shallow draughts" of knowledge are worse than ignorance. The mass of the people, it is said, can go to the bottom of nothing; and the result of stimulating them to thought will be the formation of a dangerous set of half-thinkers. To this argument I reply, first, that it has the inconvenience of proving too much; for, if valid, it shows that none of any class ought to think. For who, I would ask, can go to the bottom of anything? Whose "learning" is not "little"? Whose "draughts" of knowledge are not "shallow"? Who of us has fathomed the depths of a single product of nature or a single event in history? Who of us is not baffled by the mysteries in a grain of sand? How contracted the range of the widest intellect! But is our knowledge, because so little, of no worth? Are we to despise the lessons which are taught us in this nook of creation, in this narrow round of human experience, because an infinite universe stretches around us, which we have no means of exploring, and in which the earth, and sun, and planets dwindle to a point? We should remember that the known, however little it may be, is in harmony with the boundless unknown, and a step towards it. We should remember, too, that the gravest truths may be gathered from a very narrow compass of information. God is revealed in his smallest work as truly as in his greatest. The principles of human nature may be studied better in a family than in the history of the world. The finite is a manifestation of the infinite. The great ideas, of which I have formerly spoken, are within the reach of every man who thirsts for truth, and seeks it with singleness of mind. I will only add, that the laboring class are not now condemned to draughts of knowledge so shallow as to merit scorn. Many of them know more of the outward world than all the philosophers of antiquity; and Christianity has opened to them mysteries of the spiritual world which kings and prophets were not privileged to understand. And are they, then, to be doomed to spiritual inaction, as incapable of useful thought?

It is sometimes said, that the multitude may think on the common business of life, but not on higher subjects, and especially on religion. This, it is said, must be received on authority; on this, men in general can form no judgment of their own. But this is the last subject on which the individual should be willing to surrender himself to others' dictation. In nothing has he so strong an interest. In nothing is it so important that his mind and heart should be alive and engaged. In nothing has he readier means of judging for himself. In nothing, as history shows, is he more likely to be led astray by such as assume the office of thinking for him. Religion is a subject open to all minds. Its great truths have their foundation in the soul itself, and their proofs surround us on all sides. God has not shut up the evidence of his being in a few books, written in a foreign language, and locked up in the libraries of colleges and philosophers; but has written his name on the heavens and on the earth, and even on the minutest animal and plant; and his word, taught by Jesus Christ, was not given to scribes and lawyers, but taught to the poor, to the mass of men, on mountains, in streets, and on the sea-shore. Let me not be told that the multitude do actually receive religion on authority, or on the word of others. I reply, that a faith so received seems to me of little worth. The precious, the living, the effectual part of a poor man's faith, is that of which he sees the reasonableness and excellence; that which approves itself to his intelligence, his conscience, his heart; that which answers to deep wants in his own soul, and of which he has the witness in his own inward and outward experience. All other parts of his belief, those which he takes on blind trust, and in which he sees no marks of truth and divinity, do him little or no good. Too often they do him harm, by perplexing his simple reason, by substituting the fictions and artificial systems of theologians for the plain precepts of love, and justice, and humility, and filial trust in God. As long as it was supposed that religion is to benefit the world by laying restraints, awakening fears, and acting as a part of the system of police, so long it was natural to rely on authority and tradition as the means of its propagation; so long it was desirable to stifle thought and inquiry on the subject. But now that we have learned that the true office of religion is to awaken pure and lofty sentiments, and to unite man to God by rational homage and enlightened love, there is something monstrous in placing religion beyond the thought and the study of the mass of the human race.

I proceed to another prejudice. It is objected, that the distinction of ranks is essential to social order, and that this will be swept away by calling forth energy of thought in all men. This objection, indeed, though exceedingly insisted on in Europe, has nearly died out here; but still enough of it lingers among us to deserve consideration. I reply, then, that it is a libel on social order to suppose that it requires for its support the reduction of the multitude of human beings to ignorance and servility; and that it is a libel on the Creator to suppose that he requires, as the foundation of communities, the systematic depression of the majority of his intelligent offspring. The supposition is too grossly unreasonable, too monstrous, to require labored refutation. I see no need of ranks, either for social order or for any other purpose. A great variety of pursuits and conditions is indeed to be desired. Men ought to follow their genius, and to put forth their powers in every useful and lawful way. I do not ask for a monotonous world. We are far too monotonous now. The vassalage of fashion, which is a part of rank, prevents continually the free expansion of men's powers. Let us have the greatest diversity of occupations. But this does not imply that there is a need of splitting society into castes or ranks, or that a certain number should arrogate superiority, and stand apart from the rest of men as a separate race. Men may work in different departments of life, and yet recognize their brotherly relation, and honor one another, and hold friendly communion with one another. Undoubtedly, men will prefer as friends and common associates those with whom they sympathize most. But this is not to form a rank or caste. For example, the intelligent seek out the intelligent; the pious, those who reverence God. But suppose the intellectual and the religious to cut themselves off by some broad, visible distinction from the rest of society, to form a clan of their own, to refuse admission into their houses to people of inferior knowledge and virtue, and to diminish as far as possible the occasions of intercourse with them; would not society rise up, as one man, against this arrogant exclusiveness? And if intelligence and piety may not be the foundations of a caste, on what ground shall they, who have no distinction but wealth, superior costume, richer equipages, finer houses, draw lines around themselves and constitute themselves a higher class? That some should be richer than others is natural and is necessary, and could only be prevented by gross violations of right. Leave men to the free use of their powers, and some will accumulate more than their neighbors. But to be prosperous is not to be superior; and should form no barrier between men. Wealth ought not to secure to the prosperous the slightest consideration. The only distinctions which should be recognized are those of the soul, of strong principle, of incorruptible integrity, of usefulness, of cultivated intellect, of fidelity in seeking for truth. A man in proportion as he has these claims, should be honored and welcomed everywhere. I see not why such a man, however coarsely if neatly dressed, should not be a respected guest in the most splendid mansions, and at the most brilliant meetings. A man is worth infinitely more than the saloons, and the costumes, and the show of the universe. He was made to tread all these beneath his feet. What an insult to humanity is the present deference to dress and upholstery, as if silk-worms, and looms, and scissors, and needles could produce something nobler than a man! Every good man should protest against a caste founded on outward prosperity, because it exalts the outward above the inward, the material above the spiritual; because it springs from and cherishes a contemptible pride in superficial and transitory distinctions; because it alienates man from his brother, breaks the tie of common humanity, and breeds jealousy, scorn, and mutual ill-will. Can this be needed to social order?

It is true, that in countries where the mass of the people

are ignorant and servile, the existence of a higher and a worshipped rank tends to keep them from outrage. It infuses a sentiment of awe, which prevents more or less the need of force and punishment. But it is worthy of remark that the means of keeping order in one state of society may become the chief excitement of discontent and disorder in another, and this is peculiarly true of aristocracy or high rank. In rude ages, this keeps the people down; but when the people by degrees have risen to some consciousness of their rights and essential equality with the rest of the race, the awe of rank naturally subsides, and passes into suspicion, jealousy, and sense of injury, and a disposition to resist. The very institution which once restrained, now provokes. Through this process the Old World is now passing. The strange illusion, that a man, because he wears a garter or a riband, or was born to a title, belongs to another race, is fading away; and society must pass through a series of revolutions, silent or bloody, until a more natural order takes place of distinctions which grew originally out of force. Thus aristocracy, instead of giving order to society, now convulses it. So impossible is it for arbitrary human ordinations permanently to degrade human nature or subvert the principles of justice and freedom.

I am aware that it will be said, "that the want of refinement of manners and taste in the lower classes will necessarily keep them an inferior caste, even though all political inequalities be removed." I acknowledge this defect of manners in the multitude, and grant that it is an obstacle to intercourse with the more improved, though often exaggerated. But this is a barrier which must and will yield to the means of culture spread through our community. The evil is not necessarily associated with any condition of human life. An intelligent traveller tells us, that in Norway, a country wanting many of our advantages, good manners and politeness are spread through all conditions; and that the "rough way of talking to and living with each other, characteristic of the lower classes of society in England, is not found there." Not many centuries ago, the intercourse of the highest orders in Europe was sullied by indelicacy and fierceness; but time has worn out these stains, and the same cause is now removing what is repulsive among those who toil with their hands. I cannot believe that coarse manners, boisterous conversation, slovenly negligence, filthy customs, surliness, indecency, are to descend by necessity from generation to generation in any portion of the community. I do not see why neatness, courtesy, delicacy, ease, and deference to others' feelings, may not be made the habits of the laboring multitude. A change is certainly going on among them in respect to manners. Let us hope that it will be a change for the better; that they will not adopt false notions of refinement; that they will escape the servile imitation of what is hollow and insincere, and the substitution of outward shows for genuine natural courtesy. Unhappily they have but imperfect models on which to form themselves. It is not one class alone which needs reform in manners. We all need a new social intercourse, which shall breathe genuine refinement; which shall unite the two great elements of politeness, self-respect, and a delicate regard to the rights and feelings of others; which shall be free without rudeness, and earnest without positiveness; which shall be graceful, yet warm-hearted; and in which communication shall be frank, unlabored, overflowing, through the absence of all assumption and pretence, and through the consciousness of being safe from heartless ridicule. This grand reform, which I trust is to come, will bring with it a happiness little known in social life; and whence shall it come? The wise and disinterested of all conditions must contribute to it; and I see not why the laboring classes may not take part in the work. Indeed, when I consider the greater simplicity of their lives and their greater openness to the spirit of Christianity, I am not sure but that the "golden age" of manners is to begin among those who are now despaired of for their want of refinement.

In these remarks, I have given the name of "prejudices" to the old opinions respecting rank, and respecting the need of keeping the people from much thought. But allow these opinions to have a foundation in truth; suppose high fences of rank to be necessary to refinement of manners; suppose that the happiest of all ages were the feudal, when aristocracy was in its flower and glory, when the noble, superior to the laws, committed more murders in one year than the multitude in twenty. Suppose it best for the laborer to live and die in thoughtless ignorance. Allow all this, and that we have reason to look with envy on the past; one thing is plain, the past is gone, the feudal castle is dismantled, the distance between classes greatly reduced. Unfortunate as it may be, the people have begun to think, to ask reasons for what they do and suffer and believe, and to call the past to account. Old spells are broken, old reliances gone. Men can no longer be kept down by pageantry, state-robes, forms, and shows. Allowing it to be best that society should rest on the depression of the multitude, the multitude will no longer be quiet when they are trodden under foot, but ask impatiently for a reason why they too may not have a share in social blessings. Such is the state of things, and we must make the best of what we cannot prevent. Right or wrong, the people will think; and is it not important that they should think justly? that they should be inspired with the love of truth, and instructed how to seek it? that they should be established by wise culture in the great principles on which religion and society rest, and be protected from scepticism and wild speculation by intercourse with enlightened and virtuous men? It is plain that in the actual state of the world, nothing can avail us but a real improvement of the mass of the people. No stable foundation can be laid for us but in men's minds. Alarming as the truth is, it should be told, that outward institutions cannot now secure us. Mightier powers than institutions have come into play among us,—the judgment, the opinions, the feelings of the many; and all hopes of stability which do not rest on the progress of the many must perish.

But a more serious objection than any yet considered, to the intellectual elevation of the laboring class, remains to be stated. It is said, "that the laborer can gain subsistence for himself and his family only by a degree of labor which forbids the use of means of improvement. His necessary toils leave no time or strength for thought. Political economy, by showing that population outstrips the means of improvement, passes an irrepealable sentence of ignorance and degradation on the laborer. He can live but for one end, which is to keep himself alive. He cannot give time and strength to intellectual, social, and moral culture, without starving his family, and impoverishing the community. Nature has laid this heavy law on the mass of the people, and it is idle to set up our theories and dreams of improvement against nature."

This objection applies with great force to Europe, and is not without weight here. But it does not discourage me. I reply, first, to this objection, that it generally comes from a suspicious source. It comes generally from men who abound, and are at ease; who think more of property than of any other human interest; who have little concern for the mass of their fellow-creatures; who are willing that others should bear all the burdens of life, and that any social order should continue which secures to themselves personal comfort or gratification. The selfish epicure and the thriving man of business easily discover a natural necessity for that state of things which accumulates on themselves all the blessings, and on their neighbor all the evils, of life. But no man can judge what is good or necessary for the multitude but he who feels for them, and whose equity and benevolence are shocked by the thought that all advantages are to be monopolized by one set of men, and all disadvantages by another. I wait for the judgment of profound thinkers and earnest philanthropists on this point,—a judgment formed after patient study of political economy, and human nature and human history; nor even on such authority shall I readily despair of the multitude of my race.

In the next place, the objection under consideration is very much a repetition of the old doctrine, that what has been must be; that the future is always to repeat the past, and society to tread for ever the beaten path. But can any thing be plainer than that the present condition of the world is peculiar, unprecedented? that new powers and new principles are at work? that the application of science to art is accomplishing a stupendous revolution? that the condition of the laborer is in many places greatly improved, and his intellectual aids increased? that abuses, once thought essential to society, and which seemed entwined with all its fibres, have been removed? Do the mass of men stand where they did a few centuries ago? And do not new circumstances, if they make us fearful, at the same time keep us from despair? The future, be it what it may, will not resemble the past. The present has new elements, which must work out new weal or woe. We have no right, then, on the ground of the immutableness of human affairs, to quench, as far as we have power, the hope of social progress.

Another consideration, in reply to the objection that the necessary toils of life exclude improvement, may be drawn not only from general history, but from the experience of this country in particular. The working classes here have risen and are still rising intellectually, and yet there are no signs of starvation, nor are we becoming the poorest people on earth. By far the most interesting view of this country is the condition of the working multitude. Nothing among us deserves the attention of the traveller so much as the force of thought and character, and the self-respect awakened by our history and institutions in the mass of the people. Our prosperous classes are much like the same classes abroad, though, as we hope, of purer morals; but the great working multitude leave far behind them the laborers of other countries. No man of observation and benevolence can converse with them without being struck and delighted with the signs they give of strong and sound intellect and manly principle. And who is authorized to set bounds to this progress? In improvement the first steps are the hardest. The difficulty is to wake up men's souls, not to continue their action. Every accession of light and strength is a help to new acquisitions.

Another consideration, in reply to the objection, is, that as yet no community has seriously set itself to the work of improving all its members, so that what is possible remains to be ascertained. No experiment has been made to determine how far liberal provision can be made at once for the body and mind of the laborer. The highest social art is yet in its infancy. Great minds have nowhere solemnly, earnestly undertaken to resolve the problem, how the multitude of men may be elevated. The trial is to come. Still more, the multitude have nowhere comprehended distinctly the true idea of progress, and resolved deliberately and solemnly to reduce it to reality. This great thought, however, is gradually opening on them, and it is destined to work wonders. From themselves their salvation must chiefly come. Little can be done for them by others, till a spring is touched in their own breasts; and this being done, they cannot fail. The people, as history shows us, can accomplish miracles under the power of a great idea. How much have they often done and suffered in critical moments for country, for religion! The great idea of their own elevation is only beginning to unfold itself within them, and its energy is not to be foretold. A lofty conception of this kind, were it once distinctly seized, would be a new life breathed into them. Under this impulse they would create time and strength for their high calling, and would not only regenerate themselves, but the community.

Again, I am not discouraged by the objection, that the laborer, if encouraged to give time and strength to the elevation of his mind, will starve himself and impoverish the country, when I consider the energy and efficiency of mind. The highest force in the universe is mind. This created the heavens and earth. This has changed the wilderness into fruitfulness, and linked distant countries in a beneficent ministry to one another's wants. It is not to brute force, to physical strength, so much as to art, to skill, to intellectual and moral energy, that men owe their mastery over the world. It is mind which has conquered matter. To fear, then, that by calling forth a people's mind, we shall impoverish and starve them, is to be frightened at a shadow. I believe, that with the growth of intellectual and moral power in the community, its productive power will increase, that industry will become more efficient, that a wiser economy will accumulate wealth, that unimagined resources of art and nature will be discovered. I believe that the means of living will grow easier, in proportion as a people shall become enlightened, self-respecting, resolute, and just. Bodily or material forces can be measured, but not the forces of the soul; nor can the results of increased mental energy be foretold. Such a community will tread down obstacles now deemed invincible, and turn them into helps. The inward moulds the outward. The power of a people lies in its mind; and this mind, if fortified and enlarged, will bring external things into harmony with itself. It will create a new world around it, corresponding to itself. If, however, I err in this belief; if, by securing time and means for improvement to the multitude, industry and capital should become less productive, I still say, Sacrifice the wealth, and not the mind of a people. Nor do I believe that the physical good of a community would in this way be impaired. The diminution of a country's wealth, occasioned by general attention to intellectual and moral culture, would be followed by very different effects from those which would attend an equal diminution brought about by sloth, intemperance, and ignorance. There would indeed be less production in such a country, but the character and spirit of the people would effect a much more equal distribution of what would be produced; and the happiness of a community depends vastly more on the distribution than on the amount of its wealth. In thus speaking of the future, I do not claim any special prophetical gift. As a general rule, no man is able to foretell distinctly the ultimate, permanent results of any great social change. But as to the case before us, we ought not to doubt. It is a part of religion to believe that by nothing can a country so effectually gain happiness and lasting prosperity as by the elevation of all classes of its citizens. To question this seems an approach to crime.

> "If this fail,
> The pillar'd firmament is rottenness,
> And earth's base built on stubble."

I am aware that, in reply to all that has been said in favor of the possibility of uniting self-improvement with labor, discouraging facts may be brought forward from our daily experience. It may be said that in this country, under advantages unknown in other lands, there is a considerable number on whom the burden of toil presses very heavily, who can scarcely live with all their efforts, and who are cut off by their hard condition from the means of intellectual culture; and if this take place now, what are we to expect hereafter in a more crowded population? I acknowledge that we have a number of depressed laborers, whose state is exceedingly unpropitious to the education of the mind; but this argument will lose much of its power when we inquire into the causes of this evil. We shall then see that it comes, not from outward necessity, not from the irresistible obstacles abroad, but chiefly from the fault or ignorance of the sufferers themselves; so that the elevation of the mind and character of the laborer tends directly to reduce, if not remove, the evil. Of consequence, this elevation finds support in what is urged against it. In confirmation of these views, allow me just to hint at the causes of that depression of many laborers which is said to show that labor and self-improvement cannot go on together.

First, how much of this depression is to be traced to intemperance? What a great amount of time, and strength, and money, might multitudes gain for self-improvement, by a strict sobriety! That cheap remedy, pure water, would cure the chief evils in very many families of the ignorant and poor. Were the sums which are still lavished on ardent spirits appropriated wisely to the elevation of the people, what a new world we should live in! Intemperance not only wastes the earnings, but the health and the minds of men. How many, were they to exchange what they call moderate drinking for water, would be surprised to learn that they had been living under a cloud, in half-stupefaction, and would become conscious of an intellectual energy of which they had not before dreamed! Their labors would exhaust them less; and less labor would be needed for their support; and thus their inability to cultivate their high nature would in a great measure be removed. The working class, above all men, have an interest in the cause of temperance, and they ought to look on the individual who lives by scattering the means and excitements of drunkenness not only as the general enemy of his race, but as their own worst foe.

In the next place, how much of the depression of laborers may be traced to the want of a strict economy! The prosperity of this country has produced a wastefulness that has extended to the laboring multitude. A man, here, turns with scorn from fare that in many countries would be termed luxurious. It is, indeed, important that the standard of living in all classes should be high; that is, it should include the comforts of life, the means of neatness and order in our dwellings, and such supplies of our wants as are fitted to secure vigorous health. But how many waste their earnings on indulgences which may be spared, and thus have no resource for a dark day, and are always trembling on the brink of pauperism! Needless expenses keep many too poor for self-improvement. And here let me say, that expensive habits among the more prosperous laborers often interfere with the mental culture of themselves and their families. How many among them sacrifice improvement to appetite! How many sacrifice it to the love of show, to the desire of outstripping others, and to habits of expense which grow out of this insatiable passion! In a country so thriving and luxurious as ours, the laborer is in danger of contracting artificial wants and diseased tastes; and to gratify these he gives himself wholly to accumulation, and sells his mind for gain. Our unparalleled prosperity has not been an unmixed good. It has inflamed cupidity, has diseased the imagination with dreams of boundless success, and plunged a vast multitude into excessive toils, feverish competitions, and exhausting cares. A laborer, having secured a neat home and a wholesome table, should ask nothing more for the senses; but should consecrate his leisure, and what may be spared of his earnings, to the culture of himself and his family, to the best books, to the best teaching, to pleasant and profitable intercourse, to sympathy and the offices of humanity, and to the enjoyment of the beautiful in nature and art. Unhappily, the laborer, if prosperous, is anxious to ape the rich man, instead of trying to rise above him, as he often may, by noble acquisitions. The young in particular, the apprentice and the female domestic, catch a taste for fashion, and on this altar sacrifice too often their uprightness, and almost always the spirit of improvement, dooming themselves to ignorance, if not to vice, for a vain show. Is this evil without remedy? Is human nature always to be sacrificed to outward decoration? Is the outward always to triumph over the inward man? Is nobleness of sentiment never to spring up among us? May not a reform in this particular begin in the laboring class, since it seems so desperate among the more prosperous? Cannot the laborer, whose condition calls him so loudly to simplicity of taste and habits, take his stand against that love of dress which dissipates and corrupts so many minds among the opulent? Cannot the laboring class refuse to measure men by outward success, and pour utter scorn on all pretensions founded on outward show or condition? Sure I am that, were they to study plainness of dress and simplicity of living, for the purpose of their own true elevation, they would surpass in intellect, in taste, in honorable qualities, and in present enjoyment, that great proportion of the prosperous who are softened into indulgence or enslaved to empty show. By such self-denial, how might the burden of labor be lightened, and time and strength redeemed for improvement!

Another cause of the depressed condition of not a few laborers, as I believe, is their ignorance on the subject of health. Health is the working man's fortune, and he ought to watch over it more than the capitalist over his largest investments. Health lightens the efforts of body and mind. It enables a man to crowd much work into a narrow compass. Without it, little can be earned, and that little by slow, exhausting toil. For these reasons I cannot but look on it as a good omen that the press is circulating among us cheap works, in which much useful knowledge is given of the structure, and functions, and laws of the human body. It is in no small measure through our own imprudence that disease and debility are incurred, and one remedy is to be found in knowledge. Once let the mass of the people be instructed in their own frames; let them understand clearly that disease is not an accident, but has fixed causes, many of which they can avert, and a great amount of suffering, want, and consequent intellectual depression will be removed.—I hope I shall not be thought to digress too far, when I add, that were the mass of the community more enlightened on these points, they would apply their knowledge, not only to their private habits, but to the government of the city, and would insist on municipal regulations favoring general health. This they owe to themselves. They ought to require a system of measures for effectually cleansing the city; for supplying it with pure water, either at public expense or by a private corporation; and for prohibiting the erection or the letting of such buildings as must generate disease. What a sad thought is it, that in this metropolis, the blessings which God pours forth profusely on bird and beast, the blessings of air, and light, and water, should, in the case of many families, be so stinted or so mixed with impurities, as to injure instead of invigorating the frame! With what face can the great cities of Europe and America boast of their civilization, when within their limits thousands and ten thousands perish for want of God's freest, most lavish gifts! Can we expect improvement among people who are cut off from nature's common bounties, and want those cheering influences of the elements which even savages enjoy? In this city, how much health, how many lives are sacrificed to the practice of letting cellars and rooms which cannot be ventilated, which want the benefits of light, free air, and pure water, and the means of removing filth! We forbid by law the selling of putrid meat in the market. Why do we not forbid the renting of rooms in which putrid, damp and noisome vapors are working as sure destruction as the worst food? Did people understand that they are as truly poisoned in such dens as by tainted meat and decaying vegetables, would they not appoint commissioners for houses as truly as commissioners for markets? Ought not the renting of untenantable rooms, and the crowding of such numbers into a single room as must breed disease, and may infect a neighborhood, be as much forbidden as the importation of a pestilence? I have enlarged on this point, because I am persuaded that the morals, manners, decencies, self-respect, and intellectual improvement, as well as the health and physical comforts of a people, depend on no outward circumstances more than on the quality of the houses in which they live. The remedy of the grievance now stated lies with the people themselves. The laboring people must require that the health of the city shall be a leading object of the municipal administration, and in so doing they will protect at once the body and the mind.

I will mention one more cause of the depressed condition of many laborers, and that is, sloth, "the sin which doth most easily beset us." How many are there who, working languidly and reluctantly, bring little to pass, spread the work of one hour over many, shrink from difficulties which ought to excite them, keep themselves poor, and thus doom their families to ignorance as well as to want!

In these remarks I have endeavored to show that the great obstacles to the improvement of the laboring classes are in themselves, and may therefore be overcome. They want nothing but the will. Outward difficulty will shrink and vanish before them, just as far as they are bent on progress, just as far as the great idea of their own elevation shall take possession of their minds. I know that many will smile at the suggestion, that the laborer may be brought to practise thrift and self-denial, for the purpose of becoming a nobler being. But such sceptics, having never experienced the power of a grand thought or generous purpose, are no judges of others. They may be assured, however, that enthusiasm is not wholly a dream, and that it is not wholly unnatural for individuals or bodies to get the idea of something higher and more inspiring than their past attainments.

III. Having now treated of the elevation of the laborer, and examined the objections to it, I proceed, in the last place, to consider some of the circumstances of the times which encourage hopes of the progress of the mass of the people. My limits oblige me to confine myself to very few.—And, first, it is an encouraging circumstance, that the respect for labor is increasing, or rather that the old prejudices against manual toil, as degrading a man or putting him in a lower sphere, are wearing away; and the cause of this change is full of promise; for it is to be found in the progress of intelligence, Christianity, and freedom, all of which cry aloud against the old barriers created between the different classes, and challenge especial sympathy and regard for those who bear the heaviest burdens, and create most of the comforts of social life. The contempt of labor of which I have spoken is a relic of the old aristocratic prejudices which formerly proscribed trade as unworthy of a gentleman, and must die out with other prejudices of the same low origin. And the results must be happy. It is hard for a class of men to respect themselves who are denied respect by all around them. A vocation looked on as degrading will have a tendency to degrade those who follow it. Away, then, with the idea of something low in manual labor. There is something shocking to a religious man in the thought that the employment which God has ordained for the vast majority of the human race should be unworthy of any man, even to the highest. If, indeed, there were an employment which could not be dispensed with, and which yet tended to degrade such as might be devoted to it, I should say that it ought to be shared by the whole race, and thus neutralized by extreme division, instead of being laid, as the sole vocation, on one man or a few. Let no human being be broken in spirit or trodden under foot for the outward prosperity of the State. So far is manual labor from meriting contempt or slight, that it will probably be found, when united with true means of spiritual culture, to foster a sounder judgment, a keener observation, a more creative imagination, and a purer taste, than any other vocation. Man thinks of the few, God of the many; and the many will be found at length to have within their reach the most effectual means of progress.

Another encouraging circumstance of the times is the creation of a popular literature, which puts within the reach of the laboring class the means of knowledge in whatever branch they wish to cultivate. Amidst the worthless volumes which are every day sent from the press for mere amusement, there are books of great value in all departments, published for the benefit of the mass of readers. Mines of inestimable truth are thus open to all who are resolved to think and learn. Literature is now adapting itself to all wants; and I have little doubt that a new form of it will soon appear for the special benefit of the laboring classes. This will have for its object to show the progress of the various useful arts, and to preserve the memory of their founders, and of men who have laid the world under obligation by great inventions. Every trade has distinguished names in its history. Some trades can number, among those who have followed them, philosophers, poets, men of true genius. I would suggest to the members of this Association whether a course of lectures, intended to illustrate the history of the more important trades, and of the great blessings they have conferred on society, and of the eminent individuals who have practised them, might not do much to instruct, and, at the same time, to elevate them. Such a course would carry them far into the past, would open to them much interesting information, and at the same time introduce them to men whom they may well make their models. I would go farther. I should be pleased to see the members of an important trade setting apart an anniversary for the commemoration of those who have shed lustre on it by their virtues, their discoveries, their genius. It is time that honor should be awarded on higher principles than have governed the judgment of past ages. Surely the inventor of the press, the discoverer of the compass, the men who have applied the power of steam to machinery, have brought the human race more largely into their debt than the bloody race of conquerors, and even than many beneficent princes. Antiquity exalted into divinities the first cultivators of wheat and the useful plants, and the first forgers of metals; and we, in these maturer ages of the world, have still greater names to boast in the records of useful art. Let their memory be preserved to kindle a generous emulation in those who have entered into their labors.

Another circumstance, encouraging the hope of progress in the laboring class, is to be found in the juster views they are beginning to adopt in regard to the education of their children. On this foundation, indeed, our hope for all classes must chiefly rest. All are to rise chiefly by the care bestowed on the young. Not that I would say, as is sometimes rashly said, that none but the young can improve. I give up no age as desperate. Men who have lived thirty, or fifty years, are not to feel as if the door was shut upon them. Every man who thirsts to become something better has in that desire a pledge that his labor will not be in vain. None are too old to learn. The world, from our first to our last hour, is our school, and the whole of life has but one great purpose,—education. Still, the child, uncorrupted, unhardened, is the most hopeful subject; and vastly more, I believe, is hereafter to be done for children, than ever before, by the gradual spread of a simple truth, almost too simple, one would think, to need exposition, yet up to this day wilfully neglected: namely, that education is a sham, a cheat, unless carried on by able, accomplished teachers. The dignity of the vocation of a teacher is beginning to be understood; the idea is dawning on us that no office can compare in solemnity and importance with that of training the child; that skill to form the young to energy, truth, and virtue, is worth more than the knowledge of all other arts and sciences; and that, of consequence, the encouragement of excellent teachers is the first duty which a community owes to itself. I say the truth is dawning, and it must make its way. The instruction f the children of all classes, especially of the laboring class, has as yet been too generally committed to unprepared, unskilful hands, and of course the school is in general little more than a name. The whole worth of a school lies in the teacher. You may accumulate the most expensive apparatus for instruction; but without an intellectual, gifted teacher, it is little better than rubbish; and such a teacher, without apparatus, may effect the happiest results. Our university boasts, and with justice, of its library, cabinets, and philosophical instruments; but these are lifeless, profitless, except as made effectual by the men who use them. A few eminent men, skilled to understand, reach, and quicken the minds of the pupils, are worth all these helps. And I say this, because it is commonly thought that the children of the laboring class cannot be advanced, in consequence of the inability of parents to furnish a variety of books and other apparatus. But in education, various books and implements are not the great requisites, but a high order of teachers. In truth, a few books do better than many. The object of education is not so much to give a certain amount of knowledge, as to awaken the faculties, and give the pupil the use of his own mind; and one book, taught by a man who knows how to accomplish these ends, is worth more than libraries as usually read. It is not necessary that much should be taught in youth, but that a little should be taught philosophically, profoundly, livingly. For example, it is not necessary that the pupil be carried over the history of the world from the deluge to the present day. Let him be helped to read a single history wisely, to apply the principles of historical evidence to its statements, to trace the causes and effects of events, to penetrate into the motives of actions, to observe the workings of human nature in what is done and suffered, to judge impartially of action and character, to sympathize with what is noble, to detect the spirit of an age in different forms from our own, to seize the great truths which are wrapped up in details, and to discern a moral Providence, a retribution, amidst all corruptions and changes; let him learn to read a single history thus, and he has learned to read all histories; he is prepared to study, as he may have time in future life, the whole course of human events; he is better educated by this one book than he would be by all the histories in all languages as commonly taught. The education of the laborer's children need never stop for want of books and apparatus. More of them would do good, but enough may be easily obtained. What we want is, a race of teachers acquainted with the philosophy of the mind, gifted men and women, who shall respect human nature in the child, and strive to touch and gently bring out his best powers and sympathies; and who shall devote themselves to this as the great end of life. This good, I trust, is to come, but it comes slowly. The establishment of normal schools shows that the want of it begins to be felt. This good requires that education shall be recognized by the community as its highest interest and duty. It requires that the instructors of youth shall take precedence of the money-getting classes, and that the woman of fashion shall fall behind the female teacher. It requires that parents shall sacrifice show and pleasure to the acquisition of the best possible helps and guides for their children. Not that a great pecuniary compensation is to create good teachers; these must be formed by individual impulse, by a genuine interest in education; but good impulse must be seconded by outward circumstances; and the means of education will always bear a proportion to the respect in which the office of teacher is held in the community.

Happily, in this country, the true idea of education, of its nature and supreme importance, is silently working and gains ground. Those of us who look back on half a century, see a real, great improvement in schools and in the standard of instruction. What should encourage this movement in this country is, that nothing is wanting here to the intellectual elevation of the laboring class but that a spring should be given to the child, and that the art of thinking justly and strongly should be formed in early life; for, this preparation being made, the circumstances of future life will almost of themselves carry on the work of improvement. It is one of the inestimable benefits of free institutions, that they are constant stimulants to the intellect; that they furnish, in rapid succession, quickening subjects of thought and discussion. A whole people at the same moment are moved to reflect, reason, judge, and act on matters of deep and universal concern; and where the capacity of thought has received wise culture, the intellect, unconsciously, by an almost irresistible sympathy, is kept perpetually alive. The mind, like the body, depends on the climate it lives in, on the air it breathes; and the air of freedom is bracing, exhilarating, expanding, to a degree not dreamed of under a despotism. This stimulus of liberty, however, avails little, except where the mind has learned to think for the acquisition of truth. The unthinking and passionate are hurried by it into ruinous excess.

The last ground of hope for the elevation of the laborer, and the chief and the most sustaining, is the clearer development of the principles of Christianity. The future influences of this religion are not to be judged from the past. Up to this time it has been made a political engine, and in other ways perverted. But its true spirit, the spirit of brotherhood and freedom, is beginning to be understood, and this will undo the work which opposite principles have been carrying on for ages. Christianity is the only effectual remedy for the fearful evils of modern civilization,—a system which teaches its members to grasp at everything, and to rise above everybody, as the great aims of life. Of such a civilization the natural fruits are, contempt of others' rights, fraud, oppression, a gambling spirit in trade, reckless adventure, and commercial convulsions, all tending to impoverish the laborer and to render every condition insecure. Relief is to come, and can only come, from the new application of Christian principles, of universal justice and universal love, to social institutions, to commerce, to business, to active life. This application has begun, and the laborer, above all men, is to feel its happy and exalting influences.

Such are some of the circumstances which inspire hopes of the elevation of the laboring classes. To these might be added other strong grounds of encouragement, to be found in the principles of human nature, in the perfections and providence of God, and in the prophetic intimations of his word. But these I pass over. From all I derive strong hopes for the mass of men. I do not, cannot see, why manual toil and self-improvement may not go on in friendly union. I do not see why the laborer may not attain to refined habits and manners as truly as other men. I do not see why conversation under his humble roof may not be cheered by wit and exalted by intelligence. I do not see why, amidst his toils, he may not cast his eye around him on God's glorious creation, and be strengthened and refreshed by the sight. I do not see why the great ideas which exalt humanity—those of the Infinite Father, of perfection, of our nearness to God, and of the purpose of our being—may not grow bright and strong in the laborer's mind. Society, I trust, is tending towards a condition in which it will look back with astonishment at the present neglect or perversion of human powers. In the development of a more enlarged philanthropy, in the diffusion of the Christian spirit of brotherhood, in the recognition of the equal rights of every human being, we have the dawn and promise of a better age, when no man will be deprived of the means of elevation but by his own fault; when the evil doctrine, worthy of the arch-fiend, that social order demands the depression of the mass of men, will be rejected with horror and scorn; when the great object of the community will be to accumulate means and influences for awakening and expanding the best powers of all classes; when far less will be expended on the body and far more on the mind; when men of uncommon gifts for the instruction of their race will be sent forth to carry light and strength into every sphere of human life; when spacious libraries, collections of the fine arts, cabinets of natural history, and all the institutions by which the people may be refined and ennobled, will be formed and thrown open to all; and when the toils of life, by a wise intermixture of these higher influences, will be made the instruments of human elevation.

Such are my hopes of the intellectual, moral, religious, social elevation of the laboring class. I should not, however, be true to myself, did I not add that I have fears as well as hopes. Time is not left me to enlarge on this point; but without a reference to it I should not give you the whole truth. I would not disguise from myself or others the true character of the world we live in. Human imperfection throws an uncertainty over the future. Society, like the natural world, holds in its bosom fearful elements. Who can hope that the storms which have howled over past ages have spent all their force? It is possible that the laboring classes, by their recklessness, their passionateness, their jealousies of the more prosperous, and their subserviency to parties and political leaders, may turn all their bright prospects into darkness, may blight the hopes which philanthropy now cherishes of a happier and holier social state. It is also possible, in this mysterious state of things, that evil may come to them from causes which are thought to promise them nothing but good. The present anxiety and universal desire is to make the country rich, and it is taken for granted that its growing wealth is necessarily to benefit all conditions. But is this consequence sure? May not a country be rich, and yet great numbers of the people be wofully depressed? In England, the richest nation under heaven, how sad, how degraded the state of the agricultural and manufacturing classes! It is thought that the institutions of this country give an assurance that growing wealth will here equally benefit and carry forward all portions of the community. I hope so; but I am not sure. At the present time a momentous change is taking place in our condition. The improvement in steam navigation has half annihilated the space between Europe and America, and by the progress of invention the two continents are to be more and more placed side by side. We hail this triumph of the arts with exultation. We look forward to the approaching spring, when this metropolis is to be linked with England by a line of steamboats, as a proud era in our history. That a great temporary excitement will be given to industry, and that our wealth and numbers will increase, admits no dispute; but this is a small matter. The great question is, Will the mass of the people be permanently advanced in the comforts of life, and, still more, in intelligence and character, in the culture of their highest powers and affections? It is not enough to grow, if our growth is to resemble that of other populous places. Better continue as we are, better even decline, than tread in the steps of any great city, whether of past or present times. I doubt not that, under God's providence, the approximation of Europe and America is ultimately to be a blessing to both; but without our vigilance, the nearer effects may be more or less disastrous. It cannot be doubted that for a time many among us, especially in the prosperous classes, will be more and more infected from abroad, will sympathize more with the institutions, and catch more the spirit and manners, of the Old World. As a people we want moral independence. We bow to "the great" of other countries, and we shall become for a time more and more servile in our imitation. But this, though bad, may not be the worst result. I would ask, What is to be the effect of bringing the laboring classes of Europe twice as near us as they now are? Is there no danger of a competition that is to depress the laboring classes here? Can the workman here stand his ground against the half-famished, ignorant workmen of Europe, who will toil for any wages, and who never think of redeeming an hour for personal improvement? Is there no danger that, with increasing intercourse with Europe, we shall import the striking, fearful contrasts which there divide one people into separate nations? Sooner than that our laboring class should become a European populace, a good man would almost wish that perpetual hurricanes, driving every ship from the ocean, should sever wholly the two hemispheres from each other. Heaven preserve us from the anticipated benefits of nearer connection with

Europe, if with these must come the degradation which we see or read of among the squalid poor of her great cities, among the overworked operatives of her manufactories, among her ignorant and half-brutalized peasants! Any thing, every thing should be done to save us from the social evils which deform the Old World, and to build up here an intelligent, right-minded, self-respecting population. If this end should require us to change our present modes of life, to narrow our foreign connections, to desist from the race of commercial and manufacturing competition with Europe; if it should require that our great cities should cease to grow, and that a large portion of our trading population should return to labor, these requisitions ought to be obeyed. One thing is plain, that our present civilization contains strong tendencies to the intellectual and moral depression of a large portion of the community; and this influence ought to be thought of, studied, watched, withstood, with a stern solemn purpose of withholding no sacrifice by which it may be counteracted.

Perhaps the fears now expressed may be groundless. I do not ask you to adopt them. My end will be gained if I can lead you to study, habitually and zealously, the influence of changes and measures on the character and condition of the laboring class. There is no subject on which your thoughts should turn more frequently than on this. Many of you busy yourselves with other questions, such as the probable result of the next election of President, or the prospects of this or that party. But these are insignificant, compared with the great question, Whether the laboring classes here are destined to the ignorance and depression of the lower ranks of Europe, or whether they can secure to themselves the means of intellectual and moral progress. You are cheated, you are false to yourselves, when you suffer politicians to absorb you in their selfish purposes, and to draw you away from this great question. Give the first place in your thoughts to this. Carry it away with you from the present lecture; discuss it together; study it when alone; let your best heads work on it; resolve that nothing shall be wanting on your part to secure the means of intellectual and moral well-being to yourselves, and to those who may come after you.

In these lectures, I have expressed a strong interest in the laboring portion of the community; but I have no partiality to them considered merely as laborers. My mind is attracted to them because they constitute the majority of the human race. My great interest is in human nature, and in the working classes as its most numerous representatives. To those who look on this nature with contempt or utter distrust, such language may seem a mere form, or may be construed as a sign of the predominance of imagination and feeling over the judgment. No matter. The pity of these sceptics I can return. Their wonder at my credulity cannot surpass the sorrowful astonishment with which I look on their indifference to the fortunes of their race. In spite of all their doubts and scoffs, human nature is still most dear to me. When I behold it manifested in its perfect proportions in Jesus Christ, I cannot but revere it as the true temple of the Divinity. When I see it as revealed in the great and good of all times, I bless God for those multiplied and growing proofs of its high destiny. When I see it bruised, beaten down, stifled by ignorance and vice, by oppression, injustice, and grinding toil, I weep for it, and feel that every man should be ready to suffer for its redemption. I do and I must hope for its progress. But in saying this, I am not blind to its immediate dangers. I am not sure that dark clouds and desolating storms are not even now gathering over the world. When we look back on the mysterious history of the human race, we see that Providence has made use of fearful revolutions as the means of sweeping away the abuses of ages, and of bringing forward mankind to their present improvement. Whether such revolutions may not be in store for our own times, I know not. The present civilization of the Christian world presents much to awaken doubt and apprehension. It stands in direct hostility to the great ideas of Christianity. It is selfish, mercenary, sensual. Such a civilization cannot, must not, endure for ever. How it is to be supplanted, I know not. I hope, however, that it is not doomed, like the old Roman civilization, to be quenched in blood. I trust that the works of ages are not to be laid low by violence, rapine, and the all-devouring sword. I trust that the existing social state contains in its bosom something better than it has yet unfolded. I trust that a brighter future is to come, not from the desolation, but from gradual, meliorating changes of the present. Among the changes to which I look for the salvation of the modern world, one of the chief is the intellectual and moral elevation of the laboring class. The impulses which are to reform and quicken society are probably to come, not from its more conspicuous, but from its obscurer divisions; and among these I see with joy new wants, principles, and aspirations beginning to unfold themselves. Let what is already won give us courage. Let faith in a parental Providence give us courage; and if we are to be disappointed in the present, let us never doubt that the great interests of human nature are still secure under the eye and care of an Almighty Friend.

Note for the third head.—Under the third head of the lectures, in which some of the encouraging circumstances of the times are stated, I might have spoken of the singular advantages and means of progress enjoyed by the laborer in this metropolis. It is believed that there cannot be found another city in the world in which the laboring classes are as much improved, possess as many helps, enjoy as much consideration, exert as much influence, as in this place. Had I pursued this subject, I should have done what I often wished to do; I should have spoken of the obligations of our city to my excellent friend, James Savage, Esq., to whose unwearied efforts we are chiefly indebted for two inestimable institutions,—the Provident Institution for Savings and the Primary Schools; the former giving to the laborer the means of sustaining himself in times of pressure, and the latter placing almost at his door the means of instruction for his children from the earliest age. The union of the Primary Schools with the Grammar Schools and the High Schools in this place constitutes a system of public education unparalleled, it is believed, in any country. It would not be easy to name an individual to whom our city is under greater obligations than to Mr. Savage. In the enterprises which I have named, he was joined and greatly assisted by the late Elisha Ticknor, Esq., whose name ought also to be associated with the Provident Institution and the Primary Schools. The subject of these lectures brings to my mind the plan of an institution which was laid before me by Mr. Ticknor, for teaching at once agriculture and the mechanic arts. He believed that a boy might be made a thorough farmer, both in theory and practice, and might at the same time learn a trade, and that by being skilled in both vocations he would be more useful, and would multiply his chances of comfortable subsistence. I was interested by the plan, and Mr. Ticknor's practical wisdom led me to believe that it might be accomplished.

THE POETIC PRINCIPLE

BY

EDGAR ALLAN POE

INTRODUCTORY NOTE

EDGAR ALLAN POE *(1809-49) was born in Boston, the child of actors who died while he was very young. He was adopted by a Virginian gentleman, Mr. John Allan, who put him to school in England for five years, then in Richmond, and finally sent him to the University of Virginia. He remained there only a short time, and after finding that he disliked business, and publishing a volume of poems, he enlisted in the army. Mr. Allan had him discharged and placed him in West Point, from which he got himself dismissed. After that he supported himself in a hand-to-mouth fashion by writing for and editing newspapers and periodicals, living successively in Baltimore, Richmond, Philadelphia, and New York. The publication of his remarkable poem, "The Raven," in 1845, brought him fame, and for a short time he was a literary lion. But in 1847 his wife died, and his two remaining years were a gradual descent.*

Poe's work falls into three divisions: poems, tales, and criticism. The poems are chiefly remarkable for the amazing technical skill with which haunting rhythms and studied successions of vowel and consonant sounds are made to suggest atmospheres and emotional moods, with a minimum of thought. In the writing of fiction, Poe is the great master of the weird tale, no writer having surpassed him in the power of shaking the reader's nerves with suggestions of the supernatural and the horrible. In these stories, as in the poems, he shows an extraordinary sense of form, and his effects are produced not merely by the violently sensational, but by carefully calculated attacks upon the reader's imaginative sensibilities.

In criticism Poe was, if not a scholarly, at least a stimulating and suggestive, writer, with a fine ear and, within his range, keen insight. His essay on "The Poetic Principle" is his poetic confession of faith. He makes clear and defends his conception of poetry; a conception which excludes many great kinds of verse, but which, illuminated as it is by abundant examples of his favorite poems, throws light in turn upon some of the fundamental elements of poetry.

It is worth noting that no American author seems to have enjoyed so great a European vogue as Poe.

THE POETIC PRINCIPLE

IN speaking of the Poetic Principle, I have no design to be either thorough or profound. While discussing, very much at random, the essentiality of what we call Poetry, my principal purpose will be to cite for consideration some few of those minor English or American poems which best suit my own taste, or which upon my own fancy have left the most definite impression. By "minor poems" I mean, of course, poems of little length. And here in the beginning permit me to say a few words in regard to a somewhat peculiar principle, which, whether rightfully or wrongfully, has always had its influence in my own critical estimate of the poem. I hold that a long poem does not exist. I maintain that the phrase, "a long poem," is simply a flat contradiction in terms.

I need scarcely observe that a poem deserves its title only inasmuch as it excites, by elevating the soul. The value of the poem is in the ratio of this elevating excitement. But all excitements are, through a psychal necessity, transient. That degree of excitement which would entitle a poem to be so called at all cannot be sustained throughout a composition of any great length. After the lapse of half an hour, at the very utmost, it flags—fails—a revulsion ensues—and then the poem is, in effect, and in fact, no longer such.

There are, no doubt, many who have found difficulty in reconciling the critical dictum that the "Paradise Lost" is to be devoutly admired throughout, with the absolute impossibility of maintaining for it, during perusal, the amount of enthusiasm which that critical dictum would demand. The great work, in fact, is to be regarded as poetical, only when, losing sight of that vital requisite in all works of Art, Unity, we view it merely as a series of minor poems. If, to preserve its Unity—its totality of effect or impression—we read it (as would be necessary) at a single sitting, the result is but a constant alternation of excitement and depression. After a passage of what we feel to be true poetry, there follows, inevitably, a passage of platitude which no critical prejudgment can force us to admire; but if, upon completing the work, we read it again, omitting the first book (that is to say, commencing with the second), we shall be surprised at now finding that admirable which we before condemned—that damnable which we had previously so much admired. It follows from all this that the ultimate, aggregate, or absolute effect of even the best epic under the sun is a nullity;—and this is precisely the fact.

In regard to the "Iliad," we have, if not positive proof, at least very good reason for believing it intended as a series of lyrics; but, granting the epic intention, I can say only that the work is based in an imperfect sense of art. The modern epic is, of the supposititious ancient model, but an inconsiderate and blindfold imitation. But the day of these artistic anomalies is over. If, at any time, any very long poems *were* popular in reality—which I doubt—it is at least clear that no very long poem will ever be popular again.

That the extent of a poetical work is, *ceteris paribus,* the measure of its merit, seems undoubtedly, when we thus state it, a proposition sufficiently absurd—yet we are indebted for it to the Quarterly Reviews. Surely there can be nothing in mere size, abstractly considered—there can be nothing in mere bulk, so far as a volume is concerned which has so continuously elicited admiration from these saturnine pamphlets! A mountain, to be sure, by the mere sentiment of physical magnitude which it conveys, does impress us with a sense of the sublime—but no man is impressed after *this* fashion by the material grandeur of even "The Columbiad." Even the Quarterlies have not instructed us to be so impressed by it. *As yet,* they have not *insisted* on our estimating Lamartine by the cubic foot, or Pollok by the pound—but what else are we to *infer* from their continual prating about "sustained effort"? If, by "sustained effort," any little gentleman has accomplished an epic, let us frankly commend him for the effort,—if this indeed be a thing commendable,—but let us forbear praising the epic on the effort's account. It is to be hoped that common sense, in the time to come, will prefer deciding upon a work of Art, rather by the impression it makes—by the effect it produces—than by the time it took to impress the effect, or by the amount of "sustained effort" which had been found necessary in effecting the impression. The fact is, that perseverance is one thing and genius quite another; nor can all the Quarterlies in Christendom confound them. By and by, this proposition, with many which I have been just urging, will be received as self-evident. In the mean time, by being generally condemned as falsities they will not be essentially damaged as truths.

On the other hand, it is clear that a poem may be improperly brief. Undue brevity degenerates into mere epigrammatism. A *very* short poem, while now and then producing a brilliant or vivid, never produces a profound or enduring, effect. There must be the steady pressing down of the stamp upon the wax. Béranger has wrought innumerable things, pungent and spirit-stirring; but, in general, they have been too imponderous to stamp themselves deeply into the public opinion, and thus, as so many feathers of fancy, have been blown aloft only to be whistled down the wind.

A remarkable instance of the effect of undue brevity in depressing a poem—in keeping it out of the popular view—is afforded by the following exquisite little serenade:—

I arise from dreams of thee
  In the first sweet sleep of night,
When the winds are breathing low,
  And the stars are shining bright;
I arise from dreams of thee,
  And a spirit in my feet
Hath led me—who knows how?—
  To thy chamber-window, sweet!

The wandering airs, they faint
  On the dark, the silent stream;
And the champak odors fail
  Like sweet thoughts in a dream;

The nightingale's complaint,
It dies upon her heart,
As I must on thine,
Oh, beloved as thou art!

Oh, lift me from the grass!
I die! I faint! I fail!
Let thy love in kisses rain
On my lips and eyelids pale.
My cheek is cold and white, alas!
My heart beats loud and fast:
Oh! press it to thine own again,
Where it will break at last!

Very few, perhaps, are familiar with these lines—yet no less a poet than Shelley is their author. Their warm, yet delicate and ethereal imagination will be appreciated by all; but by none so thoroughly as by him who has himself arisen from sweet dreams of one beloved, to bathe in the aromatic air of a southern midsummer night.

One of the finest poems by Willis—the very best, in my opinion, which he has ever written—has, no doubt, through this same defect of undue brevity, been kept back from its proper position, not less in the critical than in the popular view.

The shadows lay along Broadway,
'Twas near the twilight-tide—
And slowly there a lady fair
Was walking in her pride.
Alone walked she; but, viewlessly,
Walked spirits at her side.

Peace charmed the street beneath her feet,
And Honor charmed the air;
And all astir looked kind on her,
And called her good as fair;
For all God ever gave to her
She kept with chary care.

She kept with care her beauties rare
From lovers warm and true,—
For her heart was cold to all but gold,
And the rich came not to woo,—
But honored well are charms to sell
If priests the selling do.

Now walking there was one more fair—
  A slight girl, lily-pale;
And she had unseen company
  To make the spirit quail:
'Twixt Want and Scorn she walked forlorn,
  And nothing could avail.

No mercy now can clear her brow
  For this world's peace to pray;
For, as love's wild prayer dissolved in air,
  Her woman's heart gave way!—
But the sin forgiven by Christ in Heaven
  By man is cursed alway!

In this composition we find it difficult to recognize the Willis who has written so many mere "verses of society." The lines are not only richly ideal, but full of energy, while they breathe an earnestness—an evident sincerity of sentiment—for which we look in vain throughout all the other works of this author.

While the epic mania—while the idea that, to merit in poetry, prolixity is indispensable—has, for some years past, been gradually dying out of the public mind by mere dint of its own absurdity—we find it succeeded by a heresy too palpably false to be long tolerated, but one which, in the brief period it has already endured, may be said to have accomplished more in the corruption of our Poetical Literature than all its other enemies combined. I allude to the heresy of *The Didactic*. It has been assumed, tacitly and avowedly, directly and indirectly, that the ultimate object of all Poetry is Truth. Every poem, it is said, should inculcate a moral; and by this moral is the poetical merit of the work to be adjudged. We Americans, especially, have patronized this happy idea; and we Bostonians, very especially, have developed it in full. We have taken it into our heads that to write a poem simply for the poem's sake, and to acknowledge such to have been our design, would be to confess ourselves radically wanting in the true Poetic dignity and force; but the simple fact is, that, would we but permit ourselves to look into our own souls, we should immediately there discover that under the sun there neither exists nor *can* exist any work more thoroughly dignified, more supremely noble, than this very poem—this poem *per se*

—this poem which is a poem and nothing more—this poem written solely for the poem's sake.

With as deep a reverence for the True as ever inspired the bosom of man, I would, nevertheless, limit in some measure its modes of inculcation. I would limit to enforce them. I would not enfeeble them by dissipation. The demands of Truth are severe; she has no sympathy with the myrtles. All *that* which is so indispensable in Song, is precisely all *that* with which *she* has nothing whatever to do. It is but making her a flaunting paradox to wreathe her in gems and flowers. In enforcing a truth we need severity rather than efflorescence of language. We must be simple, precise, terse. We must be cool, calm, unimpassioned. In a word, we must be in that mood, which, as nearly as possible, is the exact converse of the poetical. He must be blind, indeed, who does not perceive the radical and chasmal differences between the truthful and the poetical modes of inculcation. He must be theory-mad beyond redemption who, in spite of these differences, shall still persist in attempting to reconcile the obstinate oils and waters of Poetry and Truth.

Dividing the world of mind into its three most immediately obvious distinctions, we have the Pure Intellect, Taste, and the Moral Sense. I place Taste in the middle, because it is just this position which in the mind it occupies. It holds intimate relations with either extreme, but from the Moral Sense is separated by so faint a difference that Aristotle has not hesitated to place some of its operations among the virtues themselves. Nevertheless, we find the *offices* of the trio marked with a sufficient distinction. Just as the intellect concerns itself with Truth, so Taste informs us of the Beautiful, while the Moral Sense is regardful of Duty. Of this latter, while Conscience teaches the obligation, and Reason the expediency, Taste contents herself with displaying the charms:—waging war upon Vice solely on the ground of her deformity—her disproportion—her animosity to the fitting, to the appropriate, to the harmonious—in a word, to Beauty.

An immortal instinct, deep within the spirit of man, is thus, plainly, a sense of the Beautiful. This it is which administers to his delight in the manifold forms, and sounds, and odors, and sentiments, amid which he exists. And just as the lily is repeated in the lake, or the eyes of Amaryllis in the mirror, so is the mere oral or written repetition of these forms, and sounds, and colors, and odors, and sentiments, a duplicate source of delight. But this mere repetition is not poetry. He who shall simply sing, with however glowing enthusiasm, or with however vivid a truth of description, of the sights, and sounds, and odors, and colors, and sentiments, which greet *him* in common with all mankind—he, I say, has yet failed to prove his divine title. There is still a something in the distance which he has been unable to attain. We have still a thirst unquenchable, to allay which he has not shown us the crystal springs. This thirst belongs to the immortality of Man. It is at once a consequence and an indication of his perennial existence. It is the desire of the moth for the star. It is no mere appreciation of the Beauty before us, but a wild effort to reach the Beauty above. Inspired by an ecstatic prescience of the glories beyond the grave, we struggle, by multiform combinations among the things and thoughts of Time, to attain a portion of that Loveliness whose very elements, perhaps, appertain to eternity alone. And thus when by Poetry —or when by Music, the most entrancing of the Poetic moods—we find ourselves melted into tears not as the Abbate Gravia supposes through excess of pleasure, but through a certain petulant, impatient sorrow at our inability to grasp now, wholly, here on earth, at once and forever, those divine and rapturous joys, of which *through* the poem, or *through* the music, we attain to but brief and indeterminate glimpses.

The struggle to apprehend the supernal Loveliness—this struggle, on the part of souls fittingly constituted—has given to the world all that which it (the world) has ever been enabled at once to understand and to feel as poetic.

The Poetic Sentiment, of course, may develop itself in various modes—in Painting, in Sculpture, in Architecture, in the Dance—very especially in Music,—and very peculiarly and with a wide field, in the composition of the Landscape Garden. Our present theme, however, has regard only to its manifestation in words. And here let me speak briefly on the topic of rhythm. Contenting myself with the certainty that Music, in its various modes of metre, rhythm, and rhyme, is of so vast a moment in Poetry as never to be wisely rejected—is so vitally important an adjunct, that he is simply silly who declines its assistance—I will not now pause to maintain its absolute essentiality. It is in Music, perhaps, that the soul most nearly attains the great end for which, when inspired by the Poetic Sentiment, it struggles—the creation of supernal Beauty. It may be, indeed, that here this sublime end is, now and then, attained in fact. We are often made to feel, with a shivering delight, that from an earthly harp are stricken notes which cannot have been unfamiliar to the angels. And thus there can be little doubt that in the union of Poetry with Music in its popular sense we shall find the widest field for the Poetic development. The old Bards and Minnesingers had advantages which we do not possess—and Thomas Moore, singing his own songs, was, in the most legitimate manner, perfecting them as poems.

To recapitulate, then:—I would define, in brief, the Poetry of words as *The Rhythmical Creation of Beauty.* Its sole arbiter is Taste. With the Intellect or with the Conscience, it has only collateral relations. Unless incidentally, it has no concern whatever either with Duty or with Truth.

A few words, however, in explanation. That pleasure which is at once the most pure, the most elevating, and the most intense, is derived, I maintain, from the contemplation of the Beautiful. In the contemplation of Beauty we alone find it possible to attain that pleasurable elevation, or excitement, *of the soul,* which we recognize as the Poetic Sentiment, and which is so easily distinguished from Truth, which is the satisfaction of the Reason, or from Passion, which is the excitement of the heart. I make Beauty, therefore,—using the word as inclusive of the sublime,—I make Beauty the province of the poem, simply because it is an obvious rule of Art that effects should be made to spring as directly as possible from their causes—no one as yet having been weak enough to deny that the peculiar elevation in question is at least *most readily* attainable in the poem. It by no means follows, however, that the incitements of Passion, or the precepts of Duty, or even the lessons of Truth, may not be introduced into a poem and with advantage; for they may subserve, incidentally, in various ways, the general purposes of the work; but the true artist will always contrive to tone them down in proper subjection to that *Beauty* which is the atmosphere and the real essence of the poem.

I cannot better introduce the few poems which I shall present for your consideration, than by the citation of the "Proem" to Mr. Longfellow's "Waif":

The day is done, and the darkness
  Falls from the wings of Night,
As a feather is wafted downward
  From an eagle in his flight.

I see the lights of the village
  Gleam through the rain and the mist,
And a feeling of sadness comes o'er me,
  That my soul cannot resist:

A feeling of sadness and longing,
  That is not akin to pain,
And resembles sorrow only
  As the mist resembles the rain.

Come, read to me some poem,
  Some simple and heartfelt lay,
That shall soothe this restless feeling,
  And banish the thoughts of day.

Not from the grand old masters,
  Not from the bards sublime,
Whose distant footsteps echo
  Through the corridors of Time.

For, like strains of martial music,
  Their mighty thoughts suggest
Life's endless toil and endeavor;
  And to-night I long for rest.

Read from some humbler poet,
  Whose songs gushed from his heart,
As showers from the clouds of summer,
  Or tears from the eyelids start;

Who, through long days of labor,
  And nights devoid of ease,

Still heard in his soul the music
 Of wonderful melodies.

Such songs have power to quiet
 The restless pulse of care,
And come like the benediction
 That follows after prayer.

Then read from the treasured volume
 The poem of thy choice,
And lend to the rhyme of the poet
 The beauty of thy voice.

And the night shall be filled with music,
 And the cares, that infest the day,
Shall fold their tents, like the Arabs,
 And as silently steal away.

With no great range of imagination, these lines have been justly admired for their delicacy of expression. Some of the images are very effective. Nothing can be better than—

the bards sublime,
Whose distant footsteps echo
 Through the corridors of Time.

The idea of the last quatrain is also very effective. The poem, on the whole, however, is chiefly to be admired for the graceful *insouciance* of its metre, so well in accordance with the character of the sentiments, and especially for the *ease* of the general manner. This "ease," or naturalness, in a literary style, it has long been the fashion to regard as ease in appearance alone—as a point of really difficult attainment. But not so; a natural manner is difficult only to him who should never meddle with it—to the unnatural. It is but the result of writing with the understanding, or with the instinct, that *the tone*, in composition, should always be that which the mass of mankind would adopt—and must perpetually vary, of course, with the occasion. The author who, after the fashion of the "North American Review," should be, upon *all* occasions, merely "quiet," must necessarily, upon *many* occasions, be simply silly, or stupid; and has no more right to be considered "easy," or "natural," than a Cockney exquisite, or than the sleeping Beauty in the wax-works.

Among the minor poems of Bryant, none has so much impressed me as the one which he entitles "June." I quote only a portion of it:—

There, through the long, long summer hours,
The golden light should lie,
And thick, young herbs and groups of flowers
Stand in their beauty by.
The oriole should build and tell
His love-tale, close beside my cell;
The idle butterfly
Should rest him there, and there be heard
The housewife-bee and humming-bird.

And what, if cheerful shouts at noon,
Come, from the village sent,
Or songs of maids, beneath the moon,
With fairy laughter blent?
And what, if in the evening light,
Betrothèd lovers walk in sight
Of my low monument?
I would the lovely scene around
Might know no sadder sight nor sound.

I know that I no more should see
The season's glorious show,
Nor would its brightness shine for me,
Nor its wild music flow;
But if, around my place of sleep,
The friends I love should come to weep,
They might not haste to go.
Soft airs, and song, and light, and bloom
Should keep them, lingering by my tomb.

These to their softened hearts should bear
The thought of what has been,
And speak of one who cannot share
The gladness of the scene;
Whose part, in all the pomp that fills
The circuit of the summer hills,
Is—that his grave is green;
And deeply would their hearts rejoice
To hear again his living voice.

The rhythmical flow, here, is even voluptuous—nothing could be more melodious. The poem has always affected me in a remarkable manner. The intense melancholy, which seems to well up, perforce, to the surface of all the poet's cheerful sayings about his grave, we find thrilling us to the soul, while there is the truest poetic elevation in the thrill. The impression left is one of a pleasurable sadness.

And if, in the remaining compositions which I shall introduce to you, there be more or less of a similar tone always apparent, let me remind you that (how or why we know not) this certain taint of sadness is inseparably connected with all the higher manifestations of true Beauty. It is, nevertheless,

A feeling of sadness and longing
That is not akin to pain,
And resembles sorrow only
As the mist resembles the rain.

The taint of which I speak is clearly perceptible even in a poem so full of brilliancy and spirit as the "Health" of Edward C. Pinkney:—

I fill this cup to one made up
Of loveliness alone,
A woman, of her gentle sex
The seeming paragon;
To whom the better elements
And kindly stars have given
A form so fair, that, like the air,
'Tis less of earth than heaven.

Her every tone is music's own,
Like those of morning birds,
And something more than melody
Dwells ever in her words;
The coinage of her heart are they,
And from her lips each flows
As one may see the burdened bee
Forth issue from the rose.

Affections are as thoughts to her,
The measures of her hours;
Her feelings have the fragrancy,
The freshness of young flowers;
And lovely passions, changing oft,
So fill her, she appears
The image of themselves by turns,—
The idol of past years!

Of her bright face one glance will trace
  A picture on the brain,
And of her voice in echoing hearts
  A sound must long remain;
But memory, such as mine of her,
  So very much endears,
When death is nigh, my latest sigh
  Will not be life's, but hers.

I fill this cup to one made up
  Of loveliness alone,
A woman, of her gentle sex
  The seeming paragon—
Her health! and would on earth there stood
  Some more of such a frame,
That life might be all poetry,
  And weariness a name.

It was the misfortune of Mr. Pinkney to have been born too far south. Had he been a New Englander, it is probable that he would have been ranked as the first of American lyrists by that magnanimous cabal which has so long controlled the destinies of American Letters, in conducting the thing called the "North American Review." The poem just cited is especially beautiful; but the poetic elevation which it induces we must refer chiefly to our sympathy in the poet's enthusiasm. We pardon his hyperboles for the evident earnestness with which they are uttered.

It was by no means my design, however, to expatiate upon the *merits* of what I should read you. These will necessarily speak for themselves. Boccalini, in his "Advertisements from Parnassus," tells us that Zoilus once presented Apollo a very caustic criticism upon a very admirable book; whereupon the god asked him for the beauties of the work. He replied that he only busied himself about the errors. On hearing this, Apollo, handing him a sack of unwinnowed wheat, bade him pick out *all the chaff* for his reward.

Now this fable answers very well as a hit at the critics; but I am by no means sure that the god was in the right. I am by no means certain that the true limits of the critical duty are not grossly misunderstood. Excellence, in a poem especially, may be considered in the light of an axiom, which need only be properly *put,* to become self-evident. It is *not* excellence if it requires to be demonstrated as such; and thus, to point out too particularly the merits of a work of Art, is to admit that they are *not* merits altogether.

Among the "Melodies" of Thomas Moore, is one whose distinguished character as a poem proper seems to have been singularly left out of view. I allude to his lines beginning: "Come, rest in this bosom." The intense energy of their expression is not surpassed by anything in Byron. There are two of the lines in which a sentiment is conveyed that embodies the *all in all* of the divine passion of love—a sentiment which, perhaps, has found its echo in more, and in more passionate, human hearts than any other single sentiment ever embodied in words:—

> Come, rest in this bosom, my own stricken deer,
> Though the herd have fled from thee, thy home is still here;
> Here still is the smile that no cloud can o'ercast,
> And a heart and a hand all thy own to the last.
>
> Oh! what was love made for, if 'tis not the same
> Through joy and through torment, through glory and shame?
> I know not, I ask not, if guilt's in that heart,
> I but know that I love thee, whatever thou art.
>
> Thou hast called me thy angel in moments of bliss,
> And thy angel I'll be, 'mid the horrors of this,—
> Through the furnace, unshrinking, thy steps to pursue,
> And shield thee, and save thee,—or perish there too!

It has been the fashion, of late days, to deny Moore imagination, while granting him fancy—a distinction originating with Coleridge—than whom no man more fully comprehended the great powers of Moore. The fact is that the fancy of this poet so far predominates over all his other faculties, and over the fancy of all other men, as to have induced, very naturally, the idea that he is fanciful *only.* But never was there a greater mistake. Never was a grosser wrong done the fame of a true poet. In the compass of the English language I can call to mind no poem more profoundly, more weirdly *imaginative,* in the best sense, than the lines commencing: "I would I were by that dim lake," which are the composition of Thomas Moore. I regret that I am unable to remember them.

One of the noblest—and, speaking of fancy, one of the most singularly fanciful—of modern poets, was Thomas Hood. His "Fair Ines" had always, for me, an inexpressible charm:—

O saw ye not fair Ines?
  She's gone into the West,
To dazzle when the sun is down,
  And rob the world of rest;
She took our daylight with her,
  The smiles that we love best,
With morning blushes on her cheek,
  And pearls upon her breast.

O turn again, fair Ines,
  Before the fall of night,
For fear the moon should shine alone,
  And stars unrivalled bright;
And blessèd will the lover be
  That walks beneath their light,
And breathes the love against thy cheek
  I dare not even write!

Would I had been, fair Ines,
  That gallant cavalier,
Who rode so gayly by thy side,
  And whispered thee so near!
Were there no bonny dames at home,
  Or no true lovers here,
That he should cross the seas to win
  The dearest of the dear?

I saw thee, lovely Ines,
  Descend along the shore,
With bands of noble gentlemen,
  And banners waved before;
And gentle youth and maidens gay,
  And snowy plumes they wore;
It would have been a beauteous dream—
  If it had been no more!

Alas, alas, fair Ines!
  She went away with song,
With Music waiting on her steps,
  And shoutings of the throng;
But some were sad and felt no mirth,
  But only Music's wrong,

In sounds that sang Farewell, Farewell,
To her you've loved so long.

Farewell, farewell, fair Ines!
That vessel never bore
So fair a lady on its deck,
Nor danced so light before,—
Alas, for pleasure on the sea,
And sorrow on the shore!
The smile that blest one lover's heart
Has broken many more!

"The Haunted House," by the same author, is one of the truest poems ever written; one of the *truest,* one of the most unexceptionable, one of the most thoroughly artistic both in its theme and in its execution. It is, moreover, powerfully ideal, imaginative. I regret that its length renders it unsuitable for the purposes of this Lecture. In place of it, permit me to offer the universally appreciated "Bridge of Sighs."

One more Unfortunate,
Weary of breath,
Rashly importunate,
Gone to her death!

Take her up tenderly,
Lift her with care:
Fashioned so slenderly,
Young, and so fair!

Look at her garments
Clinging like cerements;
Whilst the wave constantly
Drips from her clothing;
Take her up instantly,
Loving, not loathing,—

Touch her not scornfully;
Think of her mournfully,
Gently and humanly;
Not of the stains of her—
All that remains of her
Now, is pure womanly.

Make no deep scrutiny
Into her mutiny

Rash and undutiful:
Past all dishonor,
Death has left on her
Only the beautiful.

Still, for all slips of hers,
One of Eve's family—
Wipe those poor lips of hers
Oozing so clammily,
Loop up her tresses
Escaped from the comb,
Her fair auburn tresses;
Whilst wonderment guesses
Where was her home?

Who was her father?
Who was her mother?
Had she a sister?
Had she a brother?
Or was there a dearer one
Still, and a nearer one
Yet, than all other?

Alas! for the rarity
Of Christian charity
Under the sun!
Oh, it was pitiful!
Near a whole city full,
Home she had none.

Sisterly, brotherly,
Fatherly, motherly
Feelings had changed;
Love, by harsh evidence,
Thrown from its eminence;
Even God's providence
Seeming estranged.

Where the lamps quiver
So far in the river,
With many a light
From window and casement,
From garret to basement,
She stood, with amazement,
Houseless by night.

The bleak wind of March
Made her tremble and shiver,
But not the dark arch,
Or the black flowing river:

Mad from life's history,
Glad to death's mystery,
Swift to be hurled—
Anywhere, anywhere
Out of the world!

In she plunged boldly,
No matter how coldly
The rough river ran,—
Over the brink of it,
Picture it—think of it,
Dissolute man!
Lave in it, drink of it,
Then, if you can!

Take her up tenderly,
Lift her with care;
Fashioned so slenderly,
Young, and so fair!

Ere her limbs frigidly
Stiffen too rigidly,
Decently—kindly—
Smoothe and compose them:
And her eyes, close them,
Staring so blindly!

Dreadfully staring
Through muddy impurity,
As when with the daring
Last look of despairing
Fixed on futurity.

Perishing gloomily,
Spurred by contumely,
Cold inhumanity,
Burning insanity,
Into her rest.—
Cross her hands humbly,
As if praying dumbly,
Over her breast!
Owning her weakness,
Her evil behavior,
And leaving, with meekness,
Her sins to her Saviour!

The vigor of this poem is no less remarkable than its pathos. The versification, although carrying the fanciful to the very verge of the fantastic, is nevertheless admirably adapted to the wild insanity which is the thesis of the poem.

Among the minor poems of Lord Byron, is one which has never received from the critics the praise which it undoubtedly deserves:—

Though the day of my destiny's over,
And the star of my fate hath declined,
Thy soft heart refused to discover
The faults which so many could find;
Though thy soul with my grief was acquainted,
It shrunk not to share it with me,
And the love which my spirit hath painted
It never hath found but in *thee.*

Then when nature around me is smiling,
The last smile which answers to mine,
I do not believe it beguiling,
Because it reminds me of thine;
And when winds are at war with the ocean,
As the breasts I believed in with me,
If their billows excite an emotion,
It is that they bear me from *thee.*

Though the rock of my last hope is shivered,
And its fragments are sunk in the wave,
Though I feel that my soul is delivered
To pain—it shall not be its slave.
There is many a pang to pursue me;
They may crush, but they shall not contemn;
They may torture, but shall not subdue me;
'Tis of *thee* that I think—not of them.

Though human, thou didst not deceive me;
Though woman, thou didst not forsake;
Though loved, thou forborest to grieve me;
Though slandered, thou never couldst shake;
Though trusted, thou didst not disclaim me;
Though parted, it was not to fly;
Though watchful, 'twas not to defame me;
Nor mute, that the world might belie.

Yet I blame not the world, nor despise it,
Nor the war of the many with one—
If my soul was not fitted to prize it,
'Twas folly not sooner to shun;

And if dearly that error hath cost me,
And more than I once could foresee,
I have found that, whatever it lost me,
It could not deprive me of *thee.*

From the wreck of the past, which hath perished,
Thus much I at least may recall:
It hath taught me that what I most cherished
Deserved to be dearest of all.
In the desert a fountain is springing,
In the wide waste there still is a tree,
And a bird in the solitude singing,
Which speaks to my spirit of *thee.*

Although the rhythm here is one of the most difficult, the versification could scarcely be improved. No nobler *theme* ever engaged the pen of poet. It is the soul-elevating idea, that no man can consider himself entitled to complain of Fate while, in his adversity, he still retains the unwavering love of woman.

From Alfred Tennyson—although in perfect sincerity I regard him as the noblest poet that ever lived—I have left myself time to cite only a very brief specimen. I call him, and *think* him, the noblest of poets, *not* because the impressions he produces are, at *all* times, the most profound, *not* because the poetical excitement which he induces is, at *all* times, the most intense, but because it *is,* at all times, the most ethereal—in other words, the most elevating and the most pure. No poet is so little of the earth, earthy. What I am about to read is from his last long poem, "The Princess":—

Tears, idle tears, I know not what they mean,
Tears from the depth of some divine despair
Rise in the heart, and gather to the eyes,
In looking on the happy autumn fields,
And thinking of the days that are no more.

Fresh as the first beam glittering on a sail
That brings our friends up from the underworld;
Sad as the last which reddens over one
That sinks with all we love below the verge;
So sad, so fresh, the days that are no more.

Ah, sad and strange as in dark summer dawns
The earliest pipe of half-awakened birds
To dying ears, when unto dying eyes
The casement slowly grows a glimmering square;
So sad, so strange, the days that are no more.

Dear as remembered kisses after death,
And sweet as those by hopeless fancy feigned
On lips that are for others; deep as love,
Deep as first love, and wild with all regret;
O Death in Life, the days that are no more.

Thus, although in a very cursory and imperfect manner, I have endeavored to convey to you my conception of the Poetic Principle. It has been my purpose to suggest that, while this Principle itself is, strictly and simply, the Human Aspiration for Supernal Beauty, the manifestation of the Principle is always found in *an elevating excitement of the Soul,* quite independent of that passion which is the intoxication of the Heart, or of that Truth which is the satisfaction of the Reason. For, in regard to Passion, alas! its tendency is to degrade rather than elevate the Soul. Love, on the contrary—Love, the true, the divine Eros, the Uranian as distinguished from the Dionæan Venus—is unquestionably the purest and truest of all poetical themes. And in regard to Truth—if, to be sure, through the attainment of a truth we are led to perceive a harmony where none was apparent before, we experience, at once the true poetical effect; but this effect is referable to the harmony alone, and not in the least degree to the truth which merely served to render the harmony manifest.

We shall reach, however, more immediately a distinct conception of what the true Poetry is, by mere reference to a few of the simple elements which induce in the Poet himself the true poetical effect. He recognizes the ambrosia, which nourishes his soul, in the bright orbs that shine in Heaven, in the volutes of the flower, in the clustering of low shrubberies, in the waving of the grain-fields, in the slanting of the tall, Eastern trees, in the blue distance of mountains, in the grouping of clouds, in the twinkling of half-hidden brooks, in the gleaming of silver rivers, in the repose of sequestered lakes, in the star-mirroring depths of lonely wells. He perceives it in the songs of birds, in the harp of Æolus, in the sighing of the night-wind, in the repining voice of the forest, in the surf that complains to the shore, in the fresh breath of the woods, in the scent of the violet, in the voluptuous perfume of the hyacinth, in the suggestive odor that comes to him at eventide from far-distant, undiscovered islands, over dim oceans, illimitable and unexplored. He owns it in all noble thoughts, in all unworldly motives, in all holy impulses, in all chivalrous, generous, and self-sacrificing deeds. He feels it in the beauty of woman, in the grace of her step, in the lustre of her eye, in the melody of her voice, in her soft laughter, in her sigh, in the harmony of the rustling of her robes. He deeply feels it in her winning endearments, in her burning enthusiasms, in her gentle charities, in her meek and devotional endurances; but above all—ah! far above all—he kneels to it, he worships it in the faith, in the purity, in the strength, in the altogether divine majesty of her *love*.

Let me conclude by the recitation of yet another brief poem—one very different in character from any that I have before quoted. It is by Motherwell, and is called "The Song of the Cavalier." With our modern and altogether rational ideas of the absurdity and impiety of warfare, we are not precisely in that frame of mind best adapted to sympathize with the sentiments, and thus to appreciate the real excellence, of the poem. To do this fully, we must identify ourselves, in fancy, with the soul of the old cavalier.

Then mounte! then mounte, brave gallants, all,
  And don your helmes amaine:
Deathe's couriers, Fame and Honor, call
  Us to the field againe.
No shrewish teares shall fill our eye
  When the sword-hilt's in our hand;
Heart-whole we'll part and no whit sighe
  For the fayrest of the land;
Let piping swaine, and craven wight,
  Thus weepe and puling crye,
Our business is like men to fight,
  And hero-like to die!

WALKING

BY

HENRY DAVID THOREAU

INTRODUCTORY NOTE

HENRY DAVID THOREAU *was born at Concord, Massachusetts, July 12, 1817, and died there May 6, 1862. He was one of the most markedly individual of that group of philosophers and men of letters which has made the name of the little Massachusetts town so notable in the intellectual history of America.*

Thoreau came of a family of French descent, and was educated at Harvard. "He was bred," says his friend Emerson, "to no profession; he never married; he lived alone; he never went to church; he never voted; he refused to pay a tax to the State; he ate no flesh, he drank no wine, he never knew the use of tobacco; and, though a naturalist, he used neither trap nor gun." The individualism which is implied in these facts was the most prominent characteristic of this remarkable person. Holding that "a man is rich in proportion to the number of things which he can afford to let alone," he found that a small part of his time, devoted to making lead-pencils, carpentering, and surveying, gave him enough for his simple needs, and left him free for the rest of the year to observe nature, to think, and to write.

In 1845 Thoreau built himself a hut on the edge of Walden Pond, and for over two years lived there in solitude, composing his "Week on the Concord and Merrimac Rivers." During these years he kept a journal, from which he later drew the volume called "Walden," and these are his only two books published during his lifetime. From articles in magazines and manuscripts, some eight more volumes have been compiled since his death.

Interesting as is the philosophy which permeates the work of this solitary, his books have found readers rather on account of their minute and sympathetic observation of nature and the beauty of their style. The following essay on "Walking" represents all three elements; and in its charming discursiveness, in the absence of any structure to hinder the writer's pen from wandering at will, and in the responsiveness which it exhibits to the moods and suggestions of nature, it is a characteristic expression of its author's spirit.

WALKING

[1862]

I WISH to speak a word for Nature, for absolute freedom and wildness, as contrasted with a freedom and culture merely civil,—to regard man as an inhabitant, or a part and parcel of Nature, rather than a member of society. I wish to make an extreme statement, if so I may make an emphatic one, for there are enough champions of civilization: the minister and the school committee and every one of you will take care of that.

I have met with but one or two persons in the course of my life who understood the art of Walking, that is, of taking walks,—who had a genius, so to speak, for *sauntering:* which word is beautifully derived from "idle people who roved about the country, in the Middle Ages, and asked charity, under pretence of going *à la Sainte Terre,*" to the Holy Land, till the children exclaimed, "There goes a *Sainte-Terrer,*" a Saunterer, a Holy-Lander. They who never go to the Holy Land in their walks, as they pretend, are indeed mere idlers and vagabonds; but they who do go there are saunterers in the good sense, such as I mean. Some, however, would derive the word from *sans terre,* without land or a home, which, therefore, in the good sense, will mean, having no particular home, but equally at home everywhere. For this is the secret of successful sauntering. He who sits still in a house all the time may be the greatest vagrant of all; but the saunterer, in the good sense, is no more vagrant than the meandering river, which is all the while sedulously seeking the shortest course to the sea. But I prefer the first, which, indeed, is the most probable derivation. For every walk is a sort of crusade, preached by some Peter the Hermit in us, to go forth and reconquer this Holy Land from the hands of the Infidels.

It is true, we are but faint-hearted crusaders, even the walkers, nowadays, who undertake no persevering, never-ending enterprizes. Our expeditions are but tours, and come round again at evening to the old hearth-side from which we set out. Half the walk is but retracing our steps. We should go forth on the shortest walk, perchance, in the spirit of undying adventure, never to return—prepared to send back our embalmed hearts only as relics to our desolate kingdoms. If you are ready to leave father and mother, and brother and sister, and wife and child and friends, and never see them again—if you have paid your debts, and made your will, and settled all your affairs, and are a free man, then you are ready for a walk.

To come down to my own experience, my companion and I, for I sometimes have a companion, take pleasure in fancying ourselves knights of a new, or rather an old, order—not Equestrians or Chevaliers, not Ritters or riders, but Walkers, a still more ancient and honourable class, I trust. The chivalric and heroic spirit which once belonged to the Rider seems now to reside in, or perchance to have subsided into, the Walker,—not the Knight, but Walker, Errant. He is a sort of fourth estate, outside of Church and State and People.

We have felt that we almost alone hereabouts practised this noble art; though, to tell the truth, at least, if their own assertions are to be received, most of my townsmen would fain walk sometimes, as I do, but they cannot. No wealth can buy the requisite leisure, freedom, and independence which are the capital in this profession. It comes only by the grace of God. It requires a direct dispensation from Heaven to become a walker. You must be born into the family of the Walkers. *Ambulator nascitur, non fit.* Some of my townsmen, it is true, can remember and have described to me some walks which they took ten years ago, in which they were so blessed as to lose themselves for half an hour in the woods; but I know very well that they have confined themselves to the highway ever since, whatever pretensions they may make to belong to this select class. No doubt they were elevated for a moment as by the reminiscence of a previous state of existence, when even they were foresters and outlaws.

> "When he came to grene wode,
> In a mery mornynge,
> There he herde the notes small
> Of byrdes mery syngynge.
>
> "It is ferre gone, sayd Robyn,
> That I was last here;
> Me lyste a lytell for to shote
> At the donne dere."

I think that I cannot preserve my health and spirits, unless I spend four hours a day at least—and it is commonly more than that—sauntering through the woods and over the hills and fields, absolutely free from all worldly engagements. You may safely say, A penny for your thoughts, or a thousand pounds. When sometimes I am reminded that the mechanics and shopkeepers stay in their shops not only all the forenoon, but all the afternoon too, sitting with crossed legs, so many of them—as if the legs were made to sit upon, and not to stand or walk upon—I think that they deserve some credit for not having all committed suicide long ago.

I, who cannot stay in my chamber for a single day without acquiring some rust, and when sometimes I have stolen forth for a walk at the eleventh hour or four o'clock in the afternoon, too late to redeem the day, when the shades of night were already beginning to be mingled with the daylight, have felt as if I had committed some sin to be atoned for,—I confess that I am astonished at the power of endurance, to say nothing of the moral insensibility, of my neighbours who confine themselves to shops and offices the whole day for weeks and months, ay, and years almost together. I know not what manner of stuff they are of—sitting there now at three o'clock in the afternoon, as if it were three o'clock in the morning. Bonaparte may talk of the three-o'clock-in-the-morning courage, but it is nothing to the courage which can sit down cheerfully at this hour in the afternoon over against one's self whom you have known all the morning, to starve out a garrison to whom you are bound by such strong ties of sympathy. I wonder that about this time, or say between four and five o'clock in the afternoon, too late for the morning papers and too early for the evening ones, there is not a general explosion heard up and down the street, scattering a legion of antiquated and house-bred notions and whims to the four winds for an airing—and so the evil cure itself.

How womankind, who are confined to the house still more than men, stand it I do not know; but I have ground to suspect that most of them do not *stand* it at all. When, early in a summer afternoon, we have been shaking the dust of the village from the skirts of our garments, making haste past those houses with purely Doric or Gothic fronts, which have such an air of repose about them, my companion whispers that probably about these times their occupants are all gone to bed. Then it is that I appreciate the beauty and the glory of architecture, which itself never turns in, but forever stands out and erect, keeping watch over the slumberers.

No doubt temperament, and, above all, age, have a good deal to do with it. As a man grows older, his ability to sit still and follow indoor occupations increases. He grows vespertinal in his habits as the evening of life approaches, till at last he comes forth only just before sundown, and gets all the walk that he requires in half an hour.

But the walking of which I speak has nothing in it akin to taking exercise, as it is called, as the sick take medicine at stated hours—as the swinging of dumb-bells or chairs; but is itself the enterprise and adventure of the day. If you would get exercise, go in search of the springs of life. Think of a man's swinging dumb-bells for his health, when those springs are bubbling up in far-off pastures unsought by him!

Moreover, you must walk like a camel, which is said to be the only beast which ruminates when walking. When a traveller asked Wordsworth's servant to show him her master's study, she answered, "Here is his library, but his study is out of doors."

Living much out of doors, in the sun and wind, will no doubt produce a certain roughness of character—will cause a thicker cuticle to grow over some of the finer qualities of our nature, as on the face and hands, or as severe manual labor robs the hands of some of their delicacy of touch. So staying in the house, on the other hand, may produce a softness and smoothness, not to say thinness of skin, accompanied by an increased sensibility to certain impressions. Perhaps we should be more susceptible to some influences important to our intellectual and moral growth, if the sun had shone and the wind blown on us a little less; and no doubt it is a nice matter to proportion rightly the thick and thin skin. But methinks that is a scurf that will fall off fast enough—that the natural remedy is to be found in the proportion which the night bears to the day, the winter to the summer, thought to experience. There will be so much the more air and sunshine in our thoughts. The callous palms of the laborer are conversant with finer tissues of self-respect and heroism, whose touch thrills the heart, than the languid fingers of idleness. That is mere sentimentality that lies abed by day and thinks itself white, far from the tan and callus of experience.

When we walk, we naturally go to the fields and woods: what would become of us if we walked only in a garden or a mall? Even some sects of philosophers have felt the necessity of importing the woods to themselves, since they did not go to the woods. "They planted groves and walks of Platanes," where they took *subdiales ambulationes* in porticos open to the air. Of course it is of no use to direct our steps to the woods, if they do not carry us thither. I am alarmed when it happens that I have walked a mile into the woods bodily, without getting there in spirit. In my afternoon walk I would fain forget all my morning occupations and my obligations to society. But it sometimes happens that I cannot easily shake off the village. The thought of some work will run in my head and I am not where my body is—I am out of my senses. In my walks I would fain return to my senses. What business have I in the woods, if I am thinking of something out of the woods? I suspect myself, and cannot help a shudder, when I find myself so implicated even in what are called good works—for this may sometimes happen.

My vicinity affords many good walks; and though for so many years I have walked almost every day, and sometimes for several days together, I have not yet exhausted them. An absolutely new prospect is a great happiness, and I can still get this any afternoon. Two or three hours' walking will carry me to as strange a country as I expect ever to see. A single farmhouse which I had not seen before is sometimes as good as the dominions of the King of Dahomey. There is in fact a sort of harmony discoverable between the capabilities of the landscape within a circle of ten miles' radius, or the limits of an afternoon walk, and the threescore years and ten of human life. It will never become quite familiar to you.

Nowadays almost all man's improvements, so called, as the building of houses, and the cutting down of the forest and of all large trees, simply deform the landscape, and make it more and more tame and cheap. A people who would begin by burning the fences and let the forest stand! I saw the fences half consumed, their ends lost in the middle of the prairie, and some worldly miser with a surveyor looking after his bounds, while heaven had taken place around him, and he did not see the angels going to and fro, but was looking for an old post-hole in the midst of paradise. I looked again, and saw him standing in the middle of a boggy stygian fen, surrounded by devils, and he had found his bounds without a doubt, three little stones, where a stake had been driven, and looking nearer, I saw that the Prince of Darkness was his surveyor.

I can easily walk ten, fifteen, twenty, any number of miles, commencing at my own door, without going by any house, without crossing a road except where the fox and the mink do: first along by the river, and then the brook, and then the meadow and the wood-side. There are square miles in my vicinity which have no inhabitant. From many a hill I can see civilisation and the abodes of man afar. The farmers and their works are scarcely more obvious than woodchucks and their burrows. Man and his affairs, church and state and school, trade and commerce, and manufactures and agriculture, even politics, the most alarming of them all,—I am pleased to see how little space they occupy in the landscape.

Politics is but a narrow field, and that still narrower highway yonder leads to it. I sometimes direct the traveller thither. If you would go to the political world, follow the great road—follow that market-man, keep his dust in your eyes, and it will lead you straight to it; for it, too, has its place merely, and does not occupy all space. I pass from it as from a bean-field into the forest, and it is forgotten. In one half-hour I can walk off to some portion of the earth's surface where a man does not stand from one year's end to another, and there, consequently, politics are not, for they are but as the cigar-smoke of a man.

The village is the place to which the roads tend, a sort of expansion of the highway, as a lake of a river. It is the body of which roads are the arms and legs—a trivial or quadrivial place, the thoroughfare and ordinary of travellers. The word is from the Latin *villa,* which together with *via,* a way, or more anciently *ved* and *vella,* Varro derives from *veho,* to carry, because the villa is the place to and from which things are carried. They who got their living by teaming were said *vellaturam facere.* Hence, too, apparently, the Latin word *vilis* and our vile; also *villain.* This suggests what kind of degeneracy villagers are liable to. They are wayworn by the travel that goes by and over them, without travelling themselves.

Some do not walk at all; others walk in the highways; a few walk across lots. Roads are made for horses and men of business. I do not travel in them much, comparatively, because I am not in a hurry to get to any tavern or grocery or livery-stable or depot to which they lead. I am a good horse to travel, but not from choice a roadster. The landscape-painter uses the figures of men to mark a road. He would not make that use of my figure. I walk out into a Nature such as the old prophets and poets, Menu, Moses, Homer, Chaucer, walked in. You may name it America, but it is not America: neither Americus Vespucius, nor Columbus, nor the rest were the discoverers of it. There is a truer account of it in mythology than in any history of America, so called, that I have seen.

However, there are a few old roads that may be trodden with profit, as if they led somewhere now that they are nearly discontinued. There is the Old Marlborough Road, which does not go to Marlborough now, methinks, unless that is Marlborough where it carries me. I am the bolder to speak of it here, because I presume that there are one or two such roads in every town.

THE OLD MARLBOROUGH ROAD

Where they once dug for money,
Where sometimes Martial Miles
But never found any;
Singly files,
And Elijah Wood,
I fear for no good:
No other man,
Save Elisha Dugan,—
O man of wild habits,
Partridges and rabbits,
Who hast no cares
Only to set snares,
Who liv'st all alone,
Close to the bone,
And where life is sweetest
Constantly eatest.
When the spring stirs my blood
With the instinct to travel
I can get enough gravel
On the Old Marlborough Road.
Nobody repairs it,
For nobody wears it;
It is a living way,
As the Christians say.
Not many there be
Who enter therein,
Only the guests of the
Irishman Quin.
What is it, what is it,
But a direction out there,
And the bare possibility
Of going somewhere?
Great guide-boards of stone,
But travellers none;
Cenotaphs of the towns
Named on their crowns.
It is worth going to see
Where you *might* be.
What king
Did the thing,
I am still wondering;

Set up how or when,
By what selectmen,
Gourgas or Lee,
Clark or Darby?
They're a great endeavor
To be something forever;
Blank tablets of stone,
Where a traveller might groan,
And in one sentence
Grave all that is known;
Which another might read,
In his extreme need.
I know one or two
Lines that would do,
Literature that might stand
All over the land,
Which a man could remember
Till next December,
And read again in the Spring,
After the thawing.

If with fancy unfurled
You leave your abode,
You may go round the world
By the Old Marlborough Road.

At present, in this vicinity, the best part of the land is not private property; the landscape is not owned, and the walker enjoys comparative freedom. But possibly the day will come when it will be partitioned off into so-called pleasure-grounds, in which a few will take a narrow and exclusive pleasure only,—when fences shall be multiplied, and man-traps and other engines invented to confine men to the *public* road, and walking over the surface of God's earth shall be construed to mean trespassing on some gentleman's grounds. To enjoy a thing exclusively is commonly to exclude yourself from the true enjoyment of it. Let us improve our opportunities, then, before the evil days come.

What is it that makes it so hard sometimes to determine whither we will walk? I believe that there is a subtle magnetism in Nature, which, if we unconsciously yield to it, will direct us aright. It is not indifferent to us which way we walk. There is a right way; but we are very liable from heedlessness and stupidity to take the wrong one. We would fain take that walk, never yet taken by us through this actual world, which is perfectly symbolical of the path which we love to travel in the interior and ideal world; and sometimes, no doubt, we find it difficult to choose our direction, because it does not yet exist distinctly in our idea.

When I go out of the house for a walk, uncertain as yet whither I will bend my steps, and submit myself to my instinct to decide for me, I find, strange and whimsical as it may seem, that I finally and inevitably settle southwest, toward some particular wood or meadow or deserted pasture or hill in that direction. My needle is slow to settle,—varies a few degrees, and does not always point due southwest, it is true, and it has good authority for this variation, but it always settles between west and south-southwest. The future lies that way to me, and the earth seems more unexhausted and richer on that side. The outline which would bound my walks would be, not a circle, but a parabola, or rather like one of those cometary orbits which have been thought to be non-returning curves, in this case opening westward, in which my house occupies the place of the sun. I turn round and round irresolute sometimes for a quarter of an hour, until I decide, for a thousandth time, that I will walk into the southwest or west. Eastward I go only by force; but westward I go free. Thither no business leads me. It is hard for me to believe that I shall find fair landscapes or sufficient wildness and freedom behind the eastern horizon. I am not excited by the prospect of a walk thither; but I believe that the forest which I see in the western horizon stretches uninterruptedly toward the setting sun, and there are no towns nor cities in it of enough consequence to disturb me. Let me live where I will, on this side is the city, on that the wilderness, and ever I am leaving the city more and more, and withdrawing into the wilderness. I should not lay so much stress on this fact, if I did not believe that something like this is the prevailing tendency of my countrymen. I must walk toward Oregon, and not toward Europe. And that way the nation is moving, and I may say that mankind progress from east to west. Within a few years we have witnessed the phenomenon of a southeastward migration, in the settlement of Australia; but this affects us as a retrograde movement, and, judging from the moral and physical character of the first generation of Australians, has not yet proved a successful experiment. The eastern Tartars think that there is nothing west beyond Thibet. "The world ends there," say they; "beyond there is nothing but a shoreless sea." It is unmitigated East where they live.

We go eastward to realise history and study the works of art and literature, retracing the steps of the race; we go westward as into the future, with a spirit of enterprise and adventure. The Atlantic is a Lethean stream, in our passage over which we have had an opportunity to forget the Old World and its institutions. If we do not succeed this time, there is perhaps one more chance for the race left before it arrives on the banks of the Styx; and that is in the Lethe of the Pacific, which is three times as wide.

I know not how significant it is, or how far it is an evidence of singularity, that an individual should thus consent in his pettiest walk with the general movement of the race; but I know that something akin to the migratory instinct in birds and quadrupeds,—which, in some instances, is known to have affected the squirrel tribe, impelling them to a general and mysterious movement, in which they were seen, say some, crossing the broadest rivers, each on its particular chip, with its tail raised for a sail, and bridging narrower streams with their dead,—that something like the *furor* which affects the domestic cattle in the spring, and which is referred to a worm in their tails,—affects both nations and individuals, either perennially or from time to time. Not a flock of wild geese cackles over our town, but it to some extent unsettles the value of real estate here, and if I were a broker I should probably take that disturbance into account.

> "Than longen folk to gon on pilgrimages,
> And palmeres for to seken strange strondes."

Every sunset which I witness inspires me with the desire to go to a West as distant and as fair as that into which the sun goes down. He appears to migrate westward daily, and tempts us to follow him. He is the Great Western Pioneer whom the nations follow. We dream all night of those mountain-ridges in the horizon, though they may be of vapor only, which were last gilded by his rays. The island of Atlantis, and the islands and gardens of the Hesperides, a sort of terrestrial paradise, appear to have been the Great West of the ancients, enveloped in mystery and poetry. Who has not seen in imagination, when looking into the sunset sky, the gardens of the Hesperides, and the foundation of all those fables?

Columbus felt the westward tendency more strongly than any before. He obeyed it, and found a New World for Castile and Leon. The herd of men in those days scented fresh pastures from afar.

> "And now the sun had stretched out all the hills,
> And now was dropped into the western bay;
> At last *he* rose, and twitched his mantle blue;
> To-morrow to fresh woods and pastures new."

Where on the globe can there be found an area of equal extent with that occupied by the bulk of our States, so fertile and so rich and varied in its productions, and at the same time so habitable by the European, as this is? Michaux, who knew but part of them, says that "the species of large trees are much more numerous in North America than in Europe; in the United States there are more than one hundred and forty species that exceed thirty feet in height; in France there are but thirty that attain this size." Later botanists more than confirm his observations. Humboldt came to America to realize his youthful dreams of a tropical vegetation, and he beheld it in its greatest perfection in the primitive forests of the Amazon, the most gigantic wilderness on the earth, which he has so eloquently described. The geographer Guyot, himself a European, goes farther—farther than I am ready to follow him; yet not when he says: "As the plant is made for the animal, as the vegetable world is made for the animal world, America is made for the man of the Old World. . . . The man of the Old World sets out upon his way. Leaving the highlands of Asia, he descends from station to station towards Europe. Each of his steps is marked by a new civilization superior to the preceding, by a greater power of development. Arrived at the Atlantic, he pauses on the shore of this unknown ocean, the bounds of which he knows not, and turns upon his footprints for an instant." When he has exhausted the rich soil of Europe, and reinvigorated himself, "then recommences his adventurous career westward as in the earliest ages." So far Guyot.

From this western impulse coming in contact with the barrier of the Atlantic sprang the commerce and enterprise of modern times. The younger Michaux, in his "Travels West of the Alleghanies in 1802," says that the common inquiry in the newly settled West was, "'From what part of the world have you come?' As if these vast and fertile regions would naturally be the place of meeting and common country of all the inhabitants of the globe."

To use an obsolete Latin word, I might say, *Ex Oriente lux; ex Occidente* FRUX. From the East light; from the West fruit.

Sir Francis Head, an English traveller and a Governor-General of Canada, tells us that "in both the northern and southern hemispheres of the New World, Nature has not only outlined her works on a larger scale, but has painted the whole picture with brighter and more costly colors than she used in delineating and in beautifying the Old World. . . . The heavens of America appear infinitely higher, the sky is bluer, the air is fresher, the cold is intenser, the moon looks larger, the stars are brighter, the thunder is louder, the lightning is vivider, the wind is stronger, the rain is heavier, the mountains are higher, the rivers longer, the forests bigger, the plains broader." This statement will do at least to set against Buffon's account of this part of the world and its productions.

Linnæus said long ago, "Nescio quæ facies *læta, glabra* plantis Americanis: I know not what there is of joyous and smooth in the aspect of American plants;" and I think that in this country there are no, or at most very few, *Africanæ bestiæ,* African beasts, as the Romans called them, and that in this respect also it is peculiarly fitted for the habitation of man. We are told that within three miles of the centre of the East Indian city of Singapore, some of the inhabitants are annually carried off by tigers; but the traveller can lie down in the woods at night almost anywhere in North America without fear of wild beasts.

These are encouraging testimonies. If the moon looks larger here than in Europe, probably the sun looks larger also. If the heavens of America appear infinitely higher, and the stars brighter, I trust that these facts are symbolical of the height to which the philosophy and poetry and religion of her inhabitants may one day soar. At length, perchance, the immaterial heaven will appear as much higher to the American mind, and the intimations that star it as much brighter. For I believe that climate does thus react on man—as there is something in the mountain air that feeds the spirit and inspires. Will not man grow to greater perfection intellectually as well as physically under these influences? Or is it unimportant how many foggy days there are in his life? I trust that we shall be more imaginative, that our thoughts will be clearer, fresher, and more ethereal, as our sky—our understanding more comprehensive and broader, like our plains—our intellect generally on a grander scale, like our thunder and lightning, our rivers and mountains and forests—and our hearts shall even correspond in breadth and depth and grandeur to our inland seas. Perchance there will appear to the traveller something, he knows not what, of *læta* and *glabra,* of joyous and serene, in our very faces. Else to what end does the world go on, and why was America discovered?

To Americans I hardly need to say—

"Westward the star of empire takes its way."

As a true patriot, I should be ashamed to think that Adam in paradise was more favourably situated on the whole than the backwoodsman in this country.

Our sympathies in Massachusetts are not confined to New England; though we may be estranged from the South, we sympathize with the West. There is the home of the younger sons, as among the Scandinavians they took to the sea for their inheritance. It is too late to be studying Hebrew; it is more important to understand even the slang of to-day.

Some months ago I went to see a panorama of the Rhine.

It was like a dream of the Middle Ages. I floated down its historic stream in something more than imagination, under bridges built by the Romans, and repaired by later heroes, past cities and castles whose very names were music to my ears, and each of which was the subject of a legend. There were Ehrenbreitstein and Rolandseck and Coblentz, which I knew only in history. They were ruins that interested me chiefly. There seemed to come up from its waters and its vine-clad hills and valleys a hushed music as of Crusaders departing for the Holy Land. I floated along under the spell of enchantment, as if I had been transported to an heroic age, and breathed an atmosphere of chivalry.

Soon after, I went to see a panorama of the Mississippi, and as I worked my way up the river in the light of to-day and saw the steam-boats wooding up, counted the rising cities, gazed on the fresh ruins of Nauvoo, beheld the Indians moving west across the stream, and, as before I had looked up the Moselle, now looked up the Ohio and the Missouri and heard the legends of Dubuque and of Wenona's Cliff,—still thinking more of the future than of the past or present,—I saw that this was a Rhine stream of a different kind; that the foundations of castles were yet to be laid, and the famous bridges were yet to be thrown over the river; and I felt that *this was the heroic age itself,* though we know it not, for the hero is commonly the simplest and obscurest of men.

The West of which I speak is but another name for the Wild; and what I have been preparing to say is, that in Wildness is the preservation of the World. Every tree sends its fibres forth in search of the Wild. The cities import it at any price. Men plough and sail for it. From the forest and wilderness come the tonics and barks which brace mankind. Our ancestors were savages. The story of Romulus and Remus being suckled by a wolf is not a meaningless fable. The founders of every state which has risen to eminence have drawn their nourishment and vigor from a similar wild source. It was because the children of the Empire were not suckled by the wolf that they were conquered and displaced by the children of the northern forests who were.

I believe in the forest, and in the meadow, and in the night in which the corn grows. We require an infusion of hemlock-spruce or arbor-vitæ in our tea. There is a difference between eating and drinking for strength and from mere gluttony. The Hottentots eagerly devour the marrow of the koodoo and other antelopes raw, as a matter of course. Some of our Northern Indians eat raw the marrow of the Arctic reindeer, as well as various other parts, including the summits of the antlers, as long as they are soft. And herein, perchance, they have stolen a march on the cooks of Paris. They get what usually goes to feed the fire. This is probably better than stall-fed beef and slaughter-house pork to make a man of. Give me a wildness whose glance no civilization can endure—as if we lived on the marrow of koodoos devoured raw.

There are some intervals which border the strain of the wood-thrush, to which I would migrate,—wild lands where no settler has squatted; to which, methinks, I am already acclimated.

The African hunter Cumming tells us that the skin of the eland, as well as that of most other antelopes just killed, emits the most delicious perfume of trees and grass. I would have every man so much like a wild antelope, so much a part and parcel of Nature, that his very person should thus sweetly advertise our senses of his presence, and remind us of those parts of Nature which he most haunts. I feel no disposition to be satirical, when the trapper's coat emits the odour of musquash even; it is a sweeter scent to me than that which commonly exhales from the merchant's or the scholar's garments. When I go into their wardrobes and handle their vestments, I am reminded of no grassy plains and flowery meads which they have frequented, but of dusty merchants' exchanges and libraries rather.

A tanned skin is something more than respectable, and perhaps olive is a fitter color than white for a man—a denizen of the woods. "The pale white man!" I do not wonder that the African pitied him. Darwin the naturalist says, "A white man bathing by the side of a Tahitian was like a plant bleached by the gardener's art, compared with a fine, dark green one, growing vigorously in the open fields."

Ben Jonson exclaims,—

"How near to good is what is fair!"

So I would say—

How near to good is what is *wild!*

Life consists with wildness. The most alive is the wildest. Not yet subdued to man, its presence refreshes him. One who pressed forward incessantly and never rested from his labors, who grew fast and made infinite demands on life, would always find himself in a new country or wilderness, and surrounded by the raw material of life. He would be climbing over the prostrate stems of primitive forest trees.

Hope and the future for me are not in lawns and cultivated fields, not in towns and cities, but in the impervious and quaking swamps. When, formerly, I have analyzed my partiality for some farm which I had contemplated purchasing, I have frequently found that I was attracted solely by a few square rods of impermeable and unfathomable bog —a natural sink in one corner of it. That was the jewel which dazzled me. I derive more of my subsistence from the swamps which surround my native town than from the cultivated gardens in the village. There are no richer parterres to my eyes than the dense beds of dwarf andromeda (*Cassandra calyculata*) which cover these tender places on the earth's surface. Botany cannot go farther than tell me the names of the shrubs which grow there— the high-blueberry, panicled andromeda, lamb-kill, azalea, and rhodora—all standing in the quaking sphagnum. I often think that I should like to have my house front on this mass of dull red bushes, omitting other flower plots and borders, transplanted spruce and trim box, even graveled walks—to have this fertile spot under my windows, not a few imported barrow-fulls of soil only to cover the sand which was thrown out in digging the cellar. Why not put my house, my parlour, behind this plot, instead of behind that meagre assemblage of curiosities, that poor apology for a Nature and Art, which I call my front-yard? It is an effort to clear up and make a decent appearance when the carpenter and mason have departed, though done as much for the passer-by as the dweller within. The most tasteful front-yard fence was never an agreeable object of study to me; the most elaborate ornaments, acorn-tops, or what not, soon wearied and disgusted me. Bring your sills up to the very edge of the swamp, then (though it may not be the best place for a dry cellar), so that there be no access on that side to citizens. Front-yards are not made to walk in, but, at most, through, and you could go in the back way.

Yes, though you may think me perverse, if it were proposed to me to dwell in the neighborhood of the most beautiful garden that ever human art contrived, or else of a Dismal Swamp, I should certainly decide for the swamp. How vain, then, have been all your labors, citizens, for me!

My spirits infallibly rise in proportion to the outward dreariness. Give me the ocean, the desert, or the wilderness! In the desert, pure air and solitude compensate for want of moisture and fertility. The traveller Burton says of it—"Your *morale* improves; you become frank and cordial, hospitable and single-minded. . . . In the desert, spirituous liquors excite only disgust. There is a keen enjoyment in a mere animal existence." They who have been travelling long on the steppes of Tartary say: "On reëntering cultivated lands, the agitation, perplexity, and turmoil of civilization oppressed and suffocated us; the air seemed to fail us, and we felt every moment as if about to die of asphyxia." When I would recreate myself, I seek the darkest wood, the thickest and most interminable and, to the citizen, most dismal swamp. I enter a swamp as a sacred place,—a *sanctum sanctorum*. There is the strength, the marrow of Nature. The wild-wood covers the virgin mould,—and the same soil is good for men and for trees. A man's health requires as many acres of meadow to his prospect as his farm does loads of muck. There are the strong meats on which he feeds. A town is saved, not more by the righteous men in it than by the woods and swamps that surround it. A township where one primitive forest waves above while another primitive forest rots below,—such a town is fitted to raise not only corn and potatoes, but poets and philosophers for the coming ages. In such a soil grew Homer and Confucius and the rest, and out of such a wilderness comes the Reformer eating locusts and wild honey.

To preserve wild animals implies generally the creation of a forest for them to dwell in or resort to. So it is with man. A hundred years ago they sold bark in our streets peeled from our own woods. In the very aspect of those primitive and rugged trees there was, methinks, a tanning principle which hardened and consolidated the fibres of men's thoughts. Ah! already I shudder for these comparatively degenerate days of my native village, when you cannot collect a load of bark of good thickness; and we no longer produce tar and turpentine.

The civilised nations—Greece, Rome, England—have been sustained by the primitive forests which anciently rotted where they stand. They survive as long as the soil is not exhausted. Alas for human culture! little is to be expected of a nation, when the vegetable mould is exhausted, and it is compelled to make manure of the bones of its fathers. There the poet sustains himself merely by his own superfluous fat, and the philosopher comes down on his marrow-bones.

It is said to be the task of the American "to work the virgin soil," and that "agriculture here already assumes proportions unknown everywhere else." I think that the farmer displaces the Indian even because he redeems the meadow, and so makes himself stronger and in some respects more natural. I was surveying for a man the other day a single straight line one hundred and thirty-two rods long, through a swamp, at whose entrance might have been written the words which Dante read over the entrance to the infernal regions,—"Leave all hope, ye that enter,"—that is, of ever getting out again; where at one time I saw my employer actually up to his neck and swimming for his life in his property, though it was still winter. He had another similar swamp which I could not survey at all, because it was completely under water, and nevertheless, with regard to a third swamp, which I did *survey* from a distance, he remarked to me, true to his instincts, that he would not part with it for any consideration, on account of the mud which it contained. And that man intends to put a girdling ditch round the whole in the course of forty months, and so redeem it by the magic of his spade. I refer to him only as the type of a class.

The weapons with which we have gained our most important victories, which should be handed down as heirlooms from father to son, are not the sword and the lance, but the bush-whack, the turf-cutter, the spade, and the bog-hoe, rusted with the blood of many a meadow, and begrimed with the dust of many a hard-fought field. The very winds blew the Indian's corn-field into the meadow, and pointed out the way which he had not the skill to follow. He had no better implement with which to intrench himself in the land than a clam-shell. But the farmer is armed with plough and spade.

In Literature it is only the wild that attracts us. Dulness is but another name for tameness. It is the uncivilized free and wild thinking in "Hamlet" and the "Iliad," in all the Scriptures and Mythologies, not learned in the schools, that delights us. As the wild duck is more swift and beautiful than the tame, so is the wild—the mallard—thought, which 'mid falling dews wings its way above the fens. A truly good book is something as natural, and as unexpectedly and unaccountably fair and perfect, as a wild flower discovered on the prairies of the West or in the jungles of the East. Genius is a light which makes the darkness visible, like the lightning's flash, which perchance shatters the temple of knowledge itself,—and not a taper lighted at the hearthstone of the race, which pales before the light of common day.

English literature, from the days of the minstrels to the Lake Poets,—Chaucer and Spenser and Milton, and even Shakespeare, included—breathes no quite fresh and, in this sense, wild strain. It is an essentially tame and civilized literature, reflecting Greece and Rome. Her wilderness is a green wood, her wild man a Robin Hood. There is plenty of genial love of Nature, but not so much of Nature herself. Her chronicles inform us when her wild animals, but not when the wild man in her, became extinct.

The science of Humboldt is one thing, poetry is another thing. The poet to-day, notwithstanding all the discoveries of science, and the accumulated learning of mankind, enjoys no advantage over Homer.

Where is the literature which gives expression to Nature? He would be a poet who could impress the winds and streams into his service, to speak for him; who nailed words to their primitive senses, as farmers drive down stakes in the spring, which the frost has heaved; who derived his words as often as he used them—transplanted them to his page with earth adhering to their roots; whose words were so true and fresh and natural that they would appear to expand like the buds at the approach of spring, though they lay half-smothered between two musty leaves in a library,—aye, to bloom and bear fruit there, after their kind, annually, for the faithful reader, in sympathy with surrounding Nature.

I do not know of any poetry to quote which adequately expresses this yearning for the Wild. Approached from this side, the best poetry is tame. I do not know where to find in any literature, ancient or modern, any account which contents me of that Nature with which even I am acquainted. You will perceive that I demand something which no Augustan nor Elizabethan age, which no *culture,* in short, can give. Mythology comes nearer to it than anything. How much more fertile a Nature, at least, has Grecian mythology its root in than English literature! Mythology is the crop which the Old World bore before its soil was exhausted, before the fancy and imagination were affected with blight; and which it still bears, wherever its pristine vigor is unabated. All other literatures endure only as the elms which overshadow our houses; but this is like the great dragon-tree of the Western Isles, as old as mankind, and, whether that does or not, will endure as long; for the decay of other literatures makes the soil in which it thrives.

The West is preparing to add its fables to those of the East. The valleys of the Ganges, the Nile, and the Rhine having yielded their crop, it remains to be seen what the valleys of the Amazon, the Platte, the Orinoco, the St. Lawrence, and the Mississippi will produce. Perchance, when, in the course of ages, American liberty has become a fiction of the past—as it is to some extent a fiction of the present—the poets of the world will be inspired by American mythology.

The wildest dreams of wild men, even, are not the less true, though they may not recommend themselves to the sense which is most common among Englishmen and Americans to-day. It is not every truth that recommends itself to the common sense. Nature has a place for the wild clematis as well as for the cabbage. Some expressions of truth are reminiscent—others merely *sensible,* as the phrase is,—others prophetic. Some forms of disease, even, may prophesy forms of health. The geologist has discovered that the figures of serpents, griffins, flying dragons, and other fanciful embellishments of heraldry, have their prototypes in the forms of fossil species which were extinct before man was created, and hence " indicate a faint and shadowy knowledge of a previous state of organic existence." The Hindoos dreamed that the earth rested on an elephant, and the elephant on a tortoise, and the tortoise on a serpent; and though it may be an unimportant coincidence, it will not be out of place here to state, that a fossil tortoise has lately been discovered in Asia large enough to support an elephant. I confess that I am partial to these wild fancies, which transcend the order of time and development. They are the sublimest recreation of the intellect. The partridge loves peas, but not those that go with her into the pot.

In short, all good things are wild and free. There is something in a strain of music, whether produced by an instrument or by the human voice,—take the sound of a bugle in a summer night, for instance,—which by its wildness, to speak without satire, reminds me of the cries emitted by wild beasts in their native forests. It is so much of their wildness as I can understand. Give me for my friends and neighbors wild men, not tame ones. The wildness of the savage is but a faint symbol of the awful ferity with which good men and lovers meet.

I love even to see the domestic animals reassert their native rights,—any evidence that they have not wholly lost their original wild habits and vigor; as when my neighbor's cow breaks out of her pasture early in the spring and boldly swims the river, a cold, grey tide, twenty-five or thirty rods wide, swollen by the melted snow. It is the buffalo crossing the Mississippi. This exploit confers some dignity on the herd in my eyes—already dignified. The seeds of instinct are preserved under the thick hides of cattle and horses, like seeds in the bowels of the earth, an indefinite period.

Any sportiveness in cattle is unexpected. I saw one day a herd of a dozen bullocks and cows running about and frisking in unwieldy sport, like huge rats, even like kittens. They shook their heads, raised their tails, and rushed up and down a hill, and I perceived by their horns, as well as by their activity, their relation to the deer tribe. But, alas! a sudden loud *Whoa!* would have damped their ardor at once, reduced them from venison to beef, and stiffened their sides and sinews like the locomotive. Who but the Evil One has cried, "Whoa!" to mankind? Indeed, the life of cattle, like that of many men, is but a sort of locomotiveness; they move a side at a time, and man, by his machinery, is meeting the horse and the ox half-way. Whatever part the whip has touched is thenceforth palsied. Who would ever think of a *side* of any of the supple cat tribe, as we speak of a *side* of beef?

I rejoice that horses and steers have to be broken before they can be made the slaves of men, and that men themselves have some wild oats still left to sow before they become submissive members of society. Undoubtedly, all men are not equally fit subjects for civilization; and because the majority, like dogs and sheep, are tame by inherited disposition, this is no reason why the others should have their natures broken that they may be reduced to the same level. Men are in the main alike, but they were made several in order that they might be various. If a low use is to be served, one man will do nearly or quite as well as another; if a high one, individual excellence is to be regarded. Any man can stop a hole to keep the wind away, but no other man could serve so rare a use as the author of this illustration did. Confucius says—"The skins of the tiger and the leopard, when they are tanned, are as the skins of the dog and the sheep tanned." But it is not the part of a true culture to tame tigers, any more than it is to make sheep ferocious; and tanning their skins for shoes is not the best use to which they can be put.

When looking over a list of men's names in a foreign language, as of military officers, or of authors who have written on a particular subject, I am reminded once more that there is nothing in a name. The name Menschikoff, for instance, has nothing in it to my ears more human than a whisker, and it may belong to a rat. As the names of the Poles and Russians are to us, so are ours to them. It is as if they had been named by the child's rigmarole—*Iery wiery ichery van, tittle-tol-tan.* I see in my mind a herd of wild creatures swarming over the earth, and to each the herdsman has affixed some barbarous sound in his own dialect. The names of men are of course as cheap and meaningless as *Bose* and *Tray,* the names of dogs.

Methinks it would be some advantage to philosophy, if men were named merely in the gross, as they are known. It would be necessary only to know the genus and perhaps the race or variety, to know the individual. We are not prepared to believe that every private soldier in a Roman army had a name of his own,—because we have not supposed that he had a character of his own.

At present our only true names are nicknames. I knew a boy who, from his peculiar energy, was called "Buster" by his playmates, and this rightly supplanted his Christian name. Some travellers tell us that an Indian had no name given him at first, but earned it, and his name was his fame: and among some tribes he acquired a new name with every new exploit. It is pitiful when a man bears a name for convenience merely, who has earned neither name nor fame.

I will not allow mere names to make distinctions for me, but still see men in herds for all them. A familiar name cannot make a man less strange to me. It may be given to a savage who retains in secret his own wild title earned in the woods. We have a wild savage in us, and a savage name is perchance somewhere recorded as ours. I see that my neighbor, who bears the familiar epithet William, or Edwin, takes it off with his jacket. It does not adhere to him when asleep or in anger, or aroused by any passion or inspiration. I seem to hear pronounced by some of his kin at such a time his original wild name in some jaw-breaking or else melodious tongue.

Here is this vast, savage, howling mother of ours, Nature, lying all around, with such beauty, and such affection for her children, as the leopard; and yet we are so early weaned from her breast to society, to that culture which is exclusively an interaction of man on man—a sort of breeding in and in, which produces at most a merely English nobility, a civilization destined to have a speedy limit.

In society, in the best institutions of men, it is easy to detect a certain precocity. When we should still be growing children, we are already little men. Give me a culture which imports much muck from the meadows, and deepens the soil—not that which trusts to heating manures, and improved implements and modes of culture only!

Many a poor sore-eyed student that I have heard of would grow faster, both intellectually and physically, if, instead of sitting up so very late, he honestly slumbered a fool's allowance.

There may be an excess even of informing light. Niépce, a Frenchman, discovered "actinism," that power in the sun's rays which produces a chemical effect; that granite rocks, and stone structures, and statues of metal, "are all alike destructively acted upon during the hours of sunshine, and, but for provisions of Nature no less wonderful, would soon perish under the delicate touch of the most subtile of the agencies of the universe." But he observed that "those bodies which underwent this change during the daylight possessed the power of restoring themselves to their original conditions during the hours of night, when this excitement was no longer influencing them." Hence it has been inferred that "the hours of darkness are as necessary to the inorganic creation as we know night and sleep are to the organic kingdom." Not even does the moon shine every night, but gives place to darkness.

I would not have every man nor every part of a man cultivated, any more than I would have every acre of earth cultivated: part will be tillage, but the greater part will be meadow and forest, not only serving an immediate use, but preparing a mould against a distant future, by the annual decay of the vegetation which it supports.

There are other letters for the child to learn than those which Cadmus invented. The Spaniards have a good term to express this wild and dusky knowledge—*Gramática parda,* tawny grammar—a kind of mother-wit derived from that same leopard to which I have referred.

We have heard of a Society for the Diffusion of Useful Knowledge. It is said that knowledge is power; and the like. Methinks there is equal need of a Society for the Diffusion of Useful Ignorance, what we will call Beautiful Knowledge, a knowledge useful in a higher sense: for what is most of our boasted so-called knowledge but a conceit that we know something, which robs us of the advantage of our actual ignorance? What we call knowledge is often our positive ignorance; ignorance our negative knowledge. By long years of patient industry and reading of the newspapers,—for what are the libraries of science but files of newspapers?—a man accumulates a myriad facts, lays them up in his memory, and then when in some spring of his life he saunters abroad into the Great Fields of thought, he, as it were, goes to grass like a horse and leaves all his harness behind in the stable. I would say to the Society for the Diffusion of Useful Knowledge, sometimes,—Go to grass. You have eaten hay long enough. The spring has come with its green crop. The very cows are driven to their country pastures before the end of May; though I have heard of one unnatural farmer who kept his cow in the barn and fed her on hay all the year round. So, frequently, the Society for the Diffusion of Useful Knowledge treats its cattle.

A man's ignorance some times is not only useful, but beautiful,—while his knowledge, so called, is oftentimes worse than useless, besides being ugly. Which is the best man to deal with,—he who knows nothing about a subject, and, what is extremely rare, knows that he knows nothing, or he who really knows something about it, but thinks that he knows all?

My desire for knowledge is intermittent; but my desire to bathe my head in atmospheres unknown to my feet is perennial and constant. The highest that we can attain to is not Knowledge, but Sympathy with Intelligence. I do not know that this higher knowledge amounts to anything more definite than a novel and grand surprise on a sudden revelation of the insufficiency of all that we called Knowledge before,—a discovery that there are more things in heaven and earth than are dreamed of in our philosophy. It is the lighting up of the mist by the sun. Man cannot *know* in any higher sense than this, any more than he can look serenely and with impunity in the face of the sun: Ὡς τὶ νοῶν, οὐ κεῖνον νοήσεις,—"You will not perceive that, as perceiving a particular thing," say the Chaldean Oracles.

There is something servile in the habit of seeking after a law which we may obey. We may study the laws of matter at and for our convenience, but a successful life knows no law. It is an unfortunate discovery certainly, that of a law which binds us where we did not know before that we were bound. Live free, child of the mist,—and with respect to knowledge we are all children of the mist. The man who takes the liberty to live is superior to all the laws, by virtue of his relation to the law-maker. "That is active duty," says the Vishnu Purana, "which is not for our bondage; that is knowledge which is for our liberation: all other duty is good only unto weariness; all other knowledge is only the cleverness of an artist."

It is remarkable how few events or crises there are in our histories; how little exercised we have been in our minds; how few experiences we have had. I would fain be assured that I am growing apace and rankly, though my very growth disturb this dull equanimity,—though it be with struggle through long, dark, muggy nights or seasons of gloom. It would be well, if all our lives were a divine tragedy even, instead of this trivial comedy or farce. Dante, Bunyan, and others appear to have been exercised in their minds more than we: they were subjected to a kind of culture such as our district schools and colleges do not contemplate. Even Mahomet, though many may scream at his name, had a good deal more to live for, aye, and to die for, than they have commonly.

When, at rare intervals, some thought visits one, as perchance he is walking on a railroad, then indeed the cars go by without his hearing them. But soon, by some inexorable law, our life goes by and the cars return.

> "Gentle breeze, that wanderest unseen,
> And bendest the thistles round Loira of storms,

Traveller of the windy glens,
Why hast thou left my ear so soon?"

While almost all men feel an attraction drawing them to society, few are attracted strongly to Nature. In their relation to Nature men appear to me for the most part, notwithstanding their arts, lower than the animals. It is not often a beautiful relation, as in the case of the animals. How little appreciation of the beauty of the landscape there is among us! We have to be told that the Greeks called the world *Κόσμος*, Beauty, or Order, but we do not see clearly why they did so, and we esteem it at best only a curious philological fact.

For my part, I feel that with regard to Nature I live a sort of border life, on the confines of a world into which I make occasional and transient forays only, and my patriotism and allegiance to the State into whose territories I seem to retreat are those of a moss-trooper. Unto a life which I call natural I would gladly follow even a will-o'-the-wisp through bogs and sloughs unimaginable, but no moon nor firefly has shown me the causeway to it. Nature is a personality so vast and universal that we have never seen one of her features. The walker in the familiar fields which stretch around my native town sometimes finds himself in another land than is described in their owners' deeds, as it were in some far-away field on the confines of the actual Concord, where her jurisdiction ceases, and the idea which the word Concord suggests ceases to be suggested. These farms which I have myself surveyed, these bounds which I have set up, appear dimly still as through a mist; but they have no chemistry to fix them; they fade from the surface of the glass; and the picture which the painter painted stands out dimly from beneath. The world with which we are commonly acquainted leaves no trace, and it will have no anniversary.

I took a walk on Spaulding's Farm the other afternoon. I saw the setting sun lighting up the opposite side of a stately pine wood. Its golden rays straggled into the aisles of the wood as into some noble hall. I was impressed as if some ancient and altogether admirable and shining family had settled there in that part of the land called Concord, unknown to me,—to whom the sun was servant,—who had not gone into society in the village,—who had not been called on. I saw their park, their pleasure-ground, beyond through the wood, in Spaulding's cranberry-meadow. The pines furnished them with gables as they grew. Their house was not obvious to vision; the trees grew through it. I do not know whether I heard the sounds of a suppressed hilarity or not. They seemed to recline on the sunbeams. They have sons and daughters. They are quite well. The farmer's cart-path, which leads directly through their hall, does not in the least put them out, as the muddy bottom of a pool is sometimes seen through the reflected skies. They never heard of Spaulding, and do not know that he is their neighbor,—notwithstanding I heard him whistle as he drove his team through the house. Nothing can equal the serenity of their lives. Their coat of arms is simply a lichen. I saw it painted on the pines and oaks. Their attics were in the tops of the trees. They are of no politics. There was no noise of labor. I did not perceive that they were weaving or spinning. Yet I did detect, when the wind lulled and hearing was done away, the finest imaginable sweet musical hum,—as of a distant hive in May, which perchance was the sound of their thinking. They had no idle thoughts, and no one without could see their work, for their industry was not as in knots and excrescences embayed.

But I find it difficult to remember them. They fade irrevocably out of my mind even now while I speak and endeavor to recall them and recollect myself. It is only after a long and serious effort to recollect my best thoughts that I become again aware of their cohabitancy. If it were not for such families as this, I think I should move out of Concord.

We are accustomed to say in New England that few and fewer pigeons visit us every year. Our forests furnish no mast for them. So, it would seem, few and fewer thoughts visit each growing man from year to year, for the grove in our minds is laid waste,—sold to feed unnecessary fires of ambition, or sent to mill, and there is scarcely a twig left for them to perch on. They no longer build nor breed with us.

In some more genial season, perchance, a faint shadow flits across the landscape of the mind, cast by the *wings* of some thought in its vernal or autumnal migration, but, looking up, we are unable to detect the substance of the thought itself. Our winged thoughts are turned to poultry. They no longer soar, and they attain only to a Shanghai and Cochin-China grandeur. Those *gra-a-ate thoughts,* those *gra-a-ate men* you hear of!

We hug the earth,—how rarely we mount! Methinks we might elevate ourselves a little more. We might climb a tree, at least. I found my account in climbing a tree once. It was a tall white pine, on the top of a hill; and though I got well pitched, I was well paid for it, for I discovered new mountains in the horizon which I had never seen before,—so much more of the earth and the heavens. I might have walked about the foot of the tree for three-score years and ten, and yet I certainly should never have seen them. But, above all, I discovered around me,—it was near the end of June,—on the ends of the topmost branches only, a few minute and delicate red cone-like blossoms, the fertile flower of the white pine looking heavenward. I carried straightway to the village the topmost spire, and showed it to stranger jurymen who walked the streets,—for it was court-week,—and to farmers and lumber-dealers and wood-choppers and hunters, and not one had ever seen the like before, but wondered as at a star dropped down. Tell of ancient architects finishing their works on the tops of columns as perfectly as on the lower and more visible parts! Nature has from the first expanded the minute blossoms of the forest only toward the heavens, above men's heads and unobserved by them. We see only the flowers that are under our feet in the meadows. The pines have developed their delicate blossoms on the highest twigs of the wood every summer for ages, as well over the heads of Nature's red children as of her white ones; yet scarcely a farmer or hunter in the land has ever seen them.

Above all, we cannot afford not to live in the present. He is blessed over all mortals who loses no moment of the passing life in remembering the past. Unless our philosophy hears the cock crow in every barn-yard within our horizon, it is belated. That sound commonly reminds us that we are growing rusty and antique in our employments and habits of thought. His philosophy comes down to a more recent time than ours. There is something suggested by it that is a newer testament,—the gospel according to this moment. He has not fallen astern; he has got up early and kept up early, and to be where he is is to be in season, in the foremost rank of time. It is an expression of the health and soundness of Nature, a brag for all the world,—healthiness as of a spring burst forth, a new fountain of the Muses, to celebrate this last instant of time. Where he lives no fugitive slave laws are passed. Who has not betrayed his master many times since last he heard that note?

The merit of this bird's strain is in its freedom from all plaintiveness. The singer can easily move us to tears or to laughter, but where is he who can excite in us a pure morning joy? When, in doleful dumps, breaking the awful stillness of our wooden sidewalk on a Sunday, or, perchance, a watcher in the house of mourning, I hear a cockerel crow far or near, I think to myself, "There is one of us well, at any rate,"—and with a sudden gush return to my senses.

We had a remarkable sunset one day last November. I was walking in a meadow, the source of a small brook, when the sun at last, just before setting, after a cold gray day, reached a clear stratum in the horizon, and the softest, brightest morning sunlight fell on the dry grass and on the stems of the trees in the opposite horizon and on the leaves of the shrub-oaks on the hillside, while our shadows stretched long over the meadow eastward, as if we were the only motes in its beams. It was such a light as we could not have imagined a moment before, and the air also was so warm and serene that nothing was wanting to make a paradise of that meadow. When we reflected that this was not a solitary phenomenon, never to happen again, but that it would happen forever and ever an infinite number of evenings, and cheer and reassure the latest child that walked there, it was more glorious still.

The sun sets on some retired meadow, where no house is visible, with all the glory and splendor that it lavishes on cities, and perchance as it has never set before,—where there is but a solitary marsh-hawk to have his wings gilded by it, or only a musquash looks out from his cabin, and there is some little black-veined brook in the midst of the marsh, just beginning to meander, winding slowly round a decaying stump. We walked in so pure and bright a light, gilding the withered grass and leaves, so softly and serenely bright, I thought I had never bathed in such golden flood, without a ripple or a murmur to it. The west side of every wood and rising ground gleamed like the boundary of Elysium, and the sun on our backs seemed like a gentle herdsman driving us home at evening.

So we saunter toward the Holy Land, till one day the sun shall shine more brightly than ever he has done, shall perchance shine into our minds and hearts, and light up our whole lives with a great awakening light, as warm and serene and golden as on a bankside in autumn.

ABRAHAM LINCOLN

DEMOCRACY

BY

JAMES RUSSELL LOWELL

INTRODUCTORY NOTE

JAMES RUSSELL LOWELL, *poet, essayist, diplomatist, and scholar, was born at Cambridge, Massachusetts, on February 22, 1819, the son of a Unitarian minister. Educated at Harvard College, he tried the law, but soon gave it up for literature. His poem on "The Present Crisis," written in 1844, was his first really notable production, and one that made a deep impression on the public mind. In the twenty years of troubled politics that followed, one finds it constantly quoted. The year 1848 saw four volumes from Lowell's pen—a book of "Poems," the "Fable for Critics," "The Biglow Papers," and the "Vision of Sir Launfal." The second of these exhibited the author as wit and critic, the third as political reformer, the fourth as poet and mystic; and these various sides of his personality continue to appear with varying prominence throughout his career.*

On the retirement of Longfellow from the chair of belles-lettres at Harvard in 1854, Lowell was elected to succeed him, and by way of preparation spent the next two years in Europe studying modern languages and literatures. In 1857 he became the first editor of the "Atlantic Monthly," and after 1864 he collaborated with Charles Eliot Norton in the editorship of the "North American Review." Throughout the period of the war Lowell wrote much both in prose and verse on behalf of the Union; his work on the "North American" was largely literary criticism.

In 1877 Lowell went to Spain as American Minister, and in 1880 to London, where for five years he represented the United States with great distinction, and did much to improve the relations of the two countries. Six years after his return, on August 12, 1891, he died in Elmwood, the house in Cambridge where he was born.

Lowell's literary gifts were so various that it is difficult to say on which of them his final reputation will rest. But it is certain that he will long be esteemed for the grace, vivacity, and eloquence of the prose in which he placed before the world his views of such great American principles and personalities as are dealt with in the two following essays on "Democracy" and on "Abraham Lincoln."

ABRAHAM LINCOLN

1864–1865

THERE have been many painful crises since the impatient vanity of South Carolina hurried ten prosperous Commonwealths into a crime whose assured retribution was to leave them either at the mercy of the nation they had wronged, or of the anarchy they had summoned but could not control, when no thoughtful American opened his morning paper without dreading to find that he had no longer a country to love and honor. Whatever the result of the convulsion whose first shocks were beginning to be felt, there would still be enough square miles of earth for elbow-room; but that ineffable sentiment made up of memory and hope, of instinct and tradition, which swells every man's heart and shapes his thought, though perhaps never present to his consciousness, would be gone from it, leaving it common earth and nothing more. Men might gather rich crops from it, but that ideal harvest of priceless associations would be reaped no longer; that fine virtue which sent up messages of courage and security from every sod of it would have evaporated beyond recall. We should be irrevocably cut off from our past, and be forced to splice the ragged ends of our lives upon whatever new conditions chance might leave dangling for us.

We confess that we had our doubts at first whether the patriotism of our people were not too narrowly provincial to embrace the proportions of national peril. We felt an only too natural distrust of immense public meetings and enthusiastic cheers.

That a reaction should follow the holiday enthusiasm with which the war was entered on, that it should follow soon, and that the slackening of public spirit should be proportionate to the previous over-tension, might well be foreseen by all who had studied human nature or history. Men acting gregariously are always in extremes. As they are one moment capable of higher courage, so they are liable, the next, to baser depression, and it is often a matter of chance whether numbers shall multiply confidence or discouragement. Nor does deception lead more surely to distrust of men than self-deception to suspicion of principles. The only faith that wears well and holds its color in all weathers is that which is woven of conviction and set with the sharp mordant of experience. Enthusiasm is good material for the orator, but the statesman needs something more durable to work in,—must be able to rely on the deliberate reason and consequent firmness of the people, without which that presence of mind, no less essential in times of moral than of material peril, will be wanting at the critical moment. Would this fervor of the Free States hold out? Was it kindled by a just feeling of the value of constitutional liberty? Had it body enough to withstand the inevitable dampening of checks, reverses, delays? Had our population intelligence enough to comprehend that the choice was between order and anarchy, between the equilibrium of a government by law and the tussle of misrule by *pronunciamiento?* Could a war be maintained without the ordinary stimulus of hatred and plunder, and with the impersonal loyalty of principle? These were serious questions, and with no precedent to aid in answering them.

At the beginning of the war there was, indeed, occasion for the most anxious apprehension. A President known to be infected with the political heresies, and suspected of sympathy with the treason, of the Southern conspirators, had just surrendered the reins, we will not say of power, but of chaos, to a successor known only as the representative of a party whose leaders, with long training in opposition, had none in the conduct of affairs; an empty treasury was called on to supply resources beyond precedent in the history of finance; the trees were yet growing and the iron unmined with which a navy was to be built and armored; officers without discipline were to make a mob into an army; and, above all, the public opinion of Europe, echoed and reinforced with every vague hint and every specious argument of despondency by a powerful faction at home, was either contemptuously sceptical or actively hostile. It would be hard to over-estimate the force of this latter element of disintegration and discouragement among a people where every citizen at home, and every soldier in the field, is a reader of newspapers. The pedlers of rumor in the North were the most effective allies of the rebellion. A nation can be liable to no more insidious treachery than that of the telegraph, sending hourly its electric thrill of panic along the remotest nerves of the community, till the excited imagination makes every real danger loom heightened with its unreal double.

And even if we look only at more palpable difficulties, the problem to be solved by our civil war was so vast, both in its immediate relations and its future consequences; the conditions of its solution were so intricate and so greatly dependent on incalculable and uncontrollable contingencies; so many of the data, whether for hope or fear, were, from their novelty, incapable of arrangement under any of the categories of historical precedent, that there were moments of crisis when the firmest believer in the strength and sufficiency of the democratic theory of government might well hold his breath in vague apprehension of disaster. Our teachers of political philosophy, solemnly arguing from the precedent of some petty Grecian, Italian, or Flemish city, whose long periods of aristocracy were broken now and then by awkward parentheses of mob, had always taught us that democracies were incapable of the sentiment of loyalty, of concentrated and prolonged effort, of far-reaching conceptions; were absorbed in material interests; impatient of regular, and much more of exceptional restraint; had no natural nucleus of gravitation, nor any forces but centrifugal; were always on the verge of civil war, and slunk at last into the natural almshouse of bankrupt popular government, a military despotism. Here was indeed a dreary outlook for persons who knew democracy, not by rubbing shoulders with it lifelong, but merely from books, and America only by the report of some fellow-Briton, who, having eaten a bad dinner or lost a carpet-bag here, had written to the "Times" demanding redress, and drawing a mournful inference of democratic instability. Nor were men wanting among ourselves who had so steeped their brains in London literature as to mistake Cockneyism for European culture, and contempt of their country for cosmopolitan breadth of view, and who, owing all they had and all they were to democracy, thought it had an air of high-breeding to join in the shallow epicedium that our bubble had burst.

But beside any disheartening influences which might affect the timid or the despondent, there were reasons enough of settled gravity against any over-confidence of hope. A war—which, whether we consider the expanse of the territory at stake, the hosts brought into the field, or the reach of the principles involved, may fairly be reckoned the most momentous of modern times—was to be waged by a people divided at home, unnerved by fifty years of peace, under a chief magistrate without experience and without reputation, whose every measure was sure to be cunningly hampered by a jealous and unscrupulous minority, and who, while dealing with unheard-of complications at home, must soothe a hostile neutrality abroad, waiting only a pretext to become war. All this was to be done without warning and without preparation, while at the same time a social revolution was to be accomplished in the political condition of four millions of people, by softening the prejudices, allaying the fears, and gradually obtaining the coöperation, of their unwilling liberators. Surely, if ever there were an occasion when the heightened imagination of the historian might see Destiny visibly intervening in human affairs, here was a knot worthy of her shears. Never, perhaps, was any system of government tried by so continuous and searching a strain as ours during the last three years; never has any shown itself stronger; and never could that strength be so directly traced to the virtue and intelligence of the people,—to that general enlightenment and prompt efficiency of public opinion possible only under the influence of a political framework like our own. We find it hard to understand how even a foreigner should be blind to the grandeur of the combat of ideas that has been going on here,—to the heroic energy, persistency, and self-reliance of a nation proving that it knows how much dearer greatness is than mere power; and we own that it is impossible for us to conceive the mental and moral condition of the American who does not feel his spirit braced and heightened by being even a spectator of such qualities and achievements. That a steady purpose and a definite aim have been given to the jarring forces which, at the beginning of the war, spent themselves in the discussion of schemes which could only become operative, if at all, after the war was over; that a popular excitement has been slowly intensified into an earnest national will; that a somewhat impracticable moral sentiment has been made the unconscious instrument of a practical moral end; that the treason of covert enemies, the jealousy of rivals, the unwise zeal of friends, have been made not only useless for mischief, but even useful for good; that the conscientious sensitiveness of England to the horrors of civil conflict has been prevented from complicating a domestic with a foreign war;—all these results, any one of which might suffice to prove greatness in a ruler, have been mainly due to the good sense, the good humor, the sagacity, the large-mindedness, and the unselfish honesty of the unknown man whom a blind fortune, as it seemed, had lifted from the crowd to the most dangerous and difficult eminence of modern times. It is by presence of mind in untried emergencies that the native metal of a man is tested; it is by the sagacity to see, and the fearless honesty to admit, whatever of truth there may be in an adverse opinion, in order more convincingly to expose the fallacy that lurks behind it, that a reasoner at length gains for his mere statement of a fact the force of argument; it is by a wise forecast which allows hostile combinations to go so far as by the inevitable reaction to become elements of his own power, that a politician proves his genius for statecraft; and especially it is by so gently guiding public sentiment that he seems to follow it, by so yielding doubtful points that he can be firm without seeming obstinate in essential ones, and thus gain the advantages of compromise without the weakness of concession; by so instinctively comprehending the temper and prejudices of a people as to make them gradually conscious of the superior wisdom of his freedom from temper and prejudice,—it is by qualities such as these that a magistrate shows himself worthy to be chief in a commonwealth of freemen. And it is for qualities such as these that we firmly believe History will rank Mr. Lincoln among the most prudent of statesmen and the most successful of rulers. If we wish to appreciate him, we have only to conceive the inevitable chaos in which we should now be weltering, had a weak man or an unwise one been chosen in his stead.

"Bare is back," says the Norse proverb, "without brother behind it"; and this is, by analogy, true of an elective magistracy. The hereditary ruler in any critical emergency may reckon on the inexhaustible resources of *prestige,* of sentiment, of superstition, of dependent interest, while the new man must slowly and painfully create all these out of the unwilling material around him, by superiority of character, by patient singleness of purpose, by sagacious presentiment of popular tendencies and instinctive sympathy with the national character. Mr. Lincoln's task was one of peculiar and exceptional difficulty. Long habit had accustomed the American people to the notion of a party in power, and of a President as its creature and organ, while the more vital fact, that the executive for the time being represents the abstract idea of government as a permanent principle superior to all party and all private interest, had gradually become unfamiliar. They had so long seen the public policy more or less directed by views of party, and often even of personal advantage, as to be ready to suspect the motives of a chief magistrate compelled, for the first time in our history, to feel himself the head and hand of a great nation, and to act upon the fundamental maxim, laid down by all publicists, that the first duty of a government is to defend and maintain its own existence. Accordingly, a powerful weapon seemed to be put into the hands of the opposition by the necessity under which the administration found itself of applying this old truth to new relations. Nor were the opposition his only nor his most dangerous opponents.

The Republicans had carried the country upon an issue in which ethics were more directly and visibly mingled with politics than usual. Their leaders were trained to a method of oratory which relied for its effect rather on the moral sense than the understanding. Their arguments were drawn, not so much from experience as from general principles of right and wrong. When the war came, their system continued to be applicable and effective, for here again the reason of the people was to be reached and kindled through their sentiments. It was one of those periods of excitement, gathering, contagious, universal, which, while they last, exalt and clarify the minds of men, giving to the mere words *country, human rights, democracy,* a meaning and a force beyond that of sober and logical argument. They were convictions, maintained and defended by the supreme logic of passion. That penetrating fire ran in and roused those primary instincts that make their lair in the dens and caverns of the mind. What is called the great popular heart was awakened, that indefinable something which may be, according to circumstances, the highest reason or the most brutish unreason. But enthusiasm, once cold, can never be warmed over into anything better than cant,—and phrases, when once the inspiration that filled them with beneficent power has ebbed away, retain only that semblance of meaning which enables them to supplant reason in hasty minds. Among the lessons taught by the French Revolution there is none sadder or more striking than this, that you may make everything else out of the passions of men except a political system that will work, and that there is nothing so pitilessly and unconsciously cruel as sincerity formulated into dogma. It is always demoralizing to extend the domain of sentiment over questions where it has no legitimate jurisdiction; and perhaps the severest strain upon Mr. Lincoln was in resisting a tendency of his own supporters which chimed with his own private desires, while wholly opposed to his convictions of what would be wise policy.

The change which three years have brought about is too remarkable to be passed over without comment, too weighty in its lesson not to be laid to heart. Never did a President enter upon office with less means at his command, outside his own strength of heart and steadiness of understanding, for inspiring confidence in the people, and so winning it for himself, than Mr. Lincoln. All that was known of him was that he was a good stump-speaker, nominated for his *availability,*—that is, because he had no history,—and chosen by a party with whose more extreme opinions he was not in sympathy. It might well be feared that a man past fifty, against whom the ingenuity of hostile partisans could rake up no accusation, must be lacking in manliness of character, in decision of principle, in strength of will; that a man who was at best only the representative of a party, and who yet did not fairly represent even that, would fail of political, much more of popular, support. And certainly no one ever entered upon office with so few resources of power in the past, and so many materials of weakness in the present, as Mr. Lincoln. Even in that half of the Union which acknowledged him as President, there was a large and at that time dangerous minority, that hardly admitted his claim to the office, and even in the party that elected him there was also a large minority that suspected him of being secretly a communicant with the church of Laodicea. All that he did was sure to be virulently attacked as ultra by one side; all that he left undone, to be stigmatized as proof of lukewarmness and backsliding by the other. Meanwhile, he was to carry on a truly colossal war by means of both; he was to disengage the country from diplomatic entanglements of unprecedented peril undisturbed by the help or the hindrance of either, and to win from the crowning dangers of his administration, in the confidence of the people, the means of his safety and their own. He has contrived to do it, and perhaps none of our Presidents since Washington has stood so firm in the confidence of the people as he does after three years of stormy administration.

Mr. Lincoln's policy was a tentative one, and rightly so. He laid down no programme which must compel him to be either inconsistent or unwise, no cast-iron theorem to which circumstances must be fitted as they rose, or else be useless to his ends. He seemed to have chosen Mazarin's motto, *Le temps et moi.* The *moi,* to be sure, was not very prominent at first; but it has grown more and more so, till the world is beginning to be persuaded that it stands for a character of marked individuality and capacity of affairs. Time was his prime-minister, and, we began to think, at one period, his general-in-chief also. At first he was so slow that he tired out all those who see no evidence of progress but in blowing up the engine; then he was so fast, that he took the breath away from those who think there is no getting on safely while there is a spark of fire under the boilers. God is the only being who has time enough; but a prudent man, who knows how to seize occasion, can commonly make a shift to find as much as he needs. Mr. Lincoln, as it seems to us in reviewing his career, though we have sometimes in our impatience thought otherwise, has always waited, as a wise man should, till the right moment brought up all his reserves. *Semper nocuit differre paratis* is a sound axiom, but the really efficacious man will also be sure to know when he is *not* ready, and be firm against all persuasion and reproach till he is.

One would be apt to think, from some of the criticisms made on Mr. Lincoln's course by those who mainly agree with him in principle, that the chief object of a statesman should be rather to proclaim his adhesion to certain doctrines, than to achieve their triumph by quietly accomplishing his ends. In our opinion, there is no more unsafe politician than a conscientiously rigid *doctrinaire,* nothing more sure to end in disaster than a theoretic scheme of policy that admits of no pliability for contingencies. True, there is a popular image of an impossible He, in whose plastic hands the submissive destinies of mankind become as wax, and to whose commanding necessity the toughest facts yield with the graceful pliancy of fiction; but in real life we commonly find that the men who control circumstances, as it is called, are those who have learned to allow for the influence of their eddies, and have the nerve to turn them to account at the happy instant. Mr. Lincoln's perilous task has been to carry a rather shaky raft through the rapids, making fast the unrulier logs as he could snatch opportunity, and the country is to be congratulated that he did not think it his duty to run straight at all hazards, but cautiously to assure himself with his setting-pole where the main current was, and keep steadily to that. He is still in wild water, but we have faith that his skill and sureness of eye will bring him out right at last.

A curious, and, as we think, not inapt parallel might be drawn between Mr. Lincoln and one of the most striking figures in modern history,—Henry IV. of France. The career of the latter may be more picturesque, as that of a daring captain always is; but in all its vicissitudes there is nothing more romantic than that sudden change, as by a rub of Aladdin's lamp, from the attorney's office in a country town of Illinois to the helm of a great nation in times like these. The analogy between the characters and circumstances of the two men is in many respects singularly close. Succeeding to a rebellion rather than a crown, Henry's chief material dependence was the Huguenot party, whose doctrines sat upon him with a looseness distasteful certainly, if not suspicious, to the more fanatical among them. King only in name over the greater part of France, and with his capital barred against him, it yet gradually became clear to the more far-seeing even of the Catholic party that he was the only centre of order and legitimate authority round which France could reorganize itself. While preachers who held the divine right of kings made the churches of Paris ring with declamations in favor of democracy rather than submit to the heretic dog of a Béarnois, —much as our *soi-disant* Democrats have lately been preaching the divine right of slavery, and denouncing the heresies of the Declaration of Independence,—Henry bore both parties in hand till he was convinced that only one course of action could possibly combine his own interests and those of France. Meanwhile the Protestants believed somewhat doubtfully that he was theirs, the Catholics hoped somewhat doubtfully that he would be theirs, and Henry himself turned aside remonstrance, advice, and curiosity alike with a jest or a proverb (if a little *high,* he liked them none the worse), joking continually as his manner was. We have seen Mr. Lincoln contemptuously compared to Sancho Panza by persons incapable of appreciating one of the deepest pieces of wisdom in the profoundest romance ever written; namely, that, while Don Quixote was incomparable in theoretic and ideal statesmanship, Sancho, with his stock of proverbs, the ready money of human experience, made the best possible practical governor. Henry IV. was as full of wise saws and modern instances as Mr. Lincoln, but beneath all this was the thoughtful, practical, humane, and thoroughly earnest man, around whom the fragments of France were to gather themselves till she took her place again as a planet of the first magnitude in the European system. In one respect Mr. Lincoln was more fortunate than Henry. However some may think him wanting in zeal, the most fanatical can find no taint of apostasy in any measure of his, nor can the most bitter charge him with being influenced by motives of personal interest. The leading distinction between the policies of the two is one of circumstances. Henry went over to the nation; Mr. Lincoln has steadily drawn the nation over to him. One left a united France; the other, we hope and believe, will leave a reunited America. We leave our readers to trace the further points of difference and resemblance for themselves, merely suggesting a general similarity which has often occurred to us. One only point of melancholy interest we will allow ourselves to touch upon. That Mr. Lincoln is not handsome nor elegant, we learn from certain English tourists who would consider similar revelations in regard to Queen Victoria as thoroughly American in their want of *bienséance*. It is no concern of ours, nor does it affect his fitness for the high place he so worthily occupies; but he is certainly as fortunate as Henry in the matter of good looks, if we may trust contemporary evidence. Mr. Lincoln has also been reproached with Americanism by some not unfriendly British critics; but, with all deference, we cannot say that we like him any the worse for it, or see in it any reason why he should govern Americans the less wisely.

People of more sensitive organizations may be shocked, but we are glad that in this our true war of independence, which is to free us forever from the Old World, we have had at the head of our affairs a man whom America made, as God made Adam, out of the very earth, unancestried, unprivileged, unknown, to show us how much truth, how much magnanimity, and how much state-craft await the call of opportunity in simple manhood when it believes in the justice of God and the worth of man. Conventionalities are all very well in their proper place, but they shrivel at the touch of nature like stubble in the fire. The genius that sways a nation by its arbitrary will seems less august to us than that which multiplies and reinforces itself in the instincts and convictions of an entire people. Autocracy may have something in it more melodramatic than this, but falls far short of it in human value and interest.

Experience would have bred in us a rooted distrust of improvised statesmanship, even if we did not believe politics to be a science, which, if it cannot always command men of special aptitude and great powers, at least demands the long and steady application of the best powers of such men as it can command to master even its first principles. It is curious, that, in a country which boasts of its intelligence, the theory should be so generally held that the most complicated of human contrivances, and one which every day becomes more complicated, can be worked at sight by any man able to talk for an hour or two without stopping to think.

Mr. Lincoln is sometimes claimed as an example of a ready-made ruler. But no case could well be less in point; for, besides that he was a man of such fair-mindedness as is always the raw material of wisdom, he had in his profession a training precisely the opposite of that to which a partisan is subjected. His experience as a lawyer compelled him not only to see that there is a principle underlying every phenomenon in human affairs, but that there are always two sides to every question, both of which must be fully understood in order to understand either, and that it is of greater advantage to an advocate to appreciate the strength than the weakness of his antagonist's position. Nothing is more remarkable than the unerring tact with which, in his debate with Mr. Douglas, he went straight to the reason of the question; nor have we ever had a more striking lesson in political tactics than the fact, that, opposed to a man exceptionally adroit in using popular prejudice and bigotry to his purpose, exceptionally unscrupulous in appealing to those baser motives that turn a meeting of citizens into a mob of barbarians, he should yet have won his case before a jury of the people. Mr. Lincoln was as far as possible from an impromptu politician. His wisdom was made up of a knowledge of things as well as of men; his sagacity resulted from a clear perception and honest acknowledgment of difficulties, which enabled him to see that the only durable triumph of political opinion is based, not on any abstract right, but upon so much of justice, the highest attainable at any given moment in human affairs, as may be had in the balance of mutual concession. Doubtless he had an ideal, but it was the ideal of a practical statesman,—to aim at the best, and to take the next best, if he is lucky enough to get even that. His slow, but singularly masculine, intelligence taught him that precedent is only another name for embodied experience, and that it counts for even more in the guidance of communities of men than in that of the individual life. He was not a man who held it good public economy to pull down on the mere chance of rebuilding better. Mr. Lincoln's faith in God was qualified by a very well-founded distrust of the wisdom of man. Perhaps it was his want of self-confidence that more than anything else won him the unlimited confidence of the people, for they felt that there would be no need of retreat from any position he had deliberately taken. The cautious, but steady, advance of his policy during the war was like that of a Roman army. He left behind him a firm road on which public confidence could follow; he took America with him where he went; what he gained he occupied, and his advanced posts became colonies. The very homeliness of his genius was its distinction. His kingship was conspicuous by its workday homespun. Never was ruler so absolute as he, nor so little conscious of it; for he was the incarnate common-sense of the people. With all that tenderness of nature whose sweet sadness touched whoever saw him with something of its own pathos, there was no trace of sentimentalism in his speech or action. He seems to have had but one rule of conduct, always that of practical and successful politics, to let himself be guided by events, when they were sure to bring him out where he wished to go, though by what seemed to unpractical minds, which let go the possible to grasp at the desirable, a longer road.

Undoubtedly the highest function of statesmanship is by degrees to accommodate the conduct of communities to ethical laws, and to subordinate the conflicting self-interests of the day to higher and more permanent concerns. But it is on the understanding, and not on the sentiment, of a nation that all safe legislation must be based. Voltaire's saying, that "a consideration of petty circumstances is the tomb of great things," may be true of individual men, but it certainly is not true of governments. It is by a multitude of such considerations, each in itself trifling, but all together weighty, that the framers of policy can alone divine what is practicable and therefore wise. The imputation of inconsistency is one to which every sound politician and every honest thinker must sooner or later subject himself. The foolish and the dead alone never change their opinion. The course of a great statesman resembles that of navigable rivers, avoiding immovable obstacles with noble bends of concession, seeking the broad levels of opinion on which men soonest settle and longest dwell, following and marking the almost imperceptible slopes of national tendency, yet always aiming at direct advances, always recruited from sources nearer heaven, and sometimes bursting open paths of progress and fruitful human commerce through what seem the eternal barriers of both. It is loyalty to great ends, even though forced to combine the small and opposing motives of selfish men to accomplish them; it is the anchored cling to solid principles of duty and action, which knows how to swing with the tide, but is never carried away by it,—that we demand in public men, and not obstinacy in prejudice, sameness of policy, or a conscientious persistency in what is impracticable. For the impracticable, however theoretically enticing, is always politically unwise, sound statesmanship being the application of that prudence to the public business which is the safest guide in that of private men.

No doubt slavery was the most delicate and embarrassing question with which Mr. Lincoln was called on to deal, and it was one which no man in his position, whatever his opinions, could evade; for, though he might withstand the clamor of partisans, he must sooner or later yield to the persistent importunacy of circumstances, which thrust the problem upon him at every turn and in every shape.

It has been brought against us as an accusation abroad and repeated here by people who measure their country rather by what is thought of it than by what it is, that our war has not been distinctly and avowedly for the extinction of slavery, but a war rather for the preservation of our national power and greatness, in which the emancipation of the negro has been forced upon us by circumstances and accepted as a necessity. We are very far from denying this; nay, we admit that it is so far true that we were slow to renounce our constitutional obligations even toward those who had absolved us by their own act from the letter of our duty. We are speaking of the government which, legally installed for the whole country, was bound, so long as it was possible, not to overstep the limits of orderly prescription, and could not, without abnegating its own very nature, take the lead in making rebellion an excuse for revolution. There were, no doubt, many ardent and sincere persons who seemed to think this as simple a thing to do as to lead off a Virginia reel. They forgot what should be forgotten least of all in a system like ours, that the administration for the time being represents not only the majority which elects it, but the minority as well,—a minority in this case powerful, and so little ready for emancipation that it was opposed even to war. Mr. Lincoln had not been chosen as general agent of an antislavery society, but President of the United States, to perform certain functions exactly defined by law. Whatever were his wishes, it was no less duty than policy to mark out for himself a line of action that would not further distract the country, by raising before their time questions which plainly would soon enough compel attention, and for which every day was making the answer more easy.

Meanwhile he must solve the riddle of this new Sphinx, or be devoured. Though Mr. Lincoln's policy in this critical affair has not been such as to satisfy those who demand an heroic treatment for even the most trifling occasion, and who will not cut their coat according to their cloth, unless they can borrow the scissors of Atropos, it has been at least not unworthy of the long-headed king of Ithaca. Mr. Lincoln had the choice of Bassanio offered him. Which of the three caskets held the prize that was to redeem the fortunes of the country? There was the golden one whose showy speciousness might have tempted a vain man; the silver of compromise, which might have decided the choice of a merely acute one; and the leaden,—dull and homely looking, as prudence always is,—yet with something about it sure to attract the eye of practical wisdom. Mr. Lincoln dallied with his decision perhaps longer than seemed needful to those on whom its awful responsibility was not to rest, but when he made it, it was worthy of his cautious but sure-footed understanding. The moral of the Sphinx-riddle, and it is a deep one, lies in the childish simplicity of the solution. Those who fail in guessing it, fail because they are over-ingenious, and cast about for an answer that shall suit their own notion of the gravity of the occasion and of their own dignity, rather than the occasion itself.

In a matter which must be finally settled by public opinion, and in regard to which the ferment of prejudice and passion on both sides has not yet subsided to that equilibrium of compromise from which alone a sound public opinion can result, it is proper enough for the private citizen to press his own convictions with all possible force of argument and persuasion; but the popular magistrate, whose judgment must become action, and whose action involves the whole country, is bound to wait till the sentiment of the people is so far advanced toward his own point of view, that what he does shall find support in it, instead of merely confusing it with new elements of division. It was not unnatural that men earnestly devoted to the saving of their country, and profoundly convinced that slavery was its only real enemy, should demand a decided policy round which all patriots might rally,—and this might have been the wisest course for an absolute ruler. But in the then unsettled state of the public mind, with a large party decrying even resistance to the slaveholders' rebellion as not only unwise, but even unlawful; with a majority, perhaps, even of the would-be loyal so long accustomed to regard the Constitution as a deed of gift conveying to the South their own judgment as to policy and instinct as to right, that they were in doubt at first whether their loyalty were due to the country or to slavery; and with a respectable body of honest and influential men who still believed in the possibility of conciliation,—Mr. Lincoln judged wisely, that, in laying down a policy in deference to one party, he should be giving to the other the very fulcrum for which their disloyalty had been waiting.

It behooved a clear-headed man in his position not to yield so far to an honest indignation against the brokers of treason in the North as to lose sight of the materials for misleading which were their stock in trade, and to forget that it is not the falsehood of sophistry which is to be feared, but the grain of truth mingled with it to make it specious,—that it is not the knavery of the leaders so much as the honesty of the followers they may seduce, that gives them power for evil. It was especially his duty to do nothing which might help the people to forget the true cause of the war in fruitless disputes about its inevitable consequences.

The doctrine of state rights can be so handled by an adroit demagogue as easily to confound the distinction between liberty and lawlessness in the minds of ignorant persons, accustomed always to be influenced by the sound of certain words, rather than to reflect upon the principles which give them meaning. For, though Secession involves the manifest absurdity of denying to a State the right of making war against any foreign power while permitting it against the United States; though it supposes a compact of mutual concessions and guaranties among States without any arbiter in case of dissension; though it contradicts common-sense in assuming that the men who framed our government did not know what they meant when they substituted Union for Confederation; though it falsifies history, which shows that the main opposition to the adoption of the Constitution was based on the argument that it did not allow that independence in the several States which alone would justify them in seceding;—yet, as slavery was universally admitted to be a reserved right, an inference could be drawn from any direct attack upon it (though only in self-defence) to a natural right of resistance, logical enough to satisfy minds untrained to detect fallacy, as the majority of men always are, and now too much disturbed by the disorder of the times to consider that the order of events had any legitimate bearing on the argument. Though Mr. Lincoln was too sagacious to give the Northern allies of the Rebels the occasion they desired and even strove to provoke, yet from the beginning of the war the most persistent efforts have been made to confuse the public mind as to its origin and motives, and to drag the people of the loyal States down from the national position they had instinctively taken to the old level of party squabbles and antipathies. The wholly unprovoked rebellion of an oligarchy proclaiming negro slavery the corner-stone of free institutions, and in the first flush of over-hasty confidence venturing to parade the logical sequence of their leading dogma, "that slavery is right in principle, and has nothing to do with difference of complexion," has been represented as a legitimate and gallant attempt to maintain the true principles of democracy. The rightful endeavor of an established government, the least onerous that ever existed, to defend itself against a treacherous attack on its very existence, has been cunningly made to seem the wicked effort of a fanatical clique to force its doctrines on an oppressed population.

Even so long ago as when Mr. Lincoln, not yet convinced of the danger and magnitude of the crisis, was endeavoring to persuade himself of Union majorities at the South, and to carry on a war that was half peace in the hope of a peace that would have been all war,—while he was still enforcing the Fugitive Slave Law, under some theory that Secession, however it might absolve States from their obligations, could not escheat them of their claims under the Constitution, and that slaveholders in rebellion had alone among mortals the privilege of having their cake and eating it at the same time,—the enemies of free government were striving to persuade the people that the war was an Abolition crusade. To rebel without reason was proclaimed as one of the rights of man, while it was carefully kept out of sight that to suppress rebellion is the first duty of government. All the evils that have come upon the country have been attributed to the Abolitionists, though it is hard to see how any party can become permanently powerful except in one of two ways,—either by the greater truth of its principles, or the extravagance of the party opposed to it. To fancy the ship of state, riding safe at her constitutional moorings, suddenly engulfed by a huge kraken of Abolitionism, rising from unknown depths and grasping it with slimy tentacles, is to look at the natural history of the matter with the eyes of Pontoppidan. To believe that the leaders in the Southern treason feared any danger from Abolitionism would be to deny them ordinary intelligence, though there can be little doubt that they made use of it to stir the passions and excite the fears of their deluded accomplices. They rebelled, not because they thought slavery weak, but because they believed it strong enough, not to overthrow the government, but to get possession of it; for it becomes daily clearer that they used rebellion only as a means of revolution, and if they got revolution, though not in the shape they looked for, is the American people to save them from its consequences at the cost of its own existence? The election of Mr. Lincoln, which it was clearly in their power to prevent had they wished, was the occasion merely, and not the cause, of their revolt. Abolitionism, till within a year or two, was the despised heresy of a few earnest persons, without political weight enough to carry the election of a parish constable; and their cardinal principle was disunion, because they were convinced that within the Union the position of slavery was impregnable. In spite of the proverb, great effects do not follow from small causes,—that is, disproportionately small,—but from adequate causes acting under certain required conditions. To contrast the size of the oak with that of the parent acorn, as if the poor seed had paid all costs from its slender strong-box, may serve for a child's wonder; but the real miracle lies in that divine league which bound all the forces of nature to the service of the tiny germ in fulfilling its destiny. Everything has been at work for the past ten years in the cause of anti-slavery, but Garrison and Phillips have been far less successful propagandists than the slaveholders themselves, with the constantly growing arrogance of their pretensions and encroachments. They have forced the question upon the attention of every voter in the Free States, by defiantly putting freedom and democracy on the defensive. But, even after the Kansas outrages, there was no wide-spread desire on the part of the North to commit aggressions, though there was a growing determination to resist them. The popular unanimity in favor of the war three years ago was but in small measure the result of anti-slavery sentiment, far less of any zeal for abolition. But every month of the war, every movement of the allies of slavery in the Free States, has been making Abolitionists by the thousand. The masses of any people, however intelligent, are very little moved by abstract principles of humanity and justice, until those principles are interpreted for them by the stinging commentary of some infringement upon their own rights, and then their instincts and passions, once aroused, do indeed derive an incalculable reinforcement of impulse and intensity from those higher ideas, those sublime traditions, which have no motive political force till they are allied with a sense of immediate personal wrong or imminent peril. Then at last the stars in their courses begin to fight against Sisera. Had any one doubted before that the rights of human nature are unitary, that oppression is of one hue the world over, no matter what the color of the oppressed,—had any one failed to see what the real essence of the contest was,—the efforts of the advocates of slavery among ourselves to throw discredit upon the fundamental axioms of the Declaration of Independence and the radical doctrines of Christianity could not fail to sharpen his eyes.

While every day was bringing the people nearer to the conclusion which all thinking men saw to be inevitable from the beginning, it was wise in Mr. Lincoln to leave the shaping of his policy to events. In this country, where the rough and ready understanding of the people is sure at last to be the controlling power, a profound common-sense is the best genius for statesmanship. Hitherto, the wisdom of the President's measures has been justified by the fact that they have always resulted in more firmly uniting public opinion. One of the things particularly admirable in the public utterances of President Lincoln is a certain tone of familiar dignity, which, while it is perhaps the most difficult attainment of mere style, is also no doubtful indication of personal character. There must be something essentially noble in an elective ruler who can descend to the level of confidential ease without forfeiting respect, something very manly in one who can break through the etiquette of his conventional rank and trust himself to the reason and intelligence of those who have elected him. No higher compliment was ever paid to a nation than the simple confidence, the fireside plainness, with which Mr. Lincoln always addresses himself to the reason of the American people. This was, indeed, a true democrat, who grounded himself on the assumption that a democracy can think. "Come, let us reason together about this matter," has been the tone of all his addresses to the people; and accordingly we have never had a chief magistrate who so won to himself the love and at the same time the judgment of his countrymen. To us, that simple confidence of his in the right-mindedness of his fellow-men is very touching, and its success is as strong an argument as we have ever seen in favor of the theory that men can govern themselves. He never appeals to any vulgar sentiment, he never alludes to the humbleness of his origin; it probably never occurred to him, indeed, that there was anything higher to start from than manhood; and he put himself on a level with those he addressed, not by going down to them, but only by taking it for granted that they had brains and would come up to a common ground of reason. In an article lately printed in "The Nation," Mr. Bayard Taylor mentions the striking fact, that in the foulest dens of the Five Points he found the portrait of Lincoln. The wretched population that makes its hive there threw all its votes and more against him, and yet paid this instinctive tribute to the sweet humanity of his nature. Their ignorance sold its vote and took its money, but all that was left of manhood in them recognized its saint and martyr.

Mr. Lincoln is not in the habit of saying, "This is *my* opinion, or *my* theory," but, "This is the conclusion to which, in my judgment, the time has come, and to which, accordingly, the sooner we come the better for us." His policy has been the policy of public opinion based on adequate discussion and on a timely recognition of the influence of passing events in shaping the features of events to come.

One secret of Mr. Lincoln's remarkable success in captivating the popular mind is undoubtedly an unconsciousness of self which enables him, though under the necessity of constantly using the capital *I,* to do it without any suggestion of egotism. There is no single vowel which men's mouths can pronounce with such difference of effect. That which one shall hide away, as it were, behind the substance of his discourse, or, if he bring it to the front, shall use merely to give an agreeable accent of individuality to what he says, another shall make an offensive challenge to the self-satisfaction of all his hearers, and an unwarranted intrusion upon each man's sense of personal importance, irritating every pore of his vanity, like a dry northeast wind, to a goose-flesh of opposition and hostility. Mr. Lincoln has never studied Quinctilian; but he has, in the earnest simplicity and unaffected Americanism of his own character, one art of oratory worth all the rest. He forgets himself so entirely in his object as to give his *I* the sympathetic and persuasive effect of *We* with the great body of his countrymen. Homely, dispassionate, showing all the rough-edged process of his thought as it goes along, yet arriving at his conclusions with an honest kind of every-day logic, he is so eminently our representative man, that, when he speaks, it seems as if the people were listening to their own thinking aloud. The dignity of his thought owes nothing to any ceremonial garb of words, but to the manly movement that comes of settled purpose and an energy of reason that knows not what rhetoric means. There has been nothing of Cleon, still less of Strepsiades striving to underbid him in demagogism, to be found in the public utterances of Mr. Lincoln. He has always addressed the intelligence of men, never their prejudice, their passion, or their ignorance.

On the day of his death, this simple Western attorney, who according to one party was a vulgar joker, and whom the *doctrinaires* among his own supporters accused of wanting every element of statesmanship, was the most absolute ruler in Christendom, and this solely by the hold his good-humored sagacity had laid on the hearts and understandings of his countrymen. Nor was this all, for it appeared that he had drawn the great majority, not only of his fellow-citizens, but of mankind also, to his side. So strong and so persuasive is honest manliness without a single quality of romance or unreal sentiment to help it! A civilian during times of the most captivating military achievement, awkward, with no skill in the lower technicalities of manners, he left behind him a fame beyond that of any conqueror, the memory of a grace higher than that of outward person, and of a gentlemanliness deeper than mere breeding. Never before that startled April morning did such multitudes of men shed tears for the death of one they had never seen, as if with him a friendly presence had been taken away from their lives, leaving them colder and darker. Never was funeral panegyric so eloquent as the silent look of sympathy which strangers exchanged when they met on that day. Their common manhood had lost a kinsman.

DEMOCRACY

INAUGURAL ADDRESS ON ASSUMING THE PRESIDENCY OF THE BIRMINGHAM AND MIDLAND INSTITUTE, BIRMINGHAM, ENGLAND, 6 OCTOBER, 1884

HE must be a born leader or misleader of men, or must have been sent into the world unfurnished with that modulating and restraining balance-wheel which we call a sense of humor, who, in old age, has as strong a confidence in his opinions and in the necessity of bringing the universe into conformity with them as he had in youth. In a world the very condition of whose being is that it should be in perpetual flux, where all seems mirage, and the one abiding thing is the effort to distinguish realities from appearances, the elderly man must be indeed of a singularly tough and valid fibre who is certain that he has any clarified residuum of experience, any assured verdict of reflection, that deserves to be called an opinion, or who, even if he had, feels that he is justified in holding mankind by the button while he is expounding it. And in a world of daily—nay, almost hourly—journalism, where every clever man, every man who thinks himself clever, or whom anybody else thinks clever, is called upon to deliver his judgment point-blank and at the word of command on every conceivable subject of human thought, or on what sometimes seems to him very much the same thing, on every inconceivable display of human want of thought, there is such a spendthrift waste of all those commonplaces which furnish the permitted staple of public discourse that there is little chance of beguiling a new tune out of the one-stringed instrument on which we have been thrumming so long. In this desperate necessity one is often tempted to think that, if all the words of the dictionary were tumbled down in a heap and then all those fortuitous juxtapositions and combinations that made tolerable sense were picked out and pieced together, we might find among them some poignant suggestions towards novelty of thought or expression. But, alas! it is only the great poets who seem to have this unsolicited profusion of unexpected and incalculable phrase, this infinite variety of topic. For everybody else everything has been said before, and said over again after. He who has read his Aristotle will be apt to think that observation has on most points of general applicability said its last word, and he who has mounted the tower of Plato to look abroad from it will never hope to climb another with so lofty a vantage of speculation. Where it is so simple if not so easy a thing to hold one's peace, why add to the general confusion of tongues? There is something disheartening, too, in being expected to fill up not less than a certain measure of time, as if the mind were an hour-glass, that need only be shaken and set on one end or the other, as the case may be, to run its allotted sixty minutes with decorous exactitude. I recollect being once told by the late eminent naturalist, Agassiz, that when he was to deliver his first lecture as professor (at Zürich, I believe) he had grave doubts of his ability to occupy the prescribed three quarters of an hour. He was speaking without notes, and glancing anxiously from time to time at the watch that lay before him on the desk. "When I had spoken a half hour," he said, "I had told them everything I knew in the world, everything! Then I began to repeat myself," he added, roguishly, "and I have done nothing else ever since." Beneath the humorous exaggeration of the story I seemed to see the face of a very serious and improving moral. And yet if one were to say only what he had to say and then stopped, his audience would feel defrauded of their honest measure. Let us take courage by the example of the French, whose exportation of Bordeaux wines increases as the area of their land in vineyards is diminished.

To me, somewhat hopelessly revolving these things, the undelayable year has rolled round, and I find myself called upon to say something in this place, where so many wiser men have spoken before me. Precluded, in my quality of national guest, by motives of taste and discretion, from dealing with any question of immediate and domestic concern, it seemed to me wisest, or at any rate most prudent, to choose a topic of comparatively abstract interest, and to ask your indulgence for a few somewhat generalized remarks on a matter concerning which I had some experimental knowledge, derived from the use of such eyes and ears as Nature had been pleased to endow me withal, and such report as I had been able to win from them. The subject which most readily suggested itself was the spirit and the working of those conceptions of life and polity which are lumped together, whether for reproach or commendation, under the name of Democracy. By temperament and education of a conservative turn, I saw the last years of that quaint Arcadia which French travellers saw with delighted amazement a century ago, and have watched the change (to me a sad one) from an agricultural to a proletary population. The testimony of Balaam should carry some conviction. I have grown to manhood and am now growing old with the growth of this system of government in my native land, have watched its advances, or what some would call its encroachments, gradual and irresistible as those of a glacier, have been an ear-witness to the forebodings of wise and good and timid men, and have lived to see those forebodings belied by the course of events, which is apt to show itself humorously careless of the reputation of prophets. I recollect hearing a sagacious old gentleman say in 1840 that the doing away with the property qualification for suffrage twenty years before had been the ruin of the State of Massachusetts; that it had put public credit and private estate alike at the mercy of demagogues. I lived to see that Commonwealth twenty odd years later paying the interest on her bonds in gold, though it cost her sometimes nearly three for one to keep her faith, and that while suffering an unparalleled drain of men and treasure in helping to sustain the unity and self-respect of the nation.

If universal suffrage has worked ill in our larger cities, as it certainly has, this has been mainly because the hands that wielded it were untrained to its use. There the election of a majority of the trustees of the public money is controlled by the most ignorant and vicious of a population which has come to us from abroad, wholly unpractised in self-government and incapable of assimilation by American habits and methods. But the finances of our towns, where the native tradition is still dominant and whose affairs are discussed and settled in a public assembly of the people, have been in general honestly and prudently administered. Even in manufacturing towns, where a majority of the voters live by their daily wages, it is not so often the recklessness as the moderation of public expenditure that surprises an old-fashioned observer. "The beggar is in the saddle at last," cries Proverbial Wisdom. "Why, in the name of all former experience, doesn't he ride to the Devil?" Because in the very act of mounting he ceased to be a beggar and became part owner of the piece of property he bestrides. The last thing we need be anxious about is property. It always has friends or the means of making them. If riches have wings to fly away from their owner, they have wings also to escape danger.

I hear America sometimes playfully accused of sending you all your storms, and am in the habit of parrying the charge by alleging that we are enabled to do this because, in virtue of our protective system, we can afford to make better bad weather than anybody else. And what wiser use could we make of it than to export it in return for the paupers which some European countries are good enough to send over to us who have not attained to the same skill in the manufacture of them? But bad weather is not the worst thing that is laid at our door. A French gentleman, not long ago, forgetting Burke's monition of how unwise it is to draw an indictment against a whole people, has charged us with the responsibility of whatever he finds disagreeable in the morals or manners of his countrymen. If M. Zola or some other competent witness would only go into the box and tell us what those morals and manners were before our example corrupted them! But I confess that I find little to interest and less to edify me in these international bandyings of "You're another."

I shall address myself to a single point only in the long list of offences of which we are more or less gravely accused, because that really includes all the rest. It is that we are infecting the Old World with what seems to be thought the entirely new disease of Democracy. It is generally people who are in what are called easy circumstances who can afford the leisure to treat themselves to a handsome complaint, and these experience an immediate alleviation when once they have found a sonorous Greek name to abuse it by. There is something consolatory also, something flattering to their sense of personal dignity, and to that conceit of singularity which is the natural recoil from our uneasy consciousness of being commonplace, in thinking ourselves victims of a malady by which no one had ever suffered before. Accordingly they find it simpler to class under one comprehensive heading whatever they find offensive to their nerves, their tastes, their interests, or what they suppose to be their opinions, and christen it Democracy, much as physicians label every obscure disease gout, or as cross-grained fellows lay their ill-temper to the weather. But is it really a new ailment, and, if it be, is America answerable for it? Even if she were, would it account for the phylloxera, and hoof-and-mouth disease, and bad harvests, and bad English, and the German bands, and the Boers, and all the other discomforts with which these later days have vexed the souls of them that go in chariots? Yet I have seen the evil example of Democracy in America cited as the source and origin of things quite as heterogeneous and quite as little connected with it by any sequence of cause and effect. Surely this ferment is nothing new. It has been at work for centuries, and we are more conscious of it only because in this age of publicity, where the newspapers offer a rostrum to whoever has a grievance, or fancies that he has, the bubbles and scum thrown up by it are more noticeable on the surface than in those dumb ages when there was a cover of silence and suppression on the cauldron. Bernardo Navagero, speaking of the Provinces of Lower Austria in 1546, tells us that "in them there are five sorts of persons, Clergy, Barons, Nobles, Burghers, and Peasants. Of these last no account is made, *because they have no voice in the Diet.*"[1]

Nor was it among the people that subversive or mistaken doctrines had their rise. A Father of the Church said that property was theft many centuries before Proudhon was born. Bourdaloue reaffirmed it. Montesquieu was the inventor of national workshops, and of the theory that the State owed every man a living. Nay, was not the Church herself the first organized Democracy? A few centuries ago the chief end of man was to keep his soul alive, and then the little kernel of leaven that sets the gases at work was religious, and produced the Reformation. Even in that, far-sighted persons like the Emperor Charles V. saw the germ of political and social revolution. Now that the chief end of man seems to have become the keeping of the body alive, and as comfortably alive as possible, the leaven also has become wholly political and social. But there had also been social upheavals before the Reformation and contemporaneously with it, especially among men of Teutonic race. The Reformation gave outlet and direction to an unrest already existing. Formerly the immense majority of men —our brothers—knew only their sufferings, their wants, and their desires. They are beginning now to know their opportunity and their power. All persons who see deeper than their plates are rather inclined to thank God for it than to bewail it, for the sores of Lazarus have a poison in them against which Dives has no antidote.

There can be no doubt that the spectacle of a great and prosperous Democracy on the other side of the Atlantic must react powerfully on the aspirations and political theories of men in the Old World who do not find things to their mind; but, whether for good or evil, it should not be overlooked that the acorn from which it sprang was ripened on the British oak. Every successive swarm that has gone out from this *officina gentium* has, when left to

[1] Below the Peasants, it should be remembered, was still another even more helpless class, the servile farm-laborers. The same witness informs us that of the extraordinary imposts the Peasants paid nearly twice as much in proportion to their estimated property as the Barons, Nobles, and Burghers together. Moreover, the upper classes were assessed at their own valuation, while they arbitrarily fixed that of the Peasants, who had no voice. ("Relazioni degli Ambasciatori Veneti," Serie I., tomo i., pp. 378, 379, 389.)

its own instincts—may I not call them hereditary instincts?—assumed a more or less thoroughly democratic form. This would seem to show, what I believe to be the fact, that the British Constitution, under whatever disguises of prudence or decorum, is essentially democratic. England, indeed, may be called a monarchy with democratic tendencies, the United States a democracy with conservative instincts. People are continually saying that America is in the air, and I am glad to think it is, since this means only that a clearer conception of human claims and human duties is beginning to be prevalent. The discontent with the existing order of things, however, pervaded the atmosphere wherever the conditions were favorable, long before Columbus, seeking the back door of Asia, found himself knocking at the front door of America. I say wherever the conditions were favorable, for it is certain that the germs of disease do not stick or find a prosperous field for their development and noxious activity unless where the simplest sanitary precautions have been neglected. "For this effect defective comes by cause," as Polonius said long ago. It is only by instigation of the wrongs of men that what are called the Rights of Man become turbulent and dangerous. It is then only that they syllogize unwelcome truths. It is not the insurrections of ignorance that are dangerous, but the revolts of intelligence:—

> "The wicked and the weak rebel in vain,
> Slaves by their own compulsion."

Had the governing classes in France during the last century paid as much heed to their proper business as to their pleasures or manners, the guillotine need never have severed that spinal marrow of orderly and secular tradition through which in a normally constituted state the brain sympathizes with the extremities and sends will and impulsion thither. It is only when the reasonable and practicable are denied that men demand the unreasonble and impracticable; only when the possible is made difficult that they fancy the impossible to be easy. Fairy tales are made out of the dreams of the poor. No; the sentiment which lies at the root of democracy is nothing new. I am speaking always of a sentiment, a spirit, and not of a form of government; for this was but the outgrowth of the other and not its cause. This sentiment is merely an expression of the natural wish of people to have a hand, if need be a controlling hand, in the management of their own affairs. What is new is that they are more and more gaining that control, and learning more and more how to be worthy of it. What we used to call the tendency or drift—what we are being taught to call more wisely the evolution of things—has for some time been setting steadily in this direction. There is no good in arguing with the inevitable. The only argument available with an east wind is to put on your overcoat. And in this case, also, the prudent will prepare themselves to encounter what they cannot prevent. Some people advise us to put on the brakes, as if the movement of which we are conscious were that of a railway train running down an incline. But a metaphor is no argument, though it be sometimes the gunpowder to drive one home and imbed it in the memory. Our disquiet comes of what nurses and other experienced persons call growing-pains, and need not seriously alarm us. They are what every generation before us—certainly every generation since the invention of printing—has gone through with more or less good fortune. To the door of every generation there comes a knocking, and unless the household, like the Thane of Cawdor and his wife, have been doing some deed without a name, they need not shudder. It turns out at worst to be a poor relation who wishes to come in out of the cold. The porter always grumbles and is slow to open. "Who's there, in the name of Beelzebub?" he mutters. Not a change for the better in our human housekeeping has ever taken place that wise and good men have not opposed it,—have not prophesied with the alderman that the world would wake up to find its throat cut in consequence of it. The world, on the contrary, wakes up, rubs its eyes, yawns, stretches itself, and goes about its business as if nothing had happened. Suppression of the slave trade, abolition of slavery, trade unions,—at all of these excellent people shook their heads despondingly, and murmured "Ichabod." But the trade unions are now debating instead of conspiring, and we all read their discussions with comfort and hope, sure that they are learning the business of citizenship and the difficulties of practical legislation.

One of the most curious of these frenzies of exclusion was that against the emancipation of the Jews. All share in the government of the world was denied for centuries to perhaps the ablest, certainly the most tenacious, race that had ever lived in it—the race to whom we owed our religion and the purest spiritual stimulus and consolation to be found in all literature—a race in which ability seems as natural and hereditary as the curve of their noses, and whose blood, furtively mingling with the bluest bloods in Europe, has quickened them with its own indomitable impulsion. We drove them into a corner, but they had their revenge, as the wronged are always sure to have it sooner or later. They made their corner the counter and banking-house of the world, and thence they rule it and us with the ignobler sceptre of finance. Your grandfathers mobbed Priestley only that you might set up his statue and make Birmingham the headquarters of English Unitarianism. We hear it said sometimes that this is an age of transition, as if that made matters clearer; but can any one point us to an age that was not? If he could, he would show us an age of stagnation. The question for us, as it has been for all before us, is to make the transition gradual and easy, to see that our points are right so that the train may not come to grief. For we should remember that nothing is more natural for people whose education has been neglected than to spell evolution with an initial "r." A great man struggling with the storms of fate has been called a sublime spectacle; but surely a great man wrestling with these new forces that have come into the world, mastering them and controlling them to beneficent ends, would be a yet sublimer. Here is not a danger, and if there were it would be only a better school of manhood, a nobler scope for ambition. I have hinted that what people are afraid of in democracy is less the thing itself than what they conceive to be its necessary adjuncts and consequences. It is supposed to reduce all mankind to a dead level of mediocrity in character and culture, to vulgarize men's conceptions of life, and therefore their code of morals, manners, and conduct—to endanger the rights of property and possession. But I believe that the real gravamen of the charges lies in the habit it has of making itself generally disagreeable by asking the Powers that Be at the most inconvenient moment whether they are the powers that ought to be. If the powers that be are in a condition to give a satisfactory answer to this inevitable question, they need feel in no way discomfited by it.

Few people take the trouble of trying to find out what democracy really is. Yet this would be a great help, for it is our lawless and uncertain thoughts, it is the indefiniteness of our impressions, that fill darkness, whether mental or physical, with spectres and hobgoblins. Democracy is nothing more than an experiment in government, more likely to succeed in a new soil, but likely to be tried in all soils, which must stand or fall on its own merits as others have done before it. For there is no trick of perpetual motion in politics any more than in mechanics. President Lincoln defined democracy to be "the government of the people by the people for the people." This is a sufficiently compact statement of it as a political arrangement. Theodore Parker said that "Democracy meant not 'I'm as good as you are,' but 'You're as good as I am.'" And this is the ethical conception of it, necessary as a complement of the other; a conception which, could it be made actual and practical, would easily solve all the riddles that the old sphinx of political and social economy who sits by the roadside has been proposing to mankind from the beginning, and which mankind have shown such a singular talent for answering wrongly. In this sense Christ was the first true democrat that ever breathed, as the old dramatist Dekker said he was the first true gentleman. The characters may be easily doubled, so strong is the likeness between them. A beautiful and profound parable of the Persian poet Jellaladeen tells us that "One knocked at the Beloved's door, and a voice asked from within 'Who is there?' and he answered 'It is I.' Then the voice said, 'This house will not hold me and thee;' and the door was not opened. Then went the lover into the desert and fasted and prayed in solitude, and after a year he returned and knocked again at the door; and again the voice asked 'Who is there?' and he said 'It is thyself;' and the door was opened to him." But that is idealism, you will say, and this is an only too practical world. I grant it; but I am one of those who believe that the real will never find an irremovable basis till it rests on the ideal. It used to be thought that a democracy was possible only in a small territory, and this is doubtless true of a democracy strictly defined, for in such all the citizens decide directly upon every question of public concern in a general assembly. An example still survives in the tiny Swiss canton of Appenzell. But this immediate intervention of the people in their own affairs is not of the essence of democracy; it is not necessary, nor indeed, in most cases, practicable. Democracies to which Mr. Lincoln's definition would fairly enough apply have existed, and now exist, in which, though the supreme authority reside in the people, yet they can act only indirectly on the national policy. This generation has seen a democracy with an imperial figurehead, and in all that have ever existed the body politic has never embraced all the inhabitants included within its territory, the right to share in the direction of affairs has been confined to citizens, and citizenship has been further restricted by various limitations, sometimes of property, sometimes of nativity, and always of age and sex.

The framers of the American Constitution were far from wishing or intending to found a democracy in the strict sense of the word, though, as was inevitable, every expansion of the scheme of government they elaborated has been in a democratical direction. But this has been generally the slow result of growth, and not the sudden innovation of theory; in fact, they had a profound disbelief in theory, and knew better than to commit the folly of breaking with the past. They were not seduced by the French fallacy that a new system of government could be ordered like a new suit of clothes. They would as soon have thought of ordering a new suit of flesh and skin. It is only on the roaring loom of time that the stuff is woven for such a vesture of their thought and experience as they were meditating. They recognized fully the value of tradition and habit as the great allies of permanence and stability. They all had that distaste for innovation which belonged to their race, and many of them a distrust of human nature derived from their creed. The day of sentiment was over, and no dithyrambic affirmations or fine-drawn analyses of the Rights of Man would serve their present turn. This was a practical question, and they addressed themselves to it as men of knowledge and judgment should. Their problem was how to adapt English principles and precedents to the new conditions of American life, and they solved it with singular discretion. They put as many obstacles as they could contrive, not in the way of the people's will, but of their whim. With few exceptions they probably admitted the logic of the then accepted syllogism,—democracy, anarchy, despotism. But this formula was framed upon the experience of small cities shut up to stew within their narrow walls, where the number of citizens made but an inconsiderable fraction of the inhabitant , where every passion was reverberated from house to house and from man to man with gathering rumor till every impulse became gregarious and therefore inconsiderate, and every popular assembly needed but an infusion of eloquent sophistry to turn it into a mob, all the more dangerous because sanctified with the formality of law.[2]

Fortunately their case was wholly different. They were to legislate for a widely scattered population and for States already practised in the discipline of a partial independence. They had an unequalled opportunity and enormous advantages. The material they had to work upon was already democratical by instinct and habitude. It was tempered to their hands by more than a century's schooling in self-government. They had but to give permanent and conservative form to a ductile mass. In giving impulse and direction to their new institutions, especially in supplying them with checks and balances, they had a great help and safeguard in their federal organization. The different,

[2] The effect of the electric telegraph in reproducing this trooping of emotion and perhaps of opinion is yet to be measured. The effect of Darwinism as a disintegrator of humanitarianism is also to be reckoned with.

sometimes conflicting, interests and social systems of the several States made existence as a Union and coalescence into a nation conditional on a constant practice of moderation and compromise. The very elements of disintegration were the best guides in political training. Their children learned the lesson of compromise only too well, and it was the application of it to a question of fundamental morals that cost us our civil war. We learned once for all that compromise makes a good umbrella but a poor roof; that it is a temporary expedient, often wise in party politics, almost sure to be unwise in statesmanship.

Has not the trial of democracy in America proved, on the whole, successful? If it had not, would the Old World be vexed with any fears of its proving contagious? This trial would have been less severe could it have been made with a people homogeneous in race, language, and traditions, whereas the United States have been called on to absorb and assimilate enormous masses of foreign population, heterogeneous in all these respects, and drawn mainly from that class which might fairly say that the world was not their friend, nor the world's law. The previous condition too often justified the traditional Irishman, who, landing in New York and asked what his politics were, inquired if there was a Government there, and on being told that there was, retorted, "Thin I'm agin it!" We have taken from Europe the poorest, the most ignorant, the most turbulent of her people, and have made them over into good citizens, who have added to our wealth, and who are ready to die in defence of a country and of institutions which they know to be worth dying for. The exceptions have been (and they are lamentable exceptions) where these hordes of ignorance and poverty have coagulated in great cities. But the social system is yet to seek which has not to look the same terrible wolf in the eyes. On the other hand, at this very moment Irish peasants are buying up the worn-out farms of Massachusetts, and making them productive again by the same virtues of industry and thrift that once made them profitable to the English ancestors of the men who are deserting them. To have achieved even these prosaic results (if you choose to call them so), and that out of materials the most discordant,—I might say the most recalcitrant,—argues a certain beneficent virtue in the system that could do it, and is not to be accounted for by mere luck.

Carlyle said scornfully that America meant only roast turkey every day for everybody. He forgot that States, as Bacon said of wars, go on their bellies. As for the security of property, it should be tolerably well secured in a country where every other man hopes to be rich, even though the only property qualification be the ownership of two hands that add to the general wealth. Is it not the best security for anything to interest the largest possible number of persons in its preservation and the smallest in its division? In point of fact, far-seeing men count the increasing power of wealth and its combinations as one of the chief dangers with which the institutions of the United States are threatened in the not distant future. The right of individual property is no doubt the very corner-stone of civilization as hitherto understood, but I am a little impatient of being told that property is entitled to exceptional consideration because it bears all the burdens of the State. It bears those, indeed, which can most easily be borne, but poverty pays with its person the chief expenses of war, pestilence, and famine. Wealth should not forget this, for poverty is beginning to think of it now and then. Let me not be misunderstood. I see as clearly as any man possibly can, and rate as highly, the value of wealth, and of hereditary wealth, as the security of refinement, the feeder of all those arts that ennoble and beautify life, and as making a country worth living in. Many an ancestral hall here in England has been a nursery of that culture which has been of example and benefit to all. Old gold has a civilizing virtue which new gold must grow old to be capable of secreting.

I should not think of coming before you to defend or to criticise any form of government. All have their virtues, all their defects, and all have illustrated one period or another in the history of the race, with signal services to humanity and culture. There is not one that could stand a cynical cross-examination by an experienced criminal lawyer, except that of a perfectly wise and perfectly good despot, such as the world has never seen, except in that white-haired king of Browning's who

> "Lived long ago
> In the morning of the world,
> When Earth was nearer Heaven than now."

The English race, if they did not invent government by discussion, have at least carried it nearest to perfection in practice. It seems a very safe and reasonable contrivance for occupying the attention of the country, and is certainly a better way of settling questions than by push of pike. Yet, if one should ask it why it should not rather be called government by gabble, it would have to fumble in its pocket a good while before it found the change for a convincing reply. As matters stand, too, it is beginning to be doubtful whether Parliament and Congress sit at Westminster and Washington or in the editors' rooms of the leading journals, so thoroughly is everything debated before the authorized and responsible debaters get on their legs. And what shall we say of government by a majority of voices? To a person who in the last century would have called himself an Impartial Observer, a numerical preponderance seems, on the whole, as clumsy a way of arriving at truth as could well be devised, but experience has apparently shown it to be a convenient arrangement for determining what may be expedient or advisable or practicable at any given moment. Truth, after all, wears a different face to everybody, and it would be too tedious to wait till all were agreed. She is said to lie at the bottom of a well, for the very reason, perhaps, that whoever looks down in search of her sees his own image at the bottom, and is persuaded not only that he has seen the goddess, but that she is far better-looking than he had imagined.

The arguments against universal suffrage are equally unanswerable. "What," we exclaim, "shall Tom, Dick, and Harry have as much weight in the scale as I?" Of course, nothing could be more absurd. And yet universal suffrage has not been the instrument of greater unwisdom than contrivances of a more select description. Assemblies could be mentioned composed entirely of Masters of Arts and Doctors in Divinity which have sometimes shown traces of human passion or prejudice in their votes. Have the Serene Highnesses and Enlightened Classes carried on the business of Mankind so well, then, that there is no use in trying a less costly method? The democratic theory is that those Constitutions are likely to prove steadiest which have the broadest base, that the right to vote makes a safety-valve of every voter, and that the best way of teaching a man how to vote is to give him the chance of practice. For the question is no longer the academic one, "Is it wise to give every man the ballot?" but rather the practical one, "Is it prudent to deprive whole classes of it any longer?" It may be conjectured that it is cheaper in the long run to lift men up than to hold them down, and that the ballot in their hands is less dangerous to society than a sense of wrong in their heads. At any rate this is the dilemma to which the drift of opinion has been for some time sweeping us, and in politics a dilemma is a more unmanageable thing to hold by the horns than a wolf by the ears. It is said that the right of suffrage is not valued when it is indiscriminately bestowed, and there may be some truth in this, for I have observed that what men prize most is a privilege, even if it be that of chief mourner at a funeral. But is there not danger that it will be valued at more than its worth if denied, and that some illegitimate way will be sought to make up for the want of it? Men who have a voice in public affairs are at once affiliated with one or other of the great parties between which society is divided, merge their individual hopes and opinions in its safer, because more generalized, hopes and opinions, are disciplined by its tactics, and acquire, to a certain degree, the orderly qualities of an army. They no longer belong to a class, but to a body corporate. Of one thing, at least, we may be certain, that, under whatever method of helping things to go wrong man's wit can contrive, those who have the divine right to govern will be found to govern in the end, and that the highest privilege to which the majority of mankind can aspire is that of being governed by those wiser than they. Universal suffrage has in the United States sometimes been made the instrument of inconsiderate changes, under the notion of reform, and this from a misconception of the true meaning of popular government. One of these has been the substitution in many of the States of popular election for official selection in the choice of judges. The same system applied to military officers was the source of much evil during our civil war, and, I believe, had to be abandoned. But it has been also true that on all great questions of national policy a reserve of prudence and discretion has been brought out at the critical moment to turn the scale in favor of a wiser decision. An appeal to the reason of the people has never been known to fail in the long run. It is, perhaps, true that, by effacing the principle of passive obedience, democracy, ill understood, has slackened the spring of that ductility to discipline which is essential to "the unity and married calm of States." But I feel assured that experience and necessity will cure this evil, as they have shown their power to cure others. And under what frame of policy have evils ever been remedied till they became intolerable, and shook men out of their indolent indifference through their fears?

We are told that the inevitable result of democracy is to sap the foundations of personal independence, to weaken the principle of authority, to lessen the respect due to eminence, whether in station, virtue, or genius. If these things were so, society could not hold together. Perhaps the best forcing-house of robust individuality would be where public opinion is inclined to be most overbearing, as he must be of heroic temper who should walk along Piccadilly at the height of the season in a soft hat. As for authority, it is one of the symptoms of the time that the religious reverence for it is declining everywhere, but this is due partly to the fact that state-craft is no longer looked upon as a mystery, but as a business, and partly to the decay of superstition, by which I mean the habit of respecting what we are told to respect rather than what is respectable in itself. There is more rough and tumble in the American democracy than is altogether agreeable to people of sensitive nerves and refined habits, and the people take their political duties lightly and laughingly, as is, perhaps, neither unnatural nor unbecoming in a young giant. Democracies can no more jump away from their own shadows than the rest of us can. They no doubt sometimes make mistakes and pay honor to men who do not deserve it. But they do this because they believe them worthy of it, and though it be true that the idol is the measure of the worshipper, yet the worship has in it the germ of a nobler religion. But is it democracies alone that fall into these errors? I, who have seen it proposed to erect a statue to Hudson, the railway king, and have heard Louis Napoleon hailed as the saviour of society by men who certainly had no democratic associations or leanings, am not ready to think so. But democracies have likewise their finer instincts. I have also seen the wisest statesman and most pregnant speaker of our generation, a man of humble birth and ungainly manners, of little culture beyond what his own genius supplied, become more absolute in power than any monarch of modern times through the reverence of his countrymen for his honesty, his wisdom, his sincerity, his faith in God and man, and the nobly humane simplicity of his character. And I remember another whom popular respect enveloped as with a halo, the least vulgar of men, the most austerely genial, and the most independent of opinion. Wherever he went he never met a stranger, but everywhere neighbors and friends proud of him as their ornament and decoration. Institutions which could bear and breed such men as Lincoln and Emerson had surely some energy for good. No, amid all the fruitless turmoil and miscarriage of the world, if there be one thing steadfast and of favorable omen, one thing to make optimism distrust its own obscure distrust, it is the rooted instinct in men to admire what is better and more beautiful than themselves. The touchstone of political and social institutions is their ability to supply them with worthy objects of this sentiment, which is the very tap-root of civilization and progress. There would seem to be no readier way of feeding it with the elements of growth and vigor than such an organization of society as will enable men to respect themselves, and so to justify them in respecting others.

Such a result is quite possible under other conditions than those of an avowedly democratical Constitution. For I take it that the real essence of democracy was fairly enough defined by the First Napoleon when he said that the French Revolution meant 'la carrière ouverte aux talents"—a clear pathway for merit of whatever kind. I should be inclined to paraphrase this by calling democracy that form of society, no matter what its political classification, in which every man had a chance and knew that he had it. If a man can climb, and feels himself encouraged to climb, from a coalpit to the highest position for which he is fitted, he can well afford to be indifferent what name is given to the government under which he lives. The Bailli of Mirabeau, uncle of the more famous tribune of that name, wrote in 1771: "The English are, in my opinion, a hundred times more agitated and more unfortunate than the very Algerines themselves, because they do not know and will not know till the destruction of their over-swollen power, which I believe very near, whether they are monarchy, aristocracy, or democracy, and wish to play the part of all three."

England has not been obliging enough to fulfil the Bailli's prophecy, and perhaps it was this very carelessness about the name, and concern about the substance of popular government, this skill in getting the best out of things as they are, in utilizing all the motives which influence men, and in giving one direction to many impulses, that has been a principal factor of her greatness and power. Perhaps it is fortunate to have an unwritten Constitution, for men are prone to be tinkering the work of their own hands, whereas they are more willing to let time and circumstance mend or modify what time and circumstance have made. All free governments, whatever their name, are in reality governments by public opinion, and it is on the quality of this public opinion that their prosperity depends. It is, therefore, their first duty to purify the element from which they draw the breath of life. With the growth of democracy grows also the fear, if not the danger, that this atmosphere may be corrupted with poisonous exhalations from lower and more malarious levels, and the question of sanitation becomes more instant and pressing. Democracy in its best sense is merely the letting in of light and air. Lord Sherbrooke, with his usual epigrammatic terseness, bids you educate your future rulers. But would this alone be a sufficient safeguard? To educate the intelligence is to enlarge the horizon of its desires and wants. And it is well that this should be so. But the enterprise must go deeper and prepare the way for satisfying those desires and wants in so far as they are legitimate. What is really ominous of danger to the existing order of things is not democracy (which, properly understood, is a conservative force), but the Socialism, which may find a fulcrum in it. If we cannot equalize conditions and fortunes any more than we can equalize the brains of men—and a very sagacious person has said that "where two men ride of a horse one must ride behind"—we can yet, perhaps, do something to correct those methods and influences that lead to enormous inequalities, and to prevent their growing more enormous. It is all very well to pooh-pooh Mr. George and to prove him mistaken in his political economy. I do not believe that land should be divided because the quantity of it is limited by nature. Of what may this not be said? *A fortiori,* we might on the same principle insist on a division of human wit, for I have observed that the quantity of this has been even more inconveniently limited. Mr. George himself has an inequitably large share of it. But he is right in his impelling motive; right, also, I am convinced, in insisting that humanity makes a part, by far the most important part, of political economy; and in thinking man to be of more concern and more convincing than the longest columns of figures in the world. For unless you include human nature in your addition, your total is sure to be wrong and your deductions from it fallacious. Communism means barbarism, but Socialism means, or wishes to mean, coöperation and community of interests, sympathy, the giving to the hands not so large a share as to the brains, but a larger share than hitherto in the wealth they must combine to produce—means, in short, the practical application of Christianity to life, and has in it the secret of an orderly and benign reconstruction. State Socialism would cut off the very roots in personal character—self-help, forethought, and frugality—which nourish and sustain the trunk and branches of every vigorous Commonwealth.

I do not believe in violent changes, nor do I expect them. Things in possession have a very firm grip. One of the strongest cements of society is the conviction of mankind that the state of things into which they are born is a part of the order of the universe, as natural, let us say, as that the sun should go round the earth. It is a conviction that they will not surrender except on compulsion, and a wise society should look to it that this compulsion be not put upon them. For the individual man there is no radical cure, outside of human nature itself, for the evils to which human nature is heir. The rule will always hold good that you must

> "Be your own palace or the world's your gaol."

But for artificial evils, for evils that spring from want of thought, thought must find a remedy somewhere. There has been no period of time in which wealth has been more sensible of its duties than now. It builds hospitals, it establishes missions among the poor, it endows schools. It is one of the advantages of accumulated wealth, and of the leisure it renders possible, that people have time to think of the wants and sorrows of their fellows. But all these remedies are partial and palliative merely. It is as if we should apply plasters to a single pustule of the small-pox with a view of driving out the disease. The true way is to discover and to extirpate the germs. As society is now constituted these are in the air it breathes, in the water it drinks, in things that seem, and which it has always believed, to be the most innocent and healthful. The evil elements it neglects corrupt these in their springs and pollute them in their courses. Let us be of good cheer, however, remembering that the misfortunes hardest to bear are those which never come. The world has outlived much, and will outlive a great deal more, and men have contrived to be happy in it. It has shown the strength of its constitution in nothing more than in surviving the quack medicines it has tried. In the scales of the destinies brawn will never weigh so much as brain. Our healing is not in the storm or in the whirlwind, it is not in monarchies, or aristocracies, or democracies, but will be revealed by the still small voice that speaks to the conscience and the heart, prompting us to a wider and wiser humanity.